GOO

Parenting is *the* most important, challenging, and rewarding role in the world. But the only training most parents get for it is on-the-job. To make it easier for you, the authors have compiled the latest results-oriented techniques for promoting good behavior in one easy-to-use reference. Their positive attitudes, clear-sighted approach, and in-depth knowledge are all here for the benefit of "ideal" parents—those willing to learn for the sake of their children.

THE AUTHORS

Stephen W. Garber, Ph.D., a clinical behavioral psychologist, has worked with children with various learning and behavior problems and has been a consultant to parents, teachers, pediatricians, and a variety of child-care institutions. **Marianne Daniels Garber, Ph.D.,** an educational consultant in private practice with her husband, also serves as co-director of the Atlanta Hyperactivity Clinic. The Garbers are the parents of three children.

Robyn Freedman Spizman is the author of numerous books and articles on children's learning. The mother of two, she appears on television weekly on NBC-affiliate WXIA's "Noonday."

The authors write "Good Behavior," a regular parenting column featured in the *Atlanta Journal & Constitution*.

GOOD
BEHAVIOR

STEPHEN W. GARBER, Ph.D.
MARIANNE DANIELS GARBER, Ph.D.
ROBYN FREEDMAN SPIZMAN

St. Martin's Paperbacks

Published by arrangement with Villard Books

GOOD BEHAVIOR

Library of Congress Catalog Card Number: 86-40298

ISBN: 0-312-95263-5

Printed in the United States of America

Villard Books edition/June 1987
St. Martin's Paperbacks edition/February 1991

10 9 8 7

This Book Is Dedicated to Our Families

To our parents—Al and Gerry Garber, Rooks and Dan Daniels, and Phyllis and Jack Freedman—who gave us our first lessons in parenting.

To our children—Amy, Adam, and Arielle Garber, and Justin and Ali Spizman—from whom we learn daily.

To Robyn's husband, Willy Spizman, who has provided endless support to all of us.

Acknowledgments

WHEN we began this book, we had strong beliefs about how children can be raised. We still do. We believe that for children to reach happy adulthood, their self-image must be built on a history of experiences in which their efforts toward good behavior are noticed and appreciated. Our families tried to do that for us, and we try to do that for our children. There are many other people through the years who taught us, believed in us, and reinforced our efforts in many ways, and by so doing, they contributed to this book—our teachers and professors—especially Dr. Teodore Ayllon and Dr. MaryAnne Hall, family members and friends, and the parents, teachers, and children we have worked with. Each in his own way taught us and supported us in this project so that we believed we could accomplish this goal.

Then, too, there have been many individuals who have directly contributed to this project. We wish to express our sincere appreciation to them.

We thank the professionals who contributed information, reviewed sections of the book, and always gave their warm support, including: H. Ted Ballard, Ph.D., Stanley A. Cohen, M.D., William Doverspike, Ph.D., Brenda Galina, Ph.D., Robert Garner, M.D., Peter A. Gordon, M.D., Stan Hibbs, Ph.D., Stephen King, M.D., Mark Kogut, D.D.S., Ron Lorber, D.D.S., M.S., Marc

vii

McElheney, Ph.D., Robert Margolis, Ph.D., Wayne Parker, Ph.D., Melinda Parrill, Ph.D., John Parrino, Ph.D., Marvin B. Rothenberg, M.D., Samuel Spizman, M.D., Roy Stulting, M.D., Jonathan D. Winner, M.D., W. W. Reeves, Jr., R.Ph., and to staff members of The Georgia Academy of Music, The American Academy of Pediatrics, The American Dental Association, The Scottish Rite Hospital for Cripple Children, Atlanta, Georgia, The Society to Prevent Blindness, Cindy Gelb, executive producer of "Noonday," WXIA, Sonia Roy of Oxford Book Store, Atlanta, Georgia, and Ellen Rafeedie.

A special thank you to those friends and family members who shared their experiences and comments, among them: Regina and Gus Spizman, Pauline Blonder, Lisa Bluestein, Ziva Blum, Brenda and Stanley Daniels, Lorie Goldklang, Susan and Steve Freedman, Genie and Doug Freedman, Debra and Marc McElheney, Margie Rawn, Frances Ritchkin, Linda Reisman, Ava Wilensky, Irene Shellington, and Kathy Shellington.

We are very grateful to our wonderful support staff who made Xerox copies, typed, and freed us in a myriad of other ways at the office and in our homes so we could complete this book: Pat Hunnicutt, Mary Henderson, Suzanne Tennyson, Renae Rogers, and especially Doris Dozier and Bettye Storne.

Finally, but definitely not last or least, there are three people whose efforts in our behalf made this book possible: Diane Reverand, senior editor of Villard Books, for her direction and sustained belief; Meredith Bernstein, our literary agent, for her unwavering support and guidance; and Joan R. Heilman, for her invaluable assistance in the preparation of the final manuscript.

Contents

The names of individuals involved in examples and experiences used in this book have been changed. We have interchanged the pronouns used in the book, alternating gender. Except where indicated, the pronouns could have been easily interchanged. When reading the information and incidents, feel comfortable to think of the children you know best.

Introduction

WE have come together as a team, a child psychologist, an educational consultant, and a teacher, parents ourselves, who have worked professionally with parents and children for many years in a variety of settings. In private practice, in the classroom, and in the community, we have helped parents solve hundreds of childhood problems. Parents have sought our advice for behaviors and habits that range from tantrums to back talk, bed-wetting to pilfering, picky eating to jealousy and head banging, from morning dawdling to fear of the dark, from poor grades to daydreaming, and school phobias to biting and fighting. In the process, we have collected from our own experience, from the literature, and from the shared ideas of the many we have worked with thousands of solutions for changing behaviors and habits. We have collaborated on this book to share this knowledge with you, to be a ready source that will help you be a parent who acts with love and authority as you develop your child's good behavior.

We are not offering only theory. We have discovered that though our solutions are based on sound philosophy and research, what parents want is help *now*. You need to know how to cope today with unacceptable behaviors that take the joy out of family life. You want effective answers to specific situations.

Everyone has questions about his or her child's actions and the

best approach to discipline. With our own children, we all sometimes feel like novices. We have worked with doctors, lawyers,
electricians and salespeople, single parents and intact families,
stepparents and guardians. The only common denominator across
the people we meet is concern about their children.

A psychologist asked our advice about dealing with his child's
reluctance to go to bed and stay there. Fully aware of the theoretical principles, he didn't know how to reduce his little boy's nighttime fears and expedite a pleasant bedtime. Another family had
four children, one of whom wasn't performing well at school and
was difficult to handle at home. It didn't make the parents feel
better that their relationship with the other children was smooth.
They felt like failures with this one child. They needed reassurance
and specific guidance in how to improve the situation. A distraught
mother of a hyperactive boy, a single parent, had many questions
about how to cope with her child's negative behaviors. She was
exhausted from extricating him from precarious places, including
the roof of the house, and their relationship had deteriorated to
yelling and threats. With this case, and most we see, what is needed
is a consistent approach and an effective set of strategies incorporated into specific solutions appropriate to the problems and personalities involved.

Our goal is to provide a practical, down-to-earth guide for any
parent who needs information, wants solutions, or just wonders
what are reasonable expectations for a child's behavior. *Good Behavior* is not designed to be read from beginning to end, but to be
used as a quick reference to problem solving and for knowing when
you should seek professional help. Because every child, parent, and
situation is unique, there is no single "right" answer. What works
today for your child may not work tomorrow, and what is effective
with one of your offspring may not do anything for another. Therefore, we offer several options as solutions for each of the unwanted
behaviors you may encounter in raising your children.

In creating this book, we have tried to include as many childhood behaviors as possible. A panel of parents reviewed our original list and offered suggestions. The results are comprehensive, but
we suggest you use the index if the behavior you are seeking is not

defined in the table of contents. Chapter titles reflect an attempt to organize the book around common themes. From morning to night, you can find the behaviors that exasperate, bewilder, and worry you at home and away, that are fearsome to your child or annoying to others.

Chapters 1 and 2 provide the basic approach, discussing the strategy and techniques you should adopt. Begin your reading there. After that, simply look up the troubling behavior and select an answer from the several choices we suggest. The format will help you quickly identify the background information you need, the possible solutions, and the steps involved.

Good Behavior offers you a means to stand back from the emotion of the moment and respond sensibly rather than just react to each situation. It gives you an opportunity to act confidently and positively to change your child's behavior. The solutions have worked for hundreds of parents and their children. They can work for you, too.

CHAPTER 1

Steps To Changing
Your Child's
Behavior

THERE'S no such thing as perfect children or perfect parents, and we've never met parents who didn't have doubts, at least occasionally, about their own abilities and talents as mothers and fathers. Children don't always behave as parents would like, and when parents can't seem to change their children's habits, they become frustrated, confused, and uncertain.

Although this is the best-educated and informed generation of parents in history, we don't have all the answers. What should you do when Caroline changes her mind fifteen times about what she's going to wear to school and continually misses the bus? How do you act when Kent misbehaves in the supermarket? When the baby won't eat? When Sam constantly punches his little sister? When Ellen wakes up and calls all night long or David's nails are bitten down to the quick?

There *are* solutions that have worked for parents who have consulted us, but before you use them, read the following guidelines and the techniques described in Chapter 2. The concepts presented here will make the solutions easier to understand and apply. Remember not to expect too much too fast, but set your goals according to your child's age, personality, abilities, sex, and development. All children don't go through the same stages at the same ages, nor are they equally malleable. Since you know your child best, rely on your own judgments and instincts.

DEFINE THE PROBLEM

Before you can make changes, you must know exactly what it is you want to change. It won't help simply to label a child annoying or wild or stubborn or uncooperative, because those labels are generalities and you can't change anything so amorphous. Besides, you don't want to change the whole child, merely his behavior or attitude. Get specific. Step back from the emotion. Define and isolate the problem.

Exactly what is it that your child repeatedly does or doesn't do that dissatisfies you? Exactly what is it that you'd like him to do *less* often or *more* often? Reflect on what it is that your child does that drives you wild. If you believe that Lucy never gets anything done, dissect what she does to make you think that. Break the behavior down into small parts: Lucy doesn't finish her homework; and she never picks up her clothes. You can't deal with never getting anything done, but you *can* manage to change the way she copes with her homework and her clothes.

Take a piece of paper and divide it in half lengthwise. At the top of one half write *Less Often.* At the top of the other half, write *More Often.* In the first column, list the specific behaviors or habits you'd like your child to engage in less often. In the second column, write the reverse or parallel of these behaviors, those you'd like to see more often. Each item must have its parallel. For example:

Less Often	More Often
talk back	speak respectfully
stall or question	act on requests promptly
leave room messy	put clothes in hamper

FOCUS ON ONE PROBLEM AT A TIME

Once you've decided exactly what it is your child does or doesn't do that you wish to change, you may be tempted to tackle all of the problems on the list at once. Resist the urge. Focus on only one problem at a time, and solve that problem before going on to the next.

We help the parents who come to us with their list of undesirable behaviors rank the problems from most important to least. Then we select one, not necessarily from the top of the list, to work on first. When you make your choice, you may pick a difficult behavior or one that bothers you the most. That's fine, but sometimes it's helpful to begin with a less significant problem that can be resolved quickly, so everyone starts off with a feeling of success.

In the weeks or months ahead, as you move down your list, you'll probably discover that your priorities tend to change. New problems come up and old ones vanish or seem less important. Each change you manage to make will have an effect on your youngster's overall behavior—for the better. Each change means you are on your way to a more cooperative child. So take it one step at a time. The old patterns will change. And you'll see, both you and your child will quickly feel better about yourselves and each other.

THINK SMALL

It's rare that a child's problem is solved overnight. Changes in both children and adults tend to come about slowly and in stages. If a child previously wouldn't practice the piano at all and then starts to play for ten minutes a day, be pleased—and show it. You've made real progress. She will feel good about herself and will be encouraged to work longer. If you've been having difficulty getting your son out of the house on time in the morning, be happy when he catches his bus two days in a row and don't expect him to make his bed, too. That comes later. It's much more productive to both be delighted by small signs of progress than to be disappointed when too-high expectations aren't met.

BE CONSISTENT

Your ultimate success in changing your child's behaviors requires consistency: *Mean what you say, say what you mean, and make sure everyone says the same thing.* You and your spouse must come to an agreement about the problem and the plan *before* you begin using the solutions. In addition, it will help enormously if you can enlist the same consistency from baby-sitters, teachers, other family members, and anyone else who interacts regularly with the child.

Always try a solution long enough to give it a chance to work. We have found that parents tend to give up much too quickly, and their children know it. Inconsistent parents don't exude authority, and their children don't respect their wishes because they know they don't have to. If they whine or scream or resist long enough, they will get their own way. Once you've made your decision about how you will deal with a problem, don't waver or quit (within reason, of course). For example, if you've decided to use systematic ignoring (see Section 2.2) when your child whines for goodies in the supermarket, and if, after two trips to the store, you can't stand the crying and pleading or the hostile stares of your fellow shoppers and you give in, you have not solved the problem. In fact, you have reinforced it.

To assist yourself in applying consistency, measure and record the changes. Often, these are less obvious than you would expect, but they are there. If your child throws tantrums, for example, keep a record of their frequency and duration. We think you'll be surprised to discover that the fits of anger are becoming briefer and fewer after a few days of applying a technique. When you realize you are making progress, it will be easier to continue what you are doing.

Record keeping helps, too, if the solution you've chosen is *not* working in your case. Choose one of the suggested alternatives.

BE POSITIVE

Try to view your child's general behavior in a positive light. You don't dislike everything about him, just those behaviors that annoy and frustrate you. You will be working on those one at a time. In the meantime, make sure your child knows you love him and appreciate him and remember to let him know when he's behaving nicely. If Johnny has been making noise in the restaurant and then calms down, tell him you like the way he's acting now. A positive comment accomplishes far more than any amount of criticism. Never undervalue the effectiveness of praise, especially for children. Youngsters, whatever their age or stage, desperately want their parents' approval (though, we'll admit, this is sometimes hard to detect).

LET THE CHILD KNOW WHAT TO EXPECT

After you have chosen the behavior you want to change and selected your strategy or solutions from those we offer in this book, find a quiet time to explain to the child what is going to happen. Keep it positive. You are simply explaining a new event.

Describe the goal in simple words that the child can easily understand. Parents, we've found, often talk to their children in adult terms, telling them they must be more *responsible* or *trustworthy* or *cooperative*. That means very little to small people. Skip the abstracts and deal only in specifics. Tell the child exactly what it is you are going to do and what you expect of him: "Joey, from now on we are going to work on picking up your dirty clothes and putting them in the hamper." Talk about what you want him to do more often and less often.

Don't reveal your entire strategy, but let him know in a friendly, loving, and nonthreatening manner what goal you both will be working toward. Depending on the strategy or solutions you have selected, as well as the age of the child, you may have more information to impart, such as details about charts or rewards.

CHAPTER 2

The Basic Techniques
of Discipline

TO most parents, discipline is punishment. But the word *discipline* really means training or teaching and combines both positive and negative techniques. When you discipline children, you *teach* them how to behave. You give instructions before you ask them to try a skill. You model behaviors for them so they may see what's expected. You tell them over and over again what they are doing well. And when necessary, you tell them what it is they do that is not appropriate.

Effective discipline is signaling, "That's fine," when your child glances over at you for reassurance when he's exploring. It's a firm no when your toddler reaches for the electrical outlet. It's ignoring a little one's repeated attempts to interrupt your telephone conversation, but quick attention after she patiently waits her turn. And it's letting an older child know you recognize that it's difficult for him to give up an argument. And sometimes it's allowing negative natural consequences to follow his behavior when it is not what you'd like it to be. The yesses are often more important than the nos because they let the child know when he's behaving as you wish.

Parenting isn't complete in one day, and discipline is not a one-time effort. Both must be constant and consistent efforts to be lovingly effectual with your child.

There is much to teach a child—values, beliefs, and skills—and it takes time. Besides, your child won't always be ready for the lesson. So we suggest that first, you learn to relax (see Section 2.10). That way, you may handle unexpected events and unsuccessful efforts more calmly and effectively. Second, you should examine your parenting goals and your child's needs so you know what you expect. Third, you should strive to be consistent, saying what you mean and meaning what you say and sticking with it. And finally, you should maintain a positive approach to parenting, keeping a picture in your mind of how you want your child to act and then remembering to tell him what it is he's doing that you like. You'll have opportunities to point out what you don't like, but a positive focus will strengthen your disapproval when you must use it.

The basic skills and techniques of discipline are discussed in detail in this chapter, then repeatedly used in the solutions throughout the book. They are the foundation of *Good Behavior*. You must understand them thoroughly before you begin to use them, so you will become a more confident, secure, and effective parent and your child will practice the good behavior you admire.

2.1 HOW TO PRAISE

It's easy for parents to focus only on what their children are doing wrong and fail to notice what they are doing right. For example, Mike and Leah are playing quietly in the den and no one comments on how nicely they are sharing the toys. But a few minutes later, when they quarrel, Dad quickly finds his voice.

Parents are so busy teaching and caring for their children that it's easy to take good behavior for granted, but when everything goes wrong, it's easy for them to come up with ten other misdeeds. They get stuck in the usual web of criticism, and everyone ends up feeling bad.

Constant criticism combined with little praise has other results, too. Your child wants your attention, and he'll get it in any way he can. If your focus is negative, then he'll use negative means to reach you. If you concentrate on the positive, you will get more good behavior in response because *that's* what gets the attention.

If you're not used to praising your child, it may be difficult for you to do at first, and in the midst of an already hectic day, it may seem like one more thing to remember. But the more you use it, the more natural and easy it will become. You will quickly learn that praise is such a powerful influence that only a little of it can shape a new behavior and even less will maintain the change.

Parents sometimes fear that children will become dependent on praise. It's quite possible for the wrong kind of praise to lead to problems with a child who's insecure or has always been the center of attention. But it is our experience that most children get too *little* praise rather than too much and that praise can perform miracles.

If you use these guidelines when you apply it, you will quickly see that praise is a remarkably effective discipline technique:

Praise Behavior, Not Personality.

When parents consult us because they are having problems dealing with their child, they are often so exasperated that they have nothing positive to say about that child. They describe his personality with words like *rebellious, lazy,* and *selfish.* That's a vicious cycle that leads nowhere. Behavior can be altered, and that is where the focus belongs. Personality is more resistant to change. When you center your efforts on behavior, you are much more likely to reach your goal.

Don't say, "That's a good girl!" which sends a message that being good all the time is the goal, an impossible expectation. Say instead, "I like the way you spoke to Granny just now." No amount of "good boy" or "good girl" will build a positive self-concept unless the child receives specific feedback on his actual good behaviors, because his self-image is composed of his accomplishments.

The most effective way to build good behavior is to shape it with praise. Shaping with praise is a teaching tool that you must use repeatedly to show your approval of your child's newly established behaviors.

Use Specific Praise.

The purpose of praise is to increase desirable behaviors, so you must emphasize the specific behaviors that please you. The more specific your praise is, the better the child will understand what he's doing right and the more likely he will be to repeat it. One morning, for example, you notice your child has made her bed. At that moment, she's brushing her hair. If you simply say, "Looks nice," she won't know whether you are referring to her bed or her hair. Say, "I really like the way you made your bed so neatly this morning. Thanks."

When parents have a difficult time finding something positive to say about their child, we ask them to keep a good behavior diary, where they will record all the good things the child does. We've had parents exclaim, "The pages will be blank!" but they are usually amazed to see how many positive behaviors they can note down and how much it helps them in learning to praise their child.

When you use this technique, share your notes with your child at the end of each day. It's a good way to talk about the events of the day, and you'll both feel good.

Praise Progress.

Start praising every little step toward the target behavior, making a point of catching the child at being good. Suppose you have told your child he must clean up his toys when he's through playing with them, though he's never done this before. Praise every bit of progress, however minor. At first, praise him for picking up one toy from the floor even though he's left three others there. You might say, "It was great the way you picked up your truck and put it in the toy box. Let me help you pick up the others." The next time, praise him for picking up two items, and so on.

Or suppose your child is accustomed to instant attention and won't let you finish a telephone conversation without interrupting you. The first time she waits thirty seconds, pause in your conversation and thank her for not interrupting. Respond to her before continuing to talk. At the next opportunity, wait a little longer before pausing, praising, and responding, so that her waiting is "shaped." You may have to begin with lower expectations so you can reach your goal.

When the new behavior is well established, less praise will be needed to maintain it. You needn't continue to praise the child constantly. Instead, praise him randomly, perhaps every fifth or tenth time he performs appropriately. This will be sufficient to keep the new behavior reinforced and will soon feel natural to both of you. Never, however, stop praising completely.

Praise Appropriately.

If it's going to elicit the response you want, the praise must fit the child. Hugs, kisses, and other physical signs of affection paired with the proper words are very effective for little ones. Some children a little older, however, like to be praised privately, and in that case it's better to keep a quiet tally or to use special secret signals. A wink or a thumbs-up will tell your child, without focusing unwanted attention on her, that you've noticed the good work. Later, let her know how well she did.

Many older children accept joking comments better than straight praise. Saying, "I wonder what cleaning crew passed through here" may elicit a better response from a preteen than, "You really made your bed nicely and cleaned up so beautifully."

What we're saying is that you must judge your own youngster's reactions to praise to see if you're striking the right chord. If a child plays down your comments but later repeats the good behavior, then you'll know this form of praise did its job.

Remember that anyone will tire of too much of a good thing. The same phrases used over and over again will lose their effectiveness. Be creative. Little notes left under a pillow or in a lunch box can make your comments special. Or let your child overhear you raving about his accomplishments to a friend.

For an added boost, accompany your praise with a reward. Tell your child what he did that you liked and reward him with a little gift, but save the surprises for special occasions so they won't be expected.

Give Praise Immediately.

Praise is most effective, especially with very young children, when it's delivered promptly. Don't let time go by between the child's approved behavior and your response, though older children can appreciate delayed recognition.

The gap between a child's action and your feedback can be bridged with a gesture if necessary, and the good behavior diary can lead to a private signal between you. When you record what your child is doing well and show the diary to her, say something to her too, like, "I'm glad to see you are sharing your paper with your sister." Later, you may keep a number tally without long written comments, and eventually the tally can turn into a silent signal of praise written in the air that is personally meaningful.

Mix Praise with Unconditional Love.

Children crave your praise when that's the only time they get attention from you. Some parents begin to worry that their children will behave nicely only if they receive the recognition. When you are working on establishing a new behavior, praise this behavior constantly at the beginning, then gradually fade it. When the behavior has been taught, praise it randomly. You can't be present every time the child does something right, anyway. The times when you do comment specifically and positively on her behavior will give the child a positive view of herself, so she becomes secure in her accomplishments.

At the same time, show the child you value and love her unconditionally even when you are not working on her behavior. Hug her, pay attention to her, listen to her, appreciate her. This will reassure her that she doesn't need to "earn" your love, because she already has it.

2.2 HOW TO IGNORE

An effective way to eliminate specific irritating behaviors is simply to ignore them. You may feel, when you use this technique, that you're doing absolutely nothing to alter the situation, but you will find that by systematically ignoring certain behaviors, consistently acting as though they weren't happening, you will have astonishing results.

When they want to, children will do just about anything to get your total and immediate attention. They know exactly what will startle you or irritate you the most, especially at your most vulnerable moments—in the front hall just as the guests arrive, for example, or when you are on the phone or at the check-out counter in the supermarket. If you can ignore the annoying behavior every time it happens, children will stop doing it because it doesn't get the results they are looking for.

Systematic ignoring is the art of ignoring the behaviors you don't like and paying positive attention to those you do like. One should never be done without the other.

Before you try this strategy, however, you must classify the behavior and decide whether you can safely ignore it. Obviously, you cannot ignore dangerous actions like running into the street or climbing on top of the refrigerator, and you can't ignore actions you simply can't tolerate, like hitting and biting.

Another point to consider: Systematic ignoring is a technique that some parents like and can use effectively. For others, it only increases the stress because their tolerance for ignoring is too low. If this is the case with you, try another of our solutions for handling the problem.

Here are the guidelines for successful systematic ignoring:

Decide What You Can and Cannot Ignore.

Is this a behavior that you can, should, or wish to ignore? Is it safe to ignore it? Or is the behavior hazardous to the child, someone else, or property? If Johnny throws heavy objects or plays with electrical outlets, this is not a situation that calls for ignoring.

Don't start anything you can't finish. If this is a behavior you know you cannot manage to ignore for hours, then don't even start. Most behaviors get worse before they get better. Ask yourself: "What's the worst that can happen?" "Can I bear it?" Will you be able to put up with the screams for Doodle Delights in the supermarket while other shoppers turn to stare at you and shake their head at your hardheartedness? If your child uses profanity in front of Grandma, can you turn a deaf ear? If you can't, then it would be better to choose another option for dealing with this behavior.

Ignoring is most effective with behaviors that have previously been nurtured by attention from you and will not work well on those that are normal at certain ages or stages of development. Most two- or three-year-olds throw some tantrums, and no matter how well you ignore them, it's unrealistic to expect them to disappear. However, systematic ignoring of early tantrums will reduce their persistence later.

Ignoring usually works well to stop a behavior that has always provoked attention and has allowed the child to "get his way" before. Tantrums are a good example. Your child wants a piece of candy, but you say, "No, not now." She cries, she falls on the floor, she kicks and screams. You try to resist, but you finally can't stand it anymore and you give in. You give her the candy to stop the tantrum. The tears dry up, and her tactics have worked. You have reinforced her reliance on tantrums for the future.

Next time, try walking out of the room instead. You may be surprised at how quickly those tears stop. Mrs. J. came to us for a consultation because her two daughters, ages seven and eight and a half, were constantly fighting. Since the girls seemed to fight much more when their mother was around, we suggested systematic ignoring. Now, when the fights began, Mrs. J. became very occupied with other matters and paid no attention. The girls tried to get her involved, to intervene or take sides. But she told them to settle their disputes themselves and left the room. When the fighting stopped, she returned to talk or play. If another argument ensued, she left again. Before long, the girls got the idea that their fighting didn't get them the results they wanted and it diminished considerably.

You might think a toddler couldn't be so sophisticated, but this is a true story: Noah would have a tantrum when he was strapped into his car seat. On the eve of his third birthday, his father commented as he buckled up his son, "Tomorrow you will be three. No more tantrums." Noah stopped screaming and said, "No way, Jose!" before resuming his tears. Systematic ignoring changed this pattern, too.

Pay No Attention to the Behavior.

Do not react to the unwanted behavior in any way, verbally or nonverbally. Don't say anything about it. Don't look at the child when he's making his performance. Don't display any facial expressions or gestures in response to it. Look away, pretend you're doing something else, leave the room. If you can't leave, casually move as far away as you can. Continue for as long as he continues the behavior.

This doesn't mean giving him the cold shoulder, because that is another form of attention. Don't smile with amusement, either, because the patronizing attitude will make him more defiant. Just become so involved with what you are doing that you don't notice anything.

One little boy used to put his head into his plate and cry when he didn't get more of his favorite food. His parents learned to talk to each other, discussing the dust on the chandelier or their dinner plans, and ignore his crying. Eventually, when he realized he wasn't likely to get more of that particular food right then, the toddler picked up his spoon and began eating something else on his plate. Now the habit has vanished.

Consider any attempt to catch your attention to be a sign of progress, and double your efforts to appear uninterested. Don't respond. Hum, turn up the radio, look at the ceiling, talk to yourself about your chores—all are effective ways of maintaining your inattention.

Expect Behaviors to Get Worse Before They Get Better.

When you first start ignoring an undesirable behavior, your child will do her best to get the attention she's accustomed to receiving. She will increase the intensity, volume, and frequency to the point where she is sure you will respond. But you must not give in. Don't let her know that her antics can drive you to acquiesce as they always have before.

Try timing or counting the occurrences of the behavior to get you through it; this will show you the progress you are making. Though tantrums and nagging may seem to last for eternity, you can measure them in seconds or minutes. Over a few days' time, you will probably see that the behavior intensifies and then wanes. When you notice that the whining lasted ten minutes yesterday when you didn't give your child a cookie and only eight minutes today, you'll be encouraged to continue the tactic. Before too long, whining in response to your no to a snack will be just a memory.

Keep in mind, then, that the more consistent you are and the more completely you remove your attention from the target behavior, the sooner it will subside.

Reinforce Desirable Behaviors.

You can speed the extinction of the undesirable behaviors by reinforcing good behavior that you like with praise and rewards. If you are trying to cut down on whining, praise your child immediately for playing nicely when she stops the whining for a few seconds and picks up a toy. Move closer to her and show interest in what she's doing. If the whining starts again, ignore her until it stops. If the child plays with his food and you are ignoring what's happening, go into action when he picks up his fork. Tell him how much you like the way he's eating his peas.

Sometimes, you can encourage positive behavior by pointing it out glowingly in someone else so that the offender will be prompted to imitate that person. Take, for example, a household where one child continually gets up and down from the dinner table while the other sits politely. The proper move is to praise the behavior of the child who is sitting properly at the table and withhold acknowledgment of the one jumping up and down. One caution: If this tactic backfires and encourages the poor behavior, stop! However, keep it in your repertoire. It will work another time.

2.3 HOW TO USE THE BROKEN RECORD TECHNIQUE

Don't try to reason forever with a child who refuses to accept no for an answer. This child has learned that persistence will get results, so he continues to carry on until you give in. "But why can't I?" repeated enough times can become extremely annoying, especially after you've given several answers.

Don't get angry; that often leads to guilt rather than success. Don't give in, either. If ignoring isn't your style or you can't stick with it, try the broken record technique. This means you counter the demands with an adult version of the same behavior.

Let's say Brian is clamoring for a snack right before dinner. You decide he can't really be that hungry and you don't want him to ruin his meal. You explain the reasons for your decision reasonably and fully—just once. Then, in response to additional demands, you repeat the same explanation in abbreviated form, such as, "No snack before dinner."

No matter how creative Brian's arguments become, say only, "No snack before dinner." This technique is most effective when you seem to be paying scant attention to the pleas. Continue whatever you are doing, singsonging the phrase whenever a new demand is made.

We assure you that you'll get some interesting results. The child may first respond by getting angry. He may throw a tantrum, scream, or complain. But eventually, the demands will decrease because he'll tire of asking and getting the same answer. If he does misbehave so badly that you feel additional action is needed, apply time-out (see Section 2.7) or another form of punishment (Section 2.6). Do not lose your temper.

2.4 HOW TO REWARD

Rewards for desirable behavior act as reinforcers that make the child feel good about how she's acted and make her want to do the same thing more often. A reinforcer can be anything that follows a behavior and causes it to happen more often. It provides motivation.

The first time your baby said Mama or Dada, you reinforced those sounds with smiles and hugs. You were thrilled, and your baby knew it. The first time she climbed onto the kitchen counter and reached the cookie jar, her climb was reinforced by the taste of the cookies. In both cases, her initial behavior was reinforced by the results.

Choosing an appropriate reward for your child's desirable behavior is not always easy. It's a matter of detective work, common sense, and a little guessing to find just the thing that will please her. We suggest you ask an older child what he'd like so you'll have the information you need and can still maintain control over the selection.

Make a Survey.

To help you accomplish this, we suggest you make a survey of your child's wishes, like the one below. Because children's preferences change frequently, repeat the process from time to time.

REINFORCER SURVEY
1. If you could wish for three things, what would they be?
   1.
   2.
   3.

2. If you had the following amount of money, how would you spend it?
   —$ .05
      .10
      .25
      .50
      1.00
      5.00
      more

3. If you could do something alone with Dad, what would it be?

4. If you could do something special with Mom, what would it be?

5. What extra privileges would you like to earn (extra TV time, later bedtime, etc.)?

6. What would you like to do with a friend (go to a movie, play miniature golf, get ice cream cones, etc.)

The survey will give you a menu of potential rewards. Separate them into lists of small rewards that could be used on a daily basis and larger rewards, which would be appropriate for weekly or monthly progress. For example:

Daily Rewards	Weekly Rewards	Monthly Rewards
stickers	book	doll
dessert	movie	game

Vary the Rewards.

There are some strategies that will make your selection of rewards most effective. One is to vary the rewards so they don't lose their appeal. Bradley was very excited when he earned a small plastic animal every time he used the potty instead of his pants, and he earned a lot of them. But after a couple of weeks, he lost interest in these toys.

Select many different kinds of rewards from the menu you've developed with the survey. Then alternate the tangible material rewards with activities and special privileges.

When you can, choose rewards appropriate to the behavior you are reinforcing. Staying up thirty minutes later at night could be a logical reward for getting ready for school on time and in good cheer.

Always Deliver.

And always deliver quickly. To a child, especially a small child, the nonfulfillment or delay of a promised reward is a betrayal. Don't make promises you can't keep, and don't make substitutions. When a reward is earned, give it. Your child must know you will come through.

Remember: It Takes Time.

Changing a child's behavior takes time and the proper motivation. At first, reward any progress, using the reward to shape the new behavior. Later, less reinforcement will be required to maintain it.

Let us tell you about Cheryl, a little girl who wanted to do everything right the first time and was afraid to admit she needed help sometimes. Despite reassurance from her parents and teachers, tears were her usual response to frustration in school.

We set up a system to help her ask for help or persist at a task without crying. Cheryl was told she could earn one point each time she asked for help or persisted at a task without crying. Her teacher helped her keep the tally. Every evening, she earned a small reward from her list—ribbons, fancy barrettes, plastic charms, a chance to ride her bike with Daddy's help after dinner, or extra reading time before going to sleep. Her points also could be used to earn the right to color in one section of a graph toward a bigger reward. Watery eyes were rewarded at first, then no tears at all. Slowly, the points required for the rewards increased so she was able to earn a reward every other day, then twice a week.

The changes in Cheryl's behavior were remarkable. She cried less, tried longer, asked for help when she needed it, and smiled more. As her tolerance for frustration increased and her new mature behavior stabilized, the frequency of rewards decreased even more and her teacher sent home weekly notes instead of daily notes. Smily faces on the family calendar replaced the chart, and finally, even the weekly notes were discontinued at Cheryl's insistence. Her parents still occasionally surprise her with a reward to let her know they notice.

Her progress demonstrates the basic rules that will help you use rewards effectively.

• Define exactly what you want your child to do more often. As precisely as possible, define what he must do to earn the reward. Do not say, "Be more responsible." Instead say, "Please make your bed neatly in the morning."

• Reward initial progress with immediate or daily rewards, combined with long-term rewards. The child's earning power should be dual when the program first begins. The first time he picks up his toys, he might earn a sticker—plus a point toward a reward that "costs" five points. Use marks or stars on a chart to note the points, or let him color in a portion of a rocketship shaped like the one in Figure 1. The younger the child, the more important the visual measures of success are.

Fig. 1 Chad's Rocket Chart

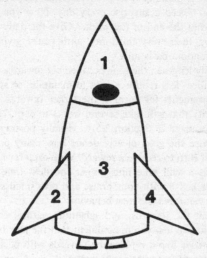

Color one section each time teeth are brushed

• Gradually increase the requirements as the child shows improvement. For example, if your goal is to have the child put all of her toys in the correct place when she's finished with them, at first give her a small immediate reward for putting away one toy. Then when she's earned several rewards, change the criteria so she must put away two or three toys to earn a reward. Over time, slowly increase your expectations even more to shape the child's behavior, but don't make the changes too fast.

• Don't accept a poor performance after you've raised the ante. Once you have upped the requirements, if the child doesn't earn a reward one day, tell her how sorry you are but that she will have another chance tomorrow. Then ask her to get busy picking up the toys she forgot to put away.

• Gradually fade out the daily rewards. When you have concluded that the new behavior is well established, slowly fade the daily rewards, explaining it in positive terms: "You are doing so well, you don't need a surprise every day. Now you can earn a bigger reward at the end of the week." Give the daily rewards on alternate days, then every third day, until you're giving small rewards on a random basis only.

• Gradually lengthen the time between big rewards. Established behavior requires less reinforcement to maintain, so start increasing the requirements for earning the larger rewards. Choose an item or activity that will take several weeks to earn. Using one of the charts discussed in Section 2.5 to visually portray the child's progress toward the goal, clearly define how many points on the chart he must earn to receive a reward. With each reward, increase the "cost" so it will take him longer the next time to earn it. Meantime, be lavish with your praise and give small surprises occasionally to reinforce the new behavior.

• Phase out the rewards, and substitute natural consequences and recognition. When you're confident that the new behavior has become a positive habit, replace the rewards with positive natural consequences and recognition to maintain it. A natural consequence for learning to sit politely at the dinner table would be to let the child select a favorite restaurant to go to because he has such good table manners. Comment on how nicely he's behaving, and encourage other people to do the same.

2.5 HOW TO USE CHARTS

Callie proudly displays her chart to all visitors. It's covered with the stars she has earned for brushing her teeth after every meal without reminders from her parents. Joshua carries a small index card divided into columns to school every day. His teacher initials the card each time he completes an assignment on time. He rushes home after school every afternoon and transfers his earnings to the chart on the refrigerator, because he's working toward a new video game.

Many professionals use charts and graphs to portray profits, research findings, and test results. Charts are an excellent way for you to illuminate your child's new behaviors clearly and simply. To be effective, charts must be simple and easy to read. We've had parents show us charts with which they have had little success and it was quite obvious to us why they didn't work. They were complicated flow charts and graphs of multiple behaviors that only an engineer could possibly follow. Our charts are not designed to complicate the lives of parents or children. Their object is to give you a simple visual way to track each child's behaviors.

Here are our suggestions. Let each child decorate his own chart with drawings, cutouts, stickers, or designs. The whole chart may be in the shape of something the child likes, the behavior he's learning, or the reward he's working toward. It may be posted wherever the child wants it—on display in the kitchen, on the bedroom mirror, or hidden away in a drawer.

Each chart must be part of a system for earning short-term and long-term rewards, as discussed in Section 2.4. The charts should follow these guidelines:

Focus on Only One Behavior (or Cluster of Behaviors) at a Time.

It's impossible to change everything at once, and trying to do it will overwhelm everyone involved. Take one problem at a time, then add to it appropriately. Jamie, one of our patients, had morning problems. He got up late, wouldn't make his bed, and didn't have time for breakfast. We tackled getting up on time first. When he began to get up with the alarm clock consistently, we added bed making to the chart, and then the criteria for earning a point included both behaviors. When he had these under control, we added breakfast to the list. All three of these behaviors were grouped together on the chart as A.M. Responsibilities. (Figure 2)

Make the Chart Easy to Use, Read, and Maintain.

In dealing with a daily behavior, try a chart based on the calendar, perhaps like the one in Figure 2.

Fig. 2 Jamie's A.M. Chart

WEEK	MON	TUES	WED	THURS	FRI	TOTAL CHECKS
1						
2						
3						
4						

Jamie earns a check if he gets up by 7:00 A.M. without reminder.

When the target behavior is the kind that occurs often during the day, then a daily chart divided into appropriate time intervals works better. (Figure 3) The chart in Figure 3 was used to teach Aileen not to whine. Because whining doesn't occur at scheduled times, this chart allowed her to earn stars for each hour she hadn't whined. Aileen's mom made the chart on bright colored paper with stickers and drawings to make it more appealing.

Fig. 3 Aileen's Chart

TIME	SUN	MON	TUES	WED	THURS	FRI	SAT
8:00							
9:00							
10:00							
11:00							
12:00							
1:00							
2:00							
3:00							
4:00							
5:00							
6:00							
7:00							
TOTAL							

Aileen earns a point for each hour she doesn't whine.

Sometimes, especially with older children, the target periods are early morning, late afternoon, and evening. This chart was designed to encourage Timothy to follow instructions better. Because he was working toward an airplane kit, he designed his chart in the shape of a plane (Figure 4).

Fig. 4 Timothy's Chart

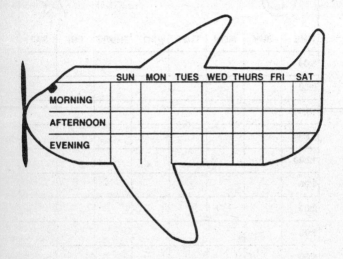

	SUN	MON	TUES	WED	THURS	FRI	SAT
MORNING							
AFTERNOON							
EVENING							

Timothy earns points for following instructions.

Be Absolutely Consistent Until the Behavior Is Established.

Use the chart faithfully, without missing a day, reinforcing the new behavior with plenty of praise and natural consequences. Then, when a new habit has been established, phase out the rewards, as we've already described in Section 2.4.

To summarize the technique of using charts effectively, let's use Jamie, the boy with the morning problem, as an example. Jamie originally earned a small reward for each check earned each day, with one check per good behavior. Later he had to accomplish all three behaviors (getting up on time, making his bed, and eating breakfast) to earn a check.

In addition to the daily rewards, each of his checks allowed him to earn part of a larger reward—a football—by accumulating his checks until he had six of them. With a little backsliding, he earned the checks and got his football. The next reward cost seven checks, and the one after that, eight. In this way, the rewards became less frequent, until they were finally phased out, though his parents occasionally surprised him with a small reward for doing so well.

2.6 HOW TO PUNISH

All parents have strong opinions about punishment, and all parents, whether they admit it or not, use punishment as a way to teach their children appropriate behavior. If you have ever sent your child to her room, restricted television time, taken away a beloved toy, or firmly exclaimed, "No!" when your toddler reached for the hot stove, then you have used the punishment principle to change behavior.

It would be wonderful if we could raise our children using only positive techniques—but we can't. It takes both positive and negative consequences to teach them desirable behavior patterns. We do not think punishment is necessarily good or bad. We are not against its use. We are *for* the effective use of punishment when that discipline technique is appropriate.

Punishment alone, however, won't effect the desired results. That's because it is entirely negative. It teaches a child what *not* to do; it doesn't teach him what he *should* do. When it's used alone, without the balance of positive reinforcement of appropriate behavior, it doesn't teach the child how to replace the poor behavior with a more acceptable one.

Three-year-old Heather climbs onto a chair to reach a glass. Her mother pulls her off the chair and scolds her for climbing. Heather cries and says, "I no do it anymore, Mommy." That's fine for now, but did she learn that there are cups at a safer level or that she should ask for help the next time? She learned what *not* to do but not what she should do in the future.

In addition, the effects of punishment are at best temporary, and when a punishment is used too often, it loses its effectiveness. Parents frequently tell us things like, "The first time I spanked Carl, he cried bitterly and then behaved very well for a long time. Now it seems like I am always spanking him—hard, too—but it has no effect on him. He doesn't even seem to care." That's the classic adaptation effect, and it is one of the reasons we don't recommend spanking as a form of punishment.

Because punishment is sometimes a necessary management technique, however, the question becomes: When and how should you use it? We suggest these principles:

Choose a Punishment That Decreases the Undesired Behavior.

Punishment is effective only if it makes the inappropriate behavior less likely to recur. All too often, children are sent to the principal's office as punishment, but it doesn't work as intended. The student avoids assignments and enjoys waiting for the principal, so his misbehavior is inadvertently reinforced. This is especially true if he receives little praise for positive actions. If you use physical punishment, grounding, restrictions, or removal of toys or privileges, it's not punishment if it doesn't work.

The classic example is nine-year-old Mike. He was sent to his room for hitting his sister. There, he played with his robots and computer. When his mother told him he could come out, he was watching his favorite superhero show on TV. He couldn't have cared less about being sent to his room. Besides, when he did come out, he hit his sister for getting him in trouble.

So our advice is to observe the effect of the punishment. If the target behavior has decreased, then the consequence must have been punishing. If not, then it's no use repeating that action. Try another technique.

Use Punishment Sparingly.

If you use punishment too often, your child will get used to it and it will not continue to be effective. Any action—even if it is effective—including grounding, loss of television, and spankings, will be weakened with overuse and won't have the desired effect when you need it.

Use Punishment in Combination with Positive Techniques.

When you choose to use punishment, be sure you give positive discipline as well. Applied by itself, punishment does not automatically teach a child good behavior. To encourage a child to act the way you would like, you must define, teach, and reward the positive behaviors you wish to develop. If, say, you punish your child for running into the street, also teach her how to stop, look, and listen before crossing the road. Praise her for staying in the yard or looking carefully before crossing the street. This will make punishment for undesired actions more effective.

Don't Delay Punishment.

If you are going to punish your child, do it as soon as possible after the misbehavior. Behavior is controlled by immediate consequences, both positive and negative, so don't wait till "Daddy comes home." Don't wait until afternoon or tomorrow or next week. Any punishment loses its influence in the waiting, and the child may not connect it with what he did wrong.

Always Explain the Consequences.

The child must know what behavior displeases you and what you will do if he continues to do it. Tell him your rule and the consequence for ignoring it.

Be Consistent.

Effectual punishment is not only swift, it is also predictable. It must occur each and every time the misbehavior occurs. If your child has been told that if he throws a block, he will lose it, then the block should be taken away immediately after he throws it.

Don't Make Empty Threats.

Don't threaten a child with punishment and then fail to follow through. Don't give her a second, third, or a twelfth chance before taking action. Say what you mean and mean what you say—every time. Inconsistency and empty threats lead to misbehavior that becomes more firmly established and more resistant to change.

Give an Opportunity to Practice Good Behavior.

The flip side of punishment is teaching the child what is appropriate, but she must get the chance to show what she's learned. Prolonged punishment prevents that from happening. Take grounding, for example. The child comes home very late or has ignored repeated calls to come inside for dinner. In your anger, you ground her for a month. For that month, she can't show you she's learned to come home on time or respond punctually to calls. She may resent the punishment so much that she sneaks out or acts like a caged animal. If, however, she is punished by having to come directly home from school for two days, then she soon has the opportunity to show you she's learned the rules. Within a month's time, she will have many chances to regain your trust.

If You Use Physical Punishment, Make It Brief and Controlled.

As a general principle, we do not recommend physical punishment, but there are a few isolated exceptions. If, for example, your two-year-old tries to stick a bobbypin into an electrical outlet, you might shout, "No!," grab the bobbypin, and give the child a quick slap on the hand. For a toddler, this consequence is more appropriate than a lecture on the dangers of electricity.

An alternate approach, really more effective with some children, is to hold the child's hand still as you say no emphatically. Momentary restraint often works well with young children. It is also a good alternative when you become so frustrated that you feel you may lose your cool and strike the child too hard.

Never apply physical punishment in anger. If you choose to use spanking, do it as a conscious selection rather than an emotional response of the moment. Your action should then be purposeful, brief, and controlled. We believe the outside limits of physical punishment must be a slap on the hand or the bottom with an open hand. Anything more than that can be dangerous. *Never* use paddles, belts, switches, or any other object to spank a child.

Try, instead, to use nonphysical management techniques such as time out, overcorrection, and response cost, and other forms of punishment such as restrictions and loss of privileges or objects. Remember: The best discipline techniques include both positive and negative consequences *planned* as a way to change a behavior.

2.7 HOW TO USE TIME-OUT

Most parenting techniques are not brand new. Time-out has been around for a long time. Do you remember the nursery rhyme "Sulky Sue, what shall we do? Turn her face to the wall till she comes to." Time-out really means time out from positive reinforcement. In practical terms, it means removing the child from an activity or situation so he can't be part of the action or receive praise or attention. As a punishment technique, it can be very effective when it is used correctly. It works best when the child feels he is missing something.

Build these steps into your plan:

1. Choose the time-out location carefully.

For time-out to be effective, your child must feel he is missing out on something better than what he's experiencing in time-out.

Therefore, a time-out location should be boring—not cruel, dark, or scary, just boring. Any safe place in the house that is uninteresting will do. A "thinking corner" will work, too, if it's removed from the mainstream of family activity. A bedroom is fine if the child can be restricted to his bed. The actual location is less important, however, than the fact that the child prefers to be elsewhere. If Sandy desperately wants to watch a certain TV program, play with his brother, or ride his bicycle, then even a bedroom full of toys is a good location for time-out.

2. Explain the time-out rules to the child.

At a quiet time before you need to use this technique, tell your child that she will be sent to time-out if she continues to do whatever it is you have asked her not to do. Explain that this will help her break this habit. Then follow through *every* time the behavior occurs.

At first, apply time-out for one behavior at a time. When that behavior has changed, then use it for another. If you use it for many misbehaviors at once, the child will become confused about why he is now in time-out. Besides, time-out, like any punishment technique, loses its effectiveness when it is overused.

3. Set a time limit to the time-out according to the child's age.

Long periods of time spent in a room or weeks of grounding are nonproductive, leaving a child resentful and behavior unchanged. A short time-out usually works very well and need last only for minutes. According to Drs. Vance and Marilyn Hall in their booklet "How to Use Time-Out," a child should stay in time-out for one minute per year of age. We have found this to be a very good rule of thumb. Accordingly, this means four minutes for a four-year-old, five for a five-year-old, with one more minute for each additional year. For a child, that's a long time with nothing to do. It interrupts his activity but gives him a chance to cool down and stop doing whatever sent him there.

4. Add minutes for resistance.

The shorter length of time also gives you leverage. If you have difficulty putting your child in time-out or keeping him there, add a minute to the time-out period for each instance of resistance. If Marshall refuses to go to time-out, he should be led there and told, "That's one more minute." Supervise as needed. If he leaves without permission, he must be led back and given another minute. Try not to exceed three one-minute penalties, because at this point it will be more effective to add another consequence.

5. Add backup consequences for excessive resistance.

If you reach the point where it's necessary to back up your words and actions, inform the child that if he doesn't do his time-out, he will lose a favorite toy or privilege for a few days. Then follow through. Often, the knowledge that a backup consequence exists will curb the resistance.

6. Use a timer.

Keep track of the passing minutes with a kitchen timer. Tell the child how long he must remain in time-out and that he may come out when the bell rings if he has quieted down. If you've added time, reset the timer. If he has not calmed down before the time is up, don't allow him to leave until he has controlled himself.

7. Don't let time-out become a way to avoid responsibilities.

When the time is up, have the child do whatever he was asked to do before time-out began or to show the appropriate behavior. When he cooperates, praise him warmly. This, too, will work best when the child is eager to rejoin the activity he has been missing.

8. Adapt the procedure for older children.

Although time-out works best with children between the ages of two and about twelve, the same principles apply to grounding or other forms of time-out that are more appropriate for older children. Brief periods of grounding are better than weeks or months, and can always be reactivated if the child reverts to his old habits. For example, if a youngster's grades drop, he can be grounded for a few days until he shows he's studying harder and more consistently. If he slacks off once the grounding has been lifted, it can be reapplied. If the child misuses the telephone, it can be timed out so she may make or receive no calls for that evening. The next night, the rules for using the telephone can be reinstated and she can try again. When the time-out period is shorter, she is motivated again and she feels the punishment is fair.

2.8 HOW TO USE OVERCORRECTION

Overcorrection, as used by Dr. Nathan Azrin, a psychologist, is a powerful set of techniques designed to put an end to persistent undesirable behaviors. It uses natural consequences to break bad habits and to teach appropriate behaviors at the same time. It's an extremely effective alternative to yelling, nagging, spanking, or any other punishment in your efforts to turn unpleasant or difficult behaviors into those you can accept. It works well for common annoying behaviors and more serious nervous habits or even aggressive and possibly harmful behaviors.

When you use overcorrection, you have the child "undo" the damage she has done and then practice (and practice and practice) the right way to approach the request or task. She repeats the "antidote" to the point where she doesn't want to revert to the undesirable behavior again. Meanwhile, you ignore resisting, crying, throwing a tantrum, and you follow through to the end. This may not be easy for you, but it is essential.

Consider this example: Your child draws on the wall—once again. Tell her that the wall looks dirty because of the writing and that "somebody" must clean it so it will look nice again. Give the child the proper cleaning materials and then supervise the cleaning process. Then, explain that the cleaned spot now looks lighter than the rest of the wall and so that part must also be cleaned (within reason, of course).

If the child refuses, calmly but firmly inform her that you understand how she feels, but it's obvious that she hasn't had enough practice cleaning and you will gladly show her how to do it. Take the child's hands and manually guide her through the procedures, even if she resists or complains. When the area is clean once again, ask her to show you the proper place for her to draw. If she writes on the wall again, repeat the entire process: "Oh no! The wall is dirty again. You need more practice cleaning walls! When you're finished, you can show me again where you may draw."

In most cases, this is enough motivation for even the most oppositional child to stop writing on walls. This technique is effective with younger and older children.

Overcorrection sometimes works wonders with behaviors that approach obsession. Cathy, an active four-year-old, was fascinated by electrical switches and plugs, playing with light switches, unplugging appliances, flicking on garbage disposals and fans. Her parents had found all the lights on in the middle of the night and the freezer quietly defrosting at noon. They punished her and restricted her, but nothing worked for very long.

We suggested that overdoing this same behavior could put an end to it. When a switch was turned on or a plug disconnected, Cathy had to check every plug and switch in the house over and over again. After the fourth round of checking, she tired of the game. "One more time. I'm not sure about the switches in the hall," her mother said. After three more passes, Cathy was told she'd practiced enough for the day. A few more days, a few more practice sessions, and she lost her interest in plugs and switches.

This power-packed technique will be suggested throughout this book. Here is how to apply it:

1. Have the Child Undo or Correct the Social or Physical Damage.

Examples: cleaning the wall, picking up clothes from the floor, apologizing for biting.

2. Have the Child Practice Positive Behaviors.

For example, if he doesn't come in from outdoors when he's called, have him go back outside and come in after being called ten times in succession. Repeat this from several locations and directions around the yard.

3. Supervise the Practice Session.

This may take a little time, but it's well worth the investment.

4. Use Manual Guidance if Necessary.

If the child resists practicing, manually guide her through the correct actions. If she won't pick up toys, hold her hands and guide them like robots, picking up toys and depositing them in the right place. Ignore crying, tantrums, or resisting. Be calm but firm until the job is done or the child begins to do it by herself.

5. Praise and Reinforce Compliance.

As the child begins to behave better and less practice is needed, let her know what a great job you think she is doing. Praise lavishly. Give her a little reward for her progress.

6. Resist the Urge to Do It for Her.

Be consistent. Don't start cleaning the wall yourself or picking up the toys, or you will have lost the benefits you've gained. Instead, remind her she can always put in some extra practice if she needs it. And if that's the case, supervise the practice once again.

2.9 HOW TO LISTEN AND TALK TO YOUR CHILD

Keeping the lines of communication open between parents and children is extremely important for a good relationship. We want our youngsters to share their thoughts and feelings so we can understand and help them through life's crises. We want them to express themselves appropriately rather than act out their feelings in destructive ways. And we want them to listen to us and hear what we are saying to them.

Children are not born knowing how to express their thoughts and feelings appropriately. Nor are they automatically ready to listen to what we say and follow our directions. They must be taught to express themselves and to listen to others. Parents, too, often need to improve their communicating skills.

There are several excellent books, some of which we have listed at the end of this chapter, on the subject of communication with children. Read them and consider the points we make here. But first, a few words of caution:

• Remember that talking isn't everything. All behavior problems cannot be solved by talk, no matter how good a listener you are, how clearly you speak, or how well the child appears to listen. Children need to know the limits for their behavior, and merely explaining them is not usually enough. Many parents try too often to instruct their children or reason with them. Many times they say the same things over and over again—only louder—but it isn't any more effective. A better approach is to *speak softly but carry a real consequence.*

• Alter your tactics with the child's age and maturity. A major mistake many parents make is to talk too much. They employ their communication skills too early in their child's life, using words before the child wants to listen or is able to comprehend. Young children respond better to management techniques than to endless words.

While it is true that you should start building a base for communicating with your children at an early age, you can't expect a payoff until later. Making the shift from more consequences with less talk to more communication with fewer consequences is appropriate as the child becomes an adolescent. At that time, you will gradually have less and less control over the consequences in his life.

When the order of these two child-rearing processes is reversed, the results can be disastrous. Parents who always try to reason with a very young child often find the child becoming more and more difficult as he grows older. Then, when the youngster starts to act out as an adolescent, they try to get tough with strong consequences. But the adolescent who is accustomed to words only often rebels against the new restrictions even more than the typical teen.

In general, it is best to use more *management* with a younger child and more *communication* with an older child. For example, telling your two-year-old that the stove is hot may eventually bring him to understanding, but pulling his hand away and firmly saying no gives him immediate comprehension of exactly what you mean. On the other hand, a thirteen-year-old who is found drinking beer may need grounding, but it won't do any good without a great deal of communication about alcohol and drugs.

2.9-1 How to Listen So Your Child Will Talk to You.

1. Listen to behavior.

Parents become experts at reading their infants' body language, but they often don't realize that children continue communicating through their behavior long after they have mastered the art of speech.

Older children and teenagers communicate nonverbally, frequently acting out their feelings when under pressure or in conflict. An eight-year-old girl was brought to see us because she had become destructive, breaking toys and family possessions. We discovered that she was extremely anxious about her father's health, which was poor and never discussed in her presence. With our help, she was able to label her feelings and stop acting out her fears.

When your child starts acting in a new way, it may not be a stage. She may be trying to tell you something. Jessica, six, insisted on pushing her baby brother's stroller at the mall. She also had reverted to whining, a habit she'd abandoned long ago. True, her baby brother was six months old, but Jessica was feeling the need for attention. She wanted compliments from passersby, and she wanted a little extra love from her mother.

Put yourself in your child's shoes for a moment and try to discover what he's attempting to communicate through his actions. Then talk about it.

2. Label feelings.

Samuel, four, is trying to fit two parts of a toy together and getting frustrated. Finally, he throws the toy across the room. You know you must respond, but how? Certainly, a consequence for throwing objects is appropriate, but you must help the child find a different way to express his frustrations. With young children like Samuel, the best approach is to help him label his emotion. Tell him you know he must feel "frustrated," and when he feels that way, he should ask for help. Add a consequence such as, "When you throw things, you'll lose them for two days." (See sections on punishment, natural consequences, and overcorrection for management suggestions.)

You may also suggest a positive consequence, like, "When you do need help and ask for it, I will be very proud of you and will gladly help." Of course, then you must do so, kindly and promptly.

A technique that helps small children learn how to identify feelings is the feeling tree. Draw the trunk and limbs of a large tree on a big piece of paper. As you and the child identify feeling words, draw a face representing that feeling on the tree with the word written next to it. Cut out pictures of faces and situations that represent the feelings and paste them on the tree. Then use the tree as a prompt when the child wants to label what he's feeling. Praise him when he uses his new words correctly.

The process of teaching a child to identify and express his feelings takes years and much repetition. But you will have many opportunities to help her interpret them. As she grows older, start becoming a detective rather than simply supplying the label: "It sounds like you're angry with Billy," or, "You look like you're bothered by something. What do you suppose it is?" Then, with some discussion, she might offer the information that she's "jealous" of Billy because he's more popular. Identifying feelings is a skill that continues to need refining, so be patient.

3. Take time to listen.

Sometimes it's hard to find a few uninterrupted moments to listen to your child, but it's essential that you do it if you're going to build good communication with him and have the channels available when you really need them. It is also essential for him to get the opportunity to talk with each parent individually, especially in single-parent, blended, or divorced families. By the time adolescence arrives, it may be difficult to start listening and talking. But if you have begun early, then good communication can smooth the way.

Children must be allowed to discuss the everyday occurrences of their lives and their feelings with you, to feel free to fill you in on the details of what's happening. One deep or meaningful discussion now and then is not sufficient. Communication is a matter of quantity as well as quality. This is an extremely important point and one we cannot emphasize enough. One great conversation will not make up for years of silence.

These steps will help you provide both quantity and quality communication with your child.

• Communicate regularly. Set aside time every day to talk with your child. Even if it's only five minutes at bedtime, sit down and talk. The time will vary, but the place should be forged in your schedules.
• Make appointments for talking. When your child asks to talk

with you or nonverbally gives you cues that something is bothering him, sit down privately with him as soon as possible or make an appointment to talk to him later in the day. Especially with young children, right now is the best time to talk. It usually takes only a few minutes, and it lets the child know that what she has to say is important enough for you to stop and listen.

If you must delay your talk, set a time for later: "We can't talk now because it's too noisy, but let's talk about this in your room tonight as soon as the dinner dishes are put away." Then be sure to keep the appointment.

• Give your undivided attention. Tell the rest of the family not to disturb you, go to a private place, and act like you have all the time in the world to listen. Give your child the same attention you would give a friend who's come to discuss an important problem.

• Use conversation openers. Sometimes when children want to talk, it's hard for them to get started. So openers, like "Let's talk" or "Tell me what's bothering you," can help. But the more specific the lead, the better. You might say, for example, "When you came home from school today, you looked very sad. Do you want to talk about what happened?" If the child indicates that something did happen at school but he doesn't want to talk about it now, let him know you are free to talk later.

If your child usually responds to added prompting, push gently to get him started. Try telling him a story or reading a book, fictional or true, about a similar situation. Sometimes just sitting with your arm around him and waiting quietly for him to start is the best opener of all.

• Keep it going. Once you've started talking, use your skills to keep the conversation alive. Adults have a tendency to offer solutions, advice, even lectures to children. *Resist the temptation.* Many children tell us they can't communicate with their parents because every time they try, they get a lecture. Just listen!

Use questions to promote confidence and keep the child talking. "What happened then?" "What did he say?" Or make empathetic statements that show you understand how he's feeling. "I bet that really made you mad." "It would have really hurt my feelings if somebody did that to me." Or even short exclamations such as "Oh no!" or "Ugh!" can advance conversation.

Try reflecting back to the child what he is saying as a way to persuade the child to share more of his feelings. Originally developed by Dr. Carl Rogers many years ago, this technique is used by many therapists who work with adults as well as children. It is also called active listening by Dr. Thomas Gordon in his book *Parent Effectiveness Training*.

Active listening is repeating to the child what he has said or an interpretation of what he has said. If the child says, "Billy hit me," you reply, "He hit you!" Then, to elicit deeper feelings, you could respond with an interpretation like, "Billy is your best friend, so I bet it hurt your feelings that he hit you, of all people!" Though you may guess wrong, even an inaccurate interpretation will usually earn additional feedback. Go with whatever response the child offers, being the friendly scientist and friend rather than an interrogating policeman. Keep in mind that you are looking for the child's view of the world, not necessarily the exact "truth" about what happened.

Don't overdo this or any other technique. If you repeat every statement the child makes or you ask too many questions, he may get annoyed or balk.

• Let the child know you appreciate the sharing. When your child talks to you about critical issues in her life, let her know you think it's great. You can simply say, "Thanks for talking to me about this." Or perhaps, "I know it was difficult for you to talk about that. I'm so glad you feel you can come to me when something's bothering you." Or simply share your feelings with a hug.

2.9-2 How to Talk to Your Child.

Do your children continually turn a deaf ear to your requests? This is not loss of hearing but the tendency to tune out whatever you are saying until the volume reaches a certain critical point when the child knows the parent means business.

Curing this problem requires two essential ingredients: Parents must say what they mean and mean what they say. So choose your words carefully, and then back them up with fair, consistent, and meaningful actions. Your child will quickly learn to listen to you the first time you say something.

To accomplish this:

1. Establish eye contact.

Because children are so easily distracted, make sure they look at you when you speak to them. This may be the most important factor in getting your child to follow your instructions or simply listen to you. Show them what you mean by eye contact. Teach the young child with the staring game: Sit a few feet apart from each other, then see who looks away first. Time your child and tell her how long she met your eyes.

If your child is very shy or becomes uncomfortable looking directly into your eyes, teach her to look at your mouth or your whole face.

Sometimes you must use physical contact to get a child's attention. Touch him lightly on the shoulder or, if necessary, orient him toward you by placing your hands on his shoulders and gently turning him toward you. Use this technique sparingly and try to phase out its use quickly. For the older child, anything more than a tap on the shoulder may lead to a quick confrontation instead of good listening.

When your child looks at you when you are speaking, praise her for it and let her know you appreciate it. Later you may praise her for looking at you and then doing what you ask quickly.

2. Speak in a calm, firm voice.

If you always raise your voice or speak harshly when you ask your child to do something, he will learn to tune you out until you reach your ceiling volume. If you find yourself getting louder and louder, stop, take a deep breath, reestablish eye contact, speak slowly and very distinctly. Say, "Andy (with a long pause between words, eye contact), I . . . want . . . you . . . to . . . pick . . . up . . .

your . . . clothes . . . now . . . and . . . put . . . them . . . in . . . the . . . hamper . . . now." Be sure to put a "period" at the end of your statement.

3. Avoid question statements.

If you say to your child, "How about picking up your clothes?" then don't be surprised if he answers, "Not now!" If you say, "Let's do the dishes now," it gives him an opening for "Let's not." When there is no question in your mind about what you want your child to do, then make definite statements that tell him exactly what to do as well as when, where, and how to do it.

4. Keep it simple.

Don't use words your child doesn't understand. Speak clearly and simply. Don't talk too much. With long instructions or explanations, the child may lose interest or forget what you said at the beginning. Young children have a limited ability to recall long strings of verbal information. Short and simple communications with a natural consequence will be understood and remembered infinitely better than a long speech. Instead of carrying on about responsibility, the meaning of a dollar, and worldwide inflation, give the child a clear choice: "You can either put your bicycle away now or lose it for one week."

5. Tell how you feel.

Tell your child how you feel about his actions or attitudes instead of criticizing him directly. For example, "It makes me really angry when you leave the bathroom a mess for me to clean up." Or, "I was scared that you were lost when you didn't come home on time." If you begin your statement with "I" rather than "You," you can avoid criticizing, blaming, or attacking the child and still express strong emotion very effectively.

2.10 HOW TO TEACH YOUR CHILD TO RELAX (OR HOW TO KEEP YOUR COOL)

Adults tend to remember childhood as a carefree time when there were no responsibilities, worries, or problems. But children in today's world feel tremendous pressure from many sources. They are pressured to learn things, such as reading and arithmetic, even before they enter elementary school. They know they are expected to finish high school and go on to college. They must often manage the stresses created by divorce, single parents, working parents, day care, or hours spent alone at home. The dangers of nuclear war, kidnapping, murder, and muggings are impressed upon them by their parents and the media.

The stresses in a child's world may manifest themselves in physical symptoms such as insomnia, tension headaches, bed-wetting, or a nervous stomach. Or they may show up as emotional manifestations—anger, withdrawal, fear—that may be interpreted as a discipline problem. As parents, you can't always alleviate all of your child's frustrations, but you can learn stress-management techniques that will help you and the child cope with tension.

In our practice, we teach parents and children ways to relax and keep their cool. We know from personal and professional experience that stress-reduction training will make a difference in your life and your child's. Learning these techniques takes practice, so plan to spend time. It will be worth it.

Try our program and check out the suggested readings and tapes listed at the end of this section. *Kiddie QR,* developed by Dr. Charles Stroebel, is designed for parents and children to do together and is especially worthwhile.

1. Recognize stress reactions. Craig has a headache every day after school. Sherry loses her temper over minor things. John wakes up with a stomachache in the morning. Amy has a hard time getting to sleep. It's a good guess that all of these problems are symptoms of tension and stress.

The following checklist can help you identify some of the physiological and behavioral manifestations of stress. Keep in mind that these same symptoms may be the result of medical problems, so before assuming that a persistent symptom is psychological, check it out with your physician. Sometimes, too, they are used as a means to get attention or avoid tasks. If this is your suspicion, read the sections of this book dealing with these problems.

There are also times when reactions are a combination of all of these factors. A child may start with an illness that causes her to miss school. She enjoys the extra attention she receives, she has difficulties in school that she would like to avoid—feigned illness seems like the perfect solution. In her case, a combination of stress-reduction training and other interventions will elicit the best results.

STRESS SIGNALS CHECKLIST

1. headaches
2. stomachaches, upset stomach, gas, ulcers
3. nausea, vomiting
4. hyperventilation (includes rapid breathing, breathlessness, dizziness, tingling)
5. tachycardia (rapid heartbeats)
6. sweaty, clammy, or cold hands
7. nervous habits (nail-biting, skin pulling, hair pulling, teeth grinding, etc.)
8. insomnia and other sleep problems
9. fears and anxieties
10. shyness and avoidance of social situations
11. temper outbursts
12. oversensitivity to criticism or teasing
13. low frustration tolerance
14. lack of concentration because of anxiety

2. Help the child recognize and understand stress reactions. When you have concluded that your child's symptom or behavioral reaction is stress-induced, the next step is to help her label her

feelings and figure out why they occur. One little girl was referred to us by her pediatrician, who couldn't find a medical cause for her stomachaches and vomiting on school mornings. With her parents' help, she began to recognize her anxieties about being accepted by the other children in her new class and understood why she was having stomach pains. Her parents learned to listen to her problems and talk over her fears; they encouraged her to invite classmates home to play; and they showed her how to relax her body. Her physical symptoms soon subsided, along with the stress.

Sometimes, it's hard for parents to understand how stress works. At first, Cynthia was anxious about being accepted by the other children. When the stomachaches and vomiting started, she began to worry that these reactions would be embarrassing at school and the fear made the cycle self-perpetuating. Stress management gave her the control she needed over her own responses.

If your child has a reaction that you believe is stress-induced, explain to him how stress works. We often use this story to help children understand their reactions:

In the olden days, one of the cave people's worst enemies was the saber-toothed tiger. Because of what the cave people had heard about the tiger, they were afraid before they ever saw one. The first time the cave person finally heard a real saber-toothed tiger growl, his heartbeat quickened, he began breathing faster, and he clenched his teeth. His arms and legs tightened so he was ready to run away or fight the tiger. His stomach churned and he felt weak-kneed because he was so frightened.

Cave people didn't have much time to be frightened. The tiger would eat the person, the cave person would kill the tiger, or they would both run away.

Our problems are a little different in the modern world. Our "tigers" are smaller, but they don't go away so easily. A kid at school who bothers you will be there every day. Our body reacts just like the cave person's. A big bully threatens you. Just thinking about him, your stomach starts to knot up. It may tighten up and hurt. You haven't gone to recess yet, but you know you will have to face that bully when you go outside. That's like the cave person anticipating the tiger. We are luckier, though, because no tiger will eat us. We can teach our bodies to relax so we won't have the stomachaches or headaches or other reactions that bother us.

Determining the cause of a child's stress requires good communication skills. Let's assume your youngster has been tossing and turning for several days before he can fall asleep at night. You talk to him about how the cave person couldn't sleep if he was worried about the tiger he ran into today or the one he might see at the river tomorrow. You explain that sometimes you have trouble clearing your mind, too. Give some examples of what worries you. Your child starts talking about the trouble he's having with math and his fear of the exam on Friday.

The child starts relaxing as he talks about his fears. You work out a plan to help him with math, rub his back, show him how to use the relaxation techniques described below. And he falls asleep.

3. Try to remove the sources of stress. The ultimate stress eliminator is to get rid of the reasons for the tension. Perhaps your child is overscheduled, bored, getting to bed too late, or worrying about a remark he's overheard. With discussion, rearranging, and rescheduling, these stressors can be reduced. One child we worked with had had insomnia for years. She was "cured" when her parents recognized her fears. They put locks on her windows and doors so she felt secure at night.

Many stresses children experience stem from problems at home. When we ask them what their parents might do to help them relax, the answer almost invariably is: "Don't yell so much." You can do much to reduce the stress level in your home if you try the techniques and solutions in this book instead of "yelling."

4. Teach relaxation techniques. Teach yourself and your child to react differently to stressful situations and emotions. Here are some basic techniques that we have found to work well with both adults and children. Read everything through first before starting. Go slowly, adding new steps when the first steps have been assimilated. Relate the instructions to your child in a calm, gentle voice.

Our explanations will be marked off with (————). Your instructions to the child appear between quotation marks.

Quiet Time.

(Your purpose is to teach the child to lie still for as many minutes as his age. Use a stopwatch or timer to let the child know how long he can be quiet.)

"I want you to lie down on the floor (or bed). Close your eyes. Now let's see how long you can lie quietly. (Wait.) That's terrific, you were still for   seconds. Now try to beat that time."

(Lie down with your child to show how important you consider the relaxation skills and to develop a sense of closeness. Increase the time with back rubs, imaginary walks, music.)

The Breathing Technique.

(Breathing is a very important aspect of relaxation training and can have profound effects on the level of relaxation. Using the cave-person story, explain why breathing is important.)

"Remember how the cave person breathed so fast when he was scared? Breathe in and out very quickly, as if you were scared by a tiger."

(Wait for ten breaths, no more. Then ask:)

"How do you feel? Dizzy or weak? That's the way being scared or stressed can make you feel. Sometimes you can feel even worse.

"Lie down on your back and settle into a comfortable and calm state of mind. Close your eyes. Put one hand on your chest and the other one on your stomach. Breathe in and out. Can you feel your hands move? Now, breathe in as I count, then wait and breathe out as I count."

(Lengthen the count gradually, so the child is breathing in to the count of 4, pausing for 2, then slowly exhaling to the count of 4. Pause again for a count of 2, then start the cycle again.)

"Inhale 1, 2, 3, 4. Hold it 1, 2. Exhale 1, 2, 3, 4. Hold it 1, 2. Inhale 1, 2, 3, 4 . . . Say the word *relax* to yourself as you breathe out. Imagine the word *relax* written in big white letters by a sky-writer against a clear blue sky.

"Keep breathing in and out very slowly. Feel your hands on your chest and stomach. Which hand moves the most? Try to breathe air into your stomach so it fills up like a balloon. Push down gently on your stomach as you breathe out so it deflates like a balloon."

(Have the child practice till he doesn't have to push down on his stomach as he exhales but feels it deflate and then inflate again on its own. Soon, the hand on the stomach will begin to move more than the hand on the chest. It may require a few practice sessions to develop this skill. Be patient and reinforce the progress. Keep sessions short enough to maintain the child's motivation.)

"Now that you know how to breathe the relaxing way while you are lying down, let's try it sitting in the chair. Remember to whisper the word *relax* as you breathe out . . . that's right."

(Use the same count as above to prompt correct breathing. Have the child practice several times a day, in several locations of the house, and in several positions—lying down, sitting, standing—so he can use this new skill when he needs it. Remember to praise him for practicing.

(When he has mastered relaxed breathing, explain to him that he can use this skill when he feels himself getting tense or upset. Record the times he uses it on a chart, or ask him to keep his own chart. Reinforce him with praise and rewards. Arrange a special signal so you can remind him silently to use it—a pull on the ear, perhaps, or a secret phrase like, "John, can you go see what time it is for me?" Again, praise and reward a gradual increase in the use of this skill.)

Progressive Muscle Relaxation.

Now your child is ready to combine correct breathing with deep muscle relaxation. Borrowing from Dr. Edmund Jacobson's step-by-step guide to progressive relaxation, *You Must Relax,* we give a child's version of this important technique.

A few suggestions: Have your child copy each motion as you

demonstrate it. Do the facial movements while looking in a mirror. Teach one step at a time, practicing it for a few days before adding another. Eventually, you and the child will learn the entire series of four steps. Do them twice each, which will take no more than ten minutes to complete.

STEP 1: SPAGHETTI ARMS

"Lie down and get into your relaxing position. Practice your breathing for a few moments: Inhale 1, 2, 3, 4 . . . and now *r e l a x* . . . (fade prompts). Make a fist for me. Bend your arm so you can show me your muscle."

(Show her how to raise her fist toward her arm as she lifts her elbow.)

"Slowly tighten your muscles in your arm as hard as possible. Count to 10—1, 2, 3, 4, 5, 6, 7, 8, 9, 10. Take a deep breath. Hold it. Then slowly say *relax* as you exhale and quickly let your hand open and drop your arm—all at once." (The sudden release is very important.) "Let your hand flop like a giant noodle. You can't hold it up or even move it." (Check her relaxation by picking her arm up at the wrist and letting it drop. It should be limp.) "Good. Your arm should be feeling tingly and maybe warm. That's very good."

(Repeat this exercise with both arms a few times until the child learns how to make her arms limp and relaxed. At the end of each session, as the closing step ask her to continue lying on her back, close her eyes, and do relaxed breathing. Then lead her through an imaginary scene, such as the one suggested here.)

"Imagine we're walking down the beach. All you can see is sand and ocean, and your arms are getting very heavy. The weather is warm, and your arms (substitute other body parts) are getting heavier and heavier . . . you are feeling very calm and very relaxed. . . ."

(Let her lie there as long as she likes, perhaps even fall asleep.)

STEP 2: LEGS OF STEEL

(Now, teach the child to relax her legs. Caution: If she has a known back problem or if this exercise causes back strain or discomfort, stop. Check with your physician before continuing. Skip the feet and legs, and go on to another part of the body.)

"Lie on your back on the floor. Focus all your attention on your feet and legs. Straighten your right leg, flexing your foot up and pointing your toes toward your head to tighten your calf muscles. Keeping it straight, lift your leg a few inches off the floor." (If your child has difficulty raising her leg, lift it for her.) "Hold it tight so it feels like a bar of steel. . . . 1, 2, 3, 4, 5. Take a deep breath. Hold it like a steel bar . . . 1, 2, 3, 4, 5. Let go! Drop your leg with a thud. Exhale, saying *r-e-l-a-x.* Good!"

(Shorten the time if the child can't hold her leg up very long. Be sure the leg is dropped in one clean movement so the tension is released all at once. Have her raise, tense, and relax each leg twice, focusing on the feeling of heaviness and warmth. If she doesn't understand the concept of suddenly dropping the leg, demonstrate with a piece of wood tied to a string, so she may watch one end of the wood being raised and dropped.)

STEP 3: STOMACH HARD AS A ROCK AND BACK UP

(Now you are ready to add stomach relaxation exercises to the routine. Meanwhile, have the child practice the breathing, spaghetti arms, and legs of steel. Once more, a caution: If your child has potential back problems or experiences pain, skip this exercise and consult your physician.)

"Your arms and legs are very relaxed. Now, make your stomach muscles very tight as if someone is going to hit you there. Good. Pull your stomach in, making it hard as a rock. That's right. Now, hold it, counting slowly up to ten. Breathe in. Say *r-e-l-a-x* as you breathe out and relax your stomach.

"Let's do it again. Your whole body is feeling very relaxed now. Your arms and legs are heavy and warm. Your stomach has sunk into the floor. Now let's raise your back. I want you to push your head into the floor, arching your back. Bring it right up off the floor. Good! Hold it! Take a deep breath, counting 1, 2, 3, 4, 5. Let go and release your tight muscles. Rest your back on the floor. Let's try it once more."

STEP 4: FUNNY FACES

(Most of us store much of our tension in our face and head; children are no exception. Like adults, they clench their teeth, wrinkle their foreheads, tighten their necks and shoulders. Tension in the head and neck causes headaches and is a barometer of the tension in the rest of the body.

(Loosen up your face and your child's face before beginning this exercise. Each of you should look at your face in the mirror. Is your jaw tight, your forehead wrinkled; are your shoulders tense, your eyes squinted? Lead the child through a series of funny faces, first tensing and then suddenly relaxing the facial muscles. Open the eyes very wide, then squeeze them shut. Tense the teeth together, then press, release. Practice pressing lips into a fish kiss as if you were pressing your lips against a window, then relax. Wrinkle the nose like a rabbit. Now proceed with the exercises.)

"Pretend someone's shining a high-powered flashlight right into your eyes. Squint your eyes tight and wrinkle your nose like a rabbit. Good. Grit your teeth together and press your lips into the shape of an *O* like you're a fish kissing the side of your tank. Take a deep breath. Make the face, hold it as I count to five. Say *r-e-l-a-x* to yourself as you let go, breathe, and relax your whole face with your mouth open. Nicely done. Let's do it again.

"Your whole face is very relaxed, even your eyes. Raise your head, then make your chin touch your chest. Take a deep breath to the count of 5. Hold it. Now say *r-e-l-a-x* as you exhale and drop your head and relax all the way down to your toes. Think about your body—your face, neck, arms, stomach, back, legs— each part is very relaxed, very heavy, very warm. Sink to the floor and just r-e-l-a-x.

STEP 5: THOUGHT BLOCKAGE

(After the child has learned to relax his whole body by combining the steps already described, teach him—and yourself—how to block out those nagging thoughts that cause tension. Practice on yourself first. If your child can easily count backward from a hundred, start with that number; or start with whatever number works for him. If he can't count backward, ask him to count up instead.)

"Inhale as you start counting backward from a hundred. After each number, exhale and repeat the word *r e l a x* slowly: Inhale, 100, exhale, *relax,* inhale, 99. . . . Close your eyes and try to see each number as you say it. Don't think about anything else but the numbers. This is your time to relax."

(When the child has practiced this step several times, have him do thought blocking after the muscle relaxation to get into a deeper state of relaxation.)

STEP 6: PRACTICE

Now, it's important that you both practice relaxation regularly. Here are ways to make it part of your lives.

1. Schedule a time for the child to practice each day. A regular scheduled time for a relaxation break usually works best. Bedtime is ideal for most families because it helps the child wind down and ends the day pleasantly. Supervise the practice at first until the child can do it on his own. Try taping the relaxation instructions for him to use until he's memorized them. Your goal is to train him to use relaxation when he needs it. And don't forget to practice it yourself at a time when there are no other distractions. You'll soon see how it can help you keep your cool.

2. Use a chart to provide motivation. A calendar chart like the one shown in Section 2.5 may be adapted to reinforce your child's relaxation practice. Include rewards at first, too, as additional motivators. Rewards may become less frequent as the habit becomes established.

3. Use mini-relaxers in everyday situations. Teach yourself and your child how to use mini-relaxation to counteract feelings of anxiety and tension encountered throughout the day. After learning relaxation, the word *relax* will help to release tension if you simply repeat it to yourself in a stressful situation.

To enhance its effect, use this six-second relaxation technique originated by Dr. Charles Stroebel: Smile to yourself and clench your teeth. Take a deep breath and hold it. Breathe out suddenly, let your mouth drop open, and think *relax.* Consciously feel the tension draining out of your body from your head to your toes.

Teach your child to use this quick technique whenever she becomes scared, angry, tense, or jittery. And use it yourself when you need it. Arrange a secret signal that will remind the child to do mini-relaxation when she is uptight, and praise her whenever you notice her tensing, hesitating, relaxing, and then responding calmly.

BOOKS FOR PARENTS AND CHILDREN: SUGGESTED READINGS AND TAPES

Azrin, Nathan H., Ph.D., and Victoria Besalel, Ph.D. "How to Use Overcorrection." Lawrence, Kansas: H & H Enterprises, Inc., 1980. Discusses specific method and principles of overcorrection and self-correction.

Becker, Wesley C. *Parents Are Teachers.* Champaign: Research Press, 1971. A programmed text designed to teach basic behavioral parenting terms and skills.

Benson, Herbert, M.D., and Miriam Z. Klipper. *The Relaxation Response.* New York: Avon, 1976. An explanation of the concept of stress and a simple meditation technique you may wish to use in addition to the progressive muscle relaxation techniques.

Gordon, Thomas. *P.E.T. : Parent Effectiveness Training.* New York: Peter H. Wyden, 1970. Teaches communication skills in easy-to-understand and usable ways.

Hall, R. Vance, Ph.D., and Marilyn C. Hall. Ed.D., "How to Use Planned Ignoring." Lawrence, Kansas: H & H Enterprises,

Inc., 1980. A manual that teaches how to effectively ignore behavior to extinguish it.

Hall, R. Vance, Ph.D., and Marilyn C. Hall., "How to Use Systematic Attention and Approval." Lawrence, Kansas: H & H Enterprises, Inc., 1980. A booklet designed to teach parents the effective use of positive reinforcement and praise.

Hall, R. Vance and Marilyn C. Hall. "How to Use Time-Out." Lawrence, Kansas: H & H Enterprises, Inc., 1980. A step-by-step discussion of time-out. Exercises are provided for practice application.

Jacobson, Edmund, M.D. *You Must Relax.* New York: McGraw-Hill, 1976. The basics of deep muscle relaxation by the inventor of the technique. Good illustrations.

Patterson, Gerald R. *Families: Application of Social Learning to Family Life.* Champaign: Research Press, 1975. A primer of social learning theory applied to families. Good examples.

Rosen, Gerald M. *The Relaxation Book: An Illustrated Self-Help Program.* Englewood Cliffs: Prentice-Hall, 1977. A step-by-step guide to the relaxation response.

Stroebel, Charles F., M.D., Ph.D. *The Quieting Response.* Manual and audio cassette program. New York: BMA Publications, 1978. An excellent series teaching relaxation step by step.

Stroebel, Elizabeth, Ph.D., Stroebel, Charles F., M.D., Ph.D., and Margaret Holland, Ph.D. *Kiddie QR.* Wethersfield, CT: QR Institute, 119 Forest Drive, 1980. Tapes designed to help children and parents learn basic relaxation skills, in story form that is especially good for young school-age children.

Van Houton, Ron. "How to Use Reprimands." Lawrence, Kansas: H & H Enterprises, Inc., 1980. Describes how to use reprimands effectively.

CHAPTER 3

Coping
With Morning
Problems

THE day has a much better chance of turning out to be a good one for both parents and children if it gets a happy start. But we often get so frustrated by habits and hassles and our roles as alarm clocks, organizers, hygiene inspectors, short-order cooks and chauffeurs that the inevitable morning struggles threaten to ruin the entire day.

In this chapter, we're going to discuss a variety of parent-child problems that frequently contribute to a typical morning's frustrations—and the ways to avoid or change them. Try the suggested solutions as you need them, and you'll soon see what a difference these techniques can make in starting your family off each morning with a much more positive attitude toward each other and the day ahead.

3.1 EARLY MORNING RISERS

If your child consistently wakes up too early in the morning to suit you, what can you do? If your child tends to keep you from getting enough sleep yourself or worries you by wandering unsupervised around the house while you're still in bed, you can train him to go back to sleep or to play quietly in bed until it's time to get up. But first you must determine whether he's getting sufficient sleep. The fact is, some children require much less sleep than others. A good night's sleep may mean a full twelve hours for one child and eight for another. Sometimes, the need for less sleep is a sign of hyperactivity (see Section 11.15), but usually, it simply reflects individual patterns.

If your child is not getting enough sleep to spend the day in good shape, your job is to teach him how to sleep longer or how to go back to sleep when he wakes up early. If he exists happily on less sleep than the average child, however, then your goal is to train him to play in bed or another safe place until it's a reasonable time for you to get up.

To identify your child's general sleep patterns, ask yourself these questions:

1. Has he always slept fewer hours than other children his age?
2. How many hours per night does he sleep? Keep a record for one week, then average the numbers. What is the nightly average?
3. Is there a consistent pattern, or do the hours vary significantly from day to day?
4. Is he usually in a good mood in the morning? Does he "last" until naptime or bedtime?

If your child gets approximately the same amount of sleep every night and is usually in a happy mood, then he's probably getting enough sleep for him and must be taught to play quietly in bed longer, either before sleeping at night or after awakening in the morning. If, on the other hand, he appears to require more sleep, you can use these tactics to attempt to change his sleeping habits so he'll sleep longer.

3.1-1 Training Children to Sleep Longer.

For children who go to bed without difficulty and tend to sleep well but have developed the habit of waking up before they "should," the following solutions are designed to teach them to go back to sleep until a more appropriate hour in the morning.

• Be direct. Tell the child firmly to go back to sleep when he awakens early. Or tell him he must stay in his bed until you come to get him. For some children, this is all that's needed if they know you really mean it.

• Don't expect miracles. The best you can hope for is a gradual increase in sleeping time. If your toddler has been waking up at 6 A.M., don't expect her to start sleeping until 8! If she makes it until 6:15, then 6:30, that's wonderful. Try to accomplish a little at a time.

• Be reassuring. Some children worry that they will oversleep. Reassure them that you'll wake them up if necessary, or set an alarm clock for them.

• Impose the five-minute rule. You may have to restrain yourself instead of the child. Don't run to her immediately when you hear her stirring, or even crying. Wait five or ten minutes after she calls before going to her room unless, of course, you think she's in trouble. After a few days, you may find she goes back to sleep or sleeps a little later. If it is still early, then apply the rule again.

• Reward her. With a child who understands language, you can try rewarding her for sleeping later in the morning. This often works well with children over about three years of age. See Section 2.5 for the chart and procedures, selecting small goals for her to achieve. If you reward your child with a toy, make sure it is safe for unsupervised play. Don't leave young children with toys that are easily disassembled into pieces that could be swallowed. Also use caution with toys that have cords. You may wish to combine the reward chart with the next suggestion.

• Use positive practice. This technique gives your child the opportunity to master a skill so he will have it when he needs it. Many children don't know *how* to go back to sleep once they wake up, so you must help them with positive practice. During the day, lie down with your child and talk to him about how to fall asleep. Tell him to close his eyes. In a quiet and soothing voice, tell him a story about how the waves at the beach follow one another out to play and then back home again, over and over again. At bedtime, remind him to lie quietly with his eyes closed and think of the waves just like he did during your practice sessions. Teach older children to count sheep or design their own soothing sleep scenes during the practice sessions.

• Use relaxation techniques. Teach a child five years old or over to use the relaxation techniques outlined in Section 2.10. Use positive practice to rehearse these techniques so she'll know what to do when she wakes up too early.

3.1-2 Training Your Child to Play in Bed.

Many small children don't know how to spend the time until they are allowed to get up in the morning. So you must come up with some creative ideas for keeping them occupied. Plan ahead. Decide the night before how the morning will be handled. Then, remember to praise your child for playing quietly and independently in the morning. Refer to sections 2.1, 2.4, and 2.5. Then try these ideas.

• Exploring for infants. When you go in to cover the baby for the night, put a surprise crib toy in the bed for her to discover in the morning. Rotate the toys every day or so.

• Fun with faces. Tape some pictures of babies—or yourself or the infant's siblings—on the crib where she can see them easily. Or try an unbreakable mirror so she can look at herself.

• Use positive practice. Ask a toddler to describe to you what he will do when he wakes up early in the morning. Practice using the tape recorder or playing with other items he mentions.

• Provide an A.M. kit. Take a soft pouch or a pillowcase and stuff it with toys or busywork that will keep a child occupied quietly in the morning. Attach it safely to the side of the mattress. Change the contents every few days. Be sure the child knows the purpose of the kit and how to play with whatever's inside it.

• Give her time. If your child can't tell time, draw a clock on a paper plate. By drawing the hands or writing the digital numerals, make the play clock read the time when the child may wake you up. Set the paper clock next to a real one where it can be easily seen. Tell her to play quietly in bed until the two times match up.

• Tape a story. A tape-recorded story will provide a wonderful morning activity for toddlers or older children. Read one of the child's favorite stories or books into the tape, and be sure to show him how to use the recorder. This is even more entertaining if you leave the book too, so he can look at the pictures while you read.

• Use the TV baby-sitter. Of course, the television or radio may also provide amusement for the child. Preset the channel or station for him and make sure he's able to operate the TV.

• Use the early-bird chart. All of the solutions that are appropriate for toddlers and older children can be used in combination with an early-bird chart, which will encourage him to entertain himself for longer and longer periods of time in the mornings. Use the information in Section 2.5 to design your own. Set a goal together with your child before he goes to sleep at night. Use a paper-plate clock if he can't tell time. Then reward him for playing in bed until the appropriate time.

3.2 SLEEPYHEADS

Sometimes, especially with older children, the tables are turned and the children tend to sleep *later* in the morning than their parents would like them to. It's hard to have to pull someone else's strings, especially in the morning, because you have things to do and places to go. This section is for parents whose child is a sleepyhead, who is chronically difficult to wake up in the morning and then can't seem to get moving. Because this throws the family out of whack, the day begins with frustration and irritation.

Before deciding to try our solutions, you must first determine whether your child gets enough sleep—or perhaps too much sleep. Experiment with putting him to bed earlier or later to find out how many hours he really needs. If he seems to get enough sleep but is sluggish and tired throughout the entire day, have the pediatrician check him out for possible medical problems.

When you have established that there aren't any other problems, then you must recognize one important fact: You can't always turn a sleepyhead into a little person who wakes up easily. You can, however, make waking up and getting going much more pleasant for all of you.

Some of the solutions are more appropriate for very young children, while others are designed for older children who are capable of assuming responsibility for the consequences of being sleepyheads.

3.2-1 Observe and Adjust.

Try not to wake the child in the middle of a dream. If her eyelids are fluttering, wait a few minutes so that her dream won't be rudely interrupted. All of us dream on the average of five to six times a night and each dream—though it may seem long—lasts only a short time.

3.2-2 Use Positive Motivation.

Make it as pleasant as possible for your sleepyhead child to wake up and get going. Prepare a special breakfast, or suggest he listen to his favorite music. Speak to him quietly, calmly, and lovingly. If you are always impatient, he'll be less likely to want to get up and face the day.

3.2-3 Try a Snooze Alarm.

Use a snooze alarm clock and set it earlier than the child must get up. Then allow him to push the snooze alarm several times while he gradually comes out of the sleep cycle. It provides periodic reminders that it's almost time to get up and can make the occasion less traumatic.

3.2-4 Encourage Independence.

When a child becomes responsible for his own actions in the morning, he often motivates himself to follow through. Make a special event out of going out together to buy his own alarm clock and tell him how proud you are that he'll be using the clock all by himself very soon. Teach him how to use it, and do some positive practicing during the day. For example, have him set the alarm while he's playing or reading. When the clock goes off, he'll know the time is up. Remember to praise him in the morning when he manages to get up on time.

3.2-5 Try Physical Stimulation.

Some deep sleepers need physical movement to help them wake up. Have your sleepy child wash her face and then lead her through some morning exercises, like stretching and bending, to get her circulation going and her body moving. If she's using an alarm clock, place it so she'll have to get out of bed to turn it off.

3.2-6 Apply Consequences.

When you feel your child is mature enough to be responsible for himself in the morning, perhaps when he's seven or eight years old, then you must provide the appropriate consequences for nonperformance. Let him know pleasantly that you expect him to get up and prepare for the day on his own and help him set a realistic time goal.

• Use natural consequences. The consequences of failure should seem logical and fair to him. A logical consequence is one that results quite naturally from an action. If the child has a pattern of not getting up for breakfast, for example, tell him exactly when breakfast will be served and inform him that you will prepare it for him at that time only. Then if he doesn't get to the table on time, he doesn't eat that morning.

Perhaps he often misses the school bus because of dawdling. The consequence could be that he must call a taxicab and earn back the money it costs.

• Use response cost. Many parents have found that the "you owe me the time" technique works well. This means that the child understands he *owes* you however many minutes he runs late (or runs *you* late) in the morning. He must then pay them back by doing household chores or errands. Or he pays the minutes back by having to get up that many minutes earlier the next morning.

3.3 MORNING GROUCH

Some people wake up full of good cheer and chatter in the morning, but others are not morning people. Instead, they are morning grouches and tend to take the happy edge off everyone else's mood.

Everyone—including children—has the right to be grouchy once in a while. And there are even some stages of growing up that may be interpreted as grouchiness. At about age two, for example, children start asserting themselves and their growing independence with the classic response: "No!" This can easily be taken by their parents as a negative and grouchy attitude, but it really isn't. As children approach puberty, they tend to get moody and touchy, and that, too, is quite normal behavior.

If your child is usually happy in the morning but unexpectedly becomes a morning grouch, it may be a sign that something is bothering her—perhaps too little sleep or an illness or stress. These problems can't be ignored, and other sections of the book may provide additional insight and solutions.

This section is designed to provide a variety of solutions for dealing with habitual morning grouches, the children who always seem to wake up on the wrong side of the bed. Try them, too, for the occasional sufferer.

3.3-1 Systematically Ignore.

Refer to Section 2.2 to refresh yourself on how to simply ignore this behavior. In this case, don't mention the child's mood, but openly recognize and comment on the pleasant behaviors of others in the family. Praise the child when she tries to be pleasant. Do so just as soon as it occurs: "Susie, it's great to see your smile again. That was a really nice thing to say to your brother. Welcome back."

3.3-2 Vary the Wake-up Time.

Some children get up in a bad mood in the morning because they always are awakened during a period of deep sleep. Try changing the time by a few minutes, earlier or later. Or let the child use a snooze alarm or wake up slowly to music.

3.3-3 Try Humor.

You may be able to humor a child out of his grumpiness, so you might try jokes and laughs to get him going in the morning. We'll have to admit, however, that sometimes humor has just the opposite effect, making a grouch even more irascible. If it does in your case, drop the comedy act immediately!

- Onstage! This is your chance to act up, so go for it with your interpretation of the grouch in your house. Do your grouchiest caveman act, or maybe Daddy the Hun.
- Name the Grump contest. At the breakfast table, organize a contest to come up with the best name for the grouch who sometimes visits your house. Gather all the suggestions and then use the winning name to help dispel the mood: "Uh-oh, Griselda the Monster is back!"
- Squeeze out the Meanies. This one often works with small children: Hold your child in your arms and gently "love her up" while you tell her you're squeezing out her unhappy feelings.

3.3-4 Show Him Himself.

A young child usually doesn't understand the effect his perennial bad moods can have on the other people in his life. Later in the day, when he's feeling more cheerful, discuss it with him and help him model his behavior. Read a book together, like *Alexander and the Terrible, Horrible, No Good, Very Bad Day* by Judith Viorst (New York: Atheneum, 1972), and then talk about how a bad mood can mess up the day for everyone. Ask for the child's suggestions for changing it.

3.3-5 Set a Time Limit.

Tell your child she can be just as grouchy as she likes, but she has only five minutes in which to be that way. Let the others in the family join in, too. Set a timer for five minutes while you all complain and harangue, grumping away the black clouds.

3.3-6 Say It Instead!

Tell the older child you're going to treat her like an adult. Everyone gets grouchy occasionally and you understand that, but it becomes most unpleasant for everyone else. Therefore, instead of making everyone else suffer, ask her to say out loud that she is in a bad mood and is trying her best to work her way out of it.

3.3-7 Apply Time-out.

Ask the child to excuse himself from the presence of others until he is feeling better, but be sure to provide him with the means of rejoining the group when he's ready. For example, you might say, "Perhaps it would be better for you to work this mood out alone. When you feel up to it, please hurry back because we'll miss you!"

3.3-8 Goodbye, Grumps Chart.

For some children, being grumpy in the morning has become a habit and may take strong measures to overcome. We suggest setting up a reward chart with gold stars applied for better attitudes in the morning. Don't expect instant success, but set your goals realistically. Perhaps the goal for the first few days or even a week could be limited to a "neutral" attitude or no arguments with siblings. Make sure the child understands the criteria, and decide together what the reward is going to be. For more information, see sections 2.4 and 2.5.

3.4 SPEEDING UP SLOW DRESSERS

Getting a child dressed in the morning is an everyday routine that is guaranteed to drive many parents wild. Picture this scene: Two-year-old Bradley's mom enters his room to dress him for the day. After dealing with several delay tactics, she loses her patience when he insists on wearing short sleeves in the middle of the winter. This encourages Bradley to play hide-and-seek with his shoes. His mother, infuriated, screams, "Bradley, you are either getting dressed or you are in big trouble!" Bradley kicks and screams. His mother threatens him with a spanking. It has become a battle of wills and common in their daily routine. Only a negative approach finally gets this little boy into his clothes.

Or how about this scene: Breakfast is on the table, the eggs are getting cold, and your ten-year-old is still in her room trying to decide what she wants to wear.

With very young children, the best you can expect is to get through the dressing process as simply and enjoyably as possible. So in our solutions, we've included suggestions to help make dressing fun for them as well as some steps to help you teach your child to dress independently. Between the ages of two and four, little ones can learn to master most of the techniques involved in dressing. By two, they can remove a coat or dress. By about three, they can put them on. At three and a half or so, they will master buttons. By five, most children can dress themselves, except for tying shoelaces.

If you allow these first attempts at getting dressed to be pleasant, they will result in less resistance and more cooperation later. Once the skills are learned, then you can deal with making the process happen at a faster pace. Realistic expectations together with positive motivation and planning will speed it along.

We will also offer solutions for children who dress themselves inappropriately or take an inordinately long time to put their clothes on.

Before you try any of these methods, make sure you're allotting adequate time in the morning for your child to get dressed! You may be able to solve your problems simply by waking him up a little earlier.

3.4-1 Make It Fun.

Dressing should be fun right from the beginning of a baby's life. While you dress your infant, talk to her or sing to her. When she's a little older, give her something interesting to look at or play with, such as mobiles, musical toys, pictures, or stuffed animals.

3.4-2 Teach with Cues.

Encourage a small child to sing along with you as you put each piece of clothing on: "This is the way we put on our socks, put on our socks, put on our socks. This is the way we put on our socks so early in the morning . . ." Eventually, she will know the song and the order of getting dressed.

3.4-3 Teach Techniques.

When your child seems ready for learning new techniques involved in dressing himself, show him how to do them. Practice with a stuffed animal or doll, encouraging him to remove the clothing first. Then help him put it back on. Give him lots of praise for each accomplishment and plenty of opportunities to try his skill. Let him practice special skills like mastering snaps, zippers, hooks, buttons and, finally, laces. Don't be impatient or expect too much progress at once—he'll eventually manage to do it.

3.4-4 Choose Appropriate Clothing.

While your child is in the process of learning to dress herself, choose clothes that are easy to put on and take off. Skirts and pants with an elastic waist and pullover shirts are easier for a child to manipulate than overalls with buttons or snowsuits with zippers. When she's mastered the simpler clothes, then you can move on to more complicated versions.

3.4-5 Try Parallel Dressing.

Children enjoy learning by following your example. If you get dressed together, you'll not only show the child how to put on clothes, but you'll also set the pace. Later, sharing this time with same-sex children provides special woman-to-woman or man-to-man experiences in the midst of busy schedules.

3.4-6 Use Positive Practice.

Assess what your child can easily do for himself in getting dressed and then expect only that much independence in the morning. Then practice those skills together. The morning rush doesn't usually lend itself to teaching, so do your positive practicing at a more relaxed time of day, when you can take him slowly through the procedure with a smile and a song.

3.4-7 Resistance Busters.

There are many ways to channel your child's attention, help him focus on getting dressed, and make it fun. If she enjoys it, the dressing routine will be much easier.

• **Twenty Questions.** If your little one resists getting dressed, help her look forward to it with a game of Twenty Questions, one for each article of clothing she's putting on. Ask her what shape it is, the color, the pattern, the purpose. See if she can point out other things that are the same color.

• **The Name Game.** Let her make up names for each piece of clothing as she gets dressed—the sillier, the better, such as Kurt the Shirt and Lance the Pants. By placing her focus on the positive aspects of a routine activity, you'll smooth the way.

• **The Color Game.** Trace the figure of a child in clothes on a sheet of white paper or cardboard. Let him color in each piece of clothing in the picture as he learns how to put it on himself. Display the picture in a prominent place so the child understands how proud you are of his accomplishments.

3.4-8 Fire Attire.

When your child has mastered the skills of getting dressed himself, help him to gain some momentum. Ring a "fire bell" and let him pretend he's a fireman who must get dressed fast and go to the fire. Reward his speed with a visit to a real firehouse.

3.4-9 Clothes to Go.

The night before, decide together what clothes he's to wear in the morning—and lay them out. Children should have a voice in buying their own clothes, and they'll be happier wearing them if they've helped choose their favorite colors and styles. Lay the ground rules for clothes selection to help the child make decisions. Explain what is appropriate to wear when, according to occasion and weather. If she has a favorite shirt or pair of pants that have become too shabby for school, make sure she understands when and where she may wear them—after school or on weekends— because we all have favorites we can't part with.

3.4-10 Play Tracy Allen.

To motivate the slow dresser, pretend there's a child just her age across town who's also getting dressed. Tell your child you want to see whether she or "Tracy Allen" will get all dressed first. Start the race. Be your child's cheering squad, coaching her to a close finish —which, of course, she wins.

3.4-11 Beat the Clock.

Ask the child how long she thinks it will take her to get dressed, then time her while she does it. The next morning, ask her if she can beat her own record. Help her set a reasonable time, set a timer for that number of minutes, and go! Keep a chart of the daily times, and remember to give her lots of praise for her efforts.

3.4-12 Setting Realistic Goals.

You've undoubtedly got your own pattern of activity in the morning. You may be a rusher, getting dressed in record time, or perhaps you are a dawdler who enjoys taking lots of time. Discuss with an older child just how much time he thinks he needs to get himself into his clothes in the morning and then, working backward, help him plan exactly when he must start in order to make the deadline. He may need to get up a little earlier to make it or to spend less time doing other things before he begins. A child who surpasses his goal may spend the time before breakfast watching television. Use a chart to reward the goals met, letting the child earn points toward a fun activity or a new toy (see sections 2.4 and 2.5).

3.4-13 Make It the Child's Problem.

Let's face it: There are some children who *can* but *won't* get dressed. When your child has the skills but refuses to use them, define the consequences. Tell her that for every minute over five she takes to finish dressing, she goes to bed a minute earlier or loses television time. And tell her that breakfast will no longer be held for her. Breakfast is scheduled for a specific time and she must get there or miss it.

3.5 BREAKFAST REFUSENIKS

Would your child rather not have breakfast? Do you face a morning hassle every day trying to get her to eat a healthy meal before she goes off to school or to play? Take a close look at your own breakfast habits, because example is the best teacher. If you sit down at the table every morning to a tasty meal, your offspring will almost undoubtedly do the same. Try to eat together as a family, never rushing, being pleasant. *Expect* that you all enjoy breakfast, and show her that you certainly do.

If, in spite of setting a good example, your child will still not eat breakfast, don't make this into a major power struggle between you. Try some of these solutions:

3.5-1 Make It Fun.

Attempt to allot enough time for a leisurely breakfast, and try to make it enjoyable rather than simply an occasion for stuffing down nutrition. Small children enjoy having their own bowls and drinking cups. They love to participate in the preparation by decorating a piece of whole wheat toast with a funny face made of yellow cheese. Add whipped cream and a cherry to pancakes. Draw pictures on top with the syrup.

3.5-2 Let Him Help Plan.

If you allow your child to help plan the breakfast menus for the week and perhaps assist you when you shop for the food at the market, he'll be much more likely to want to eat it. We're assuming, of course, that you provide the nutritional guidelines.

3.5-3 Down with Tradition!

If your child won't eat a conventional breakfast, try something different. Whip up a milkshake and let her drink a liquid meal. Smear some peanut butter on apple slices, serve a cheesy baked potato or a slice of pizza with a glass of milk. As long as it's fortified with nutrition, does the form matter?

3.5-4 Make It Smaller.

If your child prefers lunch to breakfast, offer her a small breakfast and a larger lunch. It doesn't matter as long as the first meal of the day provides enough energy for the morning and, by the end of the day, she has consumed sufficient calories through a balanced diet.

3.5-5 Offer a Variety of Foods.

Introduce new foods to the breakfast menu every so often to preclude boredom. If the child suddenly refuses a food she used to enjoy in the morning, don't force the issue. Forget it for a while, then offer it again later or include it in new combinations or recipes. Don't get hung up on certain foods for breakfast.

3.5-6 Be a Breakfast Buddy.

Small children shouldn't be left alone to eat, and older children like to have company, too. Even if you can't sit with your child while he eats, always remain in the room and give him "a breakfast buddy" to keep him company at the table. A doll or a stuffed animal will usually do the job, but it could even be the comics, a book, the radio, or perhaps the television set. Supervised television, on an *occasional* basis, needn't be a negative influence. Just be sure you don't make it a habit.

3.5-7 Jazz Up the Cereal.

Choose a nutritious cereal with the help of your child, then repackage it into breakfast-size portions in clear plastic bags. In each package, include a surprise—a colorful sticker, a coupon good for a visit to the library, a trinket. She earns the surprise if she eats all of the cereal or a prearranged acceptable portion of it.

3.5-8 Build a Blockbuster.

For every bite of breakfast your child eats, present him with a small building block. When he's finished eating, he may use the blocks for building a castle. Or if he prefers, let him build the castle block by block as he eats.

3.5-9 Fill It with Sunshine.

Each time your little one takes a bite, let her draw on a piece of paper with a marker. Encourage her to complete a picture and fill up her paper as well as her tummy. Make a sunshine chart: Draw a circle—the sun—on a piece of paper. With each bite, add a ray of sunshine to the circle. If you make this an ongoing project, you can add rays each morning, and when the sun is shining very brightly, your child earns a special reward, like a trip to the park. (See Section 2.5.)

3.5-10 Time It.

Try motivating a slow eater with a kitchen timer, setting it for about the time it usually takes him to eat and encouraging him to finish breakfast before the bell rings. Then gradually shorten the time, subtracting a minute or two every morning, until you've reached a reasonable time for him to get through his meal.

3.6 WASHUP WASHOUTS

A clean child is a joy, but try to be reasonable about just how spick-and-span you expect your little child to be—and when. Getting dirty is perfectly acceptable some of the time, and getting cleaned up shouldn't be treated as a punishment. On the other hand, every child should develop a sense of pride in his own body and learn how to take care of it. Setting a good example yourself will help your child pick up good cleanliness habits along with the idea that washing is lots of fun.

Small children try to wash up without any help from you, but most can't manage to do a good job of unsupervised hand washing until they are almost four years old. An acceptable unassisted face wash doesn't usually occur until about six months later, while the skills involved in giving themselves an adequate bath all alone tend to develop by about age six (see Section 9.1). Cleanliness doesn't have the priority for children that it does for their parents, but nurtured during the early years, it eventually becomes part of their daily routine.

Our solutions begin with suggestions for teaching very little children to wash themselves, incorporated into your own daily routine, so they become a natural way to learn. Don't rush. Show your child that the washup routines can be fun. If you think your child forgot to wash his face, don't ask if he did, just ask him to wash because his face is dirty. Specify what you expect, and then encourage him in a positive noncritical way.

3.6-1 Make Things Reachable.

Because your sink is too high for the child to use all by himself, have a small, sturdy stepladder available and bring it out when it's time for a washup. Make the washing materials, such as the washcloth and fingernail brush, readily available. Teach him how to use them. Do the job together. Let him practice on you as well as on himself.

3.6-2 Begin Early.

Even when you are potty training, make it second nature to wash hands after toileting.

3.6-3 Allow Choices.

Let the child choose the washing supplies, and he will have more fun using them. Toddlers, for example, love washcloths decorated with fantasy characters and soap that dispenses from a pump. Use soap that won't sting the eyes. Sew two washcloths together and slip in all those used little pieces of soap to make an "automatic" soap machine. Let your child finger-paint his face clean with liquid soap.

3.6-4 Reward Cleanliness.

Keep a chart in the bathroom. Before meals and after your child toilets, have him check that he washed his hands. Smily faces can be earned for arriving at the table with clean hands and face, and the cleanest hands get dessert first. When a child earns x points, let him choose the menu for dinner or a special dessert.

3.6-5 Stage a Daily Inspection.

Pretend to be the private investigator or ham it up as a drill sergeant and give your child a close inspection after he's finished washing himself. Make it fun, give him special praise when he's done a good job, and be quite specific about areas that need more work.

3.6-6 Apply Consequences.

If, even though he is old enough to be quite capable of washing himself adequately, the child refuses, then it's time to apply some logical consequences. Tell a young child, for example, that you'll have to wash his face and hands for him if he can't manage to do it for himself. After two or three times, he'll prefer to do his own washing up. Or use overcorrection. If the child doesn't wash himself the first time, then supervise the activity as he practices it once, twice, three times.

3.7 TOOTHBRUSH REBELS

Tooth brushing obviously isn't a subject for debate—every child must learn to brush his teeth at least twice a day, preferably after every meal, and to do a good job besides. Flossing is a must. But for some parents, getting their children to brush their teeth quite automatically every morning as part of their daily routine becomes a constant everyday struggle.

Most parents understand the importance of dental care. However, since baby teeth are not permanent, sometimes they don't take them seriously. Baby teeth or primary teeth create the foundation for the permanent set. Decay in these teeth is not only painful but also potentially dangerous, because it can lead to infection or too-early loss of teeth that then affects the position of the permanent teeth.

3.7-1 Establish the Habit Early.

If your child sees you brushing your own teeth regularly, he'll be eager to do it, too. Long before he can really brush, give your baby his own toothbrush. Put a little toothpaste on it and let him go at it. By the age of two, he will be making the motions as you do. And don't forget to floss after brushing. There are floss holders shaped like small slingshots, which make flossing easier for a child. More fun, too, is flavored floss.

3.7-2 Teach the Child How to Brush.

As the toddler gains skill, encourage him to improve his technique.

• Tell him the brush is a little car he must drive all over his teeth.
• Substitute the words *brush, brush, brush your teeth* for *row, row, row your boat,* and sing while he works.
• Let him "inspect" your teeth when you are finished, and you inspect his.
• Brush your teeth together, so he can model himself on you.
• Use disclosing liquid to let the child see the dirty spots and brush them away, as directed by your dentist.
• Teach him to run his tongue along his teeth to *feel* how smooth and slick his clean teeth feel.

3.7-3 Build the Habit with Positive Motivation.

• Praise, praise, praise all of the child's early efforts to brush.
• Let your child choose his own brush and toothpaste. Most children love the pumps.

• Include brushing in your nighttime routine so it is naturally rewarded with a bedtime story afterward.

• Use a timer. Set the time for seconds longer than the child usually brushes and encourage him to brush until the bell rings.

• Chart the progress. Make a happy-tooth chart. Each time the child brushes, add a sticker or star to the chart. When it is filled, he earns a treat (which will be carefully brushed away afterward!)

3.7-4 Use the Dentist to Motivate Brushing.

To prevent dental phobias and encourage your child to get in the habit of brushing, schedule an appointment with the dentist *before* there are any problems. Opinions vary on the right age to do this, ranging from twelve to eighteen months or when the child has twelve teeth, to age two or three.

• Prepare the child for the visit. Play dentist, or read a book about going to the dentist. Talk about what she will see and do there.

• Ask the dentist to explain how to brush teeth and why it's so important.

SUGGESTED READING FOR PARENTS AND CHILDREN
Barnett, Naomi. *I Know a Dentist.* New York: Putnam, 1978. A children's book about the dentist and dental procedures.
Berenstain, Stan and Jan. *The Berenstain Bears Visit the Dentist.* New York: Random House, 1981. The bears visit the dentist and learn about procedures and loose teeth.
Moss, Stephen J. *Your Child's Teeth.* Boston: Houghton-Mifflin, 1977. A parents' guide to children's dental hygiene.

3.8 PICKING UP CLOTHES

When children are toddlers, most of them love to pick up their clothes. Helping Mommy or Daddy is not a chore but a way to have fun and feel important. They love to put dirty clothes in the hamper and trash in the wastebasket. But very often, little children don't get in the habit of picking up after themselves because it's so much more efficient if someone else does it for them. Then, when they've grown up a little, their parents shift gears and suddenly it's "your job."

Obviously, it's best if everyone in the house is responsible for himself right from the beginning, but with the proper planning and some consistent guidance and encouragement, even the sloppiest child will reform!

3.8-1 Make It Fun.

Small children love the game of picking up clothes and helping put away the laundry. A two-year-old can match up socks, carry folded underwear, and guess which piece of clothing belongs to what member of the household. Tell the child to make a train of his shoes in the closet as he puts them away. Let him decorate shoe boxes cut down to be drawer dividers. Let him decide which drawer he wants for his socks, underwear, or shorts. Play Follow the Leader as your child picks up his clothes around the room.

3.8-2 Use Praise.

Be sure you're consistent in praising the child's efforts when he picks up his clothes and puts them where they belong. Tell him exactly what he did that you liked: "Jeremy, I really like the way you picked up your pants and put them in the hamper. That really helps me a lot."

3.8-3 Model the Behavior.

This may not seem like a solution, but modeling sets the standard in the household. If your child knows you do it too, there's no way he can say, "You don't pick up your clothes!" Lead the path to the hamper.

3.8-4 Make It Easy.

If you make it easy for her to do her own picking up and putting away, it will be so much simpler for her to be tidy. For example, add a lower rack or bar for hanging clothes in her closet. Place the most commonly used items on the lowest shelves, and organize the drawers in the dresser so she can reach them without your help. (Make the upper drawers off limits if she must climb up to reach them, or bolt the dresser to the wall so it can't fall over.) Attach clothes hooks at her level in the bathroom and in her own room. Attach another near the front door, where she can hang her coat when she comes home. Provide a small bench or table or shelf that is her special place to keep belongings she needs frequently, such as school supplies.

3.8-5 Rate the Room.

Schedule "room inspections" that can be fun, but also let the child know you like him to pick up his clothes. Give him points for each passing grade, noting them on a chart, and present rewards for a set number of "clean floors" (see Section 2.5). Let the child check out your room, too, rating the neatness. This, after all, is a household goal!

3.8-6 Apply Overcorrection.

If you've tried the positive approach without too much luck, you may add overcorrection to the consequences for not picking up clothes. If your child doesn't do what you've asked him to do, then overcorrect him by having him check for dropped clothes under the bed, in the closet, in the corners, etc. He'll see that it would have been easier to have done it right the first time around. See Section 2.8 for more on using overcorrection.

3.8-7 Apply Natural Consequences.

When your child reaches the age when she likes clothes or has special favorites, then you have a very natural consequence to apply. Don't wash clothes that haven't been placed in the hamper. Gather them in your "weekend box." When she asks for a certain piece of clothing, tell her, "I didn't wash it because it wasn't in the hamper." Then let her help you wash the clothes in the box before going out to play.

3.8-8 Be Very Specific.

Always let the child know exactly what it is you expect of her, and criticize her action rather than her character. For example, don't say, "You're a slob," but instead, "It really bothers me to see your new pants on the floor." A child who is labeled soon begins to believe the name. Explain that it's what he's doing that you don't like, and discuss with him how to change this behavior. You might even let an older child help decide the consequences.

CHAPTER 4

Nighttime Problems

IT'S been a long day and you've worked hard. It's time for the little ones to climb into bed, give you a big hug and a kiss, close their eyes, and go off to sleep for the night, waking up refreshed and happy at a reasonable hour in the morning. But in your house, it doesn't work out that way. Your child wants another story, a drink of water, one more trip to the potty, another half hour of television. He wants to stay up till nine o'clock, just like his friend Jimmy does.

Asleep at last! But an hour after you've nodded off yourself, he's up again, wandering into your room. He wants to sleep in your bed. Still later, you wake up to sobs and plaintive calls: "Mommy! Daddy!"

Whatever the nighttime problems in your family, you are not alone. Many parents have the same problems getting their children into bed and keeping them there. In his informative book *Sleepless Children: A Handbook for Parents,* Dr. David Haslam reports the results of a survey of the sleep patterns of 124 children. One quarter of the school-age children consistently got up during the night, while 35 percent refused to go to bed before their parents.

In every household, there are at least occasional bedtime problems and nights when sleep for Mommy and perhaps Daddy, too, seems out of the question. Sleepwalking, night terrors, separation anxiety, and sleeplessness caused by illness or overexcitement can happen in any family at any time.

Nighttime would be a lot easier if all children had the same sleep needs as their parents, but they don't. Everyone requires periods of sleep characterized by REM (rapid eye movements) as well as "orthodox" sleep, which has four progressively deeper stages of sleep, occurring in adults and older children in cycles of about ninety minutes throughout the night. Babies experience the same phases, but the cycle is complete in only about fifty minutes. This means that babies and younger children have more opportunities to experience periods of light sleep. Eighty percent of adult sleep is deep while only 50 percent of baby sleep is deep.

As for general patterns of sleep, according to many pediatricians, the typical two-year-old requires an average of twelve hours per night, plus a one- to two-hour nap. At age six, the child still needs about twelve hours but with shorter naps. At nine, the average sleep time is eleven hours, and by twelve, it is ten hours. Remember that these are average sleep times and that a child who sleeps more hours or fewer hours is not abnormal.

For everyone in the family to function well during the day, we need the best night's sleep we can get. Nighttime shouldn't be a constant battle of wills between parents and children in an effort to keep the small people in bed or asleep. Follow the suggestions in this chapter for more peaceful nights for your family.

4.1 CHILDREN WHO WON'T GO TO BED

Children resist bedtime for many reasons. Perhaps they're afraid of the dark or fear they won't wake up or feel insecure when they are alone. Undoubtedly, they'd rather play or watch television and certainly, they'd like your company and attention. When they get older, their social life takes precedence. Nevertheless, all children must have a bedtime, and if there is to be peace in the house, their parents can't allow a choice in the matter. Parents who say, "Hey, kids, don't you think it's time for bed?" have chosen not to take charge, and their children are certainly not going to get right into bed. Parents who always give in, who can be counted on to allow the children to stay up "just a little longer," are always going to have problems with bedtime. If a choice is even hinted at, red-blooded children are going to grab it. For many parents, getting the children into bed is one more struggle at the end of a long day, just when they need some time to themselves.

If you are new parents, follow the suggestions outlined here so you can head off nighttime problems before they begin. If bedtime is already a problem, plan a new initiative for putting your child to sleep. Decide what you will do, let the child know a change is imminent, and on day one, put the plan into effect.

4.1-1 Set a Bedtime.

Decide on a specific bedtime for your child and then stick with it. That doesn't mean you must be absolutely rigid and insist that your child is always in his bed at eight o'clock on the dot even if his Daddy just came home or Uncle Joe is visiting, but the more you are able to define a bedtime, the easier it will be to get your child to sleep at a regular time. Hint: Don't use "dark" as your bedtime, because summertime and daylight savings time will cause problems.

4.1-2 Use Security Rituals to Your Advantage.

Small children, especially toddlers, find reassurance in sameness. They like the security of rituals and certain objects they can count on. For example, among the children we know, Alan likes to have his blue hammer in bed with him every night, Sarah must kiss everyone before she goes to her room and then have everyone come to kiss her in bed, while Sissy arranges her dolls under a yellow blanket by her side. Both the rituals and the comforting security items, such as ragged blankets or stuffed dogs, that some children depend upon help the child separate from loved ones and help make the transition from wakefulness to sleep. Don't make fun of your child's rituals, and on the other hand, don't let them become too cumbersome. Limit the number of toys your child takes to bed. "Joey, you may take one book and one toy. Choose." Some children are quite capable of chaining the action so it takes an extra fifteen minutes to get them into bed.

4.1-3 Establish a Bedtime Routine.

Children like to know what is going to happen next. A regular nighttime routine will let them know that bedtime is approaching and it's time to wind down. Follow these guidelines to establish a nighttime routine:

• Keep it simple. Take into consideration your family's usual schedule and your child's preferences. Don't start a pattern you don't plan to continue. The bedtime routine should provide a feeling of warm security, a comforting closure for the day. Perhaps it's only a discussion of the day that's ending and plans for the next one. Setting out tomorrow's clothes and getting school books together will work for older children. Choosing a bedtime story or having a snack will help others understand that now it is time for bed.

• Use signals to highlight the routine. Let your child know when the bedtime routine is to begin. It could be as simple as saying, "Bedtime is when this TV show is over." Or try visual cues. For example: Draw a circle on a sheet of colored paper. Sector the circle into wedges labeled *playtime, bedtime,* and *story time.* Make a paper spinner and attach it to the center with a brad. Point the spinner to the appropriate section when the time comes. Or draw a homemade clock with the hands pointing to the bedtime hour and place it near a real clock. When the hands of the real clock match the fake, the child will know it's time to get ready for bed.

• Keep it calm. Roughhousing and active play immediately before bedtime are not conducive to sleep. Start a period of quiet activities about a half hour before bedtime so the child will be relaxed when the moment comes. Rather than a pillow fight or a game of ball, the winding-down routine could include normal hygiene, reading, storytelling, or music. The quiet routine that smooths the way to bed will be useful, too, if it's followed when a baby-sitter or Grandma is putting him to sleep that night or when the day runs late and the overtired child needs help in calming down for the night.

• Make it special. Ideally, getting ready for bed should be a warm and cozy time for you and your child, a time of warmth and security. Many children love hearing the same book over and over again before bed. Some children love to hear made-up stories, and others like nursery rhymes as a bedtime routine.

Don't assume that older children don't need the bedtime routine. Even preteens love to be read to or to use the time to discuss something important or ask a question before something becomes a problem. Bedtime is an excellent opportunity to be close. Bedtime rituals that begin in youth will aid the children throughout life. Some begin a nighttime reading habit, others keep diaries or plan for the next day. Some do relaxation exercises.

• Be flexible, but know how to end the routine. If you don't know how to make the final decision on when it's time to turn out the lights and go to sleep, the nighttime routine could become tiresome and endless. Don't allow stalling. Don't be persuaded to keep on reading "one more story." Instead, set the number of stories you will read tonight in advance, and stick to it. If setting limits is a problem for you, let your clock or kitchen timer help you. Tell your child, "When the clock says seven-thirty, that's it. Lights out." Or, "In fifteen minutes, the timer will ring and that means lights out."

4.1-4 Discuss the Fears and Anxieties.

Everyone, including children, has fears and worries that tend to surface at night. Encourage your child to talk about her problems and concerns so you can alleviate them and help her fall asleep. (And try a little back rub, too!)

4.1-5 Cope with the Pop-up Syndrome.

You've followed the bedtime routine and Jamie is tucked into bed, but he doesn't stay there! Within ten minutes, he's back in the living room, asking for juice. Try the following techniques. For some children, one will do the trick, for others, it will take all of the suggestions to keep them in bed.

• Tuck him in again and set the kitchen timer for one minute. Tell him you'll return to his room before it rings. Reward him with a back rub for staying in bed. Gradually lengthen the time he must stay in his bed before he gets the reward, whether it's a back rub or something else, like ice cream for breakfast. If necessary, set the timer again, then sit and read in the room until he falls asleep.

• Teach your child how to go to sleep (see Section 3.1). Some youngsters don't know how to relax enough to fall asleep, so teach the techniques described in Section 2.10.

• Give him a P.M. kit with everything he may need right there by his bed: a glass of water and a box containing a flashlight, a favorite toy, and a cassette or radio to listen to before he goes to sleep.

• For babies who are still in the crib but old enough to talk, the nighttime routine often requires some definitive action that takes strength on your part. Let's assume you have covered your toddler and kissed her good night for the fourth time. As you leave the room, say, "Good night. I am going to bed now. Good night." Close the door and don't go back in, no matter how much she screams (unless, of course, you have reason to believe she is in real trouble) for twenty minutes. If after twenty minutes she is still crying, go back to her room and tell her to go to sleep now. Kiss her and leave again for another twenty minutes. If necessary, repeat this routine every night until she's discovered her tactics won't work anymore. Caution: If she stops crying, don't return to her room to check on her until you are *sure* she's sound asleep, or you'll be in for it once again!

• Use a chart. A bedtime chart works with children over the age of about three, allowing them to earn points toward a desired reward. In the beginning, give points for staying in bed for five minutes, then gradually lengthen the time required for accumulating the needed number of points. See Sections 2.4 and 2.5 for details on selecting and using rewards.

• Don't get into a hassle. If your child is used to getting his way, you may need to follow through with a few negative consequences: loss of privilege the following day or an earlier bedtime the next night.

4.1-6 Reinforce the Child's Cooperation.

Using both words and actions, give your child positive feedback for cooperating at bedtime. Plan your bedtime routine, and implement the entire plan all at once. Because it's sometimes difficult to change established behavior, you may need to offer rewards at first, perhaps using a bedtime chart if bedtime has become a nightly struggle. Give points for going through the bedtime routine and for staying in bed before falling asleep, with a reward every night at first. The rewards could include, for example, an extra TV program the next night, special bed sheets, chocolates on the pillow, or a special snack before bed tomorrow night. In the meantime, let the child accumulate points toward a larger reward that will take longer to earn. The big rewards should be chosen from the "menu" of things or activities you know the child wants. Read Section 2.4 once again for details on using these techniques effectively and appropriately.

SUGGESTED BOOKS FOR CHILDREN

Bank, Molly. *Ten, Nine, Eight.* New York: Greenwillow, 1983. A reassuring countdown to bedtime for young children (PS).

Boynton, Sandra. *Good Night, Good Night.* New York: Random House, 1985. A boatload of animals go through their bedtime routine (PS).

Brown, Margaret Wise. *Goodnight, Moon.* New York: Harper & Row, 1947. Rhyming verse describing a child's room while saying good night (PS).

Marmer, Juliet. *The Little Go to Sleep Book.* New York: Atheneum, 1986. A story about how every person and every animal goes to sleep (PS).

4.2 CHILDREN WHO GET UP DURING THE NIGHT

We've never heard of a child who doesn't get up occasionally during the night and attempt to get attention. This is a behavior, just like almost all the others discussed in this book, that shouldn't be considered a problem unless it becomes a habit. Sometimes restless sleep signals a medical or emotional problem and should be checked out if you suspect that possibility. But in most cases, a child who awakens and gets out of bed night after night has simply developed a pattern that needs to be changed. Consult with your pediatrician if our solutions aren't effective—perhaps the problem is serious enough to require medication that will help your child change his sleep pattern. If the nighttime risings include other behaviors, such as insistence on sleeping with parents or siblings, check the sections dealing with these situations.

4.2-1 Systematic Ignoring.

An infant wakes up at night and demands attention because his body is signaling him that he's hungry or wet or in pain, and he shouldn't be ignored. However, an older baby who's been carefully nurtured and loved can be helped to sleep for longer periods of time during the night with the application of systematic ignoring (see Section 6.7, on sleeping through the night, for more information about this solution).

To help you apply systematic ignoring in this situation:

• Observe the pattern. Answering these simple questions will help you determine whether your child really needs you or is simply demanding attention: What does he do when he gets up out of bed? Who does he call? What does he do if nobody responds? Does he ask for water every night? Put a cupful within reach. If you don't answer, does he turn over and go back to sleep?

• Develop a game plan. Make a plan using the principles of systematic ignoring and then stick to it, applying it consistently until there is improvement in the child's behavior pattern. Put the child to bed, firmly but lovingly bid him good night, then leave the room. (If going to bed is the problem, refer to Section 4.1.) Decide how long you will wait to go to him if he wakes up and calls. This should never be more than twenty minutes, a long time for a child in the middle of the night, and never less than five minutes, because he'll soon learn to wait you out! For most parents, this is not easy because you must listen to your wailing child, who may be waking up everyone else in the household if not the neighborhood. If your child doesn't stop crying and calling within the specified time, go to her and tell her firmly in a matter-of-fact tone of voice that she must go back to sleep now. Don't pick her up or cuddle her unnecessarily. Say good night again. Then leave. Continue the systematic ignoring, adding five minutes to your original time until you reach the maximum of about twenty minutes. It won't harm your child if you go a little longer, but it has been our personal experience that twenty minutes consistently applied will do the job in a few days.

If you don't feel comfortable letting your little one cry unless you've reassured yourselves that she is not in any trouble, then check her first. Don't talk to her or reassure her, because you do not want to reward this behavior with warm attention. Simply see that she is all right, then say good night, tell her you won't be back, and leave the room. Now start the ignoring procedure.

• Time the crying. Make a chart to record the length of time your child continues to cry or call for you, so you can spot progress. Before long, when he learns that you won't come on demand, we promise you will see an increase in tears but a decrease in their duration.

When his exhausted parents consulted us, Seth was a twenty-two-month-old little boy who had made a habit of getting up about three times a night. The first night of systematic ignoring, his mother sat nervously on the edge of her bed watching the hands of the clock tick off twenty minutes before going in and telling him to go back to sleep. The next time he woke up, she did the same, but on the third try, he went to sleep after seventeen minutes. The second night, they let Seth cry again. He cried for twenty minutes, but he awoke only once more that night. On the third night, he got up twice, crying for shorter periods, but on the fourth, he didn't call for his parents at all.

4.2-2 Help Her Go Back to Sleep.

An older child will also be helped by systematic ignoring but may also need some help in going to sleep again.

- Use relaxation techniques described in Section 2.10.
- Use positive practice. Role-play during the day, giving the child ways he might use to fall asleep at night. Suggest a peaceful, quiet, and monotonous scene for him to think about, such as ocean waves lapping at the shore or sheep jumping over a fence. Let him practice repeating the ABC's or a nursery rhyme over and over again.
- Use soothing music. Place a cassette player with a tape of soothing music by the bed. Show the child how to turn it on if he wakes up and can't go back to sleep.

4.2-3 Provide a Way to Pass the Time.

Give him several quiet bed activities—books, story tapes, stuffed animals, or dolls—to occupy him so he doesn't need you when he wakes up.

4.2-4 Reinforce and Reward.

Again, let your child earn points and rewards for getting up fewer times at night. If, for example, she's been waking up and calling three times a night, reward her for getting up only twice, then work up to once, then never. See Section 2.4 on rewards and Section 2.5 on charts. Spread out the rewards by making them cost more. At first, one night without waking may earn a reward, then it takes two nights in a row, then three.

SUGGESTED BOOKS FOR PARENTS

Cuthbertson, Joanne, and Susie Schevill. *Helping Your Child Sleep Through the Night.* New York: Doubleday, 1985. Excellent detailed guide to overcome sleeping problems.

Haslam, David. *Sleepless Children: A Handbook for Parents.* New York: Long Shadow Books, 1984. Informed information on sleep problems and sleep patterns; offers solutions.

4.3 CHILDREN WHO WANT TO SLEEP WITH YOU

Children love to sleep with their parents—it's warm and cozy and safe. Some parents never let their children get into their bed, others say, "Only on Sunday." Many take a sick child into their bed during the night so they can comfort him and doze off at the same time. Some parents allow their child into their bed till he falls asleep, then gently move him to his own bed, while others wake up to find the child there in bed with them in the morning. Still others have made a habit of sleeping in the same bed with their child.

We believe that allowing a child to sleep with you except occasionally is unhealthy for both child and parent. In our experience and that of many other mental-health professionals, the practice of allowing children to sleep regularly with their parents can lead to serious problems for the child. He may become overly dependent and unable to spend the night away from home. He may be embarrassed by the practice, confused over his role in the family and his sexual feelings, or anxious about the relationship between his parents. He may not express these concerns overtly, but he will still feel them.

There is a big difference between allowing a child to sleep with you occasionally and allowing it as a regular practice. In most cases, parents find it a difficult habit to stop once it starts, especially since it's such an easy way out of a tiring situation. It seems so much simpler to take the child to bed with you than to listen to him cry or beg. Sometimes parents use the children in their bed as a simple but perhaps unspoken way to avoid intimacy and sexual relations with each other, and therefore it is an unhealthy habit for them, too.

It is best not to let children think of their parents' bed as their own. The following are solutions designed to keep sleeping with parents from becoming a habit or for breaking that habit if it has already been established.

4.3-1 Prevent the Habit from the Start.

If the child won't go to sleep alone because she is frightened or has difficulty falling asleep, see suggestions in sections 4.1 and 14.4. When the child is sick, an intercom will allow you to hear her. Or if it's necessary or makes you feel better, one parent can sleep in the child's room. If you do allow him to sleep in your room when he's ill, discontinue the practice when he's well again.

4.3-2 Return Her to Her Bed.

If your child finds her way to your room during the night, return her firmly to her bed and tuck her in without too much TLC. The parent who is able to be the most firm and the least sympathetic should be assigned to the job.

4.3-3 Catch the Night Visitor.

Many parents report that their child sneaks into their bed while they are asleep. If this is what happens to you, try these solutions for catching the visitor before she gets into your bed and returning her to her room.

• Bell the cat. Hang bells on your door or the child's so you will hear her coming.
• Tuck yourselves in. Tuck in the sheets on your bed very tight or position the pillows so that it's almost impossible for the child to slip into your bed without waking you up.
• Block the door. Make a noisy barricade blocking your room

so the child can push the door open, but not without letting you know it.

4.3-4 Use Crowding Techniques.

This tactic requires you to be good actors. The object is to make the child so uncomfortable in your bed that her own becomes more and more attractive to her.

• Crowd her out. If you wake up to find the child has already climbed into your bed, pretend you are still asleep and roll over toward her. Still "asleep," place an arm on her nose or give her a gentle kick. If she's between you, then both of you can gently roll together, giving her less and less room. If she's on the outside, thrash around and gently nudge her to the edge.

One pair of parents came to us for help because they had tried everything they knew to induce their nine-year-old daughter to sleep in her own bed. They had begged, pleaded and punished, and redecorated her room three times. We instructed them to squeeze her out of bed—it worked. But then she began sleeping at the *side* of their bed on the floor. We suggested that the mother get up a few times during the night and "accidentally" step on the child—gently, of course. Eventually, Cindy decided that sleeping in her parents' room was much too dangerous.

• Pretend to be restless. Crowding is effective, too, if you often find yourself sleeping with your child in her room because she calls for you in the middle of the night. An adult friend, Sara, reports that when she was small, she would call for her parents and one of them would get in bed with her until she was no longer frightened of the "lions and tigers." The parent would climb into her little single bed and fall asleep immediately, then stretch out and squeeze her against the wall, snoring loudly. Very soon, she decided having them sleep with her wasn't worth it.

4.3-5 Give Rewards.

Reinforce and reward your child for sleeping alone, whether or not you choose a "formal" reward system.

• Use praise and affection. Be sure to tell your child how proud you are of him and what a "big boy" he is because he sleeps alone in his own bed. Give him extra hugs and attention in the daytime hours.

• Use rewards. If the child has been sleeping with you in your bed for a long time, you may have to reward progress toward total nighttime independence. Together, design a nighttime chart, perhaps in the shape of a bed, and give points for partial or whole nights spent sleeping alone in his own bed. See sections 2.4 and 2.5 for details. Some natural rewards for sleeping alone might include spending the night with a friend, taking a portable TV set to his room for the evening, or getting a new poster for his wall.

4.3-6 Make His Room Inviting.

Though you needn't go so far as to redecorate his room completely, make it attractive to him, so he'll feel a special attachment to it. A simple way to do this is to ask him to choose pictures from magazines to hang on the wall. When it's time to decorate, ask your child what color she'd like it to be. Take her to the fabric store or bedspread shop. Or let her choose among samples you have selected. Sit together in the middle of the room, and come up with a new furniture arrangement.

4.3-7 Get Professional Help.

If our solutions don't work, if one parent resists solving this problem, or if you realize that you are using this habit to avoid intimacy between you, seek help from the appropriate professional. See Chapter 17 on finding professional help.

4.4 CHILDREN WHO WANT TO SLEEP WITH SIBLINGS

Sometimes it's not the parents that a child wants to sleep with; instead, it's his siblings. Perhaps brothers or sisters have previously shared a room. Or this may be a second-best solution to sleeping alone because the child already knows the possibility of sleeping with his parents is nil. Climbing into bed with his brother looks pretty good. Often it doesn't matter whether the sibling is older or younger; it's someone to share the night with.

Sleeping with a sibling in the same bed can quickly become a habit, and it is not to be encouraged. First of all, children should learn to be on their own while they sleep. And second, sleeping together may stimulate sexual fantasies and sexual play between the siblings.

If your children have gotten into the habit of sleeping in the same bed, you may find the following solutions to be helpful.

4.4-1 Inform Them That They Will Now Sleep Alone.

With a matter-of-fact attitude and a firm tone, tell the children that they have their own beds and must sleep in them. Period.

4.4-2 Discuss the Fears.

If the child seems to be afraid to sleep alone, talk about his fears and try to solve problems. For fears that persist, use the suggestions in Chapter 14.

4.4-3 Provide Alternatives.

Smooth the way to sleeping alone by providing your child with company at night or an alternative sleepmate.

• A stuffed animal or doll is a natural alternative that the child can use to develop independence without being "alone."

• Allow the children to sleep in the same room but not in the same bed. This requires supervision to prevent relapses.

• Arrange an intercom or walkie-talkie connection so the children can talk to each other from their separate rooms until they fall sleep.

• Use the nighttime kit suggested in Section 4.1, so he'll have something to do in bed until he gets sleepy.

4.4-4 Reinforce Sleeping Alone.

With any desirable behavior, it's important to provide encouraging reinforcement. Praise the child for sleeping by herself. Tell her how proud you are that she is such a big girl now. Encourage her siblings to contribute to the praise. An older child will respond to natural consequences, too. For example, let her ask a friend to spend the night. Or stage an indoor camp-out for separated siblings, sleeping side by side in sleeping bags for a night. Provide breakfast in bed for the siblings, or have a picnic on the floor.

4.4-5 Use a Sandman Reward Chart.

Set up a more elaborate reward system. See sections 2.4 and 2.5 for information about using rewards and charts effectively. For this chart, tell the child that the sandman visits this house every night, and if he finds him in his own bed, he will give him a point. Start off with low numbers of points earning rewards and gradually raise the requirements. In more difficult situations, the sandman may need to visit more than once an evening to shape the desired behavior. If the child is alone in bed, he earns a reward. Slowly move toward a complete night alone to earn the reward.

4.5 SLEEPWALKERS

It's been estimated that 10 to 15 percent of all children sleepwalk at least once. Most of them outgrow it, but about 2 percent continue to be sleepwalkers right into adulthood. Somnambulism, the technical term for sleepwalking, is not the physical manifestation of a dream, nor does it seem to be associated with psychological problems or emotional upheaval, since it doesn't even occur during dream sleep. It does seem to run in families.

When a child sleepwalks, his eyes remain open but are glassy and seemingly unseeing. The walks, which may last anywhere from a few minutes to an hour, are not harmful except for the fact that children (or adults, for that matter) who wander around unsupervised while they are sound asleep can hurt themselves.

That means that you, as a parent, must devise ways to protect your child from injury when he walks in his sleep. This does not mean restraining him, because that can be more dangerous than the stroll. Instead, focus on arranging the environment to prevent injury or to allow immediate detection. Involve older children in designing their own safety measures.

4.5-1 Arrange Alerts.

If your object is to awaken both the child and yourself, hang bells on her door. Or rig up electric eye buzzers to warn you when the child is up and about.

4.5-2 Block the Way Out.

A teenager we know once sleepwalked right out the front door in his pajamas. He was so embarrassed by this that he placed a chair, a football helmet, and a trash can in front of his bedroom door so the noise would wake him up if he set forth again. It worked. For young children, try placing a door latch high enough so it cannot easily be reached; provide enough slack in the contact so the child is not locked in, but can't get out without a deliberate effort. That way he will almost surely wake up if he squeezes through, but he can get out in an emergency. Prop safety gates across stairways. Caution: Never lock a child into his room.

4.5-3 Use Suggestion.

Combine relaxation techniques (see Section 2.10) with imagery about *not* sleepwalking. Practice the techniques during a quiet period of the day or, even better, just before bedtime. When he's very relaxed, ask the child to imagine sitting up in bed, ready to sleepwalk, but when his feet touch the floor, he wakes up. Or have him imagine that grasping the doorknob is the trigger to waking up. Talk him through the scene first, then have him imagine it by himself. Have him imagine how proud and happy he feels, and be sure to praise his success.

For some children, negative imagery works best. For example, have the child imagine sleepwalking out of her room and falling down the stairs, then saying to herself, "Stop! Stop! Go back to bed! You're walking in your sleep!" Make it as real and fearful as possible, then have the child complete the scene by imagining herself safely in bed.

4.5-4 Praise and Reward Fewer Instances.

Let the child know you are happy when he sleepwalks less: "Joe, you only walked in your sleep once this week. That's wonderful! You've earned a surprise." You can also use more formal charts and rewards. If you do, let the child earn points for catching himself and waking up before walking as well as for not walking at all.

4.5-5 Try Medication.

Confer with your pediatrician if your child is a dedicated sleepwalker. Sometimes medication can alter sleep patterns.

4.6 SLEEP TALKERS

Most kids talk in their sleep occasionally, and we don't consider it a problem unless it wakes up the rest of the family. If you do, however, you may want to try our solutions.

4.6-1 Ignore It.

In most cases, the less attention sleep talking receives, the more likely it will cease. Pay no attention. Make no comments about it the next day.

4.6-2 Change Sleeping Arrangements.

If the talking disturbs anyone else in the household, block the sound by closing a door or separating children who share the same room.

4.6-3 Avoid the Cause.

If sleep talking, or somniloquy, seems to be triggered by overexcitement at bedtime, then forbid roughhousing or vigorous play in the evening. Monitor television programs so that the child isn't overstimulated or made fearful by what he watches. After an especially eventful day, use relaxation techniques (see Section 2.10) to calm him down before bed.

4.6-4 Listen and Discuss.

Sometimes, a child talks in his sleep because he is concerned or worried. Try to listen to what he is saying, and if you can understand the words, bring the subject up casually for discussion the next day.

4.7 CHILDREN WITH NIGHT TERRORS

Nightmares and night terrors are two different things. Unlike nightmares, night terrors are not fearful dreams or the result of dream activity. Instead, they are thought to reflect an immature sleep pattern in which the child has difficulty making the transition from deep sleep to lighter sleep stages. Though the child with night terrors won't remember them, these nocturnal episodes can be extremely frightening to his parents. Many children sob or scream, thrash around, run through the house, call out, their eyes wide open but unseeing and their ears seemingly not comprehending your comforting words.

There's little you can do to help the child during a night terror. You must simply wait it out, remembering that it isn't caused by stress and won't have a traumatic or lasting effect on her.

4.7-1 Comfort the Child.

Hold the child, soothe her, wash her face with a cool cloth. This will make you feel you're doing something useful and will comfort the child as she loses her glassy stare and begins to return to reality, wondering what's going on.

4.7-2 Regulate Sleep Schedules.

To help the child develop a more mature sleep pattern, make sure she has a regular sleeping schedule and gets sufficient rest.

4.7-3 Consult a Professional.

Although night terrors usually have little significance, there is a slight possibility they are the symptom of neurological abnormalities. To rule that out, discuss them—and very disturbing nightmares—with your doctor. In addition, if the terrors occur with great frequency, the doctor may wish to relieve them with carefully monitored medication.

4.8 CHILDREN WHO HAVE NIGHTMARES

Nightmares, unlike night terrors, can be very frightening for the child as well as his parents and are often the result of feelings of insecurity, anxiety, fear, or worry. They are common and normal fright reactions to scary dreams, usually beginning at about the age of three and tending to peak between the ages of four and six. Girls are likely to have them later than boys. A 1959 study by Lapouse and Monk found that 28 percent of children from six to twelve have nightmares. Around the age of ten, these bad dreams often increase in frequency again, then subside once more.

Nightmares differ from night terrors in other ways: While she may sweat, scream, and gasp, a child experiencing a nightmare can be awakened quite quickly and will usually recall the dream, at least in part. The dreams may be triggered by illness or pain, over-excitement, fear, and anxieties, violent television programs, or an ill-considered parental threat. Though the child will probably be unable to pinpoint exactly what is bothering him, you may glean some clues from her behavior and conversation. Whatever the cause, it is true that insecure, worried, or anxious children are more likely to have nightmares.

4.8-1 Soothe and Reassure.

Usually, the most a parent can do for a child with a nightmare is to wake her up, then calm, soothe, and reassure her that everything is all right. Cuddle and hug her, but don't make too much fuss over the nightmare because she may then learn to use "bad dreams" to get attention. It is also not important to discuss the dream's contents at this time.

4.8-2 Avoid Overexcitement.

All children should have a period of calm and relaxation before it's time to go to bed, and therefore it is an excellent idea not to allow overstimulating or scary television programs, not to tell them frightening stories or permit too much physical activity. Although research has not proved the relationship between television and nightmares, the experiences of many parents we know suggests that limiting TV exposure does help.

4.8-3 Discuss Problems, Fears, and Stressful Events.

Use your child's conversation and dreams as cues to any problems she may be experiencing. Talk about the nightmares during the day, and try to allay her fears and concerns. Also, look ahead and prepare her in advance for stressful events, such as going to nursery school after vacation or going on a trip. Children's fears are often caused by their lack of information.

4.8-4 Take Action Against Recurrent Nightmares.

If a child has the same dream over and over again, you can safely assume he is feeling anxious about something. See Chapter 14 for suggestions on desensitizing the child to the fears. Encourage him to talk about the dream and to role-play it in daylight—but with a happy ending.

4.8-5 Develop a Nighttime Strategy.

It often helps older children if they feel they have a defense against nightmares. One little boy we know took his "shield" to bed with him to ward off the dragons. Another found security in a night-light. Shelly, an eight-year-old girl, was able to cope better with her frightening dreams if she said a special prayer every night, asking for protection against the lions and tigers.

CHAPTER 5

Day-After-Day Problems

THOSE annoying childhood behaviors that occur day in and day out, requiring your constant attention and discipline, are the ones parents find the most exhausting. Not only does the specific behavior drive you wild, but you end the day with irritation and inadequacy, feelings that don't foster good relationships and communication between you and your child.

The good news is that there are alternative solutions for every one of these nagging everyday problems. Though overcoming them may take time, patience, and perseverance, your efforts will pay off for everyone in the family.

Let's discuss some unacceptable behaviors that are common occurrences in many households and the alternative solutions you may choose to use.

5.1 WON'T HELP WITH CHORES

Parents generally consider "chores" to be small routine jobs around the house. But their children often consider them difficult and unpleasant duties imposed on them when they'd rather be doing something else. No matter how minor the chores actually are, they can cause havoc in families, especially when it takes dozens of reminders and several arguments to get the tasks done.

We believe that everybody in the family should share the responsibility for the jobs that must be done to make life livable, especially in two-career or single-parent families. If this is an unwritten rule right from the beginning, the children will be likely to grow up assuming that helping is part of their normal daily routine. We don't, of course, think that children should be overburdened with household work, but a few simple responsibilities will help ease the load on you and teach cooperation as well.

A major complaint of parents who come to us is that their children are "irresponsible." They don't do the chores they are supposed to do, or they don't do them effectively or pleasantly without reminders or arguments. They are resentful and defiant, or they simply "forget to remember."

Other parents want to know how to instill a feeling of responsibility in their young ones. One key to remember is that the word *responsibility* means the ability to respond. In most cases, if a child is able to do something, then it's fair to ask him to try. Here's what we suggest.

5.1-1 Start Young.

Even the smallest child can learn to be responsible. With little ones, you can use their stage of development as a guide to what they are capable of doing. Toddlers, for example, love to pick things up. So harness that energy. Let them put their dirty clothes in the hamper, their clean clothes in the drawers, their toys on the shelf. Toddlers want to help Mommy and Daddy, and they can be a real asset instead of a hindrance if you let them. You'll be keeping them busy and teaching them responsibility at the same time.

When she was very small, three-year-old Lynn loved to pick up "twash" and put it in the trash can. That's a perfect chore for a toddler, who can usually spot a speck at fifty yards. When Lynn grew older and taller, she was always delighted to get things out of drawers, and by the time she was four, she could select silverware and set the table as well as any adult. That was her first real chore, but she didn't consider it to be work. To her, it was a sign of being a big girl and a natural part of life in the household.

5.1-2 Change the Chores with the Child.

Chores should be appropriate to the age and ability of the child, but it is helpful to switch chores as the child grows—especially if there is more than one young one in the house. That way, one child can't say, "Mark doesn't have to do that, so why do I?" If chores are age-related, Mark doesn't do that job now, but he once did or he will have to in the future. When chores change, children will look forward to new responsibilities. One father told his child, "You're not old enough yet to go to the street to get the newspaper, but someday you will be." His son would ask and ask if he was old enough yet, and when he finally was, he found his new chore absolutely delightful.

5.1-3 Teach the Child How to Do It.

Don't assume your child, even an older child, knows how to do what you want. Always specify what's expected, show her how to do it, and supervise her progress at the beginning. Tell her exactly how often it must be done and when it must be finished. Take bed making, for example: Nobody's born knowing how to make a bed just the way you like it made. Show the child how, then be sure to provide plenty of praise and encouragement for her efforts and improvements.

5.1-4 Don't Expect Too Much or Accept Too Little.

Try to match your expectations to your child's age and stage of development. When Lynn first started setting the table, it was wonderful that she put a utensil at each place. Of course, sometimes people got all spoons or all forks. Later, she learned which ones to put out and where to place them on the placemat, copying what her parents did. And finally, her job was to set the table completely for each meal because she knew how.

A three-year-old can put trash in the can in his room, but he obviously can't collect all the trash and take it downstairs. You know your child's capabilities. But if you are not letting your toddler help, you are underestimating his skills.

5.1-5 Monitor the Chore.

Many parents make the big mistake of expecting a job to be done correctly without supervision or assistance, at least at first. When a child is learning a new job, you'll not only have to teach him how to do it, but also monitor his work while he's doing it until he has become accomplished at it. Until it is a well-established habit, don't expect him to do it when you're not home or in another part of the house.

• Be a prompter. Provide your physical presence when little ones do their chores. They will need help, praise, and prompting whether they are picking up toys or putting clothes in the hamper. Four-year-olds may have learned to set the table, but they'll need a prompt as to when to do it. Even eleven-year-olds may need a reminder now and then.

• Provide a cue. Choose a time of day or other natural cues—such as the end of an event, perhaps a meal—to help the child know when it's time to do his task. If a child helps clear the table, then the end of dinner is a natural signal. Or if his chore is to set the table for breakfast, then he should know that is to happen just as soon as he gets dressed in the morning. If taking out the trash is the job, he knows that when dinner is over, he must collect and take out the trash.

5.1-6 Now Make the Responsibility Theirs.

As the children grow older and more capable, gradually give them the responsibility for accomplishing their tasks.

• Chart the chore, but forget the prompting. Make a chart that tells the child when he's to do his task. (You may wish to combine the chart with a reward system.) Then post the chart where he will notice it. If he's the trash disposer, the notice could be tacked on

the back door so he'll see it when he goes out (see sections 2.4 and
2.5).

• Make inspections. After you've made sure the child knows
how to do the job, tell him you won't say another word about it
until "inspection time." Let's take Joey: His nightly chores are to
wipe off the tabletop after dinner, then to remove the dishes from
the dishwasher. Your agreement with him is that you won't mention the task. However, two hours after dinner, you will hold an
inspection to be sure the job's been done. In the case of Jenny, who
is supposed to clean her room each week, picking everything up off
the floor, straightening the shelves, and arranging her closet, agree
to say nothing all week, but schedule inspections at noon on Saturday.

• Combine inspection with reminders. Some children prefer to
be reminded about chores, and our advice to parents in those cases
is to agree to a certain number of reminders at certain times. We
suggest they ask the child to choose the kind of reminders that will
help him the most. Scott vacuums out the car. He suggested that
his mom tell him what time on the weekend she'd like this job to be
finished. That serves as his reminder. Before dinner, Mom calls
Mandy once to set the table.

5.1-7 Follow Up with Natural Consequences.

Positive consequences can be used as reinforcers, after the child
has finished a chore successfully.

• Praise a job well done. The most natural consequence of a job
well done is praise and recognition. When the task is finished, let
the child know you are pleased and tell him exactly what he did
that was so terrific. If your child responds better to praise while
work is in progress, give it to him then. And if he's not the kind
who responds well to praise, then shift your tactics (see Chapter 2).

• A time to play and a time to chore. A logical consequence to
work well done is having some fun, so reward your conscientious
child with an activity she enjoys. After Susan cleans up her room,
she may watch television. When the garbage has been taken out,

Jim may go outside to play. Always be consistent, making sure the chore is completed before you give permission for the pleasurable consequence.

• Reinforce with rewards. We've mentioned many times that strong reinforcement is usually needed to establish new behavior. This is especially true when you are asking older children to accept responsibilities they've never assumed before or when you have previously had difficulty getting them to do their chores. A reward system, giving them points toward coveted rewards, can often be the magic wand.

Sarah, for example, never hangs up her clothes unless she is mercilessly nagged. Forget the nagging. Explain to Sarah exactly what you expect her to do and when it is to be done. Make a chart and tell her that when she has earned twenty-five points, she will get the new sweater she wants. Hold an inspection at seven o'clock every evening. Praise her lavishly, and put a check on her chart if all of her clothes have been hung up or put away neatly. Then give her a small reward, like permission to stay up a little later to watch a TV show or a new barrette for her hair. When she has earned twenty-five points, she gets her sweater.

5.1-8 Take Negative Action for Refusal to Do Chores.

Punishment, like removal of a privilege or toy, is always an option for frustrated parents, but we much prefer using other negative natural consequences to change your child's behavior.

• Use overcorrection. This works especially well when memory may be the problem. Joseph can't seem to remember to make his bed. Tell him that if he forgets again, he will have to make all of the beds in the house on the weekend. Then make sure he does it, even if he throws a tantrum first. Investing your time and effort a few times will etch the task in his memory and will save you the daily hassles. (See Section 2.8 for a detailed explanation of overcorrection.)

• Make deductions from her allowance. We believe that school-age children should receive an allowance. It helps them learn a healthy respect for money if they must use the allowance to pay for necessities and gifts and to save for something special. Let's assume that your child's allowance is $3.50 a week, which includes a base amount for lunch money and bus fare plus a little discretionary spending money. On Sunday evening, she will receive her allowance with twenty-five cents deducted for each day she did not do her assigned chore.

• Follow through. Make a deal with your child and then follow through, right to the end. Always. What you are trying to overcome are old habits that have become strongly ingrained in both you and the child. Don't do the chores for your child when he forgets. If your child always drops his clothes on the floor and you always pick them up, he's not the one to blame for this inconsiderate behavior—you have given him tacit approval.

Instead, tell him what the consequences will be if he forgets from now on. If his clothes are on the floor, fetch him and tell him to pick up his clothes and/or apply the prearranged consequence. In this case, the consequence could be twenty-five cents deducted from his allowance or the job of washing the clothes himself because Mom washes only the clothes in the hamper.

5.2 WON'T PRACTICE

Practice is supposed to make perfect, but instead it often produces total frustration. "Elizabeth insisted on guitar lessons, so we bought her a guitar and found a good teacher," one mother told us. "Now she says she hates it, and getting her to practice is a daily power struggle. Should we insist or surrender?"

This is a complicated situation because there are many questions that need answering before you decide what solutions are the appropriate ones to apply. When should a child start the lessons, and how does a parent choose the right teacher or class? How can you be sure the child is ready for this commitment? Is the child discouraged or defiant, or is he already overprogrammed with activities? How can you encourage the child to enjoy the experience and take the responsibility for making the required effort?

Your short-term goal in this case is to get the child to practice.

Your long-term goal, however, is to help him discover and learn new and enjoyable skills that will pay off for him in later life. To accomplish both these goals, try one or more of these solutions.

5.2-1 Match Ability with Interest.

To get the most out of this endeavor, begin with a skill that is appropriate to the age, level of development, and interest of the child.

• Expose her to appropriate choices, and let her do the choosing. Investigate and experiment before making a decision. Attend a music class that introduces many instruments to the group. Visit a gymnastics class. Attend local children's talent shows or performances. Get books or records or cassettes from the library that will serve to introduce the child to new skills. Discuss the possibilities, choices, instructors, classes, etc., with teachers and other parents. Don't make a decision until the child has been presented with real choices and seems ready to choose an activity that really excites her.

• Think it through. Make sure you have thought this through and are being realistic about whether you can support these lessons or classes or activities in terms of time, money, and energy. A child who is going to be a good figure skater, for example, must be taken to and from the rink several times a week, perhaps very early in the morning. A swimmer needs a pool and perhaps a car pool to get him there. Violin lessons cost money. Practicing the piano after school means acquiring a piano and arranging time that's undisturbed by other household happenings. In other words, to be successful, the child will need your support and enthusiasm. You and he must take it seriously.

• Make inquiries before making promises. If your child shows interest in a specific activity or skill that requires lessons, consult first with a professional in the field to determine whether this is a suitable time to begin. The youngster must be physically and mentally ready and able to master the skills. Age cannot be the sole criterion, because each child matures at a different rate.

• Invest carefully. Don't immediately go out and make a major investment in equipment simply because your child is eager to begin. Rent a violin or piano, buy one secondhand, or borrow a friend's until you know the interest is real. In this way, you can spare yourself the annoyance of having spent your hard-earned money unnecessarily if the lessons are abandoned.

• Don't force the child to continue. Even a child who is quite determined to play the piano may find, after perhaps a few years of piano lessons, that she was really destined to be a ballerina. Or a young artist for whom you've bought every brush and paint available may suddenly want to be a baton twirler. Encourage her to continue pursuing the original skill, but don't insist beyond reason. It's not worth a constant battle. However, if your child is capable and willing, make a contract with her to pursue the skill on a less strenuous basis. Remember that whatever she learns will be carried with her for life. Maybe she won't be a prima ballerina, but she can still enjoy modern jazz class once a week. The most important thing is that she feels good about herself.

5.2-2 Find the Right Teacher.

Perhaps the most important ingredient of learning a skill successfully, once interest has been established, is matching the child with the suitable teacher or class. So don't simply send your youngster to the instructor best known in town or the class your neighbor's children attend. Make your own investigation.

• Research the teacher's credentials. Talk with other parents whose children take lessons from him.

• Arrange a meeting between the teacher and the two of you. See how he interacts with your child.

• Observe the teacher in action, if possible. Does he use positive reinforcement? Does he have a sense of humor? Is he enthusiastic about the subject and can he communicate this feeling? Is he positive with his students? Does he motivate them to play?

• Ask questions: Will the teacher communicate with you about your child's progress? May the child be able to make his own choices, when appropriate, of music, recital pieces, etc.? Will there be an opportunity to perform or display his work? Are there planned meets or competitions? How many children will be in each class?

• Check on fees, payment schedules, scheduling, etc.

5.2-3 Encourage Your Child to Practice.

Before you sign your youngster up for lessons, try to make sure he understands that he is making a commitment. Ask the teacher, coach, or instructor to tell him how and how much to practice and that it is his own responsibility to do so without constant reminders from his parents. Then use this advice:

• Work out a plan together. Let the child choose the best time to practice, encouraging him to pick a time when there are few distractions. Post the plan on the piano or in the practice area.

• Make a graph (Figure 5) and keep it, along with a clock or timer, wherever he does his practicing. It will serve as a motivator to increase the time he spends at it. Have him post the number of minutes of practice every day. Connect the lines between dots to indicate increases and decreases in time.

Fig. 5 Ali's Practice Schedule

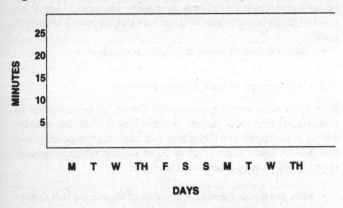

Ali records her practice time each day.

• Use a timer. A kitchen timer clicking away will help the child know how long she's been practicing. If she sets it for the length of time she's supposed to spend, the bell will let her know when she's finished.

• Follow up with reinforcement. Let the child choose an activity he enjoys after he's finished practicing.

5.2-4 Be the Audience.

It's much more fun to practice when somebody else is listening or watching. Younger children thrive on instant feedback and may even need your supervision at first. Older children enjoy it too, so let your child know you'd love to be the audience, at least occasionally. Perhaps she can practice for you while you prepare dinner, or maybe she just needs your company and would agree to your sitting in the same room while you read or listening over an intercom. Once the child no longer requires your constant presence, then you can plan to sit down and enjoy listening or watching every so often.

Unless your child is very shy, wait to be invited, and if necessary, limit your listening or watching so the child won't become dependent on your presence. Ask the child to tell you when he wants you to listen, or say, "Tell me what day this week you want me to hear you practice and I'll be happy to do it."

If you can't be there for the practicing and he wants you to hear him play, show him how to tape the session so you can listen to it later.

5.2-5 Emphasize the Positive.

It's important for a child to learn from her mistakes and know it's okay to make them. So first tell what she did right, then tell her what needs improvement, if anything. For example: "I'm so excited about how great that sounds. Do it once more, but try it a little faster in the second part," or, "Before you know it, you'll be a pro. Let's hear it again. Maybe it will help to slow up when you get to the hard part at the end."

5.2-6 Praise the Progress.

Learning anything—the piano or the computer—takes time and patience. Encourage your child to tell you what he'll be working on during the practice time, and cheer him on. Let him know you think it's wonderful that he's sticking with it, trying techniques over and over again, and finally moving ahead. Sometimes it is helpful to designate practice periods very clearly: each piece three times; scales for five minutes.

5.2-7 Make a Contract.

For some children, a written agreement encourages real commitment. They will agree to practice and to stay with the lessons for at least a certain length of time, no matter what. This is especially useful when they are learning special skills that require an investment of time before there will be noticeable results. Learning to play the violin is a good example—it takes a while to produce anything more than squeaks and screeches. If the child has worked hard but has made little progress and feels unhappy about the lessons at the end of the prescribed time, then he should be allowed to stop or change the plan.

Follow the pattern of this sample contract:

AGREEMENT

Given: John Adams will take piano lessons.

Responsibilities:

Parents	Child
Will pay for lessons	
Will rent piano	Will attend weekly piano lessons and be attentive
Will help as needed, and will serve as audience	Will practice twenty minutes every day
Will control interruptions during practice time	

Consequences: If child does not practice twenty minutes a day, then on Saturday he must make up the lost time before going out to play.

Time period: At the end of six months, parent and child will reevaluate the lessons and write a new contract.

Child's signature _____

Parent's signature _____

5.2-8 Use Natural Incentives.

For children who love what they're doing, practicing is the reward. But most youngsters must build up their interest before reaching utopia, and natural incentives will help motivate them. Again, turn to the magic powers of your kitchen timer if your child is preoccupied with how much time he must spend. The timer ticking away will reassure him that the minutes are passing and that he'll be saved by the bell! Or try making a "ticket" for admission to a favorite activity and punch a hole in it each time he practices. When he has earned a certain number of holes, he may cash in the ticket. Perhaps an activity related to the lessons, like a play, a concert, or a sports meet, could be the reward.

5.2-9 Deal with Peer Pressure.

Sometimes, practicing or rehearsing becomes a problem because your child feels different from her friends. Or perhaps her schoolmates tease her because she has to stay home and practice her harp for half an hour every afternoon while they go out to play. Fight the peer pressure by encouraging her to invite her friends to recitals, or a practice session now and then, so she'll feel special rather than different. Plan a preview party with refreshments for the audience. Ask the guests to show off their own talents.

Try to find other children with similar interests. Check out clubs or groups associated with her activity where she will feel she "belongs" because of her special skills. (See Section 13.8 for more information about peer pressure.)

5.3 WATCHES EXCESSIVE TELEVISION

Children in the United States, where virtually every home has at least one television set and over a third of the households have two, spend an astonishing number of hours a week staring at TV screens. According to *The Information Please Almanac,* youngsters ages six to eleven watch an average of twenty-four hours of television per week, while children two to five watch three hours more than that.

Television programs definitely influence children's values and their perception of the world and social reality, especially when the effect is viewed cumulatively. Adults may have the ability to distinguish fact from fiction and good from bad and to detach themselves from what is going on in front of their eyes, but children are naïve and literal. They tend to believe what they see and hear and to accept the views that are presented to them in this fascinating visual and aural manner. They are likely to identify with a favorite program's power figure, accepting his or her negative or positive views over time. Highly impulsive or impressionable children seem to be more prone to act out the aggression they see on the screen, while other children may be prompted to have nightmares instead.

Our feeling is that television has become a fact of life and cannot be ignored—even though many parents wish it could—and that it is neither innately good or bad for children. It must be used discriminately, however. To help children use it in a healthy way, we think parents must control the choice of programs and the amount of time their youngsters spend in front of the set.

5.3-1 Set the Pattern Early.

If you want television to play only a minor role in your children's life, set the model when they are very young, before there is a problem. Then remain the one in charge as they grow older. To start toddlers off correctly, we suggest you plan ahead and provide alternatives.

• Plan ahead. Try to plan your own viewing schedule as well as your child's. Turn the television set on only when there is a specific show you wish to see. Don't push the button as soon as you get up in the morning and turn it off when the test pattern appears at night, making it a constant background to everything else that's happening in the house. If you are an indiscriminate television watcher, your children will be, too.

• Provide alternatives. Don't use television as your baby-sitter, except occasionally. Make sure your child has other enjoyable activities that will keep him happy and busy, and turn on the set only for specific programs.

5.3-2 Control the Family's TV Schedule.

As your children grow older and would like to watch more television than you think is good for them, you must implement a viewing plan. First, decide how much time you will allow in front of the set, then when you will allow it. You may decide on unlimited viewing at certain times or unlimited viewing of approved programs or restricted hours, times, and programs. Your plan may be as simple as circling the shows the child may watch on the newspaper's printed schedule. Allow him to help choose the programs, but reserve final approval for yourself.

5.3-3 Implement the Plan.

Post the viewing plan near the television set. Let the child know the penalty for unscheduled watching, perhaps loss of TV privileges the next day. Follow through consistently if trust is violated.

5.3-4 Be Fair and Clear About the Rules.

Always be direct and clear when you want your child to stop watching television for any reason.

• Try to end the viewing at the end of a television program. It's very hard for children to turn off the set in the middle of a show.

• Give a warning. Let your child know when it's almost time to turn off the television. For little ones, tell them they have another ten minutes, then set the kitchen timer. When the buzzer goes off, the TV goes off, too. Or tell them, "When this show is over, TV is over."

• If a show will interfere with dinner or bedtime or other plans, don't give permission to start watching it.

5.3-5 Change the Viewing Habits in Your House.

If your children are already addicted to television and watch more than you'd like, it would be sensible to make changes.

• Alternate activities. Alternate television watching with other activities: "You may watch your favorite show at eight-thirty.

What would you like to do until then?" You might suggest board games, reading, or exercise.

• Make a family commitment. Get all the members of the family together for a conference, and make a serious group commitment to change television viewing habits. Make sure the children understand that too much television isn't good for them and why. Praise them for keeping to the schedule or watching less. One family initiated their plan with a week of no TV for anyone. They were surprised to find they didn't miss it as much as they expected. The week's vacation also broke some old viewing habits.

• Use television to stimulate reading. Since many TV shows are adapted from books, encourage the children to read these books or others that are related to the subject.

5.3-6 Use TV as a Reward.

When a child enjoys it, watching television is a natural reinforcer for other behaviors. Pair it with a behavior you are trying to increase. For example: "Jack, complete your homework and you'll have about a half hour to watch TV before dinner." Or, if you want your child to play outdoors: "Go outside and play for a half hour, then you may come in and watch TV for a half hour." At first, give equal time to the television set, but later decrease the ratio to, for example, one hour outdoors for a half hour of television.

5.3-7 Control TV Watching When You Are Not Home.

Your television viewing plan must be followed whether you are there or not. Sometimes, the schedule or a reminder stuck to the TV set will suffice. But if you really feel you can't trust your child to stick to the approved programs or if you worry about him inadvertently watching unsuitable for-adults-only material, you can make sure the set can't be turned on until your return. You can remove the tuning knob or use a removable cord or install a locking device that allows only certain channels to be seen.

5.3-8 Watch Together.

Whenever you can manage it, watch television with your child so you can talk about what you're seeing. The positive effects of television are enhanced and the negative ones decreased if a child watches and discusses the programs with an adult, who can encourage her to pay attention and will make interpretations and explanations.

• Talk about what's going on. Is this story real or a fantasy? Is what's happening dangerous or a good thing to do? What do you think these people think about each other? How do you feel about the characters? How does the show make you feel? Discuss how the characters could solve their problems without resorting to violence. Encourage the child to make up new endings.

• Discuss the news. Some of the most violent and realistic material to be seen on TV is on the news. Be aware of what your child is seeing and talk about it. In addition, discuss the content of the news so he will understand more easily what is happening in the world.

• Discuss commercials. Teach your child to view commercials with a critical eye, so she understands that their purpose is to sell her something. Ask her what she thinks the jingles are trying to get her to do. Why are there so many toy commercials? What do the commercials make you think about the product? Does a toy in the store look as good as the toy on the screen?

5.4 IS ADDICTED TO VIDEO GAMES

Let's face it, video games are fun. Children love the interaction with the action on the screen, the graphics, the sound effects, the automatic scorekeeping, the skills they acquire, and the thrill of winning or bettering their scores. Video games are educational, too. They help sharpen eye-hand coordination, improve ability to process information through several sensory channels simultaneously, and shorten reaction time. They provide a painless introduction to computer literacy.

At the other end of the scale, children sometimes spend more time playing video games than their parents would like, often shortchanging other important activities, such as schoolwork. If you think your child is too preoccupied with the games and honing his skills, then you must deal with the pattern. Keep in mind, however, that for most children, the fascination with the games is intense at first and then levels off.

5.4-1 Join the Player.

If you have never played video games, reserve judgment until you give them a try. You may find that some of them will actually help the child learn some necessary skills and subjects. Have a family outing to the local arcade and let your child show you his favorite games. Give them a try yourself, to get a sense of the competition. If you have a home computer, visit a software store together. Select a game that has educational value but uses the action tactics of the arcade games. You may both enjoy software that puts logic to use.

5.4-2 Use Video Games as Rewards.

They are a natural. Use them as an incentive to accomplish jobs, such as homework or chores: "Gerald, you can play for half an hour after your homework is finished and checked." Or let the child earn money to play games at an arcade by doing extra chores.

5.4-3 Use Satiation.

If you feel your child wants to play video games to the exclusion of other activities, make a deal with him. Allow him to play for as many hours as he wishes, as long as he does it on Friday evening— into the wee hours, if necessary (with supervision at an arcade, of course). Or challenge him to see whether you or he can play the longest. Give him the opportunity to "fill up" on games.

5.4-4 Use Negative Consequences.

When all else fails, lock up the computer or take the cord away until the child earns the play time. Let him know in advance what the consequences of abusing the privilege will be, specifying the length of time the computer will be out of bounds. Then be sure to follow through.

5.5 WANTS, WANTS, WANTS

Some children develop the "gimmes." They want what they want and they want it now! If they don't get it, they kick and scream and carry on until it is forthcoming. Though wanting is natural for all of us, giving in will soon turn requests into demands and commands that will rule your life as parents. It is helpful to listen to your child's wants and make considered decisions in response to them. If your decision is no, then it's no, not maybe. On the other hand, if there is no reason to refuse the request and you can comply, then why not say yes? Always refusing or always giving in has costly effects.

There are several reasons why a child may constantly ask for things—candy at the store, something to eat, your undivided attention, a new toy, another story—and throw a tantrum if she doesn't get them. The major reason is because she knows perfectly well that all she has to do is create enough fuss and her demands will be met. Sometimes, she wants, wants, wants because she has always been given, given, given. Sometimes, the child has developed a certain power over her parents. If your pattern is to say no to the candy in aisle two and then to say, "Oh, all right, take the candy," by aisle four because you can't hold up under the pressure any longer, then you have reinforced her persistence.

To solve a case of the wants, you must learn to say no when you mean no and then not change your mind. That's not easy, especially for parents who are busy and can't be with their children as much as they'd like. But it can be done.

5.5-1 Change the Experience.

No matter why the child has come to expect instant gratification, your first step is to alter the experience that has become the basis for his expectations.

• Use the team approach. Everyone who deals with the child must become part of the solution, and that includes baby-sitters and grandparents. Nothing perpetuates tantrums like a few well-meaning words from Grandpa: "Oh, let him have the candy." Everyone must go along with your plan and help change the pattern; if everyone won't or can't do that, you may have to limit contact for a while. The child will then learn that parents and grandparents are different.

• Evaluate your presence. Children can easily become accustomed to receiving gifts and privileges when parents use them as substitutes for their physical presence or attention, to make up for earlier harsh words, or as a way to express love. If you tend to give material things to your child to express your love, exchange that behavior for more of your time throughout the day. Give her time, attention, and unconditional love—when she's *not* demanding it or asking for things. Then add special moments, too. Make a point of reading her a special bedtime story, playing games together, or just chatting about the day's events. Let her know she is loved and valued. (See Section 2.1, on praise, and Section 2.2, on ignoring.)

5.5-2 Develop a Plan to Change the Pattern.

You must change your own behavior if the child is to change hers.

• Think ahead. Be ready for the "gimmes" wherever you may be when the attack begins. At first, avoid the public places where you may be too embarrassed to follow through with your plan to resist the demands despite the tantrums. The child must know that you mean business, so start your new plan at home. Then, before your next visit to the grocery store, tell your child that you are going to buy only those items on your shopping list. Ask him to suggest one or two favorite food choices, and add them to the list. Then praise his cooperation along the way.

• Mean what you say. Repeat the rule—no purchases except for the items on the list—before going to the store. If the child asks for Doodle Pops, stop for a few seconds to consider the request, then give a reason, perhaps, "No, they're not good for you." Don't change your mind. You may want to try the technique that cured little George, four years old, of constant whining for treats. His mother told him he could choose one thing at the grocery store when they went shopping; they decided it would be a book. To earn the book, George had to resist asking for anything else and to sit still in the shopping cart. It worked.

• Always communicate your decision clearly, telling the child what he can or cannot have (see Section 2.9–2). Suppose your youngster wants a cookie at 5:30 P.M. Look the child in the eye and in a firm, friendly tone give him a brief explanation in simple words: "It's too close to dinner to have a cookie. You may have one after dinner."

• Don't give in. Once you have made your decision and delivered it to your child, stick with it! Do not relent, even if he yells and screams and kicks his feet. Be prepared to be tested. For example, let's imagine you are now at the supermarket check-out counter and your child has been faced with fifty things he's wanted, from candy to magazines to just one piece of bubblegum. As you are paying for your groceries, he is screaming for a candy bar. Hold out; do not waver. This is an important learning experience for both of you. Apply all the steps outlined in Section 2.2, on ignoring, fortifying yourself with the knowledge that giving in under pressure will only teach him that screaming works and that he has more power than you. For further help, check back with sections 2.3 and 2.7, about the broken record technique, and time-out.

• Use praise. As you gradually wean your youngster by refusing more and more requests and teaching him to wait longer for what he wants, be sure to praise him lavishly for his efforts to cooperate —especially for accepting "No!" Surprise him occasionally with something he usually asks for, *before* he asks for it. Don't, how-

ever, make a habit of this because then he will come to expect it
and you may be right back where you started.

• Record the progress. Many parents find it very helpful to
make a chart to record their child's progress. Identify the desired
behavior and then count it. The child may earn a point for accepting no or by complying with your instructions. The points may
accumulate until he has earned enough to select a prize on the next
outing (see Section 2.5).

5.5-3 Learn to Get Unstuck.

Weathering the storm of tantrums and antisocial behavior in public
places requires determined commitment on your part. There are no
better solutions for getting out of this unpleasant pattern except to
stand by your decision. You are having a pleasant dinner at a nice
restaurant. Leslie asks for her third roll before eating a bite from
her plate. You say, "No more," and she starts to fuss. Warn her
once; then, if necessary, remove her from the situation. Take her
out to the car or to the restroom, and don't return until she stops
her tantrum and agrees to cooperate. In the worst case, if she won't
stop, you may have to take her home. Do it. If this means your
other children's fun is interrupted, give them a raincheck. Within a
short time, take them out to eat and leave Leslie home with your
spouse. The next time, take Leslie again, giving her a chance to
show she can cooperate.

For additional help, see sections 8.2 and 2.7.

5.6 CONSTANTLY FORGETS OR LOSES
      THINGS

It's only human to forget to take your lunch and to lose your
umbrella, but some of us make a habit of it. Children are especially
susceptible to the forgetting and losing syndrome, a natural occurrence that is also maddening, time-consuming, and expensive.
"Mom," says the little voice on the telephone. "I forgot my sneak-
ers. Can you bring them to school?" "Where's my math book? I
know I brought it home!"

Parents usually remember everything for their children before the youngsters reach seven. After that, they assume they can accept increasing responsibility. Nevertheless, older kids often allow themselves to be absentminded because they can count on Mom and Dad to bail them out. Some older children are highly distractible, remembering until they get sidetracked along the way. Distractibility may be a symptom of attention deficit disorder (see Section 11.15), but usually, it is simply just forgetfulness.

Remembering and planning ahead are skills to be cultivated. Try to help your child remember with these solutions:

5.6-1 Work Now, Prevent Loss Later.

Set up a framework for organization and a plan of action that cultivates independence and responsibility.

• Give the child a special place for his things. Make sure he has his own hook for his coat and hat and a special shelf for his toys and books. Label these places, and use them consistently from the very beginning. The child will copy you, and his organization skills will grow.

• Use praise. When the child needs an item and finds it in its rightful location, praise her for keeping it where it was supposed to be. When she hangs her coat on the hook or puts a toy away in its own place, comment on her efficiency and how easy it will be to find that coat or toy the next time.

• Teach her to plan ahead. As your child gets older, show her your own organizing strategies (this will inspire you to develop some, if need be). Give her a calendar, and on Sunday evenings, look over the coming week's schedule and help her plan a list of things to remember. Mark the calendar on the days and hours reports are due, parties are scheduled, etc. Sometimes a daily reminder list helps, too. Write down all the items the child will need to remember that day. Post the list on her mirror, on the refrigerator, or on her notebook—and remind her to look at it!

5.6-2 Teach Remembering Strategies.

There are several techniques that you can teach your child to help
her remember instead of forget. Teach them through role-playing,
positive-practice sessions, and modeling.

• The hesitation response. Teach your child to *stop* and say to
herself before she leaves, "Did I forget anything?" Pause at the
door, count to ten, and make sure nothing has been left behind.
Complete the process with the body scan.

• The body scan. Teach him to scan his body from head to toe,
checking for missing items. "Do I have my hat, glasses, sweater,
jacket, purse, books, gloves, bookbag, etc.?"

• The environment scan. Show him how to look around him
and note if he spots any of his belongings that he might leave
behind. Use what he sees as a cue to take things he may need
elsewhere. For example, seeing a homework assignment on the
blackboard during a scan of the classroom before going home will
remind him to take what he will need to do the homework.

• Checklists. Make a checklist of items that must be remembered that day, and have the child keep it in a prominent place to
jog his memory during the day. Small self-sticking notepapers are
wonderful for this purpose.

• Have him develop his own memory tricks. One child we know
wrote his homework assignments in a notebook every day, but he
usually forgot to take the notebook home. Eventually, he began
writing assignments on his hand because he couldn't possibly forget that! Sometimes you can't complain about success.

5.6-3 Use Natural Consequences.

The most effective way to learn to remember is to suffer the consequences of forgetting. Children often don't have to remember
many things because Mommy or Daddy remembers for them. We
don't want Joe to lose his tennis racquet, so we remind him to get
it. If he does lose it, we buy him another one. We don't want to
have to deliver the ballet shoes to the dancing school, so we remind

Mary to take them when she leaves for class. But that won't change Joe's or Mary's habit. Letting them experience the consequences of forgetting will usually do the job.

- Don't be the child's memory. If he doesn't remember his baseball glove, let him work it out. Maybe he won't be able to play in that game. Don't run home and fetch it for him.
- Make forgetting inconvenient. Let him retrieve the forgotten object himself, if possible. He can make the telephone calls to locate the lost item and make the trip (with you, if necessary) to get it. Don't make any unnecessary effort yourself.
- Use overcorrection. When your child forgets or loses something, make him practice the remembering techniques in your presence several times in a row. If Ben tends to forget his lunch, you may remind him just before he leaves the house, but then let him practice taking it from the refrigerator and putting it into his schoolbag three times. See Section 2.8 for more overcorrection techniques. If Susan forgets her coat at school, let her role-play the body-scan technique, pretending she is at school, a friend's house, or a movie.
- Don't automatically replace lost items. Let the child earn the item back by doing extra chores. Or have her replace at least part of the cost with her own savings or allowance.

5.6-4 Praise Long-term Efforts.

Praise your child for the responsibility she has accepted. Keep records of the number of days since something was left behind or lost. Praise her for using the memory techniques. Focus on keeping up the good work: "You know, you've remembered your lunch every day for the last three weeks. Keep it up! I bet you can beat your record!"

5.7 THE CHILD WHO CAN'T SIT STILL

Learning to sit quietly is one of the hardest lessons small children have to accomplish. Even a few minutes of waiting time can seem like forever. It's necessary for a child to understand what a parent means by "sitting still," and it is crucial that parents be realistic in their expectations. But even a very young child can be taught to sit for longer periods of time at the dinner table, in a house of worship, or in a social situation.

The solutions below are designed to help a child learn how to sit calmly and feel good about his accomplishment. Using a game approach, the first solutions are most appropriate for younger children and the last for the older ones. Select those that fit your child's age, skills, and personality.

5.7-1 Count and Clap.

Sit a toddler in a chair at home. Tell him you're going to see if he can sit still while you count. Displaying the numbers on your fingers, count from one to five while he sits in the chair. Applaud him, give him a hug, and let him run around for a few moments before trying again. This time, sit him down, start with, "Ready, get set, go!" and count up to ten or whatever number he is ready for. Again, clap his success, hug him, and let him run around a bit. Gradually increase the length of time he can stay in his chair, building a sense of accomplishment as you count excitedly to higher and higher numbers with obvious delight.

5.7-2 Use the Prime Timer.

When your little one can sit still during Count and Clap for sixty seconds, change the game. Count the minutes with a kitchen timer. In his chair, the child listens to the timer until the bell rings, as you very gradually increase the time over a few weeks. With an older child, begin with a training session: "We're going to see how long you can sit still." Time him and give him feedback. "Now let's see if we can beat your record!"

Caution: Don't play this game very long, and don't play it every day. A game is fun, not torment. Don't expect the child to sit quietly for long periods of time doing nothing. Adjust the game rules to allow a quiet activity, such as reading or playing with a toy. Always alternate periods of sitting still with periods of physical activity.

5.7-3 Beat the Clock.

As your child learns to relate to Prime Timer, gradually introduce the kitchen timer into other situations, such as eating dinner. Set the timer for a reasonable length of time for your child. If she rarely stays put at the table for as long as five minutes, begin with five. Gradually increase the time, praising each accomplishment. Give an occasional award for sitting still, such as an extra portion of dessert. If the child gets up before the timer rings, tell her she may try again, and reset the timer.

If you think she is about to get up before the time is up, give her an indirect reminder by praising someone else at the table for sitting so quietly. Praise her when she settles down. Ham it up for a very small child, clapping and cheering when she beats the clock. When she's successful in one place, try the technique in another.

5.7-4 Perfect Timing.

Here is a variation of Beat the Clock for an older child. Use the timer or a stopwatch, allowing the child to set her own goals. Make a small graph on a three-by-five card. On the horizontal axis, write minutes and seconds; on the vertical axis, mark the trials. Let the child keep his own record of goals.

5.7-5 Play Statue.

Sit the child in a chair facing you and ask him to place his hands on his knees. Of course he may breathe, but he must try to remain as still as a statue, not even moving a hand or his nose. With practice, he may manage a minute of stillness, and some children can achieve five minutes or more. Play the game every few days to increase his awareness of his own control over his movements. Don't forget to give him plenty of praise for his accomplishment, no matter how small.

5.7-6 Watch Time Fly.

This is a tangible way to measure time when your child will be in a situation that requires sitting still. Tell her in advance how you expect her to behave. Take along a pencil and a piece of paper. For every minute she must sit still, draw a picture of, say, a star, a circle, or a happy face. For example, ten minutes might require ten stars. As each minute passes, she may color or cross off one of the pictures. When all of the stars or faces have been crossed off, time has flown and she wins the game.

5.7-7 Happy Landing.

This is an amusing way to express graphically what you'd like your child to do. Have the child pretend he is sitting in an airplane seat with his belt buckled. Tell him you are the captain and the seat belt sign is ON. That means he must sit right there. Then "turn off" the seat belt sign, so she can stand up and stretch. Again, gradually increase the time of sitting.

5.7-8 Glue Who?

Pretend to paint the chair seat with glue before she sits down, or let her do it herself. When she is glued to her seat, ask her to notice other objects or people who are also glued and sitting very still.

5.7-9 Time Swap.

For any child who has trouble sitting still, set the expectations clearly. Then tell him that for each minute he sits appropriately you will swap time.

- For a minute of sitting nicely, swap a minute of doing an activity of his choice. Keep records.
- Praise the child profusely for his patience.
- Let the child know that when he does *not* sit nicely, you will

swap those minutes for extra chores, loss of television time, and so forth. Be sure to keep records of this time, too.

5.8 THE CHILD WHO WON'T FOLLOW DIRECTIONS

If your youngster doesn't follow instructions, it can be exasperating, frustrating, and infuriating. By the end of the day, you're exhausted from repeating, arguing, cajoling, and nagging. The first thing to remember is to keep your requests or commands to a rational number, so the children aren't asked to become your "gofers" and "do-fers." The second is to be pleasant and reasonable in tone and task.

Children sometimes get in the habit of ignoring instructions because they know perfectly well that the directions will be repeated several times before they must respond. They've learned how long it takes for their parents to become angry enough to force them to obey. They also know whether parents are likely to give up and do the job themselves. Occasionally, though, the lack of response is pure rebelliousness, and sometimes it's because we ask too much too fast and do not express our wishes clearly.

If your child understands but rarely follows directions, try these solutions, which we have found to work well. (Also see Section 11.11, which will be helpful for children who have difficulty following directions.)

5.8-1 Be Clear and Concise.

We are often so busy issuing directions that we don't realize how much we are assuming. A child may not know what "Clean up your room" means. His specifications for a clean room may not match our expectations. Also, parents sometimes give directions in a series that the child is unable to remember. And finally, parents sometimes *ask* their child to do something when their intention was to *tell* him.

• Define what you want done in simple, understandable words. Discuss what the request entails.

• Limit the number of directions. Many times, parents give too many directions at once. Give the child only as many as you know he can remember. When he has accomplished those activities, add more if necessary. If you want him to clean up his room, for example, tell him how to do it step by step: "Pick up your toys, put them away. Hang up your clothes." And so forth. Later, when he understands the whole task, then you can give only one direction: "Please go and clean up your room."

• Think before you speak. Don't give the child a choice such as, "Do you want to clean your room now?" or "Let's go to the dentist's," if you don't want to hear "No" or "Let's not." It is possible to be firm without being dictatorial, and you can use motivation; for example, "I bet you can get out of the car before I count to ten!"

5.8-2 Get the Child's Attention.

Children often become so involved in their activities that they don't really hear what you are saying. To avoid this possibility, make sure your child knows what you have said. Establish eye contact. Ask her to repeat the directions to you and then to interpret what they mean. This tactic is useful, too, if your child has a short attention span and is easily distracted.

5.8-3 Mean What You Say and Say What You Mean.

Parents are busy people, and sometimes when we ask that something be done, we assume it will be done and then we forget about it. Since this may not be the case, be sure to follow up every time you give directions, so your child will not learn to ignore you. In addition, avoid asking her to do things that really do not need to be done.

5.8-4 Make It a Game.

Most directions we issue to our children don't really take much time to accomplish, sometimes less than the time they spend arguing about them. If you start asking your little ones to help while they are still very young, they will consider their tasks quite a normal part of life. Later, you can make it a game by timing the response: "How long do you think it will take you to make your bed? On your mark, get set, go! Great, you did it in four and a half minutes! You are certainly a speedy helper. Thank you. Now you can go back to playing." In this way, you teach them in a positive way that it doesn't take very long to help.

5.8-5 Supervise.

The best way to make sure your child follows your directions correctly is to monitor the process while she's doing the job, but always in a positive, helpful manner. If you prefer, make inspections after the task is completed. The goal is not to find fault but to make sure the directions have been followed, so don't turn yourself into the unfriendly policeman.

5.8-6 Praise, Praise, Praise.

We really believe the key to inspiring your child to follow your directions consistently is to be positive: You act as if you expect your child to obey and then you give her positive feedback when she does. "Thanks for getting my glasses. I really appreciated your help." "You did a fine job cleaning your room. You put your toys and books away and straightened the closet floor. That's a good job."

When you can, associate a job well done with an activity the child likes. Alternate the work and play. "Joey, after you finish straightening your books, why not go out and ride your bike or shoot baskets?" Or, "Jessica, we've really worked hard cleaning the garden. Let's make some lemonade and popcorn."

5.8-7 Follow up Lack of Response with Consequences.

If you have tried the positive approach and you are ignored or your child responds with an uncooperative "Why should I?" then your situation has progressed to the point where you must apply negative consequences to change the pattern.

• Use a five-second response time. If your child has a history of ignoring your directions, initiate a time limit for her response. Count to five. If she has not acknowledged you and begun to respond by the time you have finished counting, repeat the directions once. Then give her a choice between two alternatives. For example: "Joanne, you may do what I asked, or I will help you do it." Or, "You must clean up now, Cassie, or you will have to go to time-out and then clean up."

• Use manual guidance. If you choose this route, repeat the directions at the end of the five-second period, then "walk" the child through the appropriate response motions. This means you will take the child's hands and put him through the actions (see Section 2.8 on overcorrection).

• Use time-out. Call time-out for an appropriate period of time. Then have the child do as he has been told. See Section 2.7 for details about this solution.

• Use overcorrection. If your child doesn't follow your instructions, tell him you can see he doesn't know how, and have him practice the task repeatedly with your supervision.

5.9 WHY, WHY, WHY?

Children begin to ask questions very early in life. Their first requests come to us in the form of questions because we, the adults, control their environment. We also control the flow of information. Conversations with our children should begin long before they can even understand language, from the moment we first hold them (if not before they are born!), and become an ongoing part of our interaction with them.

Questions are natural and normal, and they are an important

tool in a child's development. They should be answered at a level that is appropriate to his development and understanding, and with sensitivity for the real meaning behind them. They give parents a means of nurturing as well as informing. The way they are answered will influence the questions he will ask later.

One of the most important things a parent can do to stimulate language and curiosity is to answer all the child's questions. Children around the ages of two and three will ask questions about everything, but if you are always open to discussion, their questions will become more mature as they grow.

However, some children generate more questions in a short period of time than we can tolerate, and every question can't be answered at the very moment it is asked. Once the questioning machine has been turned on by these youngsters, it's almost impossible to turn it off, especially if the child is not really seeking information but is using the questions because his need to get attention, avoid a situation, or aggravate us has gone out of control.

The following solutions are suggestions for how to answer your child's questions in a helpful way and how to cope with the "whys" when they're used for the wrong reasons.

5.9-1 Use Language to Stimulate Curiosity.

Long before your child starts asking real questions, assume she is asking for information about the world around her. Use normal language, not baby talk, to discuss what you are both seeing and doing. Label objects and actions. Hold conversations as if she understands. Children learn language from language.

5.9-2 Respond to the Content of the Question.

Listen closely to the question, and try to answer the question the child is really asking. Don't simply murmur anything that comes into your head to turn off the inquiries. On the other hand, don't give too much information that the child isn't ready for.

5.9-3 Schedule a "Why" Time.

When the whys are coming fast and furiously from your four-year-old and they are starting to get to you, have a "why" time. "Cheryl," you might say, "for the next five minutes you may ask me all the questions you can think of. Then after that, I'm taking a break. Ready, get set, go . . ."

5.9-4 Don't Let "Why?" Become a Challenge.

Older children often use "Why?" as the answer to requests they don't want to fulfill. To deal with this technique, give your directions very clearly. If the response is "Why do I have to?" repeat the request with a short, succinct explanation, such as, "It is time to come in now because it is almost bedtime." If the child persists:

• Use the broken record technique (see Section 2.3). Repeat your response to the repeated question with exactly the same words as many times as necessary. Supervise your child as he walks into the house.

• Use systematic ignoring (see Section 2.2). Ignore the question. Decide in advance that this questioning of your authority won't bother you. Instead of responding to the question, reissue your first statement. Praise the child each time he follows your directions without question. It may also help you to use the six-second relaxation technique, too (see Section 2.10).

• Follow through with time-out or overcorrection. Depending on the request that is being questioned, these two techniques will usually work. However, if they don't in your case, then you have a management problem that demands a strong step-by-step approach. Reread chapters 1 and 2. Define your problems, and begin to take a stand on them one at a time. You may want to enlist the help of a specialist to get you started. See Chapter 17 for suggestions.

5.10 THE CHILD WHO WON'T CLEAN UP AFTER HIMSELF

If you're like many parents, then you've often wondered why a hurricane hasn't been named after your child. It's amazing that such little people can destroy the order in a room in such record-breaking time. Children love to make a mess and, in fact, very little ones are unaware there *is* a mess at all—the more things around to play with, the more fun they have.

Soon, however, your home looks like you are breeding toys or clothes, and you are constantly nagging your child to clean up—or cleaning up the mess yourself. You end up with one more job you shouldn't have to do. Even worse, your child learns that somebody else will clean up for him.

Everyone can become responsible for eliminating his own mess. Teach your child to understand the importance of caring for his belongings and of putting them in their proper places. He will be rewarded by being able to find his things again when he wants them and by developing a sense of pride in his neatness.

Sometimes, though, you may have to simply establish that, "This is the way it is—we all clean up after ourselves in this house." Ideally, this rule should be a natural part of life from an early age. If not, you can rectify the situation with one or more of these problem solvers.

5.10-1 Plan Ahead.

Orderliness saves time and frustration and allows you to control your environment. So spend a little time preparing your child's space to make it easy for him to be neat.

• Create places and spaces for his belongings. Tell him that just as he has a home to live in, so do each of his things. Have separate places for toys and games, sports equipment, art supplies, etc. Shoe boxes can hold smaller items, and a treasure box can be home for those precious collectibles. For larger objects, shelves or a cabinet or closet are usually better than a big toy box, where toys become jumbled and often broken. Stackable plastic bins work well for blocks or toys with many pieces. Whatever your arrangement, the goal is to provide an identifiable place for everything.

• Make the storage places accessible to the child. Scan the room from the child's point of view and make sure that shelves, cabinets, coat hooks, and closet bars are conveniently located where she can easily reach them.

• Label the places. Mark each place with a tag, self-sticking letters, or even pictures to identify where each thing belongs. In the process, the toddler will learn one purpose of print.

5.10-2 Teach and Supervise.

Provide a role model for your children—that means you, too, must be neat and orderly—and supervise their work as well. Children who have never had to clean up after themselves before cannot be expected to make a complete turnaround in a hurry. Nor will they know just what to do. All children, young or old, need to know what your standards are. Is "out of sight, out of mind" acceptable to you, or do you insist on order even behind closed doors? Keep in mind that your child will learn gradually what you want, and so you must be realistic in your expectations.

• Be prepared to help occasionally. Even the tidiest child will need assistance with putting away toys that have many pieces so they don't get lost. Try the method we learned from one mother with a two-year-old: The child was asked to clean up as best he could, then his mother returned to put all the pieces together. As the child gained expertise, he put more toys together himself until finally he could do the job himself with a great sense of pride.

• Build a habit. Encourage your child to pick up his things just as soon as he's finished with them. With very small tots, you can pick up one toy, then he picks up another, while you sing, "This is the way we pick up our toys, pick up our toys . . ." Once picking up is mastered, the next goal is to teach him where to put them. If you start doing this early, he will get the idea that this is a natural part of playing or working.

5.10-3 Give Clear Signals.

When you want your child to clean up, tell her very clearly and simply what it is you want her to do: "Marcy, please pick up all the toys and put them neatly on your toy shelf." Speak in a kind but firm voice, never issuing a command. If she doesn't respond, repeat the same request five seconds later. If she still doesn't react, though you know she has heard you both times, then apply a consequence.

5.10-4 Follow Up with Consequences.

For your requests to be meaningful, the child must know that if he doesn't do what you have asked, there will be no further discussion and you will not do the job for him. Instead, there will be a specific and immediate consequence. The consequence may be time-out, manual guidance, or overcorrection. These techniques—and others —are discussed in Chapter 2 and in Section 5.8.

Another kind of consequence is required if you have come home to find the child hasn't cleaned up. Alert him in advance that whatever of his belongings he hasn't picked up at the end of the day will be yours for a certain length of time, perhaps the rest of the week. Put the item in the time-out box until it is time to return it, making sure the child understands this will happen again if he leaves his things out of place.

5.10-5 Use Praise and Reinforcement.

Positive feedback is as helpful in this situation as it is in all others. Always praise the child's efforts when her behavior is good.

• Let your child know in words how happy it makes you when she picks up her toys. Next time you notice her doing it on her own, tell her how great that is. Next time she finds something she wants immediately because it's in its proper place, give her a pat on the back for being so wonderful.

• Reinforce with activities. "You did a great job of cleaning up without even being asked. Let's have a snack." Or, "Let's play your favorite game now."

5.10-6 Be Preventive and Inventive.

Use your imagination to encourage a sense of order.

- Use a timer. Challenge the older child to set a world's cleanup record, and time him with a kitchen timer or stopwatch.
- Ask for a surprise. Some children love to surprise you. Tell them you're leaving the room for five minutes. When you come back, you want to see if they've been able to do a magician's act and make all the toys disappear into their rightful places.
- Hold inspections. Pretend you are the world-famous detective Inspector Spickenspan, who is searching for items that aren't in their right places. Or play a game of I Spy with those items that need to be put away properly.
- Use the take-out rule. If your child loves to pull out every toy in his room at once, tell him the rules have changed. From now on, he may take out a toy, but first he must put one back. This helps, too, when two children are playing in the same room. Each child chooses a toy that he is responsible for returning to its place.
- The trade-in rule. This is especially useful with small children. Every so often, collect the toys your child hasn't been playing with recently and put them in a special place. This is the trade-in store. Each week after she has cleaned up after herself, let her trade in a toy and take out another, which will then have new appeal.

5.11 THE CHILD WITH POOR MANNERS

"Joey, please sit up straight. Don't put your feet on the table." "Denise, use your fork, not your hands." "Jonathan, please don't talk when someone else is speaking." Sound familiar? Manners have a purpose. They make human relationships more pleasant, they bring out the best in the people with whom you are communicating, and they provide an acceptable way to conduct oneself in specific situations. Most important, good manners show your consideration for other people.

You can help your child develop good manners by setting the example yourself, telling her why manners are important, and showing her just what to do. Try to keep your expectations of her behavior realistic, based on her age and stage of development, but don't underestimate her abilities, either. Of course you want her to use her knife and fork properly and to smile and say hello to your friends, but your long-term goal is to help her enjoy interaction with other people in a pleasant and acceptable manner.

5.11-1 Practice What You Preach.

Good manners begin at home, and your child will learn them quickly when he has role models to emulate. Take an honest look at your own manners and ask yourself if they are adequate. If your manners, with him or others, are poor, then that's what he will learn from you despite what you tell him. Always act the way you'd like your child to act.

5.11-2 Tackle One Manner at a Time.

It is much more effective to focus on one specific problem at a time rather than try to change everything at once. Too many messages at once can be counterproductive. If "please" and "thank you" are your priority, work on them before going on to something else.

5.11-3 Expect It and Prompt It.

Communicate to your child that good manners are important and an expected part of your life. The best way to do this is to praise them whenever they are used. When necessary, discuss the child's poor manners after they occur. Point out other people who are courteous. Use prompts to get small children to use their manners.

• Do-bees, feel-goods, and magic words. Since good manners show consideration of other people, encourage your child to join the do-bees and "do be" cooperative, kind, a good listener, polite, etc. To join the feel-goods, he must try to make other people feel good. When an appropriate occasion is approaching, ask him to tell you what he could say or do that would make somebody else happy. For example, "Grandma, that was a really good dinner." This is a wonderful way to remind a child to use good manners without embarrassing him or telling just what to say. Just smile and say, "Hey, Mark, how about a feel-good for Mrs. Harris?"

Prompt a child to say "please" or "thank you" by asking him for the magic word when making a request or receiving something. He'll enjoy it and will expect the same from you.

• State the rules in a positive way. Instead of telling the child what *not* to do, turn the rules around: "Please talk only when your mouth is empty." "Put your napkin in your lap." "Speak when nobody else is speaking."

• Role-play. Teach good manners by practicing the correct ways to behave in social situations. Act them out. Try alternating roles, letting him play the adult and you the child. You can use role-playing, too, with one of his friends. Invite another child over for a snack or a tea party, explaining that everyone is going to be very polite. Then practice your best manners.

5.11-4 Use Praise.

Praising your children for good manners will encourage their everyday use. Always tell them when they have acted considerately and politely: "That was so nice of you to get a seat for Mrs. Fox." For further help, see sections 2.1 and 2.2.

• Catch each other. Play a game with your children, catching each other using good manners. They get compliments when they behave correctly, and so do you.

• Ignore/praise. When there is more than one child in the family, emphasize the positive. Praise the child who uses good manners and ignore the child who does not.

• Use silent signals. A special signal or a pat on the back can applaud your child's good manners without calling the attention of other people.

5.11-5 Use Reinforcement Techniques.

Make a chart to assist you in teaching your child manners. For example, if you are working on table manners, make a list on the chart for all the behaviors that are necessary: napkin in the lap, utensils used properly, saying "please" and "thank you," asking to please be excused when finished eating, etc. After each meal, he will earn a check for every correct behavior. Present him with a reward, such as a favorite dessert, when he makes it through a whole meal with no mistakes. Give him a more important reward —perhaps a meal at a restaurant—when he earns a week's worth of checkmarks.

5.11-6 Correct Poor Manners.

To overcome poor manners that have been firmly established or have been picked up from your child's peers, try these consequences:

• Use positive practice. This technique will help your child realize it's easier to do something right the first time around. If she doesn't say "please," have her use the word ten times in an appropriate way: "Jenny, please make ten requests using the word please. Thank you."
• Use natural consequences. If your youngster refuses to use good table manners at home, then a logical consequence would be that he may not eat out until he makes a change in his behavior. Or if he won't sit still long enough to eat dinner at dinnertime, he won't get a second chance to have his dinner later. He will skip dinner that night or have cereal instead.

SUGGESTED READING FOR PARENTS AND CHILDREN
   Blackwelder, Nancy Harris and Martha Whitmore Hickman. *Good Manners for Boys and Girls.* New York: Crown, 1985. Four-

teen familiar situations teaching good manners told in story and color photographs (K-3).

Leaf, Munro. *Manners Can Be Fun.* New York: Harper and Row, 1958. Whimsical stick figures teach what to do and why (K-3).

Wilt, Joy. *May I? Please? Thank you!* Waco, Texas: Word Inc., 1979. One of a series of books involving the child in his own learning (elementary).

5.12 THE CHILD WHO WRITES ON WALLS AND FURNITURE

Whenever two-year-old Marvin was out of sight, he could usually be found redecorating walls with one of his creative and original drawings. No matter how many times his mother told him not to do it, Marvin was determined to continue, and did. His mother came to us for advice in dealing with this behavior, among others, and we're going to tell you what we told her.

Obviously, children like Marvin must be told what is and what is not acceptable to write or draw on, and they must know you mean what you say. (If a child writes in inappropriate places out of anger and writing on walls is not the only manifestation of his feelings, then you should refer to Section 8.3, about destroying things.)

5.12-1 Teach Him to Write Right.

Tell your child specifically where he may and may not write. Make a tour of your home, pointing out the right places and the wrong places, and if he is old enough, let him tell you why.

5.12-2 Provide Alternatives.

This is a key to a change in behavior. Children love to write and draw, and it is important for them to have the chance to do so.

• Supply art materials. Create an art cabinet in which you place a variety of materials the child can use independently when she gets a creative urge. Limit the places where she may work—the kitchen table, a desk, the floor in her room—and instruct her that these are the only places where she may work. If the materials are taken to any other part of the house, then she will lose them for a specified length of time.

• Provide writing materials. Keep a supply of paper, old stationery, cards, envelopes, notebooks, markers, pencils, pens, etc., in a special place for her use only. Encourage her to "write" whether she actually can or not. Children, given the opportunity to try, will often invent their own form of writing before they can read. The younger child could say his ideas out loud and you could print them for him. The older child can write thank-you notes or make your shopping list. You might suggest cutting out comic strips from the newspaper and writing his own clever captions.

• Prepare other places to write. Other writing and drawing alternatives include blackboards or other erasable surfaces, a roll of adding-machine tape, old pads of paper, the blank sides of junk mail, erasable books, and lift-up magic boards. For the child who likes wide open spaces such as the wall, provide a roll of brown wrapping paper as a drawing surface. Or let him use chalk on your sidewalk or the driveway.

5.12-3 Be a Supervisor.

It's not always possible or even always necessary, but it's obvious that you can avoid this destructive behavior by supervising your child's play. We firmly believe that by teaching her constructive ways to play, you can help prevent the problem by redirecting her energies. Work with her on art projects and supervise independent play until you're sure she knows the proper places to be creative.

5.12-4 Use Natural Consequences.

If, no matter what, your child continues writing on the walls and/or the furniture, you must teach him that this behavior is not acceptable. If he continues, there will be consequences.

• Use manual restraint. If you come upon your child writing on an inappropriate surface, say a firm, "No!" and restrain his hands for thirty seconds, holding them so he cannot continue. Simply hold them in a firm, uncomfortable grip, which lets the child know you do not approve of what he is doing and he must stop.

• Use overcorrection. See Section 2.8 for a lengthy discussion of this solution. Tell the child he has made the wall messy and must therefore clean it. Take his hands and guide them with yours as he cleans up. Then say, "Oh no, now there's a lighter spot on the wall. You'll have to clean the whole wall to make it match." Proceed to supervise or manually guide the cleaning process until the child is tired. Let him rest, then start again. Explain once more that he must not write on the walls.

• Use time-out. If the child persists in this unfortunate behavior, place him in a chair in another room for a specific length of time as a consequence of writing on the wall. See Section 2.7 for a fuller explanation.

5.13 THE CHILD WHO WON'T COME IN

"Alyson, time for dinner! Alyson, dinner's ready. It's getting cold. Alyson, come in right now or you'll be in big trouble!" Moments pass and finally, after ten additional minutes of bike riding, Alyson appears at the door. If this scenario seems familiar, perhaps your child is tuning you out or gets so involved with what she's doing that she doesn't hear you. Whatever the reason, she doesn't comply with your wishes, whether you want her to come in for her bath, her dinner, or her bedtime. She ignores you. And you feel powerless, the victim of your child's power plays.

5.13-1 Be Clear About Your Expectations.

Plan ahead and tell your youngster exactly what you expect her to do: "Martha, I expect you to come for lunch in ten minutes." Determine in advance how she will know the time—she will wear a watch, will listen for the dinner bell or the whistle, or come in as soon as she's gone once around the block.

• Give a warning. Some children need five-minute warnings to prepare themselves to come in. Tell them they will have one five-minute warning and then, when you say it is time, you mean business.

• Be sure your expectations are realistic. Don't expect a child to go to bed five minutes before his favorite television show is over. When you spell out the rules, make sure he understands and agrees that he will come when asked. Show him the time on the clock, discuss how long he has if that is relevant, and let him know you want him to come on your first signal.

5.13-2 Use Praise and Reinforcement.

When your child does listen and does come in on time, remember to praise her for her promptness. Next time she wants to go to her friend's house, acknowledge her previous exemplary behavior by saying, "Yes, you may go to Sean's house because the last time you remembered to come home on time." Or, "Since you've saved so much time being punctual lately, I think we'll be able to get in a game of basketball after dinner tonight."

5.13-3 Use Natural Consequences.

If none of the above work, then follow up with a natural consequence. Choose from the following, and be ready to enforce whatever you pick.

• Lose the time. If the child is ten minutes late to dinner because he didn't stop playing in time, you dock him ten minutes of play time the next day. Or he is required to sit at the table ten minutes early for the next meal. If she spends fifteen minutes finishing up a conversation on the telephone after you've called her, then she loses talking time during the next call or the right to use the phone for the rest of the day.

• Start without him. Suppose he's late again and again and again. Start eating dinner on time, then let him eat leftovers alone.

Or try a few nights of cereal and milk after everyone else has finished eating.

• Pay back the time. Every minute of lateness must be paid back with the accomplishment of a chore he normally isn't responsible for.

5.13-4 Use Positive Practice.

For repeated infractions, have the child practice ten times coming in when she is called or when a signal is given. If you usually ring a bell for dinner, have her practice responding to its ring from places inside and outside the house. Time the return. Then have her practice it again. Tell her, "Much better, but you need more practice." The repetition will help her remember next time you call her that doing it right the first time is easier.

CHAPTER 6

Earliest Childhood Problems

BABIES and small children are very special people. In a few short years, they learn more skills and use more information than they will for the rest of their lives, giving their parents the awesome job of providing a safe and nurturing environment where these precious little ones will thrive mentally, emotionally, and physically. We must give them love, warmth, and comfort along with plenty of stimulation so they develop curiosity and a desire to learn and acquire skills as they are ready for them.

The positive parenting techniques we will describe here are especially important during your child's early years. Praise and reinforcement will guide his development as you teach him to behave appropriately. They will be the main tools you use to stimulate his interest in his world and to control any hazardous or unpleasant behaviors, too, because we believe that punishment has no place in the life of a baby.

Every baby is unique right from the start, and some seem to have a harder time adjusting to life in the world. The frustration many new parents experience stems from feelings of isolation, uncertainty and, often, just plain exhaustion. To them, other babies—especially those belonging to parents down the block—appear to have arrived with an easier set of directions. It's not easy to adjust to the topsy-turvy, frequently delightful, sometimes overwhelming world of babies.

Most babies do develop according to certain stages and patterns, so give or take a few weeks or months, you will know fairly well what to expect in your own child's development. It's reassuring to know that specific behaviors are expected at certain ages and that they, too, will pass.

But at the same time, remember that you will miss those infant wails, the wobbly head, the first tottering steps, the barrage of nos, and the tears of frustration. So enjoy your baby even while you are trying to cope with the difficulties of adjusting to this brand new lifestyle.

In this chapter, we will discuss common concerns of parents during the first few years of their children's lives. Most are not problems but simply normal developmental behaviors that parents frequently find troubling or confusing. For example, a baby's game of "dropsie" is not a problem; instead, it is a learning experience for him. At the same time, we want to control it so it won't become dangerous or too difficult for the family. A baby's need to explore is natural, too, because an infant learns by looking, touching, and putting things into her mouth. Our job is to give her plenty of room to experience her surroundings while . making sure she doesn't hurt herself or anything she touches.

The "solutions" we suggest can set the tone for your attitudes and the parenting techniques you will use with your child in the future. They are designed to give you the confidence, skills—and sleep—you need to remain in control of your child's environment and behavior and, at the same time, savor those wonderful infant and toddler years.

6.1 CRIES, CRIES, CRIES

One of the things babies do best is cry. All babies cry, some more than others, and all parents seem to worry that their infant is crying too much or, occasionally, too little. What one parent thinks is a normal and natural amount of crying, another finds overwhelmingly disturbing.

Before we get into solutions to crying problems, let's list some helpful facts:

• Crying is a baby's natural way of communicating. As early as one month, an infant's cries become distinctive and a mother may start to be able to identify her own child's cries from those of other babies and to distinguish among cries of pain, hunger, anger, and fretfulness.

• Babies don't need crying to exercise their lungs. Breathing provides all the exercise their lungs require.

• You can't "spoil" an infant under about three months old. Babies get their first view of the world and relationships from the responses they get from people. If they are lovingly and attentively attended, their view is a happy one. A study by Dr. Mary Ainsworth shows that children whose cries in their first three months of life were largely ignored in the mistaken belief that responding would spoil them ended up, later in their first year, crying more frequently and for longer periods of time.

• A four- or five-month-old, however, may learn to cry to get attention. Little beings like to be with Mommy and Daddy and other family members, so when they discover that someone will respond when called, they call by crying, their only way to communicate. Why not? It works.

When your baby cries, you must be ready to respond. Practice your relaxation techniques, and rest when you can. And try some of these ideas.

6.1-1 Do a Balancing Act.

We'll assume you want your baby to feel loved and cared for but not to expect you to be a slave to his calls. This is the time to be reasonable. When you know he is not in danger, is not hungry, wet, in pain or ill, and he frets for a few minutes when you put him down for a nap, it won't hurt him to wait a little while for your attention. For example, if you're on the telephone and he starts complaining, take a moment to finish up your conversation and then go to him. If, however, the cries are piercing shrieks or heavy sobs and it sounds as if he is in trouble, then drop everything and go to him immediately. Your response is a matter of judgment. Never let an infant wail very long, whatever the situation, but let him learn help is coming, without allowing him to manipulate and enslave you.

6.1-2 How to Soothe a Fretful Baby.

Most babies have a fretting time, and it usually comes at a certain hour of the day. Often, the fretting and complaining is caused by colic—abdominal discomfort and gas—which usually begins about two to four weeks after birth and then disappears for no apparent reason at about three months. Try these methods of soothing a baby who's obviously uncomfortable:

• Swaddle the infant firmly in a receiving blanket and place her on her side in the crib. Prop her back with a rolled towel or blanket or place her back against the bumper. Some babies seem to feel more secure when they are "cornered."

• Provide some movement, because most babies find it comforting. Rock her, walk her, swing her in a mechanical seat/bed, being sure you have checked out the safety regulations and directions carefully.

• When she frets, place the infant in an infant sac worn across your chest and carry her around with you as you go about your business.

• If she seems colicky, put her on your shoulder and pat her back. Or place her across your lap and rub her small back.

• Soothe her with quiet music or, with a tape player or cassette, play her your own recorded voice talking calmly or singing.

• Try immersing her feet in lukewarm water. A study at the Princeton Center for Infancy, reported in *The Parenting Advisor* in 1978, found this seemed to soothe many babies.

6.1-3 Be Physically Close.

Hold, rock, and snuggle your infant a lot—whether or not he's crying. Cradle him when he eats even if he can hold the bottle himself. Sing or read to an older infant. Babies need to be touched and held to feel well loved.

6.1-4 Interest Her in Her Surroundings.

Let's assume your infant trusts that you'll come when "called," because we certainly don't advocate putting her down, even in a perfectly safe place, and ignoring her cries. Now it's time for her to develop some independence. Instead of relying totally on you for stimulation and amusement, she must now learn to entertain herself some of the time. Boredom will certainly make her fret, but you need your space, too.

There are many safe toys you can put in your baby's crib, but we suggest you limit them to a few at a time. Many are designed to face the child who can't sit up yet, and provide amusement from simply looking at them. Babies love mobiles and other toys that move. They love to look at faces, and you can tape magazine pictures to the sides of the crib. Be sure to use soft toys in the crib so they won't interfere with your child's sleep, and be careful that they can't be used as stepping stones for escape from the crib for babies who have learned to climb.

6.1-5 Let Him Know It's Bedtime.

When you've tried everything and you're sure there is no medical or physical problem, but your baby insists on crying when he's put into his crib, try this routine: Rock him, soothe him, then place him lovingly into his crib and pat his back. Leave the room. Let him cry for ten or fifteen minutes, then go back and repeat the same comforting motions. Leave. Wait fifteen minutes again, then repeat the same routine. Eventually, he will learn that this means bedtime and that you expect him to sleep.

6.1-6 Go One Step Further.

For a toddler who understands and uses language well, you can use words and actions to reinforce appropriate behavior and minimize unnecessary crying.

• Refer to specific sections for special problems such as refusal to go to sleep, whining, etc., where solutions are discussed in detail.

• When the child understands language, remember to continue giving her your loving attention at times when she isn't crying. If you reserve your hugs for the times she's unhappy, she'll soon develop the need to cry and complain more often.

• Be sure to give her your immediate and approving attention as soon as she stops crying and starts acting as you would like.

• When she uses crying to gain attention, try the basic techniques we've described earlier, such as systematic ignoring (see Chapter 2). Be firm and matter-of-fact.

• Investigate persistent crying that is unusual or out of character for your child, because she may be very upset or even ill. If the crying is continual, we strongly suggest you consult your pediatrician.

6.2 CLIMBING OUT OF THE CRIB

The first time your child climbs out of his crib, you'll probably be shocked that he did it and relieved that he didn't hurt himself in the process. This is something some children do, while others never even seem to consider it. Usually, you have this problem or you don't. It doesn't seem to be a sometime thing. One little boy we know climbed up and over the side of his crib when he was ten months old, though his sister wouldn't even get out of her big bed at age four without permission.

If your baby or toddler is a crib escaper, your goal must be to prevent it when you can and make it safe when you can't.

6.2-1 Prevention Tactics.

The following suggestions will help to prevent babies eighteen months or younger from climbing out of the crib:

• Lower the mattress. If the crib mattress is adjustable, place it on the lowest setting long before the child looks interested in climbing out.

• Enhance the crib. Make the crib a special place that the baby can enjoy. Use colorful sheets, toys, things that are fun to look at.

• Don't use confinement to the crib as punishment. And don't keep him there unnecessarily when he's awake. He should associate it essentially with sleeping.

• Remove the stepping-stones. When the baby is clearly big enough not to get his head caught in the bars, remove the crib bumpers. Also remove large stuffed animals and toys that could be used as an escape route.

6.2-2 Say No!

The first time your baby attempts to climb over the side of the crib, let him know in a firm voice that this is not acceptable. Tell him, "No!" Put him back into the crib and tell him he must stay there. Babies start understanding language at about eight months, and they understand tones of voice before that.

6.2-3 How to Foil a Climber.

If your child has already started climbing out of his crib and you haven't been able to stop him, then the following suggestions may help.

• Safety-proof the room. The baby's climbing out of the crib when you're not around to supervise is potentially dangerous. Try padding the floor around the crib with pillows or pads. Or do as one family we know did—put the crib mattress on the floor and make the entire room the crib. The parents of a small boy who insisted on climbing on top of the bureau, causing it to fall over on him, bolted it to the wall.

• Replace the crib with a bed. Although we don't think a baby should be rushed into a bed, you should consider the move in this case because now safety is your major concern. When you do switch, make it a big event. Give the child a lot of praise and admiration, emphasizing his new maturity. Clearly define the bed rules, and supervise him the first few days until his new behavior has been established.

• Use positive reinforcement. Each time you enter the child's room and he is awake and still in his crib, be very enthusiastic about this wonderful accomplishment.

• No restraints. We do not recommend any kind of restraint, such as a net over the crib, that is designed to keep the child from climbing out. This can be physically and psychologically hazardous.

6.3 TOUCHING, MOUTHING, EXPLORING

Exploring is a baby's job. In the earliest months, infants learn through seeing and hearing. A three-month-old will spend a lot of time just studying things nearby. His color preferences are red and blue, and he usually is especially interested in faces and bull's-eyes. When he discovers his hands, he will study them and then gradually learn to gain control of them, reaching for objects nearby. He loves to touch things with his hands, his feet, and his mouth.

The average five- to seven-month-old can rotate his head, turn his body over and back and, with his new ability to sit, can now view the world from a new position. His improving eyesight allows him to view things more than a few feet away, and his eye-hand coordination is sophisticated enough that he can pick up small objects within his reach.

Within a few months, this intense interest in the environment will be further stimulated, not only by increased manual dexterity, but by locomotion too. He is now what the English call a "runabout." He has become a toddler.

You, as his parents, have now begun one of the most trying (and enjoyable) periods of your life. This tyke must be saved from the environment, and the environment must be saved from him. Though your job is to keep him safe and sound, you also must try to encourage and stimulate his curiosity, because the early months are crucial to a child's intellectual development.

6.3-1 Safety-Proof the Environment.

Since the baby's role is to learn and explore, it's your responsibility to create a safe place for him to do it. Here's what to do first.

• Make a safety check. Patrol the areas where the child will be roaming, and remove hazardous objects. Store unsafe materials far out of his reach (it's been reported that 80 percent of all accidental poisonings happen to children between ten and thirty months of age). Prepare a list of emergency telephone numbers. These should include the phone numbers of your pediatrician, the poison control center, the hospital, the police, fire department, etc. You should also learn cardiopulmonary resuscitation (CPR), just in case of a crisis.

Pay special attention to the following areas and situations, because they are common causes of accidents. Don't assume they are safe until you have carefully considered them:

Electrical outlets; exposed cords; household-supply cabinets; medicine cabinets and closets; toilets; stairways; outside doors; fireplaces; sharp edges and corners of furniture; tiny objects; objects or furniture that may topple over when pulled; electrical appliances; self-locking cabinets and doors; faucets; plants, both indoor and outdoor.

• Teach your child what's safe and what's not. Even before a baby has a command of language, you can use words to warn her away from hazards. If she's reaching for the stove, for example, pull her back and say firmly, "No, that's hot!" If she is pulling on an electrical cord, take it away and announce in a no-nonsense voice, "No, that will hurt you." Though she may not understand your words, she will understand the tone and know she is doing something you don't like.

6.3-2 Provide Alternatives.

A child needs a stimulating environment, and you can make sure it is safe and fun. Burton White's *The First Three Years of Life* is one of many excellent reference books. It will tell you what to expect of your child as he grows, and gives suggestions to encourage maximum development. Through every stage, talk to your child in a natural way, labeling actions and items in his environment.

Babies: At first, of course, a baby responds to visual and aural stimuli and then to objects within his grasp. While a child remains stationary, it's up to you to bring the world to him. Put him on a blanket and give him some interesting objects to interact with. Make sure they are too large to fit into his mouth but small enough to focus on. Household objects like bright-colored measuring cups or plastic bowls are fun; so are doughnut-shaped rings, stacking cups, and blocks.

Toddlers: Once a baby learns to crawl, however, then everything becomes fair game. The world is his playpen. Remember to initiate and supervise his activities.

• Create a space the child knows is just for him—a cabinet, a box, a drawer, a room. If there are areas that are off limits, make a rule that the child may enter them only with an adult. One little boy named Hunter, for example, may go into his mother's home office when she's with him. Because they go there often, the territory isn't totally forbidden and so it doesn't become inordinately inviting to this curious little fellow. A desk drawer is always full of paper to tear and a ball to roll.

• Rotate the toys. Never overwhelm your child with too many stimulating objects at once. Place a few special things in his special space every day—and change them regularly. Watch to see what he especially likes to do, and give him alternative ways to practice his developing skills.

• Match child with skill. When the baby tries new skills, give him safe ways to practice them. You might, for example, practice climbing, holding his hand going up and down stairs or helping him climb onto the sofa or appropriate play equipment. Let him know firmly what he may climb on and what he may not.

• A toddler loves to pick up small objects and put them into containers. He'll play pat-a-cake and peekaboo. He loves to "read" books and look at pictures, turning the pages of sturdy books himself. He likes to study pictures of familiar objects and animals and touch them while you tell him their names. He enjoys textures, sizes, and shapes. He is a real explorer.

One year old or over: At this age, the child becomes especially interested in toys and other objects with moving parts. She loves wheels, balls, jack-in-the-boxes, page turning. She loves removing lids, stuffing one container into another, stacking and building and, of course, knocking down what she (or you) have just built. She's interested in hammering and fitting toys together, pushing and pulling, rolling cars and wagons. And she loves books she can listen to, examine, and feel. Your job is to be her assistant and to cheer her on.

6.3-3 Think It Through.

A toddler loves to explore and touch everything within his reach, but you don't want his curiosity to turn into a continuing problem. Sometimes his curiosity is perplexing. The simplest things will fascinate him, while the toys created by child experts are left unused. Many times, parents buy toys before a child is ready for them. If you've done this, put them away and bring them out again when they may be greeted with more interest. If your small child loves to play with things that you don't wish to become his toys—such as makeup—then you have to set the rules.

• Give clear signals. Clearly, firmly, and calmly let the child know what he may and may not play with. Even if he is very persistent, don't bend the rules.
• Don't start today what you may have to stop tomorrow. We have all allowed a child to play with something for the moment because it was easier than stopping him. We were busy, distracted,

not up to a confrontation. But remember that tomorrow he may go for that "toy" again, and it's not fair to become upset with him. Try to be consistent. Stop him the first time, so you won't set the stage for a future problem.

• Use distraction. When the child goes for something that is unacceptable, say no firmly and, at the same time, offer him another enticing object. Most babies are just looking for something to do or touch, and you'll distract him peacefully from his first objective if you provide something new in its place.

6.3-4 The Two- to Five-Year-Old.

When a little child becomes old enough to understand what he may or may not do, then you just provide consequences if he misbehaves—remembering, of course, that there will be occasional backsliding. If he knows what's off limits but still persists at doing it, then these alternatives will be helpful.

• Be absolutely clear and firm about what he's allowed to do and what he is not allowed to do.
• Be ready with alternatives. When you'll be in a new environment, like a waiting room or a friend's house, for example, take a toy or a book along to occupy him.
• When he insists on touching or picking up something that's off limits, hold his hand still and say a firm no. Then don't relent and allow him to touch it anyway! Provide an alternative activity, and remember that consistency is the key. If necessary, remove him from the situation and take him somewhere where you can distract him or find something else for him to do.
• Try restraint training. Hold his hand and approach the forbidden object, say no in a firm voice, and pull his hand back. Do this three or four times. The next time he restrains himself, be sure to let him know how wonderful he is.
• Use time-out. If your small child refuses to listen to your restrictions and insists on doing whatever it is you have told him not to do, say, "You didn't listen to me when I said not to touch

the lamp and so you must sit right there for one minute." Then make sure he does..

6.4 DROPPING, THROWING, BANGING

A baby who throws and bangs and drops things is only doing what comes naturally. She's exploring her world and learning about cause and effect and, at the same time, asserting her own sense of self. At around six months of age, most babies begin to achieve manual dexterity and start experimenting. They want to know, What happens when I do this? Babies will spend a lot of time practicing these simple skills. If you don't respond to the throwing, banging, and dropping too strongly, then most likely these activities won't be used as attention-getting devices, and they too shall pass.

Remember that the baby isn't trying to annoy you, even though it sometimes seems that way. She's having fun.

6.4-1 Dealing with Dropping.

Dropping things begins as an experiment, just to see what will happen. A baby drops her bottle on the floor and cries until you pick it up, and it soon becomes a game. Take it for what it is at first —a learning behavior. But don't give it too much attention, or you will reinforce it until she thinks it is a wonderful game and you think you'll go crazy.

If your child is continually dropping things, try these alternatives:

• Pick up the dropped object and give it back to her. Sometimes she is simply working on the skill of holding and hasn't quite mastered it. But once she masters holding, she learns dropping!

• Ignore it. When the dropsies become a game and you tire of it, don't be the constant retriever. Leave the object on the floor and distract her with something else.

• With an older baby, return the object, but say, "If you drop it again, it will be mine for a while." Then when it falls to the floor, keep it for a few minutes. This works well at the dinner table, when toys or forks are continually dropped from the highchair.

6.4-2 Throwing.

Though this, too, may be a form of experimentation and skills development, it isn't a behavior you can afford to ignore, because it's dangerous.

- **Be firm.** When your child throws something, whatever it is, respond with a loud and clear, "No! Don't throw."
- **Time-out the object.** If he persists, take the projectile away and tell him you're going to keep it for two minutes. If he does it again, keep it for the day.
- **Time-out the child.** If you can't remove the object and give it time-out, then remove the child from the situation and place *him* in time-out. (See Section 2.7 for time-out rules.)
- **Use overcorrection.** Make him undo what he has done. For example, if he has been throwing rocks, overcorrect him by having him pick up twice as many rocks as he threw. If necessary, take his hands and guide him through undoing what he's done. Overcorrection can include an apology for hurting someone or breaking something. If something was broken, have him clean up the pieces (see Section 2.8 for further discussion).

6.4-3 Banging.

Little children love to make noise, and they bang objects for the sheer enjoyment of it. That's fine, but often it becomes very hard on a parent's nerves. In this case, you must be preventive as well as inventive.

- **Provide the objects.** Give him toys designed to be banged upon, such as drums and workbenches. Provide him with a wooden spoon and an old pot or a rubber hammer and a tray. Rubber or plastic objects are the easiest on your ears and nerves.

Make it clear what he may bang on—"Bobby, it's fine to bang your drum, but you may not bang on the table with your spoon."

• Set circumstances. Make sure the child knows when he may and may not bang. Banging may be fine at home, but not in restaurants or at Grandpa's house. Some parents give their babies pots and pans to bang on while they prepare dinner. That way, everybody is happy and busy in the kitchen.

• Provide consequences. If the banging is too much for you and you want him to stop, time-out the banging object by taking it away for a certain amount of time.

6.5 WHINING

Whining is guaranteed to force a parent to reach deep inside for will power and patience. It hardly matters what words your child uses when he whines or what he's whining about—it's the tone of voice combined with the endless nagging that produces the problem.

Whining tends to peak at about the age of three and a half, but it can continue well into the school years if you don't find an early solution for it. We're not going to discuss the causes of the problem (some professionals believe it a sign of immaturity, spoiling, or insecurity, while others think it results from anxiety), but how to deal with it right *now*.

6.5-1 Head It Off.

To prevent whining from becoming a habit, try to circumvent it before it becomes established.

• If you're like most people, it often takes your child more than one try to get your attention. So he doesn't always have to distract you from your other activities to get it, be sure to spend some undivided time with your child every day. Don't do anything else but be with him during that special time. Give him your total concentration (unless he is whining).

• Keep him busy. Don't expect a toddler to be able to fill waiting time constructively. Try to provide him with choices and activities. When children are bored, they often resort to whining simply because they have nothing better to do. Think ahead. Find activities for him, show him how to play with new objects, let him do some simple chores in the house. Let his interests be your guide. You'll be amazed how much a toddler can do for himself—and for you. Besides, he'll learn a lot in the process.

6.5-2 Give Quick Responses.

Try to attend promptly to your little one when she tries to speak to you in an appropriate way. Don't wait until she must whine before you answer her question or request.

• Signal that you hear her when you can't respond immediately. Say, "I hear you. I'll be ready to listen in just a second." Or get her attention, look her in the eye, and use a finger signal that means "Just a moment." Then don't make her wait too long for your response—after all, what you are trying to do is head off her need to whine. If she must wait endlessly, she'll have to do something unpleasant to reach you. Free yourself up quickly and say, "Thank you for waiting. Now I can listen to you."

• Teach her *how* to ask. Let the child know the difference between whining and speaking normally. If necessary, tape-record her and let her hear herself whining. Use role-playing to show her how to ask for something correctly. When you're sure she understands just what whining is, then make it clear that whining is unacceptable.

• Reinforce with praise. Teach her how to get your attention without whining, and then praise her when she does it that way. Even a two-year-old can be taught to say "Excuse me" when interrupting you and to wait until you are ready to respond—if you don't keep her waiting too long. Even more important, reinforce this non-whining by saying, "I like the way you asked me that, Sally."

6.5-3 Don't Let Whining Succeed.

If whining works, children will continue to use it as a tactic to get what they want.

• Mean what you say. Be very clear and consistent. If a child knows the rules of the household, she will know it won't pay to try to wear you down. For example, if the rule is no snacks before dinner, she won't start whining for cookies every afternoon, because she knows she won't get them. (Of course, this doesn't mean you can't change the rules on special occasions, but let her know this is an exception.)

• Give alternatives. Say, "If you ask me your question in the right way, I will gladly answer you." If necessary, use the broken record technique (see Chapter 2), repeating the phrase over and over again until the child responds appropriately.

• Use systematic ignoring. Review Chapter 2 for details about this option. When you must respond negatively to any request, give your answer and stick to it. Ignore repeated questions or whining, remembering the behavior will get worse before it gets better. Let's say your small child asks you to take him outside to play and you say, "No, not now because I'm cooking dinner." Give him something to play with and ignore all whining. When he does stop whining, give him some attention and let him know you appreciate it.

• Apply time-out. Simply say to your child when the whining begins, "I have already answered that. You may whine all you want, but not with me." Then give him a way out: "When you stop whining, come back and we'll talk." With a toddler, pick him up and move him to a spot (perhaps called the whining chair) some distance from you, where he will feel "banished" though you can still see him. Then ignore the tears and whining and, if necessary, repeat: "When you stop whining, come back and we'll talk." If he doesn't completely stop crying or whining but really seems to be trying, let him return from time-out after a few minutes.

6.6 CLINGS OR WON'T SEPARATE FROM PARENTS

As early as the first week of life, a newborn baby will look toward the eyes of the person holding him and at about six weeks will smile at a face about six to twelve inches away. In most homes, that face belongs to a parent, and in most cases, it is the mother's. Thus begins the wonderful relationship between infant and parent.

At four or five months, the infant can distinguish his parents' from other adult faces but still doesn't get too upset if you leave him. In fact, this is usually more difficult for the parent than the child. Until he is about eight months old, even though the baby may show a preference for the person who's around him the most, he's not upset if you're there or not. For him, it's a matter of "Out of sight, out of mind."

It is during this period of time, however, that the child begins to note when people are leaving. He's beginning to learn who he is. He knows the individuals who take care of him and starts to become wary of newcomers or anyone outside the nuclear family. Anybody can become suspect in his mind if he or she doesn't live in the household or spend considerable time with him.

This is the beginning, then, of the stage when the child will look to the parent for security, especially when he encounters new people and strange places. His wariness is perfectly natural and healthy and will gradually decrease over the next few years as his own sense of self emerges. Learning to deal with strangers and new situations are skills that continue to develop all his life.

Some children have great difficulty separating from parents. Even when a stranger isn't around, they may be constantly underfoot, shadowing you around the house. If they sense your departure, they'll wrap themselves around your leg, hold tight, and shriek. Before they're grown-up, they've usually found other ways to deal with separating, but in the meantime, clinging can be an exhausting experience for everyone.

6.6-1 Encourage Her Sense of Independence.

This book is, in essence, about nurturing your child so she grows up to be a healthy, happy, and independent person. In a sentence: We suggest you do this by starting very early in her life to provide firm clear guidance, encouragement to do what she can for herself, and then praise for having done it. Every time you praise her for independent positive learning, you will encourage a sense of self she can take with her when she leaves you for a few moments.

• Give her a place to call her own. The crib, the first place an infant calls her own, should be a special place for her.

• Play peekaboo. For a baby, out of sight is "gone." Playing peekaboo—holding your hands in front of your face, then quickly removing them—is a game babies love after about the age of five months. They are truly surprised by your return from behind your fingers. Peekaboo appeals to their sense of fun and to their feeling of control over the environment, too, because they sense Mother will be back.

• Play hide-and-seek. As children get older, play hide-and-seek, slowly increasing the time and distance in the house. This way, they tend to become more comfortable being apart from you because they associate it with fun. (Caution: Don't hide so long or so far that they become frightened—this is for fun. Alarming them isn't the idea.)

• Provide a home base. Let your baby explore his environment as he becomes more mobile, gradually becoming braver as he branches out. He'll come crawling or running back to you to share or check on you. These are healthy moves, so child-proof your home (see Section 6.3) and allow some exploration while you unobtrusively supervise. Never allow a small child to roam out of your sight for more than a minute or two. And when he comes back to you, let him know you're glad to see him and have time to spend with him.

6.6-2 Prepare Him for Separation by Going and Coming.

You need time away from your child and he needs time away from you. He also needs to learn that though you leave him, you will return. Children need experiences with other adults and children to learn social skills, to find out how to act with different people and in groups. According to many psychologists, children who have been around many people since infancy and have been allowed to develop a sense of independence are less likely to be fearful when a parent leaves.

6.6-3 Prepare for the Baby-sitter.

Always be sure you have a competent and loving baby-sitter before you plan to leave your child with her. Then, when you go out through the door, don't let the baby's wailing upset you too much, because your uneasy feelings will upset him, too. Every parent feels guilty and uncertain at a time like this, but remember that learning how to separate comfortably is your goal, and it is good for both of you. Leave with assurance.

• Let child and sitter get acquainted. Ask a new baby-sitter to come to your home an hour or more before you're planning to leave so that she and the child can get to know one another. You will feel more secure, too, having seen them getting along nicely. Then try to leave while they are playing together.

• Keep everything normal. Tell the baby-sitter your schedule and patterns of activities, the baby's likes and dislikes, the usual routines, so that when you leave, everything will seem quite normal.

• Leave while he's occupied. It will be easier on both of you if you leave while your child is busy with an activity. He'll miss you less if he's in the midst of a game with a newfound friend or eating his dinner in his highchair. It is also helpful if he can look forward to a special activity planned with the baby-sitter while you're gone.

• Tell him your plans. Let your child know when you'll be leaving, where you're going, and when you'll be coming back, even if he doesn't yet have a sense of time. It will make him feel more secure. Write all of this information down for the sitter, too, so she can reassure him.

• Never leave without saying goodbye. It's not fair to simply disappear, and it can be very upsetting to the child. Some children like a two-step departure—saying goodbye and then waving from the door. Others devise their own rituals, like Lou, who always gives one hug and one kiss when Mommy or Daddy leaves him.

6.6-4 Prepare for New Places and Situations.

If you'll be leaving your child with a caretaker in a new setting, let him become familiar with the place before you leave him there. We all feel more secure when we know where we are going and what to expect when we get there.

• Visit beforehand. Go for a special get-acquainted visit before the day that you'll be leaving the child there. Take him on a tour and let him spend time with the adults who will be with him.

• Communicate. If you haven't met the teacher or sitter who will be taking care of your child, make a point of writing a note to her or talking to her on the telephone. Let her know all about the child, his preferences and dislikes, his personality and habits, and of course, discuss any special problems.

• Make friends. If possible, introduce the child to another little boy or girl who will also be in the play school or day-care center.

• Discuss what's going to happen. Talk to him about what to expect in this new place, what he'll see and do. Go to the library and find books about it to read to him.

• Do something special. Make his going to this new place a special and wonderful event. Talk about what he'll wear, get him something new to take with him, behave as though it will be great fun!

6.6-5 When It's Time to Go, Go!

Don't act uncertain, hesitant, guilty, or apprehensive. Say goodbye
confidently—and then leave promptly. The child must not feel
your departure is a matter of choice or that if she makes enough
fuss, you'll change your mind and stay with her.

• Be brave. Don't feel hurt if she is happily occupied when you
leave and hardly notices your departure. Pat yourself on the back
instead, knowing she loves and trusts you.

• Don't rock the boat. You can't let your own feelings of insecurity affect her. If you are having difficulty going through the door,
thinking, How can I leave my baby? take note of these feelings but
exude confidence *anyway*. If the child clings to one parent more
than the other, then the less clung to parent should do the leave-
taking.

• Sympathize, but leave. If your child starts getting upset at the
thought that you are leaving her, let her know you sympathize
with her feelings but that you must leave. Say very calmly, "I know
you're upset, but I know you'll be fine. You'll have fun with the
baby-sitter. I love you and I'll see you in a little while." Then *go*!
Never discuss the situation. If, for example, your child refuses to
get out of the car when he's going to school or camp, give her a
clear choice: "I will walk you in, or you may go in with the other
children. You decide." Give her five seconds to make up her mind;
then follow through.

• Deal with the second-day blues. Sometimes a child willingly
lets you go the first day but becomes very upset on the second
outing. Myra was taken to camp very happily one day, then cried
the second morning. That didn't mean she didn't enjoy herself, but
she realized that going to camp meant she must leave her mother.
Her mother followed through, said goodbye confidently, and Myra
was fine.

6.6-6 Develop a Plan to Increase Independence.

• Give your little one plenty of loving before the next leave-taking. If she clings to you when you leave her, don't assume you've "spoiled" her—she simply needs to feel more secure if she's going to be more independent. Spend *more* time with her, play with her alone, and give her lots of hugs and kisses when she is not clinging to you.

• Reinforce independence. Don't do everything for the child, but allow her to take care of herself until she asks for help. Then give that help only if she really can't do whatever it is she is attempting to accomplish; instead, encourage her to do it herself. Give her plenty of praise for her efforts and especially for her successes. And especially, don't act disappointed or angry if she doesn't manage it.

• Establish a reward system. Reward her for not crying or clinging when you go out (see sections 2.4 and 2.5 on setting up a reward system). Explain that she'll earn a star for being a big girl and saying goodbye.

6.7 SLEEPING THROUGH THE NIGHT

Newborns sleep as much as they need to, no more and no less. They have an inner biological time clock that regulates their sleep pattern, and their pattern might not match yours. It takes a while for the infant to learn about the new world he's in, and it takes parents even longer to get his inner schedule adjusted to the needs of the household.

Normal newborns sleep an average of sixteen hours a day, but it is the rare child who sleeps through the night very soon after birth. In any case, a study reported by Dr. Thomas Anders in 1979 showed that it took two-month-old infants an average of twenty-eight minutes to fall asleep, while nine-month-olds took sixteen minutes. Forty-four percent of the two-month-olds and 78 percent of the nine-month-olds slept through the night or awakened and then went back to sleep independently, just like older children and adults.

Our long-term goal as parents is to train our children to go back to sleep on their own, even if they wake up during the night. Though some parents object to helping an infant adjust to a pattern in keeping with the rest of the family, eventually their fatigue and frustration will lead them to finding a way to deal with the nights.

Although nighttime problems are discussed in Chapter 4, we're going to make some suggestions now for helping your infant develop healthy nighttime sleep habits.

6.7-1 Prepare for Sleep.

An infant's need for sleep, nourishment, and stimulation, plus a controlled environment, influences his sleeping habits. Make preparations to encourage healthy sleep patterns.

• Give an infant his own space. As we've stressed earlier, an infant needs a place to call his own. A cradle or bassinet in his parents' room is fine for the first few weeks or even months, but then he needs his own space. A safe crib provides a reliable home for many months, even if it must be placed in an alcove or in a sibling's bedroom. Try to make the crib a cheerful and interesting environment, with colorful bumpers, covers, decorations, and a few stuffed toys.

• Control the temperature. All parents worry whether their new baby is too cold or too warm, but in general, if you are wearing approximately the same amount of clothing and you are comfortable, he is too.

• Dress him comfortably. Put him to sleep in clothes that are safe (make sure they are flame-retardant) and comfortable, such as drawstring nighties and snapped sleepers, over an extra-thick diaper.

6.7-2 Encourage Healthy Sleep Habits.

You can help your infant learn healthy sleep habits by controlling certain factors in her environment.

• Help her learn the difference between day and night. Sometimes parents worry so much about waking their infant in the daytime that they tiptoe around and talk in whispers. That's not necessary or advisable, because infants can sleep through anything. Lead your life normally. Don't darken the house or the baby's room or worry about noise. The baby will soon become accustomed to the activity and start to differentiate between days and the dark, quiet nights.

• Teach her to go to sleep on her own. Don't let your baby learn to rely on you to put her to sleep with rocking, bouncing, patting, walking. First-time parents usually find this very hard to do, but you'll make it easier on yourself and the baby if you don't start a tradition that will be difficult to eliminate later. We suggest holding your infant, feeding her, changing her, rocking her, then wrapping her in a blanket and putting her on her side or stomach in the crib. (The stomach or side position, cushioned with a towel roll behind the baby's back, is safer for a newborn, who may vomit after a feeding.) If your baby prefers, place her head or back against the crib bumper—some infants like the feeling of security the contact gives them.

Leave the door open or use an intercom so you'll be reassured she's fine.

• Play only during the day. A newborn's waking periods will gradually lengthen, though she may seem to sleep all the time. Play with her only during the daytime hours. At night, be loving but businesslike, and never decide this is playtime. When she wakes up, feed and change her and then put her back to sleep as quickly as possible. What you're trying to do is to encourage her wakeful periods to occur mainly during the daytime hours.

• Develop a nighttime routine. This is discussed in more detail in Chapter 4. The routine will become more elaborate as the child grows older. For now, put your infant to sleep at approximately the same time every evening and with the same sequence of events, preferably when he first shows signs of fatigue rather than when he's overtired. Place the same toys and blankets in the crib with him each night for familiarity and comfort.

• Give him a late-night feeding. Feed your infant every night before you go to sleep, between 10 P.M. and midnight. Select your time and try to stick to it, even if you have fed him an hour or two earlier. This, according to Cuthbertson and Shevill in *Helping Your Child Sleep Through the Night,* will become a focal feeding from which the baby will begin to "stretch" the time to sleep through the night. Try to make this a complete feeding—don't be afraid to rouse him repeatedly if he falls asleep—so he'll consume enough to last him for a while.

• Don't wake him for a feeding after midnight. Unless there is a medical reason, never wake the baby up for a feeding after midnight, but let him wake up on his own. You want to encourage him to sleep as long as possible during the night.

• Do wake him during the day. In the daytime, however, we suggest you wake the infant at least every four hours for a feeding, even if you're on a demand schedule. Keep a supplementary bottle handy if you are breastfeeding and won't be home at the right times. This way, the baby will eventually consume most of her nutritional requirements during the day and will give up the night-time bottle more easily. If you wake her up in the day, you will be encouraging her longest periods of sleep to coincide with yours, at night.

6.7-3 Train the Baby to Sleep Through the Night.

If parents follow the above suggestions, their infants will naturally start sleeping through the night before very long. If yours doesn't, wait until she is about two months old, weighs ten to twelve pounds, and is gaining steadily, and then start helping her learn how to sleep through—if you want to. If you are not ready or you don't mind the nighttime disturbances, fine; what's important is that you feel comfortable and confident about what you're doing. A last point: It's easiest to train an infant to sleep through the night if you and your spouse do it together.

Here are the steps:

• Continue the late-night feeding between 10 and 12 P.M. This is very important because it will serve as the base from which the infant sleeps through the night.

• Choose a comfortable time to begin. You'll want a week when the infant is feeling well and when you can afford to lose a little sleep. If you can, start the training on the weekend and perhaps you'll have achieved your goal by Monday.

• Lengthen the time between the late-night feeding and the first middle-of-the-night feeding. When the baby wakes up and cries for his milk, one parent should go to her (if the mother is breastfeeding, the father is best for this role because he is not associated with feeding) while the other sleeps. Take your time. Change the diaper if necessary. Talk to her, sing to her, then swaddle her and put her back into her crib without feeding her.

If she settles right down, you're home free—get back in bed! If she doesn't, help her sleep without picking her up. Sing, rub her back, pat her, rock her. If you're very lucky, she may sleep another forty-five minutes or more.

When she wakes up again, stall. Offer her water if necessary. When you feel she can wait no longer, feed her and put her back into her crib. You've done a good job.

The second night, delay the late-night feeding until eleven or twelve o'clock. When the baby wakes up during the night, go through all the above procedures, stalling for time. Put her back to sleep without feeding her. The second time, stall again, giving her water once more. Put her back to bed. She may decide it's hardly worth waking up just to get water!

When she does get up again and you've changed and patted and sung and rubbed, you'll have to feed her. But by now it's probably around three or four in the morning and your infant will most likely sleep through until a decent hour in the morning.

What do you do if this doesn't work? You may want to wait another couple of weeks before trying it again. On the other hand, maybe your little one will give you a big surprise tonight and sleep through till morning. In the meantime, don't get in the habit of waking her during the night.

• Reinforce the training. Over the next few nights, continue the

same procedure: late-night feeding, then stalling tactics and back
to bed to delay the next feeding. She'll get there—and your nights
will vastly improve.

6.8 GIVING UP THE BOTTLE

Eventually, your child must give up his bottle and start drinking
exclusively from a cup. When that time comes is up to you, and it's
not unusual for parents to have a more difficult time doing it than
the child does. Parents usually worry that their child won't get
enough milk. It's true that most children who love their bottle do
drink less from a cup, but a one-year-old needs only sixteen ounces
a day and a two- to three-year-old does very well on eighteen
ounces a day. Besides, he will be eating other dairy products, too.

Once you make the big decision to give up the bottle, there are
ways to make it easier and less traumatic for both of you.

6.8-1 Plan Ahead.

• You can help your child give up the bottle by never letting
him become too dependent on it in the first place. What we mean is
that the baby should depend on *you* for his security rather than the
bottle. Don't prop it for him, but instead, hold him while he
drinks. In fact, even when he learns to hold the bottle himself, we
advise holding him as much as possible.

• Don't use the bottle as a pacifier, because that, too, will make
him more dependent on it for comfort.

• Never give him the bottle in his crib, when he's going to sleep.
This can be the cause of extensive tooth decay.

• Show him how to drink from a cup at six months. Offer him
the cup at mealtime so he'll start developing the skill. Give him his
own bright-colored cup that he will recognize, perhaps one with a
spill-proof lid or a weighted bottom.

6.8-2 Decide on the Timing.

Usually, it's up to you to make the decision about when your baby should give up his bottle, though you may want to ask your pediatrician and dentist for their advice. If your toddler shows diminishing interest in his bottle, take advantage of it. Otherwise, pick a day and go for it. Choose a time when nothing out of the ordinary is going on. Once you make the decision, you must stick with it, and before you realize it, your child will have graduated to a cup.

Try these techniques separately or in combination:

• Dilute the bottle. Two weeks before B day, start diluting the milk or juice in the bottle by adding water to make it less tasty to him. At the same time, start offering him undiluted milk or juice from a cup and encouraging him to drink it.

• Change nipples. Switch from the old familiar kind of nipple to a new shape and size.

• Stick with your plan. Once you've set forth on your mission, don't falter! Don't worry—it won't traumatize the child if he's weaned in a day. Tell him he's a big boy now and it's time to send the bottles to a little baby, who needs them. Let him help you pack them up, making an event out of it. Then get rid of the bottles and don't backslide. Even if he cries loud and long for his bottle, hold out. If you give in, you'll prolong the situation and make it more difficult for both of you later on.

• Shower him with praise. When he drinks from his cup, tell him what a big boy he is and how proud you are of him. What a fantastic achievement!

CHAPTER 7

Problems
of Elimination

CHANGING diapers, sheets, and washing little bottoms are duties a good many parents accept cheerfully because they "go with the territory." When children are infants, we don't mind helping them with their basic bodily functions. We know that eventually they will be toilet trained.

Children follow different timetables in learning to control their elimination habits, though parents sometimes worry that their own youngster will never get around to it. Why isn't Sally trained yet? And some are concerned when elimination problems reoccur in older children. Why is Billy wetting his bed again? Is he insecure, or did we do something wrong?

This chapter is designed to answer your questions about many common problems of elimination and to help you make this learning experience a positive one for both you and your child.

7.1 TOILET TRAINING

Toilet training is a subject that tends to create major anxiety for parents. New parents get confused by all of the conflicting advice they get from family, friends, and "the experts." And experienced parents worry that what worked with one child is not right for the next. Some authorities on the subject advise you to wait and let the child "train himself naturally." Others suggest you accomplish this major feat in one day.

What should you do? Will your child be psychologically damaged by toilet training or, worse, go off to college in diapers? The answer is no. All children (except those with severe physical or mental handicaps) are trained sooner or later. And even many of the profoundly retarded can learn to control their elimination habits.

Of course, some children are easier to train than others, but remember that some children walk and talk earlier or are more cooperative about picking up toys or going to bed.

As for traumatizing your child by toilet training, it is our experience that training will lead to later psychological problems only if you are punitive or abusive. Toilet training is not the cornerstone of personality development.

Let's clear up another misconception. No matter what stories you've heard from friends and family, children are rarely toilet trained in our society before eighteen months of age. Be suspicious when you hear of a child trained before a year—his parents may have trained *themselves* to recognize when he has to go and put him on the pot just in time. But the child is certainly unable to understand or to control himself at that age. Trying to train a child so early can lead to a lot of frustration for everyone.

Training must follow the development of some of the child's basic abilities. An infant has not yet developed the connections between his brain and his functions of elimination. He can't will himself to eliminate, nor is he even aware that he has eliminated. Awareness must come before control.

Control is aided by the increased ability of the bladder to hold more urine and the less frequent need to move the bowels. This is the usual order of development: nighttime bowel control; daytime bowel control; daytime bladder control; and finally, nighttime bladder control. Certainly, there are exceptions to this order and to the fact that girls usually develop control earlier than boys.

Most children are ready to be trained for daytime control between the ages of two and three years, though a few may be ready as early as twenty months. To determine if your child is ready, see the section on readiness below. And don't feel pressured to train your child until both of you have a real chance of success, no matter what little Billy next door has accomplished.

Although some children seem to train themselves by watching others, most need on-the-job training. Toileting is a complex skill —the child must be able to recognize and label the urge to eliminate, control it until he gets to the bathroom, undresses, and gets into the proper position. As adults, we take this for granted, but for a young child, a lot of learning has to have been accomplished.

In this chapter, we will present basic information and several approaches to toilet training to make the process simpler for you.

7.1-1 Teach Before You Train.

Use the points below as both a checklist for readiness and a teaching guide. Teaching your child the necessary facts and skills should begin before you actually expect her to accomplish the job.

• Body knowledge. Teach the child the different parts of the body and their functions, including those associated with elimination. Be sure she knows where urine and BMs come from. The books for children listed at the end of this section can be useful in teaching these facts. Teach them by pointing and labeling the parts of their own bodies and letting them watch you go to the bathroom. Of course, it is most helpful for them to observe someone of the same sex. Don't worry that this will traumatize them. Just act naturally, and they won't give it a second thought.

• Toileting words. The child needs a working vocabulary of toileting words and/or gestures. Late talkers will obviously use more gestures than words. It doesn't matter whether the words are *toilet, urinate* and *BM,* or *potty, peepee* and *poopy*—as long as everyone understands their meanings.

• Awareness of urges and wetness/cleanness. Can your child tell when she is about to eliminate? Whether she is wet or soiled? These are vital skills for successful toilet training. Most babies under the age of one year will give some sign or expression that they're urinating or having a bowel movement. These external signals often disappear as they get older, even though parents of toddlers may be able to detect what they are doing—especially when they always go off into a corner to have a movement in their diaper! These early signals provide an opportunity to help the child understand and label the sensations that occur before and during elimination.

Try to catch your child as early in the process as possible, and use your own words to label what is occurring. You might say, "Andrew has to make poopy! Andrew is making poopy now. Good! Now let's go change your diaper."

As the child gets older, he may start to tell you that he is wet or soiled. Respond immediately, praise him for telling you, and change him quickly. The ability to discriminate between wet and dry and clean and soiled is a very important connection that precedes the ability to inform you when he needs to go to the toilet. You can speed the process by random checks on his diaper. Have the child feel the diaper, too, and praise him for correctly deciding whether or not it is clean and dry or messy and wet.

• Cooperation and learning to follow instructions. Can your child follow simple directions and instructions? Can she imitate simple tasks, such as placing her hands on her hips? To determine if your child has the skills to begin toilet training and, in fact, understands the necessary words, ask her to carry something to the bathroom and put it on the floor next to the toilet.

If she doesn't seem to understand simple directions, start with teaching her the names of objects and places in the house and reward her for correctly following instructions before you attempt toilet training. Otherwise, it could be very confusing for her. If, however, she understands directions but is oppositional and won't do as you ask, then it's best to solve this problem first (see Chapter 2 and Section 5.8).

• Coordination and dexterity. Is your child able to walk or run quickly to the bathroom? Can she pull loose clothing off and back on again? If not, then true toilet training will be difficult and you will be required to run the child to the bathroom and pull her clothes on and off yourself. Until she can move quickly, it is probably best to wait before starting to train her. If she can pick up small objects but hasn't yet learned to take clothes off, then you can start teaching her how to do it. Buy some very loose-fitting underpants and show her how to pull them down. Praise and reward her when she does it, and soon she will practice with more difficult kinds of clothing. Don't let her get too frustrated, but allow her to do as much as she can all by herself.

• Bowel/bladder control. Does your child go for several hours without wetting? Does she have a few well-formed BMs a day rather than frequent little movements? If the answers are yes, then she may have the bowel or bladder control to begin training. If the answers are no, then it's questionable whether she can hold urine or bowel movements long enough to get to the toilet in time. Wait until she has developed better capacity and control. Be patient. As we've said, all children develop at a different rate. On the other hand, if you are concerned that she isn't developing at an appropriate age, discuss this with your doctor.

• Toileting fears. Is your child afraid of the sound of a flushing toilet? Is he afraid of falling into the water? Some little children do develop such fears, and it's important to overcome them before starting out to toilet train. Let the child flush the toilet for you. Let him become accustomed to watching the contents of a soiled diaper go into the toilet; then let him dump his BMs out of his diaper into the toilet and flush it himself. Joanna Cole, in her excellent book *Parent's Book of Toilet Teaching*, suggests making a ceremony of this, with the child waving goodbye as the toilet empties.

Explain to him that bowel movements are left over after the body has taken all of the good stuff out of the food we eat and are not part of himself. The books listed at the end of this section can help with this important concept.

Let the child "practice" by sitting on the potty or potty seat for very brief periods of time, so he can see that he won't fall in and disappear like the BMs do.

Finally, if he strains and seems to experience pain during a bowel movement, talk to your doctor about a change in diet or a mild laxative. It is important that he not have painful movements before or during the training, so be sure about this before embarking. You will be better able to separate negative reactions to toileting from physical discomfort.

7.1-2 Training.

After your child has learned the readiness skills, then you can begin toilet training.

The no-pressure method: Some experts believe that once little children have all of the skills and the desire to be cooperative, they will train themselves. Dr. T. Berry Brazelton tracked 1,170 children over a ten-year period and found that without pressure, 80 percent between the ages of two and two and a half learned to toilet with no more than one accident per week. The other 20 percent, of course, learned later. Over a hundred of the observed children learned after the age of three, and another hundred were four before they were trained.

If you have a lot of patience and have no deadlines that must be met, you may wish to try this approach. Select the child-size potty, potty seat, or toilet with step with which you both will be most comfortable. Explain how to use it and suggest that when he wants to, he may use it instead of his diapers. If he asks for help, give it, but don't prompt or pressure him. You are waiting for him to tell you when he doesn't want to use diapers anymore.

Important: If you get upset about accidents or feel compelled to rush him or pressure him to use the toilet, this is not the best method for you or your child. For this approach, you must be relaxed about the whole procedure.

The twice-a-day method: In this more direct yet gradual method, you place the child on the potty twice a day. This works best for bowel training with a child who has regular BMs. Have him sit on the toilet for a little while at the time when he usually has his bowel movements. Entertain him with books or toys that are only used while sitting on the toilet. Praise and reward him for sitting there cooperatively and, then, for having his BMs in the potty.

If he has no BM, don't scold or criticize. And if he goes in his diaper, don't fuss at him. If he doesn't want to sit long enough one day, wait for the next go-around. Don't force him to sit if he doesn't want to.

When this method works, the child usually starts making BMs in the toilet and urinating at the same time. Slowly, he will make the association between the urge to go and sitting on the potty. He will then begin to ask to use the potty at other times of the day and can be switched from diapers to training pants. The whole process usually takes several months before success is achieved.

The one-day method: This is an approach that is totally different from the others. It has been proposed by two respected behavioral psychologists, Drs. Nathan Azrin and Richard Foxx, in their book *Toilet Training in Less Than a Day.* They used this method with more than two hundred children between the ages of twenty months and four years. Some of the children had no previous toilet training, and the others had failed to learn to use the toilet after years of struggle. The authors report that all but a few children were quickly trained.

If you want to train your child quickly or have had difficulty with other methods, we strongly recommend the one-day technique. You will spend a whole day teaching toileting skills—with no other distractions. If you cannot manage to spend intensive time with your child without losing your cool, it would be wise to enlist the services of another member of the family or a patient friend the child loves.

You will have to refer to the book for the details of this method because they are too lengthy to outline here, but in general, the one-day method involves direct teaching of toileting skills learned through modeling, frequent urination stimulated by extra intake of fluids, positive reinforcement, and a correction technique for accidents.

This method may not be completely successful for all children in only one day, but it certainly is faster than any other we know.

The one-week method: If the intensive one-day method doesn't appeal to you and yet you do want to speed up your child's toilet training, there is an alternative. It gives you a little longer to accomplish your purpose. It does require some preparation:

1. Pick D day. Decide on a starting date, making sure that the week that follows is relatively clear for you and the family. If you go to work, perhaps you should start the training on Saturday morning. If you don't, Monday is probably best.

2. Plant the seed. Plant the idea in your child's mind that something big is going to happen. Tell her that on that day, she'll get a surprise because she'll learn how to use the potty like big people. Mention this at least once every day for a week before D day. Talk about how she'll be able to wear big-girl pants or fancy pants (decorated training pants) because she will learn to use the potty.

3. Buy the toileting equipment. Select a potty or potty seat. We recommend the kind that sits on the floor, because it is easiest for the child to manage on her own. Perhaps you'll want to take her to the store with you and let her help pick it out. Have it gift wrapped for the big day.

Buy several pairs of training pants that are one or two sizes larger than her size so she will be able to take them off and pull them back on easily. Take out one pair for practicing before D day. Show the child how to raise and lower them.

4. Have rewards ready. The key to overcoming resistance and making progress is to use meaningful rewards (see Section 2.4). The "potty train" works well: Let the child choose a special train, car or truck that can carry a small reward. The child may play with this toy and get the reward it brings when he uses the toilet successfully.

5. Start D day. Start the day off with a bang. Give your child her gifts—the potty and the training pants. Make a big fuss over putting on the pants and looking at herself in the mirror. Take a picture of her in her new pants if you have an instant camera. Put away the extra diapers, and tell her she gets diapers only at naptime and at night. Stick with this for the rest of the week, no matter what happens.

6. Have a potty drill. Ask the child to run to the potty, pull down his pants, sit on the potty for a few seconds, and then pull his pants back up again. Praise him and let the potty train bring him a surprise. Repeat this drill from different parts of the house a few times, but don't do it so often that he gets tired or resistant.

7. Give a reward. Whenever he has a BM, even a tiny one, or urinates in the potty, praise him profusely and bring on the potty train with a reward. Let him play with the train for a few minutes

and keep the reward. When he wants the train at other times, explain again that he only plays with it when he uses the potty.

8. Reward dryness/cleanness. On the first morning, have the child help you check his training pants to see if they are dry and clean. If they are, reward him with a little surprise (but not the train). As the week goes on, increase the intervals between checking the pants to half-hour and then hour-long spans.

9. Ignore accidents. If the child has an "accident," don't make a fuss. Simply help him change and tell him not to worry, because he will have other chances to use the potty. Ask him to run to the potty from the spot where he was when he had the accident and show you how to take down his pants and sit on the potty quickly.

10. Reward the progress. As the week goes on, the child will gradually have fewer accidents and will run to the toilet more. You may get discouraged now and then, so keep a record of the progress. Make a colorful chart and post it in a prominent spot in the house. Put a star on it whenever the child uses the potty. Tell everyone in the household that Jonathan has earned four stars (or however many) for using the potty like a big boy, while you continue to praise and reward him too.

11. Ignore negative comments. If the child says negative things about toilet training or demands his diapers back again, ignore the statements (see Section 2.2).

12. Expect accidents. Accidents will happen, so expect them and don't scold or criticize. If the child is improving with his potty-using skills, play them down. If he resists changing pants, then manually lead him through the procedure without responding to his protests. But if accidents continue to occur often or even increase in the coming weeks, then more potty drills after each accident should be a consequence. If he resists the drills, manually guide him through them until he stops resisting.

13. Phase out rewards slowly. One of the biggest mistakes parents make at this point is to give up the rewards too quickly. Even after the training week is over and the child is doing well, it's important to continue to praise and reward her for correct toileting. The rewards may be presented irregularly and less often, but be sure to include a "biggie" every so often.

14. If all else fails. If this method doesn't work for your child, try to find out why. Is she missing some readiness skill? Did you go through all of the suggested steps? If you can't find the problem, we suggest you buy *Toilet Training in Less Than a Day* by Azrin and Foxx and try that program step by step. Compatible with this approach, it outlines positive and negative consequences for each action.

SUGGESTED BOOKS FOR PARENTS

Azrin, Nathan H., Ph.D., and Richard Foxx, Ph.D. *Toilet Training in Less Than a Day.* New York: Pocket Books, 1976. A tested approach for rapid toilet training, presented in detail.

Cole, Joanna. *Parents' Book of Toilet Teaching.* New York: Ballantine, 1983. A positive approach to guiding your child to independence in toileting.

SUGGESTED BOOKS FOR CHILDREN

Frankel, Alona. *Once Upon a Potty.* Woodbury: Barron's, 1980. A picture book about a little boy (female version also available) who learns to use the potty (preschool).

Mack, Alison. *Toilet Learning: The Picture Books Technique for Children and Parents.* Boston: Little, Brown, 1978. With parent text and children's version all in one, to introduce toilet training.

Rogers, Fred. *Going to the Potty.* New York: Putnam, 1986. Uses photographs to introduce toileting concept and skill (preschool).

7.2 BED-WETTING

Most children start to stay dry at night somewhere between two and three years of age, though some, of course, take longer to develop this skill. This is a natural maturational process that indicates the development of the child's bladder capacity and motivation to stay dry.

Occasional accidents must be expected even at older ages and shouldn't be considered a problem. No matter how old your child is, *never shame or ridicule him for wetting the bed.* This will not help, and it can certainly lead to serious emotional problems.

About 75 percent of four-year-olds and 85 percent of five-year-olds no longer wet their beds except occasionally, but many children do continue to wet right into adolescence and sometimes adulthood. In fact, Drs. Azrin and Besalel have reported that four out of every hundred adolescents and one out of every hundred adults wet the bed. Boys are twice as likely as girls to have this problem.

Though we feel strongly that children must *never* be shamed or even pressured to stop wetting their bed, the situation should not be ignored. Most bed-wetting children feel great shame, though they may not admit it readily. Covering their true feelings with an I-don't-care attitude, they are often very upset and anxious about something they can't seem to control. Many children refuse invitations to sleep over with their friends or to go away to camp. Bed-wetting can harm their self-image and self-confidence. This is tragic, because today we know a great deal about the causes of bed-wetting as well as effective treatments to overcome it.

Before choosing one of our solutions for bed-wetting, you must determine the probable cause of the problem. Read the possibilities below and pick the one that best fits your child. Then use the appropriate solution or solutions.

CAUSES OF BED-WETTING

Medical: Most experts agree that medical conditions are the cause of 1 to 2 percent of all bed-wetting. Sometimes the child is suffering from such physical problems as a small bladder or weak sphincter muscles. Or if he has been dry for a long time and then begins to bed-wet, the reason could be a urinary-tract infection. When common causes like infection are ruled out by the pediatrician or family doctor and the problem persists, then it would be wise to confer with a urologist before pursuing other nonmedical causes.

Emotional: While it's true that some children who have been toilet trained do wet their beds occasionally because of emotional stress, they account for only about 20 percent of the bed wetters.

However, it is rare that a child who has always wet the bed ever does so for purely emotional reasons. This is why psychotherapy has proved a poor treatment for bed wetters.

Developmental: Though a child may seem to have no medical reason for bed-wetting, this does not automatically indicate that the cause is not physical. The child may not have developed sufficient bladder capacity to make it through the night. Or the sphincter muscle, which holds the urine in the bladder, may not have matured sufficiently. We suggest some training methods below to help in these cases.

Sleeping patterns: Many children wet the bed because they sleep so deeply that they are unaware of the bladder signal that indicates fullness. Therefore, they don't arouse themselves to go to the bathroom in the middle of the night. Some children combine deep sleeping with small bladder capacity. This pattern of deep sleep is usually hereditary, and if you look back into your family history, you will probably find relatives who had the same pattern and the same problem. This information will be reassuring to your child, and in addition, it will give you a clue to the age at which you can expect him to stop wetting the bed.

7.2-1 Medical Solutions to Bed-wetting.

There are several medical alternatives your doctor may prescribe if the symptoms warrant them. Antibiotics may clear up infections that cause intermittent bed-wetting. X rays of the bladder may indicate the need to "stretch" the bladder. Or rarely, a drug is prescribed to alter the sleep pattern so the child will wake up when he has a full bladder.

7.2-2 Solutions to Bed-wetting Caused by Emotional Problems.

If your child stays dry for weeks or months and then begins wetting again without any apparent physical reason, this problem may be caused by anxiety or oppositionalism.

The anxious child: If your youngster represses his feelings but is deeply affected by what's happening around him, then the following suggestions are appropriate:

1. Keep a diary on a calendar for a month or more. Note when the child wets, the preceding events in the family, neighborhood, and school. Be sure to log fights between siblings or friends, parental arguments, parent traveling, late nights, school tests, overwhelming homework, illnesses in the family, or any other event that may be significant to your child.

2. Show the chart to your child and tell him you're trying to figure out what's bothering him so you can help him overcome bed-wetting. Ask him to review the calendar with you and to add any other occurrences that were of concern to him.

3. Keep the chart for another month *with* your child, and use it as a means to stimulate him to talk to you about whatever has been bothering him. Set aside a special time of the day for these sharing sessions.

4. Teach him the relaxation procedures described in Section 2.10. Help him learn to relax before he goes to bed after the sharing session. Follow this with a back rub or quiet music.

5. Use a dry-bed chart made in calendar form to reinforce his progress. Be sure to follow the rules outlined in Chapter 2 for using charts and rewards.

6. If after several months of these procedures your child continues to be anxious and to wet the bed, you may wish to consider professional help. A discussion of how to select a professional is found in Chapter 17.

The oppositional child: If your child is the kind of youngster who has tantrums, doesn't follow directions, or won't take no for an answer, then you may need to deal with that problem before attending to bed-wetting itself. Sections 8.2, 8.6, and 8.7 will be helpful. When you have used these solutions to overcome oppositional behavior during his waking hours, your child may also stop bedwetting. If, however, he is now more cooperative but is still wetting his bed, try the following:

1. Totally ignore his negative comments about bed-wetting. Do not try to convince him, answer him, or even look at him when he makes statements such as, "I don't care if I wet the bed," or "It's all your fault that I do it."

2. Use a dry-bed chart to commemorate dry nights, and praise him for them. Let the child earn points toward a desired goal for staying dry or wetting the bed fewer times per night. Again, don't respond if he reacts negatively even to this praise. Place the chart where he can't tear it up!

3. Be as positive as possible. Show him how to change his bed and wash out his own sheets and pajamas. If he resists or refuses to do this, lead him through it manually if necessary. Remember: Don't lose your cool, and do not ridicule or shame the child in *any* way.

4. Even if he reacts negatively, help him become aware of the positive aspects of keeping dry, such as being able to go camping happily or to spend the night with a friend. Choose a goal, such as a new sleeping bag, to use with the dry-bed chart.

5. Stay with these procedures, rewarding and praising any progress. Expect an occasional setback and don't let it bother you.

7.2-3 Solutions to Bed-wetting Caused by Physical Factors.

It's thought that about 80 percent of bed wetters have bladder capacity/control problems and/or deep-sleep patterns. First try to increase her bladder control and capacity; if you succeed, the deep sleeping may cease to be a problem. (Of course, we must assume your doctor has ruled out medical problems first.)

1. Get a large transparent cup and clearly mark it in one-ounce increments up to sixteen ounces. Be sure it is marked in large clear numbers that your child can read easily.

2. Explain that one of the reasons she may wet the bed is that her bladder cannot hold enough urine or her sphincter muscle may not be strong enough to keep the bladder shut off all night. Draw a

little picture of the bladder with the sphincter shown as a cut-off valve.

3. Explain that the training will help her increase her bladder capacity and control. Tell her it probably won't change overnight, but that she will gradually improve with the training.

4. If you or another family member has had a bed-wetting problem as a child, talk about it with her. Just knowing that someone she loves and respects has had the same problem will relieve her of some of her negative feelings about it.

5. Place the cup in the child's bathroom and teach her how to use it to collect the urine each time she urinates during the day. Before pouring the urine from the cup into the toilet, measure the amount in the cup and let the child color in a cup chart, as in Figure 6.

6. Each time she beats her own record, praise her and tell her to color up to the proper lines.

Fig. 6 Cup Chart

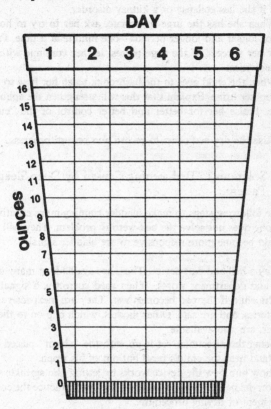

7. Help increase bladder capacity by encouraging her to drink freely all day. Explain how this will help enlarge her bladder size. To increase thirst, give her salty snacks and have her drink several glasses of liquid in an hour. Avoid drinks that contain caffeine. Water or fruit drinks are the best choices. Many bed-wetting programs suggest eliminating all caffeine, chocolate, and spicy foods from the diet.

WARNING: Do not allow the child to drink such large quantities of liquids if she has epilepsy or a kidney disorder.

8. When she has the urge to urinate, ask her to try to hold it back for longer and longer periods—one minute at a time. Praise her for her success. If the urge passes, let her continue with her other activities.

9. When the child goes to the bathroom, teach her how to start and stop her urine. Explain that this will strengthen the sphincter muscle. Praise her for better and better control of the "cut-off valve."

10. Use the dry-bed chart to record and reward progress.

7.2-4 Solutions to Bed-wetting Caused by Deep-Sleep Pattern.

Try the following steps to make bladder training more effective or if it alone does not solve the bed-wetting problem. They will help the child become more responsive to the bladder signal.

• Buy a bell-and-pad device. These are available at many drugstores and department stores. When used correctly, a signal will alert the child if the pad becomes wet. They are inexpensive, run on batteries, and are safe. Other models, which clip on to the underwear, are also available.

• Using the directions, set it up with the "alarm" placed on a nightstand near the child's head but out of his reach.

• Show him how the device works by letting him sprinkle some water on the pad or underwear. Have the child practice the correct replacement or drying procedure.

• Make a game of Beat the Buzzer. Instruct the child that he can earn points by catching himself before the buzzer sounds. Give him points on the dry-bed chart for smaller wet spots, fewer alarms during the night, and then dry nights. Be sure to reward *all* improvement.

Continue to use the device and the chart until there have been several dry weeks and your child would like to give up the buzzer. This usually takes several months, so don't give up.

7.2-5 Dry-Bed Training.

If these methods don't work singly or in combination, then try additional methods in the intensive training program described by Drs. Nathan H. Azrin and V. A. Besalel in *A Parent's Guide to Bedwetting Control: A Step-by-Step Method* (New York: Simon & Schuster, 1979).

7.3 SOILS SELF

Parents become very upset when their child does not have bowel movements on a regular schedule or in the preferred place. They fear that this is dangerous and the child will be retentive, and they don't know what to do about it. The child, too, is distressed, ashamed, and embarrassed by her lack of control.

Parents should expect a child to have occasional accidents in her pants even after she is toilet trained. Accidents happen to the two- and three-year-old most often, but older children do lose control on rare occasions, too—usually with an illness or when they are very excited or preoccupied. Depending on your child's personality, you may wish to downplay the accidents or make a point of being more careful. But keep in mind that she is more horrified by these accidents than you are. *Never* shame or punish her. Be calm and matter-of-fact about them.

If a child continues to have bowel accidents regularly after the age of three or four, then she may have encopresis, which is continued soiling of the undergarments. The soiling may be full BMs or leaky smears.

While it's true that most children outgrow this problem by the age of sixteen, it's also true that by that time the child's self-concept is severely damaged.

There are several prevalent patterns of encopresis. Some children are never completely toilet trained despite everyone's efforts. Others were trained but start soiling themselves again. Some youngsters soil almost every day, while others go for days or weeks without making any bowel movement. The latter child may only rarely have accidents and make few if any BMs in the toilet.

There are also several causes of the problem. Once in a great while, encopresis is a response to toilet training when the oppositional child gets into a power struggle with her parents and refuses to sit on the potty. This must be handled carefully and successfully, or the child can develop a lasting problem. A few children develop a fear of defecating, or "toilet phobia." This is not oppositionalism. Still others respond to life's stresses by having accidents. Though some cases of encopresis are caused by such psychological factors, most have a physical component. Many encopretic children have a parent or other close relative who also has suffered from this problem.

In addition, the vast majority of these children have chronic constipation. Whatever the reason for the constipation—emotional conflict, improper diet, pain in passing stool, or a medical condition—the result may be the same. The child retains more and more feces, the colon becomes distended and loses its muscle tone, softer stools ooze around the impaction and then seep out of the anus, which is partially opened by the pressure. Because of the seepage, the child may seem to have diarrhea and, of course, any treatment for loose bowels makes the underlying constipation worse. The child begins to lose the sensations that normally tell him he needs to go to the bathroom. And even when the bowels are emptied, it may take weeks or months before normal muscle tone is restored.

The child cannot overcome his problem by trying harder. Fussing at him won't help, either. However, there are a number of steps a parent can take to help him over it.

7.3-1 Check It Out Medically.

Before trying any of the suggestions listed here, have your child thoroughly checked by a physician. Your pediatrician or family doctor may examine her and then possibly refer you to a specialist such as a gastroenterologist or proctologist. The doctor will look for fecal impactions, distended colon, and poor muscle tone; or perhaps hypothyroidism, anatomical abnormalities, irritable bowel syndrome, malabsorption disorders, or even Hirschsprung's disease (an absence of nerve fibers). The doctor may do a barium enema to detect impactions, a biopsy to examine the nerve fibers, or other tests.

If impactions or constipation is found, the physician may prescribe a course of laxatives or enemas to clean out the intestines and keep them functioning until muscle tone returns to normal. Since laxatives may lose their effectiveness or become irritating over time, it's *essential* not to treat this problem without the help of a medical doctor.

7.3-2 Ensure Proper Diet.

Children with encopresis often experience abdominal pain and loss of appetite, which leaves them feeling listless. As a result, they may not eat enough of the fiber foods such as fruits and vegetables and grains that are necessary for good health and that encourage healthy bowel habits after constipation is overcome. Ask the doctor and/or a nutritionist to advise you on a good diet to help your child get over his problem.

7.3-3 Overcome Fears.

Children who soil themselves may have developed an avoidance pattern (toilet phobia) because of the pain associated with defecating in the past. If this is true for your child, you may have to wait for the regime of laxatives and fibrous foods to convince him that it will no longer be painful.

• Discuss the fears. See Section 2.9 for openers and ways of keeping the conversation going.

• Teach relaxation techniques (see Section 2.10). When the child has learned the basic techniques, help him learn to relax while sitting on the toilet.

• Desensitize the child to the fear of toileting. Use the fear-reduction techniques explained in Chapter 14 to desensitize her to the toilet phobia. Have her imagine having a bowel movement that doesn't hurt. Then have her relax while sitting in the bathroom near the toilet, then on the toilet.

7.3-4 Deal with Opposition.

If your child refuses to use the toilet because he is oppositional, try these solutions:

• Improve his ability to follow directions. Before trying to get your child to cooperate in using the toilet, work on improving his direction following at other times during the day. The techniques of praising, ignoring, time-out, and overcorrection will be helpful (see Section 5.8).

• Establish positive toileting. Now use the same techniques to promote sitting on the toilet. Begin with very short amounts of time on the toilet, rewarding him for sitting thirty seconds, then sixty seconds, etc. Increase the time gradually over a series of days and you may be surprised how quickly he works up to a reasonable length of time, which then allows for relaxed bowel movements.

7.3-5 Establish Regular Toileting.

After your child has started using the toilet more often, begin establishing a more regular pattern of toileting. Children who have avoided the toilet do not have regular elimination habits. Ideally, she should try to use the bathroom at least twice a day, once in the morning and again after school. Don't require her to sit for long periods of time, only long enough to relax and give her bowels a chance to work. Usually ten to fifteen minutes of sitting per day is sufficient for this to occur. At first, you must prompt the child in a friendly but firm manner and reinforce her compliance with praise and rewards. Later, reward her for remembering on her own. Set up a chart with appropriate rewards (see sections 2.4 and 2.5 on rewards and charts).

7.3-6 Reinforce Progress.

When the child sits on the toilet more regularly, you should begin to see progress. Keep track of it and then reinforce the gradual improvement.

• Number the underwear. Children who are encopretic will frequently hide their soiled underpants. To keep track of their progress, you must number each pair of pants with an indelible marker and select one for each day's use. This may seem oppressive and you may get flak from the child, but it will assure a way to measure improvement and a sense of security for her.

• Reward BMs in the toilet. The next step is to reward her not only for sitting on the toilet but also for producing BMs in it. Remember to be positive and to reinforce the gradual progress. Give a small reward for each movement made in the correct place. Then give rewards on a weekly basis for increased totals of correct toiletings. For example, if the child went in the toilet two times last week, he earns a big reward if he goes three or more times this week.

• Reward fewer accidents. As the child begins to use the toilet for BMs more regularly, he will probably have fewer accidents as well. This is your chance to reward him for fewer accidents, but because you must make sure he isn't slipping back into his old pattern of retaining feces for long periods of time, give rewards both for continuing to use the toilet regularly *and* for fewer accidents.

The next step is to start a count up, rewarding the child for two days without an accident, then three, then four, and so on. After a while, his "world record" will be weeks and then months. If he slips up, don't let him get discouraged. Accidents are to be expected for several months, until muscle tone and nerve sensitivity have returned to normal. Encourage him to start again and break his own record.

7.3-7 Correct Accidents.

When an accident occurs, remain calm. Don't fuss. Use the same correction technique used in Section 7.1 Have the child wash out his own underpants. If he resists, then calmly but firmly guide him through the process, even if this means you must do it manually. After he has changed into fresh clothing, have him practice five times going quickly to the bathroom from different locations in the house and sitting down on the toilet. He needn't sit for long periods of time, just practice the motions. Be sure he understands that this is not punishment but positive practice.

7.3-8 Be Patient.

The problem of soiling herself did not develop overnight and you are not going to solve it overnight, either. It may take several months, or there may be recurrences that will mean you'll have to reinforce diet and toileting once more. The real goal is to help the child over this large problem so that she has positive feelings about both herself and you. We recommend seeking the help of a mental-health professional if your own emotional conflicts seem to be blocking the progress toward that goal (see Chapter 17).

7.4 DAYTIME WETTING

You can expect occasional accidents even after your child has been successfully toilet trained. Daytime wetting may continue until she is five, six, or even older, especially when she is feeling tired, excited, preoccupied, or insecure. If you ignore these accidents, they will usually disappear by themselves.

As the child gets older, she will be more upset by accidents than you are. Even though daytime wetting may be frustrating to you, yelling, threatening, and punishing her will only make her more nervous or frightened to tell you about it. Besides, if you get into a power struggle, you can turn isolated occurrences into problems when none would have existed.

If a child continues to wet herself during the day very frequently, then you can't ignore it. You must help her solve her problem, whether it's physical or psychological. If she hasn't wet herself for a long time, then starts doing it repeatedly, a urinary tract infection is a plausible explanation. Or the cause may be stress in the child's life, such as the birth of a sibling or a problem at school.

7.4-1 Check Out Possible Medical Problems.

We've known many children who have been referred for psychotherapy when the cause of their daytime wetting (enuresis) was medical rather than psychological. Have your child thoroughly examined by your physician and/or a urologist before trying to solve the problem in any other way. The reason for the wetting could be a recurring urinary tract infection, a small bladder, weak muscle control, or even a neurological problem.

7.4-2 Check Out Bladder Capacity and Control.

Some children continue to wet during the day because of insufficient bladder capacity and/or control. Of course, you shouldn't expect more bladder control than is typical for your child's age. And remember that some children mature earlier or later than others.

It's not uncommon for three- and four-year-olds to wet their pants because they are too busy playing to notice that they must go to the bathroom. But if your child continues to wet consistently, make a point of observing how often he goes to the bathroom and how long he can hold his urine when he must. If he is unable to wait long enough to get to a bathroom or goes so frequently that he gets tired of using the toilet so often, then bladder training (see Section 7.2) may be the solution. Follow the directions closely. Reward the child for holding more urine longer and also for remaining dry during the daytime for more days in a row.

7.4-3 Reduce Nervous Wetting.

If your child seems to have adequate bladder capacity but loses control when he's nervous, anxious, or excited, then focus your efforts on teaching him relaxation techniques (see Section 2.10). When he has mastered basic relaxation and has lowered his overall tension level, then the wetting may stop naturally. If not, have the child practice the mini-relaxation techniques when he's in the actual situations where he sometimes loses control. One child we worked with used to get so nervous before an exam that she would often wet herself before or during one. By using the mini-relaxation techniques right there in the classroom, she was able to stop wetting and do better on the tests, besides.

7.4-4 Work on Fear of Using Other Bathrooms.

Some children are afraid to use a new or different bathroom. If you are convinced that this is the cause of your child's wetting problem, see Section 7.6.

7.4-5 Overcorrect the Intense Player.

Some children repeatedly wet themselves when they play outdoors because they become so involved in their playing that they don't notice or pay attention to the signal from their bladder. The solution lies in providing enough motivation to encourage them to notice and interrupt play long enough to come inside to use the bathroom.

If your child is old enough and mature enough to remember to toilet, if you have ruled out the other possible causes of the wetting, and if you are convinced that this is the cause of the problem, then you must provide the motivation to change the pattern of behavior. If the child is not mature enough to assume the responsibility for himself, work out a schedule with him for coming in to use the toilet at certain times. Then supervise it yourself until he is old enough to be responsible.

• Supervise scheduled checks. Explain to the child who is mature enough to assume the responsibility that if he wets himself when he's playing outside or gets involved with an interesting activity, he's proving to you that he can't play *and* remember to use the toilet all at the same time. Tell him that you are not going to scold him or punish him, but that he will not be allowed to play outside or do that particular activity until he shows you that he can remember to use the bathroom.

• Use positive practice. The next time he wets himself, restrict him from this activity for the rest of the day or, if it's already late in the day, for the next day. Don't ground him for a longer period or become angry and punitive. If you overreact, you may block this learning process and defeat your own purpose. Speak kindly and calmly, without anger or a raised voice. Remember that your role is to help him overcome his problem of wetting his pants, a practice he doesn't like, either.

When the restriction time is over, allow him to return to the activity, but have him practice stopping what he's doing and going to the bathroom for a brief visit five times in a row. Though he needn't urinate, he must pull down his clothes and stand at or sit on the toilet.

After the practice, have the child come in every fifteen minutes to check for dryness. If he refuses to do as you ask, restrict him for the rest of the day and start all over again. If he's dry, praise him and tell him he's now earned fifteen more minutes of play.

Gradually lengthen the time between checks until you reach an interval that you and the child agree is reasonable for him to check himself without coming inside or going into the bathroom. Have him agree, too, on how often he should try to urinate each day to prevent accidents. Keep daily and weekly records of accidents, and remember to praise and reward him for his progress. If he has another accident, again impose a day of restriction and practice.

We have found that most parents are successful with this procedure within several weeks, with the child having fewer and fewer accidents. If, however, you have followed the system conscientiously and it doesn't work in your case, then you should rethink the cause of your child's enuresis and seek professional help.

7.5 PLAYING WITH BMs/URINATING IN THE WRONG PLACES

It's doubtful that there are childhood behaviors that are more upsetting to parents than playing with feces or urinating in the wrong places. Playing with feces usually first occurs around the age of eighteen to thirty months, when the child becomes fascinated by bodily functions. If she hasn't been toilet trained yet, she may innocently reach into her diaper and pull out those interesting lumps. It's amazing what a mess a little one can make in her crib or play area when this happens. Older children sometimes use the BMs to finger-paint the bathroom. Occasionally, a warm bath stimulates a child to have a bowel movement in the tub and then he will play games with it until it disintegrates.

Urinating in unsuitable places, such as on the floor, the walls, or even behind the couch, sometimes occurs among children between the ages of two and four. A little boy who is still perfecting his aim may accidentally miss the toilet and become fascinated with spraying the whole bathroom. This can lead, however, to not-so-innocent urinating in other locations to see the effect on the building materials and his mother's mood.

Such exploratory urinating occurs less frequently among girls, but sometimes around the age of three, little girls try to urinate standing up. This may be just for fun or it may be modeled after Dad or brother. We do not believe this practice represents "penis envy," however. It's natural at this age for girls and boys to imitate both parents.

Playing with BMs and urinating in unsuitable places are both natural occurrences at a young age. If you don't overreact, they will probably simply fade away without any specific response from you. Though we have known an occasional eight- or ten-year-old who's urinated behind the couch or the plant stand simply as an act of defiance, in most cases these behaviors in older children indicate more serious emotional problems that should be discussed with a professional.

Whether you can take these messy and odoriferous behaviors in stride depends on your nature, but even the most relaxed person has difficulty ignoring the results of this kind of play. Whatever your personality, try not to overreact or underreact. The following suggestions may help you find the most effective response.

7.5-1 The Untrained Child.

If a toddler who is not yet toilet trained pulls BMs out of his diaper or pulls the diaper off and urinates, then this may be a signal that he's ready for training (see Section 7.1).

If he's not ready yet, then the first time it happens, say in a firm calm voice, "No! Don't do that!" Try to catch him in the act or as soon as possible after it happens. To prevent other occurrences, put him in clothes that are difficult for him to reach into or remove. Try to supervise his play more closely. At naptime, give him a special toy or stuffed animal and tell him to play with it when he wakes up. Don't mention the BMs or the diaper.

7.5-2 The Trained Child.

When the child is toilet trained, a different approach is required.

• Treat first attempts as accidents. If she urinates in wrong places or plays with her BMs, treat the behavior as an accident. The first time it happens, downplay it but ask the child to show you where she should go to the potty.

• Practice appropriate toileting. Have her practice running to the potty and sitting or, if it's a boy, standing in the correct position.

• Praise correct toileting. Praise the child for using the toilet correctly for the next several days. Increase the fun of using the toilet by making games out of sinking little pieces of toilet paper in the water. Let her play with mud, clay, or chocolate pudding to eliminate the natural inclination to play with messy substances.

7.5-3 The Oppositional Child.

If your child enjoys seeing you get upset by his behavior, then he may be urinating in strange places or playing with his BMs just to see what you'll do.

• Try systematic ignoring and praising the opposite behavior. One mother who came to us for help had already tried yelling and punishing her five-year-old for urinating on the bathroom walls. She agreed to try totally ignoring it for one week. At first, the child performed his unpleasant act even more often, but when his mother stuck to her guns and only praised him for good toileting, he quickly gave it up.

• Use overcorrection. Not every parent has the patience or the stomach to ignore such behaviors. If you can't bring yourself to ignore them, try a combination of overcorrection with positive practice. When your child makes a mess, have him "overclean" it up. This means he must not only clean up the mess he has made, but must also clean the surrounding area until it is cleaner than it was before the "accident." Keep calm. Tell him quietly and firmly that he needs practice keeping things clean. If, for example, he has urinated on the bathroom walls, he must now mop it up, clean the walls and floor with disinfectant, clean the toilet, then scrub his hands. The younger child will need help with these steps, but let him do whatever he can himself. If he resists, use manual guidance.

Now, have him practice going to the potty correctly ten times from various locations in the house (see Section 7.1). For more information on overcorrection, refer to Section 2.8.

• Praise profusely. Be generous in your praise and rewards for good toileting habits over the next several weeks. You may use a chart to reward until the habit is reestablished. Sections 2.4 and 2.5 provide all the information you will need.

7.6 WON'T USE OTHER BATHROOMS

Many newly toilet trained children feel comfortable using only the potty at home or in other very familiar places. Gradually, they expand their horizons. Some children, usually around the age of three or four, even develop a profound curiosity about bathrooms, always wanting to see where the bathroom is and what it looks like. This attention is a natural outgrowth of their interest in bodily functions and a need for security about their new toileting abilities. They want to be sure that if they need to go, they can. Sometimes they say they must go to the bathroom just to make sure the place is available.

Of course, it's infuriating for the parent who has searched a store for the restroom to discover the child didn't really need to use it. But that problem is certainly easier to deal with than the opposite one—the child who can't use any toilet but his own or maybe his grandparents'. So we suggest if your child demands to see every bathroom in town for a while, humor him.

Around the age of four, many children develop a strong need for privacy. This is quite natural and won't create a problem at home if it's understood as a sign of growing modesty. Modesty combined with fears of separation and/or fears of germs and dirt may intensify the problems of going to the bathroom away from home. The results may be accidents and reluctance to leave home for very long, compounding the difficulties of a child who's already shy or fearful.

While these concerns usually resolve themselves with time, we have seen a number of adults in therapy who have had them all their life. So if your child's fears persist, try these steps to help the child overcome them gradually without trauma.

7.6-1 Identify the Fears.

Talk to your child and find out what she is afraid of, using all of your communication skills (See Section 2.9). Go into a strange bathroom with her to get a firsthand view of what it is that's bothering her. Is it being away from you? Is it the fear of a stranger walking in and seeing her on the potty? Could it be that she's afraid of getting locked in the strange bathroom? Or does she fear dirt or germs? Never belittle her fears. Assure her you will make a plan to help her overcome them. (For more about fear reduction, see Chapter 14.)

7.6-2 Begin with Easy Bathrooms.

When you have identified the problem, start to overcome it by choosing the easiest bathroom possible. Make a list of all the bathrooms she has problems with, and let her choose where to begin. Then work your way up the list. Jessie, for example, chose her aunt's bathroom for a starter. She was afraid somebody would come in and see her on the potty. She felt most comfortable at her aunt's home, so her mother initially stood guard outside the bathroom door. As the child began to feel comfortable using this bathroom and then those of other relatives and friends, her mother praised her progress. Eventually, Jessie was willing to use the bathroom at restaurants and other public places, with her mother along, as always, for protection and to show her how to ensure her privacy.

7.6-3 Deal with Dirt/Germs.

Many older children refuse to use strange bathrooms because of an exaggerated fear of dirt or germs. Read Section 12.6 on obsessive cleanliness for pertinent information and then work specifically on the bathroom problem. It is very important to accompany the child to the particular bathrooms that concern him to see exactly what it is that bothers him.

If he is worried about unsanitary conditions, teach him how to overcome them by lining the seat with toilet paper or cleaning it before using it. Alert the authorities to improve the conditions, or get permission for the child to use another bathroom. One very neat and orderly child with whom we worked couldn't use the younger children's bathroom at school because it was always a mess. Because he wouldn't toilet at school, he began having accidents in his pants. As a remedy, his parents and teacher arranged for him to use the bathroom for the older children on the floor above. This provided a temporary solution as the child learned other coping skills.

7.6-4 Desensitize the Fears.

If your child is oversensitive to the sights and smells of a public bathroom that is quite acceptable by ordinary standards, then you must teach her coping techniques and also desensitize her fears. Go with her to find out what is bothering her. Have her relax herself (see Section 2.10). Then have her look at what's upsetting her and/or smell the air until it no longer bothers her so much. Show her that the odor becomes less noticeable if she waits a little while.

Be sure to praise and reward her for learning to stay longer and allowing the bathrooms to bother her less. Soon she will be able to go to them by herself when she needs to use them.

CHAPTER 8

Tantrums and Other Negative Behaviors

YOU have surely heard of the terrible twos, but you may not have been tipped off to the tyrannical threes, the fearless fours, the sarcastic sevens, or any of the other common "difficult" stages in childhood development. Any age spells trouble when your child has tantrums, won't take no for an answer, destroys his toys or your furniture, holds his breath till he's blue, loves to curse, or has developed other unpleasant habits.

But the terrible twos or tyrannical threes don't have to become the sarcastic sevens or the awful eights. Children can be fun and well behaved at any age, and most unacceptable behaviors are quite controllable. When you want to change them in your child and set him on the road to good behavior, try using the solutions in this chapter.

8.1 BREATH HOLDING

The first time your child holds her breath, the experience is terrifying. You've told her no, she throws a tantrum, you ignore the tears, and suddenly she turns blue, her eyes roll up, and she passes out for a few seconds. That's hard to ignore.

Breath holding rarely has a medical cause, and it is rarely an imitated behavior. Rather, it seems to be an inherited tendency that, once it occurs, usually is repeated because it's an excellent way to get everyone's attention.

Let us tell you about Suzanne, who was born prematurely and received a lot of attention from her family. One day when she was about nine months old and her mother put her down for a nap, she had a tantrum, held her breath, turned blue, and passed out. Her parents were very frightened and held her until they could get to their pediatrician. He examined the infant as the anxious parents watched, then put her down on the table. She immediately had a tantrum and held her breath again. The experienced doctor reexamined her, then explained that the child was fine but had already learned that turning blue got results. He advised the parents to put Suzanne in a safe place each time this occurred and to ignore it until she stopped. They were to pick her up only when she was not holding her breath. The doctor predicted the behavior would get worse before it got better, which it did. But the treatment worked.

If you are confronted with a child who is a breath holder, help yourself and the child by doing the following.

8.1-1 Check with Your Doctor.

Although breath holding is rarely associated with an underlying medical problem, we strongly recommend you have your child checked out by your doctor before you follow any of the suggestions. A respiratory or circulatory problem can cause the child's color to become blue when he is overexcited. When you've been assured that he is healthy, you will feel comfortable following the procedures that will eliminate the problem.

8.1-2 Provide a Safe Place.

Pick a spot where your child can't hurt herself. The crib or a carpeted floor is safe for an infant but a bed is not, because she could roll off. An older child is safer in a carpeted room where there are no sharp objects or corners to fall against. Grant was so adept at following his parents around trying to get their attention while he was turning blue that they could actually lead him into a carpeted hallway. When he finished his breath holding by falling on the floor, they knew he was fine. They stepped over him and ignored him. He soon returned to normal as though nothing at all unusual had happened.

8.1-3 Totally Ignore.

When you have assured yourself that the surroundings are safe, then ignore the breath holding (see Section 2.2). When the child again shows signs of holding her breath, turn away from her. If she continues on that route, move her or lead her to a safe place.

• Move out of sight. If possible, move out of her line of vision while surreptitiously monitoring her. If she is holding her breath for your benefit, you will soon know it. She will follow you or quit.

• Keep yourself busy. If you don't feel comfortable leaving the area, get busy. Grant's father would walk around checking light bulbs and cobwebs, talking to himself as he went. Sometimes Grant would be so distracted by his father's conversation with himself that he stopped holding his breath.

• Have patience. It may take a few bouts for the behavior to subside. You may want to count the number of incidents so you can see a decreasing pattern. Ignoring is not easy, we know that, and you may wonder during the breath holding whether the child is going to start breathing again. Talk positively to yourself about how you're doing the right thing, and practice your relaxation exercises. Your efforts will pay off.

8.1-4 Give Attention to Positive Behavior.

It's most important to give your child more attention when he's not holding his breath than you used to give him when he was. Choose something positive to make a fuss over. When you recognize a moment when he would have held his breath before but doesn't this time, move close to him and give him extra affection and attention. If, for example, he used to hold his breath when you put him into his infant seat but doesn't do it this time, take a moment to play with him. If he's older and accepts your no without a fuss, praise him, hug him, and give him a little surprise for his cooperation.

8.1-5 Use Alternatives to Ignoring if Necessary.

Some parents are unable to ignore a breath-holding child because it frightens them too much. Although systematic ignoring is the most effective solution for this problem, if you can't manage it consistently, then pay as little attention to the behavior as possible. Be detached. Don't scream, "Oh my God, Harry! Sally's turning blue again!" Instead, pick her up calmly and blow several quick puffs directly into her face. Or try a cold washcloth or a sprinkle of cold water on the face to start her breathing again. Whatever you choose to do, do it consistently. When the breath-holding episode is over, don't fuss over her or give in to the demand that prompted the incident.

8.2 TANTRUMS

The terrible twos don't always begin exactly on a child's second birthday, nor do they always end at three. One-year-olds have been known to have tantrums, and there are some forty-two-year-olds who slam doors and pound on car horns. Whether a child stamps his feet, screams, yells, kicks the furniture, throws himself on the floor, pounds his head against the wall, or pounds on car horns, he is having a temper tantrum.

Most parents have to deal with at least a few tantrums, especially when their child is between two and three and is trying to establish his individuality and wants to do everything his way and certainly not yours. This is actually a sign of growing independence and is quite normal, although that doesn't mean it's easy to take, especially in public.

Tantrums usually decrease as the child gets older, then often make a new appearance at another age. A 1959 study by Lapouse and Monk of 482 children between the ages of six and twelve found that 80 percent of them lost their temper once or more a month, 48 percent lost their temper twice a week or more, while 11 percent managed to do it once a day or more. Basic personalities and temperaments vary greatly among children even from the same family, with some rarely showing their temper and others starting to have tantrums at an early age and never stopping. Other children never have tantrums until they reach school age. A child's tendency to have tantrums may be due as much to his inherited temperament as to your child-rearing style, so don't be too quick to blame yourself if yours has tantrums, or too fast to pat yourself on the back if he doesn't.

Whatever the reason, it's not necessary to live in fear that your child will fall to the floor, kick, and scream when you turn down one of his demands. You can influence the frequency and intensity of the episodes by what you do during and after them. You can structure your responses to give you a helping hand and teach him acceptable patterns for expressing his opinions while, at the same time, you nurture the child's growing independence.

A child has tantrums for a reason. Maybe she just happened upon the behavior and found that it works. A toddler certainly isn't capable of cold-blooded, premeditated tantrums, but she knows when her behavior gets results. She may understand that she has made you change your mind about a toy she wanted, she may have avoided going to bed, or perhaps she received attention when she wanted it. So most of the time, the tantrum serves a purpose. When it no longer serves that purpose, it's less likely to occur. You may have to trust us on this one, but that is a fact 99 percent of the time.

Sometimes, of course, children throw tantrums simply because they are overtired or overstimulated and just can't handle their emotions. There are also times when the tantrum reflects the child's anger and frustration at not being able to do something he wants desperately to do.

But no matter what the reasons are for the child's tantrums and no matter how sympathetic you may feel about them, the behavior is unacceptable. The child must learn that it's inappropriate behavior that leads nowhere—it doesn't help his frustration, get him out of a responsibility, or change your mind about anything.

8.2-1 Ignore Tantrums.

This is the quickest way to get rid of tantrum behavior, because the primary purpose of most tantrums is to get our attention and nothing else. Even when it is a direct result of your "No" to a "Give me," or is prompted by an instruction to do a chore, the tantrum is not the correct response. It is not the way you wish your child to voice disapproval, nor is it the mature, rational behavior you seek to teach her. So ignore it. You can't reason with a child in the midst of an emotional outburst, so don't try. You can't make her feel better by putting your arms around her, and it's not necessary anyway. A two-year-old is fully capable of throwing a tantrum and stopping one. By ignoring it, as long as she is safe, you will teach her that tantrums are not effective and she will learn to use that response less often.

Ignoring tantrums requires a little breath holding—yours. You will hold your breath each time a tantrum occurs, waiting to see if the child is going to give in, but you will be surprised how well this works. As described in Section 2.2 on systematic ignoring, things will undoubtedly get a little worse before they get better. Hang in there.

• **Walk away.** Go about your business while the tantrum lasts. Continue your conversation or talk to yourself out loud. If it's safe, you may even walk out of the room, keeping an eye on the situation, too. If the tantrum is truly an attention-getting device, the child may even follow you because he needs his audience! Take this as a sign you are on the right track. Sing, turn on the radio or the television set, sit down and read your book, start cooking dinner. Be careful not to look at the child, because even a brief glance can prolong a tantrum.

• **Suggest a way out of the tantrum.** If you're unable to ignore the tantrum totally, as we suggest, then try the tactic of repeating a key phrase to change the behavior. Kitty, for example, wants to play with your eyeglasses and you won't let her. She promptly has a tantrum. Place her where she won't get hurt and say to her, "Kitty, you may not play with my glasses. When you've stopped crying, come back and we'll play a game." Then do not respond to her tears and demands for a while. If you have difficulty ignoring her and she's having a hard time giving up her tantrum, wait a few minutes until her tears diminish and say again, "When you've stopped crying, come back and we'll play a game." Say nothing else. Don't be surprised if she yells louder momentarily, because you have just paid attention to the tantrum. Repeat the phrase again if necessary, but don't do anything else. Your goal is to help her out of her predicament.

• Time the tantrums and count them. Though a tantrum may seem to last an eternity, it usually lasts only a few minutes and that time becomes shorter and shorter when you consistently ignore the outbursts. At first, they may get stronger until the child understands that they have lost their effectiveness. Keeping track of their duration and frequency will help you see the progress you and the child are making.

Ralph was a little boy who became an expert at having tantrums. His parents had a hard time ignoring his screams, but they managed to do it. Ralph would start fussing at the dinner table if he didn't get his way. His dad told him he would have to leave the table if he continued. He then sat Ralph on the floor in the next room while the family ate their meal. The first time this happened, the toddler screamed for five minutes and thirty-two seconds. Suddenly, he stopped and his parents called to him that his dinner was on the table. He came running back. Over the next few days, the scene replayed itself with little variations. The tantrums grew a little longer at first and then became shorter: seven minutes; four minutes and twelve seconds; five minutes; two minutes and fifty-seven seconds.

One day, Ralph had been having a tantrum for a few minutes and then suddenly stopped. He came running across the room with a sheepish grin on his face. He climbed up into his chair and touched his daddy's hand as if he were trying to make sure everything was okay and realized the tantrums weren't going to work anymore. Since then, if Ralph starts to have a tantrum and someone mentions time-out, he pulls himself together very quickly.

• When the tantrum ends, don't acknowledge it. Just welcome

the child back as though it never happened, quickly giving the child a way to get back into your good graces without mentioning the occurrence. When Jill stops crying, say, "Come on, let's go outside." Don't say, "Wasn't that silly? Now that you're acting like a big girl, I'll take you outside." Such a response only tells her that her tantrum had an effect on you, and may lead to another.

8.2-2 Give Persistent Tantrums Time-out.

If the tantrums continue until you feel you have no choice but to give in to the child's demands, then give yourself another option. Tell her it's fine if she wants to have a tantrum but that you are tired of hearing it. Place a toddler in a time-out seat in the room next to the one you are in, where she can't see you but you are close enough to monitor. An older child may be sent to her room instead, if you prefer. Tell her she must sit in time-out for x (years of age) minutes and may not get out of the chair until she has been quiet for thirty seconds.

8.2-3 Use Praise and a Reward System to Reinforce Cooperative Behavior.

Of course you must praise your child for not having a tantrum not by saying, "Thanks for not having a tantrum," but rather, "I really liked the way you listened to me and were so cooperative." Then give him attention when he is behaving nicely.

• Praise and teach alternative strategies. Teach your child the appropriate ways to get your attention and to express frustration. Role-play how you'd like her to behave: Perhaps she should tap you on the leg or say, "Mommy, I need you now," in a quiet voice. Then praise her when she does it properly. You will help her learn appropriate behavior, too, if you model it for her. She may learn to cope with frustrations by hearing you talk out your own solutions. You could say something like, "This won't fit! It must be the wrong part. Let me see if there is another part that will fit. Oh well, I can't find the part that fits. I guess I will just have to put it up for now and maybe I can fix it some other day." After a while, you may hear the child repeating similar words to herself instead of throwing the piece across the room.

• Give the child extra attention when he's not having a tantrum. As we've said before, "Catch the child being good." If you think he throws tantrums for attention, then be sure you give him plenty of attention when he's acting the way you want him to. Give him "instant" attention here and there during the day by commenting on what he's doing right. It will let him know his good behavior has been noted and appreciated. You might even keep a good-behavior diary to remind you and the child of these occurrences.

• Reward cooperation and good behavior. Some negative behaviors require a little extra push to change them. If your child has been using tantrums to get his way and your attention for years, then a reward system in addition to your new firm approach may help change the behavior more quickly. Rewards will provide a positive and formal way to declare yourself and, at the same time, make it worthwhile for the child to try a new approach too.

For example, you may tell your child that from now on you won't "hear" tantrums, but you will reward cooperation. He can earn points or stickers every time he accepts *no* without an argument or tantrum. Before you start, role-play this with him, with you playing the child and the child playing the parent who says no. The role-playing along with keeping score and rewarding improvement are often all that's needed to overcome this problem, especially in older children.

8.2-4 Don't Let the Child Use Tantrums to Avoid Responsibilities.

It's amazing how quickly a young child can learn that tantrums will distract his parents so much that they forget what it was they had asked him to do. Mom asks Brian to pick up his toys, and he stalls, "In just a minute, Mom." When she finally loses her cool and blows up, Brian throws a tantrum and is sent to his room to calm down. While he's in his room, Mom angrily picks up the toys.

When he comes out of solitary, he doesn't have to do his job, so he managed to get out of it after all.

To cope with this pattern:

• Give the child very clear signals about the task and the consequences of not doing it.

• Give fewer warnings before following through.

• After the consequences, time-out, or even overcorrection, have the child carry out the task.

Read Chapter 2 again for detailed information on giving clear signals, using time-out, and applying other consequences appropriately. As for Brian, his mother should first get his attention, maintain eye contact, and clearly tell him that she wants him to pick up his toys *now*. After waiting five seconds, she should then repeat the direction one more time. If Brian does not comply, she should send him to time-out for a specified length of time. If he has a tantrum, she should add one minute to the time-out for every minute the tantrum continues. At the end of the tantrum and the time-out, Brian must pick up the toys and *also* those in several other areas of the house.

A couple of repetitions of this pattern will undoubtedly convince this young boy that having tantrums won't get him out of any chores and, in fact, unless he cooperates he will be doing *extra* chores.

8.2-5 Don't Let Tantrums Change Your No to Yes.

Children learn from past experience that if they cry long enough or hard enough, they may get what they want. They learn this is especially true if Mom or Dad is tired, if there's company, or if the family is out in public. They find out that tantrums pay off, and they use that information. We're not saying that children consciously plan their misbehavior or even are aware that they are using it, but that you and they together become accomplices in this common pattern. They know when you are likely to give in—and so do you.

What is a parent to do? None of us can be consistent a hundred percent of the time. We can, however, start raising the odds to favor the "house" if we move toward greater consistency with the following considerations:

• Be aware when situations arise in which a tantrum response is likely to occur.

• Let the child know that you mean what you say and you will not change your mind. Tell the child that just because Aunt Mary is visiting, you won't change your no to yes, no matter what she does.

• Use an appropriate technique to deal with this negative behavior. Totally ignore what happens next after you say no. Even with a full-fledged tantrum, continue your conversation as best you can, or go about your work. Make his screams your resolve. This behavior is *not* what you want your child to do, so *don't give in to it*. Do not allow yourself to backslide.

If you can't bring yourself to totally ignore the tantrum, use the broken record technique. Warn the child only once that if he has a tantrum he will have to go to time-out and will not get the item or activity he wants for an even greater period of time. If he continues, then use time-out with *no more warnings*. (See Chapter 2 for a discussion of systematic ignoring and the other techniques; also see Section 8.7.)

8.2-6 Deal with Tantrums Where They Occur.

Most parents find tantrums hard enough to handle without a watching audience. However, the key to controlling the outbursts is to deal with the behavior where and when it occurs.

• Be realistic, and plan ahead. Don't put your child in a situation that you know will lead to problems. Most children will learn to endure a trip to the supermarket, but a full day of shopping in the mall might be more than they can take. Think about an experience before you take the child. How might you avoid problems? Can you take a toy to ward off boredom? Can you vary the situation? Get the child involved in what's going on. In the grocery store, he might help with the shopping chores. Refer to Section 5.5 (Wants, Wants, Wants) and Section 8.7 (Won't Take No for an Answer) for additional help.

• Time-out the tantrums immediately. Don't wait to deal with the behavior later. Suppose you are in the children's department of the store, shopping for clothes for your child. You have explained to Denny that you need to get his pants size and then you will be finished. He starts complaining, and soon the negative talk turns into negative behavior. You firmly tell him he must try on one pair of pants before you leave. You will wait for him to stop fussing. If you are really brave and made of steel, you could sit him down on the floor and wait right there, but it would be easier for you to take him to a remote corner or the dressing room for the time-out period. When the crying stops, try on the pants and continue on your way.

Sometimes, however, you will disturb the people around you so much that you can't consider allowing the behavior to continue publicly. Remove the child to a less public area. Suppose you are at a restaurant having dinner with the family and have already ordered your meals. Six-year-old Cynthia insists on playing with the salt and pepper shakers and then banging her fork on her plate. When you take the fork away and ask her to stop, she starts screaming. Say to her firmly, "Cynthia, it isn't fair to the people in the restaurant that you are disrupting their meal. If you continue the tantrum, you will have to do it in the restroom [or the car]."

If there's no improvement in Cynthia's behavior, take her by the hand and lead her to the restroom (or the car). Tell her she must stay there with you and not return to the restaurant until she stops. If she doesn't within a reasonable amount of time, you may have to prove you mean what you say by leaving without finishing the meal —even if there are other people with you. If you are the only adult and have other children with you, you may need to give them rainchecks. The next time you go to a restaurant, pointedly leave the one who had the tantrum home, telling her she must earn the right to go to a restaurant again.

If possible, stand your ground where you are. If you are in the check-out line at the supermarket and your child has a tantrum because you won't buy him gum, stand firm. Ignore the stares—you probably have the sympathy of many of the parents around you. Ignore the crying. Continue your business with the cashier and then leave with your head held high. Following through is the only way the child will learn that you really do mean what you say.

8.2-7 Try to Alleviate Situations That Prompt Tantrums.

There are times and situations when a child is likely to have a tantrum. If he's overtired or overstimulated, he may not be able to control his emotions very well—just like many adults. It is not always possible to prevent a temper tantrum, but it's helpful to be aware of the factors that may contribute to it and avoid them if possible.

• **Deal with the frustration directly.** Children vary greatly in their development of both gross and fine motor skills. If your child becomes very frustrated when she tries to accomplish a task or play with a toy that's too complicated for her, then it may be helpful to change the situation by varying the task to make it easier or by putting the toy away until she's more ready for it.

• **Intervene when necessary.** When you see a problem arising and you feel you can prevent it, offer your assistance. Show the child another way to turn the puzzle piece, another way to hold the scissors. Offer a few words to help diffuse a situation that's heading for rough times. Sometimes it's as simple as laying down the playing rules for two children who are having difficulty sharing or explaining how to play with a toy. Don't take over and don't do the task for the child, but do offer your help or suggest an alternative way of handling the situation.

• **Avoid fatigue or overstimulation.** Try to stop the activities before your little one is too exhausted or overexcited to cope well with his emotions. It's great fun when Uncle Jim comes over—for everyone but you. Little Bart is worn out by the time his favorite uncle leaves. He's overtired and wound up after being thrown into the air and roughhoused for the last hour and a half. Now you must settle him down before the tantrums start. Next time, explain the difficulties to Uncle Jim and set up the situation so he is a help and not a hindrance. Suggest that he play with Bart and then help wind him back down by reading a book to him or playing a quiet game before he leaves.

8.2-8 When All Else Fails.

If none of the above solutions eliminates or decreases your child's episodes of tantrums, then we suggest you seek professional help. It is possible that other underlying factors make it difficult for the child to control his emotional outbursts.

8.3 DESTROYS THINGS

We all enjoy giving our children material things, and in fact children today have more possessions than ever before in history, but we do want them to appreciate them. We don't want them to take their toys and other possessions for granted, no matter how much or how little they cost, and we certainly don't want them to destroy them. Neither do we enjoy seeing our own property damaged or assaulted.

There are many reasons for a child to destroy things. See if your child fits into any of these categories:

The active, impulsive child: The damage a child can cause is often quite accidental, the result of acting first and thinking later— or not at all. Some children have a way of creating a state of pandemonium because of their great energy (occasionally they suffer from an attention deficit disorder—check out Section 11.15). Though the damage is unintentional, you must deal with it.

The curious child: Like Kipling's elephant child, some children are extremely curious. They love to know how things work and what they are made of. They don't mean to destroy the object they are examining, but somehow it happens anyway.

The child who hasn't learned to handle emotions: Barbara throws her brush across the room because she can't get her hair "just right" or tears her blouse while yanking it off because the color is wrong. Anthony pushes over furniture because it gets in his way. Barbara and Anthony are venting their anger through destructive acts because they have not yet learned how to express themselves appropriately. Could they have picked up this habit from the adults in the family?

The unappreciative child: In our throwaway society, children often have so many possessions that they don't always realize their value. Kelly has fifteen dolls, and if she destroys one, she'll ask Grandpa for another. Samuel throws all his toys, and when one is broken, he says, "I didn't like that one anyway."

The retaliative child: There is the rare child who deliberately destroys objects in an attempt to "get even" or to make his presence and opinions known. One child with whom we worked cut off her own hair and destroyed some of her clothes to express her displeasure with her mother's new beau. Another made a habit of slashing furniture and smashing toys when he was frustrated. If your child is in the habit of deliberately destroying things, take it seriously, because sometimes it is indicative of more serious emotional problems.

Your tactics for changing a child's tendency to destroy things should vary according to the pattern of behavior.

8.3-1 Limit the Toys.

No matter how many toys your child has, try recycling them. A youngster can play with only so many at one time, and an impulsive child may be overstimulated by choices.

- Dispose of excess toys. Get rid of broken or useless toys or have them fixed and give them away. Better yet, teach the child the act of charity. Encourage him to select a few toys in good condition to give to an organization that distributes them to children who need them.

- Choose appropriate toys. Many toys, despite what the manufacturer says, will provide nothing but frustration for your child. Sometimes the toys are good but beyond the capabilities of the child; these should be saved until he is older or more able to use them properly. Others require instruction or supervision, which you must be willing to provide.

• Limit access to toys. Your child will value her toys more if you give her one or two of them at a time and have her return them to their proper storage place before getting others. This suggestion is especially helpful for children who have destroyed toys before. It requires supervision until the habit of returning the toys becomes established.

• Set playing rules. Children must be taught how to play with their toys and how to put them away so they won't get broken. All of us can think of times when a toy has been taken apart and left that way from that moment on, its appeal gone. Change the pattern of play, and be sure the child knows what the playing rules are at your house. If one of the rules is that he may play with one toy at a time, putting it away before taking another, spell it out clearly.

8.3-2 Slow Down the Overactive Child.

Use the techniques below, along with those described in Section 11.15, to slow down the overactive, impulsive child.

• Make certain areas of the house off limits. If you limit the overactive child's access to specific parts of the house, you will cut down on your monitoring duties and the child will have fewer choices to control.

• Place objects out of bounds. Remove enticing objects from your child's reach until he has been taught not to play with them, just as you would for a very young child. If necessary, use child-proof locks to keep your belongings safe.

• Reward the child for being careful. Praise him for walking slowly when he's in the house. Notice when he is trying to be careful and let him know you appreciate it. Post a chart that counts the days (or divide the days into time periods, if necessary) that your child doesn't break anything or knock things over. If he does continue to run through the house or destroy his or your possessions, apply the appropriate consequences, such as overcorrection.

8.3-3 Provide Alternative Playthings.

If your child is very curious and must learn how things work, help him put them together again or give him old items with your permission to disassemble them.

• Give him a project. There are many kits available to nurture a child's architectural and scientific interests. There are also hobby magazines and craft books that give instructions for building projects using common household materials. With the advice of the local hobby shop or woodworking store, along with the appropriate publications, help the child choose a project and the materials he needs. Then patiently help him get started or provide assistance if he needs it to complete the project.

• Be creative. Collect some old objects, such as clocks, vacuum cleaners, bicycles, that can safely be taken apart and need "just a little work." Keep these treasures in a special place and give the child permission to do what he wants with them. If, on the other hand, he disassembles or breaks other things, provide the appropriate consequence.

8.3-4 Teach Appropriate Ways to Express Emotion.

It's important for your child to know that it's okay to get angry but that it's not okay to respond in an unpleasant or antisocial manner. Encourage her to discuss her feelings with you and be sure you demonstrate to her, by your own actions, the appropriate way to express feelings. Label your feelings and your actions while you do it: "I am very angry. The dishwasher is broken again. The repairman was just here and charged us forty-five dollars and it still doesn't work. I'm going to call the repair service again. The woman who takes the calls didn't do anything wrong, so I'm going to think about what I will say and count to ten before I call."

• Teach the child to label feelings. When a child doesn't know how to express her feelings verbally, she may express them through actions. Help her learn to identify and label them. Section 2.9, on communication skills, offers many suggestions for this.

If the child is very young, you may have to verbalize for her what you think she's feeling. Let's assume your toddler is playing with her toys and can't get two pieces to fit together. She starts crying and throws the parts across the room. You may say, "No, Emily, we don't throw toys. You are frustrated because you couldn't do what you wanted. Bring them to me and I will show you how to do it." Or, "Emily, if you ask me to help you instead of crying and throwing things, I will be glad to do it." Then, of course, follow through. If she won't cooperate, then say, "I guess you're not ready for these toys, so I'll put them away for now."

• Role-play with older children. Help them identify their feelings and find appropriate ways to express them by playing out the roles together. For example, Jeremy has just come home from school very angry about the way his best friend "turned on him" in front of other children. He walks into the house and kicks his little brother's truck and breaks it. Calm him down and stage an instant replay of what happened. Discuss the alternatives, then give Jeremy the opportunity to replay the scene, expressing his anger in a nondestructive way. He might practice telling his friend that he's hurt and why. He might also replay the scene of coming into the house angry, labeling his feelings to you so he can elicit suggestions and use you as a sounding board.

• Use praise for labeling feelings and behaving appropriately. When your child expresses his frustration by saying, "I can't do it!" give him the appropriate word: "I'm glad you asked for help when you get frustrated. Let me see what you're doing. Maybe I can make a suggestion that will help you." Although you don't want to foster overdependence, a minor suggestion or a little support can ease the way.

• Teach anger control. Teach the child the relaxation techniques described in Chapter 2. When these have been learned, have her practice the mini-relaxation response as an alternative to anger when she's in a frustrating situation.

• Provide an "angry place." Some children—and some adults as well—must work off their anger or destructive feelings in a physi-

cal way. Provide a place for that to happen. Set up a punching bag
in the basement, or have pillows that may be used for a pillow
fight. When you see your child becoming angry or frustrated, you
might suggest he take a breather, walk out of the room, splash cold
water on his face, then come back.

8.3-5 Give Rewards for Caring for Toys.

Because you want your child to learn how to take care of objects,
it's always helpful to praise and reward such behavior.

• Use rewards. If your child has been destructive or careless
with material objects, now is the time to reward her when she does
treat things with respect. Make a chart to help you keep a record of
good behavior and reward her progress with natural consequences,
such as more playtime with· favorite toys or special outings with
you. If she doesn't break anything for one day, then two days, then
three days in a row, etc., let her see your appreciation and delight
by giving her little gifts or goodies.
• Let her earn access to toys. Give a destructive child access to
only very few of her toys at one time. As she learns to take care of
them, allow her to earn back the others, especially her favorites. Or
offer new toys if she is careful with her old ones, then let her earn
the right to play with them. Set up a chart, telling the child she will
earn a point after each play period that she plays with her toys
properly.

8.3-6 Use Consequences for Destructive Behavior.

If the child continues to be destructive, then you must go a step
further.

• Use time-out. If the child ignores your instructions to play
with one toy at a time or not to play with a specific toy, follow up
with time-out. Tell her, "You didn't listen to me when I told you
you may play with one toy at a time, so you must go to time-out
for three minutes." (The time should correlate with the child's age;

see Section 2.7.) Walk her to the time-out place. Tell her how long she must stay there and then time the session. When it's over, ask the child to pick up the toys and put them away properly before resuming her play.

• Time-out the toy. If a child can't play with a toy without harming it, let her know she's not ready to play with it and take it away for a specific length of time.

• Use overcorrection. If she has destroyed one of her possessions, have her glue the parts together if the item is salvageable, or clean up the broken parts and put them into the trash can. Have her practice cleaning up and straightening the toys, and in addition, tell her she must "earn" the cost of the broken object by doing a special chore. Be sure to supervise all of these steps.

8.3-7 Seek Professional Help.

If you detect a continuing pattern of destructive behavior or if the child's acts seem premeditated and/or dangerous, we strongly advise that you consult a professional (see Chapter 17).

8.4 NAME-CALLING AND CURSING

It's a rare child who doesn't name-call or use inappropriate words at least occasionally. Some children do it to express their independence, some when they are angry, while others do it for fun.

At about the age of three, words associated with bodily functions, such as *do-do* and *poopy,* creep into their conversation; then later, they progress to whatever names or words get the most attention.

In most cases, ignoring this behavior (and that means no laughing or smiling) will make it vanish before long. Bad words and names cross our minds and our lips occasionally. We have learned to control ourselves and that's what our children must learn, too. There are ways to discourage the use of inappropriate words and we will discuss them. Note, though, that we do *not* include washing a child's mouth out with soap. That age-old practice is dangerous, sometimes damaging to the lining of the esophagus or even the lungs. Besides, the soap does not wash the words out of a child's mind.

8.4-1 Be a Good Role Model.

From the very beginning, let your child know when he uses an unacceptable word. In the meantime, choose your own words wisely.

• Set a good example. Children emulate their parents, and so it's important that you behave in a way you'd like them to follow. If you curse, they will too—or they won't understand why they can't. If you explode with anger, you can't expect them to handle their feelings appropriately, either.

• Avoid name-calling. Don't label your child a *brat* or a *nerd* or anything else, because he will not only learn to call other people names, but he will also be encouraged to live up to or believe the title.

8.4-2 Don't Give Undue Attention to Name-calling or Cursing.

You may encourage this poor behavior by paying too much attention to it, so:

• Don't overreact. Tell the child firmly that you don't like him to use those words and that it is not okay for him to say them. But if you overreact, with either horror or amusement, you may motivate the child—especially a small one—to consider it a game to use words whose meaning he may not even understand.

• Ignore harmless words. Some words are just silly, and ignoring them is the best way to eradicate their use. More offensive words, of course, should not be ignored, because they will cause problems for the child outside of the household.

• Eliminate the shock value. When your child uses a "bad" word, don't yell, scream, or act shocked—you've surely heard the word before. If it is treated like forbidden fruit, the child may become even more attracted to it.

8.4-3 Teach Alternatives.

"Sticks and stones may break my bones, but names will never hurt me." That cliché has endured time and has helped many children deal with name-calling. Another way to help them is to prepare them for it so they will have a course of action and an alternative to resorting to the same tactic themselves.

• Discuss the word. Tell the child what the name or expression means and why it shouldn't be used to hurt another person's feelings. Many times the word itself is not bad, but the context makes its usage unacceptable.

• Suggest alternative strategies. Teach your child to express how he feels rather than giving somebody else a label. "Instead of calling Jess a buzzhead, tell him you're angry about how he embarrassed you in front of the other children."

• Role-play. A child of five or six is usually mature enough to act out name-calling with you, so you can encourage constructive responses. Teach him to ignore the names other children pin on him or, if that fails, how to use words to tell someone he doesn't like name-calling: "I won't play with you if you call me names."

• Encourage other words and other outlets. Your child needs an outlet for his feelings. Encourage him to express his feelings in sentences rather than damaging words, which will get him into trouble. Tell him it's okay to say those forbidden words in private only. Or silently. Help him pick a harmless word to say. One little boy we know made up his own nonsense word and trained himself to use it when he got mad.

• Praise appropriate speech. Tell your child how pleased you are when she uses constructive words to express her feelings. If Alyson is angry at Mark and, instead of calling him a name, says, "Mark, I am really mad at you. Give me back my toy or I will tell on you," let her know you are pleased with her language.

8.4-4 Apply Negative Consequences.

If swearing and name-calling can't be curtailed by the measures described above, then the following consequences may be applied:

• Time-out the child. If the child continually uses unacceptable words after you have told her not to, then use time-out (see Section 2.7). Make sure she understands that she will sit in time-out every time she name-calls or swears.

• Remove privileges. Take away a privilege if the practice continues, and give it back only when it stops.

• Have the child "pay back" for unacceptable behavior. Create a pay-back system as a consequence for continuing to use improper words. For example, you may fine him twenty-five cents out of his allowance every time he curses. Or instead of fining him money, fine him in time, perhaps the time it takes him to write a full page of sentences such as: "I promise not to swear anymore."

8.5 LYING

All of us stretch the truth at times, rationalizing our little white lies. But when one of our children tells a lie, we become very upset. Understanding the difference between truth and fiction is a difficult concept, and it takes time to develop.

Dr. Jean Piaget, the famous developmental psychologist, discovered that until about the age of four, preschoolers operate on the principle of pleasing their parents. Whatever pleases Mommy and Daddy is good; whatever upsets them is bad. If a little girl tells her mother that she just broke Mom's favorite vase, Mom will be unhappy. Since it's bad to make Mom unhappy, saying she didn't break it is the obvious solution. Similarly, it's natural for a child to look a parent straight in the face and declare she didn't get into the cookie jar, even though her face and hands are covered with crumbs.

That may be infuriating reasoning to contend with, but it takes time for a child to learn the difference between fact and fiction. Even first graders may not have mastered this ability. Dr. Arthur

Applebee, through interviews with eighty-eight children between the ages of six and nine, found that only 18.2 percent of the six-year-olds were clear about the distinction but that by the age of nine, all of the children knew that all stories are not true, and over 90 percent were sure that neither Cinderella nor giants are real.

As a child begins to distinguish between fact and fantasy, he is also learning that a lie is a lie even if you don't get caught or upset your parents. By about seven, the child feels bad about lying even when the lie goes undiscovered, though the reason isn't his values. He is concerned with crime and punishment and perhaps worries that God will punish him even if his parents don't. At eleven or twelve, he starts looking at the truth from a new perspective which, according to Piaget, reflects maturity and experience. At this age, the child develops the understanding that society is based on trust. The strong idealism of adolescence has its beginnings here.

Lying, then, means different things at different ages, and truthfulness must be treated as an evolving concept. Don't take it personally when your child lies. Instead, use the following solutions to teach him to be truthful at his level of understanding.

8.5-1 Teach the Child the Meaning of Truth.

Here are ways to help a small child of two, three, or even four learn to identify what is "pretend" and what is real.

• Use play situations. There are many opportunities during play to practice discriminating reality from fantasy. Perhaps a parent will playfully pretend to be a monster, and even though Daddy isn't wearing a costume, the child may be frightened and uncertain about what's real and what isn't. Use these occasions to talk about whether something could or couldn't really happen. Is Daddy a real monster? Do monsters exist or are they make-believe?

Real events and conversations can trigger discussion. Explain to the child that when you say he's so sweet you're going to eat him up, you're just pretending! If, however, he bites the baby, that is real and it hurts!

• Use TV programs, movies, and books to stimulate talk about the difference between fact and fiction. When you're watching television, especially cartoons and action shows, discuss whether what's going on could really happen. Why? Why not? Is the hero real or make-believe? Can people really fly? Could a cat blow up and then run away? What happens when a dog is really run over by a car?

When you read stories to your child, use this as another occasion to talk about make-believe and real life. Ask your librarian to suggest age-appropriate titles, and see the suggestions at the end of this section.

• Help the child distinguish between wishful thinking and reality. A mother recently overheard her little boy telling a friend he had a horse when, of course, he didn't. She talked this over with the child and helped him understand that though he sometimes rides ponies, he doesn't own a horse yet. She suggested he tell his friend he got carried away and then tell the story correctly. All children boast and brag when young. There is a discussion of this behavior in Section 13.10.

8.5-2 Be a Good Role Model.

Children are like video recorders—they take in everything they see and hear, then play it back later, especially when the role models are people they love. So as their parents, the people they emulate most, it's very important that you model truthful behavior for them.

If you take your child to the amusement park and lie about his age so he can get in free, he will definitely notice. He may even embarrass you by saying, "I am not three years old! I am four!" If, stopped by a policeman for passing a stop sign, you make up a lie to avoid getting a ticket, your child will wonder why you can tell a story and he can't.

As for the "little white lies" that are designed to save face or avoid hurting another person's feelings, this is a harder line to draw. With time, the child will learn the distinction between malicious lies and social amenities. Right now, avoid the problem by modeling appropriate behavior. Good manners, too, can be taught.

8.5-3 Don't Prompt Lying.

Parents often ask children about their misbehavior in a way that prompts them to lie. Little Tad is standing in the kitchen with a broken cookie jar and cookies all around him. His mother runs in, an angry look on her face, and asks, "Tad, did you climb up there and knock down the cookie jar?" He looks up innocently and says, "No." So he's in trouble for breaking the cookie jar *and* lying. Constant replays of this pattern of response can transform even the most truthful child into one who lies.

• Don't ask questions. Instead, tell the child what he did wrong. It would have been more helpful if Tad's mother had said, "I am really angry with you! You climbed up there and dropped the cookie jar!"

• Ignore denials of the obvious, and deal only with the original misbehavior. If the situation is not totally clear but you are fairly certain the child was responsible for a misdeed, don't ask questions. State what you think happened. If the vase is broken and you really don't believe it was the dog who did it, tell the child that you *believe* he did it.

8.5-4 Separate Penalties for Misbehavior and Lying.

No one ever talks about what happened to George Washington after he told the truth about the cherry tree. Explain to the child that you won't be as angry if she tells the truth. Say that lying will get her into twice the trouble. Then make sure this is the truth.

• Do not punish so severely that it's worth the risk of lying. If you punish your child too often or too severely, then she may get into the pattern of lying to avoid the punishment. She may dread the punishment so much that she's willing to take the chance on lying. We remember a boy who told us, "Things couldn't get much worse," so he lied and often he got away with it.

• Punish the action, then penalize for lying. Make the consequences for lying about a misdeed a separate punishment, and don't make it too severe. Clearly define a realistic consequence for the act, then add a penalty for lying. If the punishment for going into the cookie jar without permission is no cookies for the next day, then the punishment for lying about it should be an additional day without cookies—not a whole week. If a child is supposed to be going to a friend's house and instead goes somewhere else, an appropriate consequence may be staying inside after school for two days. The penalty for lying about where he was should be no more than the same number of days as the original restriction. If you hold to this pattern, the child will soon realize he will get into only half as much trouble if he tells the truth.

8.5-5 Reinforce Truthfullness.

Even more important than penalizing lies is remembering to reinforce the truth. You must promote the tendencies you value—in this case, truthful and honest behavior.

• Praise the truthful behavior. This is the simplest way to encourage honesty. Be sure to use praise in a way that's appropriate to the child's age (see Section 2.1). For instance, you confront your preschooler with the broken cookie jar. He pauses and then, instead of denying it as he has in the past, he says, "I'm sorry." Immediately tell him how great it is that he admitted the truth, then administer a penalty for breaking the jar.

• Make a truth book. Focus attention on your child's good behavior by using a special book to record all instances of honesty, reviewing the good deeds with the child every day. Tell other people, in the child's hearing, about them. For an older child, have him record them and reward him for accurate entries.

• Reward truthfulness with privileges and/or surprises. Use logical consequences, when possible, to reward truthfulness. If the child tells the truth about being at a certain place, tell him you will trust him to go other places. Continue this privilege as long as he returns on time and goes only to permitted places.

Give a lesser punishment to the child who voluntarily comes to you before he is caught for a misdeed and admits to it. Of course, don't let him use this to manipulate you. When a child has a history of telling lies, it is helpful to use rewards and charts to increase truthfulness. The first time Scott admits he left his math book at school, it's appropriate to reward his honesty by helping him find a solution for his predicament. As truthful behavior is established, praise and reward it less regularly. See sections 2.4 and 2.5 for details about rewards and charts.

8.5-6 Seek Professional Help for Persistent Serious Lying.

Children over the age of ten or eleven who consistently tell serious lies may be suffering from serious emotional problems. Some children can't differentiate between reality and fantasy. Others may be aware of their "stories," but do not feel remorseful or wrong. Some tell malicious lies or lies that seem designed to be detected. All of them need the attention of a professional. See Chapter 17 for information on seeking professional help.

BOOKS FOR CHILDREN AND PARENTS TO READ TOGETHER

Cohen, Miriam. *Liar Liar Pants on Fire!* New York: Greenwillow, 1985. This book is about a first grader, new to school, who lies to impress his classmates (K–3).

Levy, Elizabeth. *Lizzie Lies a Lot.* New York: Delacorte, 1976. Lizzie learns the hard way that people never trust liars (Gr. 3–5).

Ness, Evaline. *Sam, Bangs and Moonshine.* New York: Holt, Rinehart and Winston, 1966. Sam learns to draw a line between moonshine and reality (PS–2).

Sharmat, Marjorie Weinman. *A Big Fat Enormous Lie.* New York: E.P. Dutton, 1978. Lies turn into monsters, and a little boy finds the only way to make them disappear is to tell the truth.

8.6 DEMANDS EXCESSIVE ATTENTION

Everyone needs and loves attention, but some children want your attention constantly, like a puppy yapping at your heels. No matter how much attention you give them, they want more.

Why does this pattern evolve? Often, the child who's hungry for attention hasn't been getting enough from a parent. Knowing how much is enough is difficult to judge, but the child must feel that the parent will be there when he needs him, for the long term and on a regular, everyday basis.

Other children demand excessive attention because they are insecure and overly dependent. This dependency may be temporary; for example, it may occur because of a death, illness, divorce, a new sibling, or a problem in school or with friends. Or the dependency may be more permanent and, in this case, has usually been nurtured by the parents' compliance. If a parent responds instantaneously to a child's every whim, the child will quickly learn to expect such a response at all times. "Mommy, watch this!" "Daddy, play with me!" "Daddy, do this," "Mommy, do that." This child expects uninterrupted, unending, undivided attention. That is impossible and unhealthy to sustain.

The keys to coping with this problem successfully are *when* and *how* you give attention.

8.6-1 Give Plenty of Attention When the Child Is Not Demanding It.

If your child likes a lot of attention, give it when you are the one in control. Give it when she is not asking for it. Praise her and reinforce appropriate behavior (see Section 2.1) as often as you can.

• Give your child your time. Give each of your children your separate, undivided attention every day, even if only for a few minutes. Dinnertime and, especially, bedtime are usually good times for sharing, but it doesn't matter when it happens as long as your child knows you will be available consistently and regularly.

Making your attention part of his daily routine will give him security and something to look forward to.

• Give a raincheck. When you can't meet your child's reasonable needs, give her a raincheck. It could be a slip of paper on which you print, "This ticket is good for fifteen minutes of Mom's undivided attention." Tell the child exactly when you will be available for him to use it.

When a young child must wait for your attention, set the timer. When the timer rings, he knows it's his turn with you. While he waits, encourage him to make some plans for your special time together.

8.6-2 When the Child Continues to Demand Attention.

If you feel you have met your child's needs and that you've done all you can but your child still looks for excessive attention, then you must reevaluate your situation and use techniques to decrease her demands.

• Ignore the demands. Refer to Section 2.2 and apply the systematic ignoring technique. Suppose you've just picked up little Sara at school. You have spent time with her and now you are talking with your other child. Sara interrupts, demanding that you listen only to her. Ignore her requests. When she stops whining, crying, begging, and behaves appropriately, give her some attention: "Hey, Sara, I like what you're drawing. Did you learn that at school?" You have begun to teach her that she must wait her turn but that you are interested in her and what she does. Refer to Section 8.9, on interrupting, for more information on this special situation.

• Use the broken record technique. If ignoring is not your style, give yourself another out. You've been playing with Sally all afternoon, and now you want to read the newspaper before starting dinner. You tell Sally to draw some pictures while you read, but every minute, she wants you to look. Tell her you want to see her pictures when you've finished reading. From that moment on, put your feet up, continue to read, and don't look at her at all. Each time she asks you to look, say the same words: "I will look when I've finished reading." Don't change your response, no matter how many times she demands your attention. When you have finished reading, then turn to Sally and say, "Now I have finished reading, let me see your pictures." See Section 2.3 for more about this technique.

8.6-3 Help Your Child Develop Independence and Assurance.

If your child is insecure or needs to learn to operate independently:

• Shape and reinforce independence. If your child has been clamoring at you, praise him for letting you finish your task or waiting his turn. Tell him you will be reading for five minutes and to save his questions for that time. When you are ready, reward him with your interest. Use a timer to let him know how long he must wait for attention. Begin with just a few minutes' lag time, each time increasing the minutes, so he learns how to wait.

• Set up a chart and rewards. Choose an activity or a time of the day during which your child normally requires a lot of attention, for example, when you are preparing dinner. Give him a choice of activities, then tell him he can earn points for playing alone. The points can accumulate to buy some special time with you, like going to a movie, playing a favorite game, or shooting baskets. See sections 2.4 and 2.5 for more information on using charts and rewards.

• Build self-image. Keep a good-behavior diary and write down the child's good behaviors during the day. Praise him and later, in his presence, tell the rest of the family about them.

• Involve the child in activities. Get the child involved in activities that don't require help from other members of the family. Find something that she can excel in by herself, like ballet, sports, acting, or art.

• Increase your awareness of contributing problems. Sometimes the child needs your attention because he's worried or fearful. Lis-

ten to what he's really trying to tell you. See Section 6.6, on clinging, and refer to Chapter 14 on specific fears.

8.6-4 Respond to Reactions.

You need to take a special approach if the child's demands for
excessive attention are the result of a traumatic event.

• Don't overreact. Give the child the attention he needs, but
don't try to overcompensate for the disturbing events. The hunger
for extra attention usually passes, given a little time.

• Bring out the child's feelings. If something unusual is about to
occur or has happened in the child's life, try to let him know what
to expect. Prepare him for what will occur and when. Information
often alleviates insecurity. Give him the opportunity to talk about
his feelings, worries, jealousies, happiness, sadness (see Section
2.9).

• Use relaxation techniques. Reread Section 2.10, and use the
techniques described there with your child. Help her to be in tune
with herself, rather than dependent on you.

BOOKS FOR PARENTS AND CHILDREN
   Spizman, Robyn Freedman. *Lollipop, Grapes and Clothespin
Critters: Quick On-the-Spot Remedies for Restless Children 2–10*.
Reading, Mass.: Addison-Wesley, 1985. Hundreds of parent-
and-child-tested solutions for keeping children entertained in a
variety of situations.

8.7 WON'T TAKE NO FOR AN ANSWER

No matter that you've said no ten times. If your child *knows* that
eventually you will say yes, he will play the tune over and over, like
Chinese water torture, getting to you with tantrums, relentless nagging or whining—until you give in and give up. He's learned
through experience that if he keeps it up, it will pay off—probably
with surer odds than in Las Vegas. Eventually.

The only solution for this problem is that both you and your child must learn that you *mean* what you say. If her refusal to take no for an answer has become a permanent pattern, we strongly suggest you look at your previous interactions and make a real effort to change them as soon as possible. This annoying habit can turn into a serious problem in adolescence, but no matter what age your child is, begin working toward its resolution now.

8.7-1 Think Before You Speak.

Don't automatically say no to your child's requests. How often do you say no when you may mean maybe later? Better to think about your answer first and keep your nos to a minimum. Use no only when that's what you really intend. This doesn't mean you must always say yes, but rather that you should become aware of how often you tend to refuse legitimate requests without really considering them. When your child makes a demand, pause, think, then confirm the answer in your own mind before responding. If necessary, say, "Let me think about it for a minute." Once you do decide, however, clearly say what you mean, and don't change your mind.

8.7-2 Don't Offer Opportunities for Doubt.

These solutions will help you eliminate the clamoring for a change of heart:

• Don't answer with a question. "Mom, can I have an ice cream cone?" "Now, Billy, don't you think it's too close to dinner?" You are *asking* for it! Never ask. Answer! Yes or no.

• Don't offer justification. This is not the time for a debate. Avoid arguments by not setting yourself up for a discussion. Give a simple answer and don't try to explain it, or the child may try to combat your reasons one by one.

8.7-3 Show That You Mean What You Say.

Try these ideas if your child still won't take no for an answer.

• Use systematic ignoring. After you have given your answer, allow no discussion, no debate, no nothing. Just silence. Ignore responses, whys, tantrums, nagging, or whatever else is in the child's arsenal. After many months or years of success at getting you to give in, that may be a lot. Stand firm and close your ears. It will work. (See Section 2.2.)

• Apply the broken record technique. If you are unable to ignore the wheedling, reread Section 2.3, on how to use this invaluable technique. Suppose you have said "No, Sylvia, I'm not going to buy Too Sweets for breakfast," and Sylvia continues to ask for them. Simply repeat the same words in the same tone every time she asks. "No cereal, Sylvia." "No cereal, Sylvia."

• One, two, three, you're out! Explain that just like in baseball, the batter gets three tries and then he's out. The first time your child won't take no for an answer, it's strike one. The second time, it's strike two, and the only warning. The third time, it's three strikes and you're out—and into time-out. "Sorry, Timmy. I told you no cookies before dinner. If you are going to fuss, you will have to do your crying in time-out." Place him in the time-out spot and tell him when he may come out: "Timmy, when you stop whining, you may come back to the kitchen to play." (Refer to Section 2.7 for details about time-out.)

• Loss of privilege. For the older child, the loss of a privilege may be an effective tool. For example: "Jeremy, I've told you that you may not go to Carl's house now. Because you have argued about it, you may not watch the movie tonight." Or apply a natural consequence: "You may not go to Carl's house tomorrow either, because of your arguing."

8.7-4 Reinforce Cooperation.

When the child accepts no for an answer, be sure to reinforce his efforts.

• Keep a diary. Praise him promptly when he is cooperative and, in addition, mark the occurrence in a good-listening diary. At the end of the day, review the diary with your child and let him know how well he is doing.

• Give tokens or points on a chart. Every time the child takes no for an answer, let him earn a token or a point. At first, give him a surprise for two points, then for three points, gradually increasing the number of points required to earn a reward. In between, surprise him occasionally, when he doesn't expect it.

• Use natural consequences. Joey asks you for a cookie. He listens and understands when you say no. A few minutes later, reward him by saying, "Joey, I really liked the way you listened to me. You may have a cookie after lunch." Suppose you tell Joey he may not play outside because you are preparing to go shopping. He says pleasantly, "Okay, Mommy." You might reply, "Joey, I'm going to try to get home early enough so you'll have time to play later. You were such a big boy now, when you listened to me so well."

8.8 INTERRUPTING

There's one major reason why children interrupt. They want your attention *now*. Like most other behaviors, interrupting is a habit children learn to use because it works. You probably don't like it, but do you perpetuate it by allowing it? You are on the telephone. It's an important call and your child interrupts, demanding some apple juice, asking if Theo may spend the night tomorrow, or wanting to go next door. You mouth *Wait*, but he keeps asking, his voice turning into a whine, and finally you ask your caller to hold on for a minute while you listen to the child.

Interrupting is annoying and exasperating, but it can be cured. The hardest part of the cure is keeping your cool during the learning period. It will put your patience to the test, but if you prepare yourself, you will be up to the challenge. What you must do is show the child the right way to get your attention, the right times to get it, and how to wait for it.

8.8-1 Always Acknowledge the Attempt to Get Your Attention.

Don't let your child feel you are not interested in his needs. You are interested, but you simply can't attend to them at this moment.

• Respond promptly if you can. Always respond to your child's needs immediately when possible. Don't make him wait any longer than necessary, and don't ignore his appropriate attempts to get your attention.

• Give a signal. When you can't respond immediately, let her know you see or hear her. Arrange a signal that indicates your recognition, such as holding up a finger or saying, "Just one more minute." If you say, "Just one more minute," however, make sure you don't keep the child waiting ten minutes. From the time the child begins to understand language, teach her that you will answer as quickly as possible. You are, in effect, building her trust. At first, pair the gesture with words so that the gesture alone will then have meaning for her.

• Praise the child for waiting. Thank your youngster for waiting for you to finish what you are doing. Thank her for her patience, and then give her your full attention.

8.8-2 Teach the Child How to Interrupt Appropriately.

Everyone must cultivate the skill of asking for attention or help in an acceptable manner. So don't expect your child to know how to do it without your instruction.

• Teach her to say, "Excuse me." Explain to her that she should say, "Excuse me," or use another acceptable means of getting your attention and then to wait quietly for your response. Remember, however, that emergencies do arise and the child should feel free to let you know immediately in that case.

• Apply the whisper rule. This is a great technique if your child has a tendency to need you whenever you are on the telephone or conversing with someone else. Teach him to whisper his, "Excuse me," because you don't want other people to hear him asking loudly.

• Role-play. Whenever you have the opportunity, act out scenarios, teaching the child to use appropriate cues and to respond to your signal. You can also role-play inappropriate behavior, playing the annoying interrupter yourself and letting the child see how that feels. Discuss other ways you might behave, and replay the scene using the suggestions.

• Be a good role model. Practice what you preach, and that will be the best lesson of all.

8.8-3 Shape the Child's Waiting Behavior.

Waiting is a learned skill. If your child is accustomed to your immediate attention when he interrupts, you must shape his new behavior.

• Always give an acknowledgment. Use the signal that lets your child know you see or hear her.

• At first, be sure the child waits only a few seconds. Your goal is to control the situation. Do this in the beginning by giving the signal, waiting a few seconds, then interrupting your conversation or task to respond. Gradually lengthen the time between signal and response. And be sure to praise the child for waiting.

• Use a timer. Sometimes you are in the middle of a task, not a conversation, and the child may have to wait longer than a few seconds or minutes because she requires assistance rather than a verbal response. In that case, use the timer as a signal for how long she must wait. "Sally, I must finish what I'm doing. It will be only a few minutes. When the bell rings, I'll be finished." Set the timer yourself or let the child set it for a certain length of time and watch it tick away. But when the bell rings, be sure to carry out your part of the deal.

• Provide an alternative during his waiting time. Waiting can feel like forever to a child, so when he does have to wait for you, give him an activity to keep him busy. If you know you will be talking on the telephone for a while or you are going to be too busy to be interrupted, plan ahead. Let the child play at the sink with your supervision. Let him tear up lettuce for the salad or wash the dishes. Keep a toy telephone or another special toy on hand and bring it out when you are busy. Have stickers or art materials on hand so they will be readily available when you need them most. At the same time that you are saving yourself from interruption, you are teaching him how to entertain himself.

• Be realistic about the waiting time. Don't keep a child waiting too long. Time may fly when you're having a conversation at the supermarket, but it's hard for a child to wait patiently. If he acts up after a while, remember that you have precipitated his misbehavior.

• Reward the child's patience. When your youngster waits patiently even though he desperately wants your attention, reward him with something that's right at your fingertips. A glass of juice, a piece of fruit, or perhaps an interesting pot from your kitchen cabinet will keep him occupied while reinforcing his cooperation.

8.8-4 Use Systematic Ignoring.

Once the child knows how to get your attention and how to wait, stop responding to inappropriate attempts to interrupt you. Ignore them. Respond to her only when she uses the approach she has been taught. You may prompt her at first: "Jeannie, say, 'Excuse me,' and then wait till I respond." Later, phase out the prompts and respond only to correct attempts. Don't try systematic ignoring unless you can stay with it without giving in. Try it during "test calls" with your friends and be ready to be "embarrassed" if the child's requests turn into demands. If you can maintain your ignoring, the demands will probably increase first and then taper off.

CHAPTER 9

Health-Related Problems

LEARNING the value of taking care of oneself requires time to develop, but parents can't wait until their children appreciate the need. They must teach them skills like brushing their teeth, taking a bath, swallowing pills, and eating healthy foods. This chapter is devoted to solutions designed to help your child develop a healthy lifestyle.

9.1 RESISTS TAKING A BATH/WON'T WASH HAIR

For some children, a bath is the highlight of their day. For others —and as a result, their parents—it's often sheer misery. Small children may dislike baths and hair washing because they're afraid of getting soap in their eyes or slipping down the drain. Older children sometimes think they don't need washing or don't want their other activities to be interrupted. Whatever the reasons, you can help your child enjoy bathing or, at the least, get him to agree to it without a hassle.

9.1-1 Make Bathing Pleasant.

Cold hands, cold air, and a nervous or rushed parent don't make a little child feel secure in the bath. Try to make a bath an enjoyable occasion and a normal part of the day's events. (Caution: Always supervise a child in the bath. Never leave a small child in the tub alone, even for a moment.)

• Relax and enjoy. Most pediatricians will tell you that infants don't need a bath every day. But they do need a loving, relaxed time with Mom or Dad or someone else who loves them. The bath can be one of those occasions, at the same time establishing the importance and eminence of cleanliness in the household. Bathing is an activity everyone does regularly. Period.

• Make the child feel secure. If you're not sure how to bathe your new baby, take the bath class many hospitals offer for new parents. Practice on a doll. Get some experience and a few suggestions from an old pro, and before you know it, you will be one yourself. If you feel confident, both you and the baby will be more secure at bathtime. Calmly sing to the baby. Talk to him. Encourage him to splash and play. Have a good time.

• Ensure his safety and comfort. Babies usually feel more secure in a small tub or sink for their first baths. Line it with a towel and hold the baby facing you as you sponge him with the other hand. Always test the water temperature before putting the baby in the tub. Make sure the room is warm. Use nonstinging soaps and shampoos and a soft cloth or mitt. Safety-proof the faucets so the baby can't turn them on. And finish the task with a large dry towel.

• Identify preferences. Sometimes identifying a special preference is a simple way to change a child's attitude toward bathing. If your child likes to help wash himself, let him. Give him his favorite tub toys, and be very careful about getting soap in his eyes. Set the temperature to his liking. Fill the tub to the depth he prefers. In other words, let him have a say in the routine so that a bath won't be an unending power struggle.

9.1-2 Build Independence.

As soon as your child can safely sit alone in the tub, it's time to start the move toward independence. Praise and reinforce the child's efforts to do the job himself.

• Make it fun. Make the bath a time for play and laughter, not grim determination to remove dirt. Let the child choose a special tub toy. Give him clean empty squeeze bottles to play with, marked with a smily face or his name to distinguish them from household cleaning bottles. Sing songs, play games. At the same time, teach him how to wash himself, and hold inspections when he's finished. If he's old enough, let him help with hair washing, perhaps pouring the shampoo while you scrub. Make getting water in his face part of the fun. That will also help prepare him for learning to swim later.

• Respect her growing independence and sense of self. Young children must learn about private body parts. When your child is old enough, teach her to wash these special places as a normal part of the routine. Respect an older child's privacy if it's important to her, and let the same-sex parent assist with hair washing. In single-parent families, let the child wear a swimsuit during learning sessions.

• Let the child become responsible for getting the job done. When you can, encourage her to take over the responsibility for washing herself. With a toddler, sit near the tub and chat or read. Although definitely not reliable before four or five, there is no clear-cut age when a child is automatically tub-safe. Judge your child by his sitting skills, coordination, and caution. When you believe the child is tub-safe, leave for a few minutes, but stay within listening distance. Later you can remove yourself entirely and come in just to check.

Teach the child the difference between clean and dirty. Young or older, children just don't notice dirt the way their parents do. Use finger-paint soaps to show a child how to notice smudges. Later, hold lighthearted inspections.

9.1-3 Shape an Independent Routine.

Children often dislike bathing when it interrupts a preferred activity, and sometimes they learn there are ways to avoid the task altogether. If you make bathing a routine unquestionable activity in your house, the child will learn that the job can't be put off even if she puts up a real struggle.

• Make the bath a rule. Your child will have no choice if you make bathing and frequent hair washing a household routine that can't be altered by stalling or arguing.

• Set a schedule. Plan bath time at a convenient time of the day, so it doesn't interfere with other activities and yet is part of the schedule. Once that time has been agreed upon, then that's it. There will be no television, no phone calls, no playing—it's time for a bath. If the time must be altered, make the change in advance before you begin the routine.

• Use a timer. Let the child estimate how long it will take to wash thoroughly, and set the timer accordingly. Little ones are usually amazed how brief the time is. For older kids who think cleanliness approaches godliness, that's long enough to get clean but not so long that the water meter runs to exhaustion or your preteen emerges soggy and wrinkly.

9.1-4 Apply Consequences.

• Praise and reward cooperation. Tell your child what a good job she's done in the tub. Let her know how sparkling clean she is and how good she smells. Let her choose her own bath accessories and toys.

• Chart and reward good bathing habits. If getting your child to take a bath has always been a battle, then set up a new system. Define the times and the criteria for a proper bath and design a chart for the expected new behavior, letting an older child help make the decisions. Natural reinforcers include television and playtime after the bath, but sometimes more powerful rewards are needed. See Chapter 2 for details.

• Apply negative consequences if necessary. Be careful that new arguments and games don't replace the old ones. If the positive consequences don't work in your case, have a serious talk with your child and explain that you may have to take negative measures if he doesn't shape up. If he won't take a bath or wash his hair at the agreed upon time, his privileges may be lost for the evening. "Fine, if you don't want to take a bath before dinner, then no dessert." Or, "I'm sorry you don't want to take a bath. The television stays off until you do." Then stick to your guns.

SUGGESTED BOOKS FOR CHILDREN

McPhail, David. *Andrew's Bath.* Boston: Little, Brown, 1984. A picture book about a little boy who turns his hated bath into fantasy time (Ps–2).

Yolen, Jane. *No Bath Tonight.* New York: Crowell Harper and Row, 1978. A little boy changes his mind about bathtubs, with Grandma's help (K–3).

9.2 RESISTS TAKING MEDICINE

Taking medicine isn't always a pleasant experience, but it is often a necessary one. Many parents become very upset and frightened when their child spits his medicine out, gags, shuts his mouth tight, refuses to take it ever again, or throws himself on the floor screaming and kicking. And why not? This has become a trauma for everyone concerned. To avoid hassles and build a healthy respect for medication, we offer this advice.

9.2-1 Show a Positive Attitude.

Don't make apologies for having to give your youngster medicine, and don't let her know you think it's distasteful. Be positive, as if it's all part of a day's necessary routines.

• Be matter-of-fact. As far as your child knows, it's never entered your mind that she won't cooperate. When it comes to taking needed medication, you mean business and there is no choice and no problem.

• Don't pass the blame. Don't tell the child you're sorry you must be the bad guy, and don't threaten to call the doctor if he refuses to take his medicine. Use the team approach, telling him you and the doctor want him to get well and that's why he must take the medicine.

9.2-2 Make It as Easy as Possible for Both of You.

There are many ways to make the task easier and still preserve the benefits of the medication. Some drugs come in caplet, liquid, or chewable form, and you can choose the one your child copes with best. We strongly recommend that you always talk to your child's doctor when drugs are prescribed. Ask for the best way to administer the specific medication.

• If approved by your physician or pharmacist, combine medicine with something the child readily accepts. Mix a liquid medicine with a small amount of another liquid, such as milk or juice. Don't put it into a whole cup or bottle because if the child doesn't finish all of it, he won't get the proper dosage of the drug. A tablet may be crushed and mixed in a spoonful of pudding, applesauce, or jam. Don't, however, pass the medicine off as candy.

If your child has difficulty swallowing pills, see Section 9.4 for helpful hints on overcoming this problem. At some point in his life, the child must learn to take his medicine undisguised, so it won't help him to mask it perpetually.

• Try different methods. Consult your doctor or pharmacist about dosage spoons that may help you give the child his medicine. Or try an eyedropper or needleless syringe to squirt a liquid medicine into the side of an infant's mouth.

• Plan ahead. Eye drops and eardrops, among other medications, may require some strategy. Try this technique an eye specialist taught us: Have the child lie down and close his eyes. Place the drops in the inner corner of the closed eyes. When the child opens his eyes, the drops will migrate to the cornea. A six- or seven-year-old can learn to do this task himself.

When you must give eardrops, let the child focus his attention on the television screen or a story while you get the job done.

9.2-3 Explain What You Are Doing.

Even a toddler knows when she's not feeling well. Tell her about germs and the fact that medicine contains "brave little fighters" that will attack the bad germs. Let her know the medicine is necessary right now, and tell her how long she must take it.

• Be firm. Explain your action and then promptly administer the medicine without apologies or excessive sympathy. When you can, follow up with a "chaser," such as a glass of juice.

• Set the time period for medicine taking. Using a calendar, start a countdown. Mark the number of days the child will have to take the medication. Every time she takes it, she earns a star and moves closer to the end of the prescription period.

• Use a signal. Set a timer or an alarm clock to go off when it's time for taking the medicine. This way, the timer is the bad guy, not you.

9.2-4 Reinforce Cooperation.

Reinforce the child for taking the medicine and then for taking it pleasantly. Make the older child who takes it on his own feel good about it, too.

• Use natural reinforcers. Give the child a follow-up treat or chaser for being cooperative. Using the calendar approach, let the child earn other rewards, with the long-term goal of getting him to be cooperative and/or to take the medicine himself. The stars can accumulate toward the purchase of a reward.

9.3 WON'T WEAR EYEGLASSES

Many children think getting eyeglasses is really special, but others hate them or find them a bore. Your job as a parent is to help your child recognize that glasses, if he needs them, will help him see the world better.

According to the National Society to Prevent Blindness, an estimated one out of every four school-age children and one out of every twenty preschoolers has a vision problem. A child's eyes should be examined after birth and again by the age of four, with periodic examinations after that. During the growing years, a child's visual needs may change as often as every six months.

Many problems arise when a child who requires glasses doesn't want to wear them. He may tend to lose them, break them, or constantly take them off, but the bottom line must be that there is no choice. Wherever he goes, whatever he does, the glasses must safely go along with him. This is an enormous responsibility for a young child, so you must teach him the importance of wearing the glasses, motivate him positively, and then reinforce him for doing it.

9.3-1 Awareness Training.

The first step is to encourage a positive experience for the child with special vision needs, because he must have your support and encouragement. Recognize, too, how your child feels about these encumbrances. It's important for her to feel good about herself in glasses.

• Build a positive image. Make a special event out of having the glasses fitted. Point out people she knows and likes, real or on television, who wear them. Make her feel like a big girl for wearing them, and let her choose a special outing to show off her new addition. Encourage her by arranging playtime with another child who has glasses or a patch.

• Reinforce the experience with books. Many books have been

written about children's experiences with glasses. They can be very helpful. See the list of suggestions at the end of this section.

• Involve the child in choosing the glasses. If your child is old enough, let her help you pick them out, perhaps narrowing the possibilities down to an acceptable selection first. If she likes them, she will be more willing to wear them.

• Explore your options. Make yourself aware of the many styles and accessories available. Some eyeglasses are made with a loop that goes around the child's ear to help keep them on. You can buy a strap that fits around her head and holds the glasses, an accessory that is most helpful with a small child who tries to pull them off. There are also plastic lenses, which may be safer during sports or play. Investigate the possibility of contact lenses for now or the future. Educate yourself to the options before making a decision.

9.3-2 Teach the Child to Deal with Glasses.

• Prepare her for teasing. Give her suggestions for dealing with the inevitable taunts about glasses. Role-play the situation and think up rejoinders. Tell her about famous people who also wore glasses so she has role models to use as examples when needed.

• Create a support system. Talk to her teacher and discuss any special needs your child may have. For example, it may help for her to sit closer to the blackboard. Sometimes, a teacher's help in coping with teasing schoolmates is useful. Especially with younger eyeglass wearers, she can pave the way with peers with class discussions or by reading appropriate books to the class or inviting an eye specialist to speak.

9.3-3 Use Reinforcement.

Until the child realizes that he sees better with his glasses and therefore wants to wear them, you must start building a "positive dependency."

• Praise the child. Let him know how great it is that he wears his glasses so graciously (see Section 2.1).

• Reinforce his relationship with the doctor. Choose an eye doctor who can relate positively with the child and will make him feel good that he's doing what he suggests. Perhaps the doctor can be the speaker for the child's class. Encourage the child to send notes or pictures to the doctor to cement the bond.

• Reinforce with a chart. Develop a chart so the child may earn points each time he wears his glasses in the correct manner. That may mean wearing them when reading, for seeing the blackboard at school, while watching television, or always. A small child could earn stickers and wear them as badges or stick them to the chart. Another child saved his eye patches, using them on pirate drawings, reinforcing his cooperation.

If the child goes to school, you might send a stack of cards or paper slips for the teacher to send home: "Dear Mom, Timmy wore his glasses today and did a great job." Collect the cards, and when the child has a specific number of them, he can earn a treat.

• Apply natural consequences. If the child wears his glasses every day for a week or for a specific number of days, let him go on a special outing, perhaps to a movie on the weekend. Or give him a new book to read.

SUGGESTED BOOKS FOR CHILDREN AND PARENTS

Keller, Holly. *Cromwell's Glasses.* New York: Greenwillow Books, 1982. Cromwell the rabbit improves his vision with glasses and learns how to respond to teasing (K–3).

Leggett, Linda Rogers and Linda Gambee Andrews. *The Rose-Colored Glasses.* New York: Human Sciences Press, 1979. Melanie adjusts to her new glasses and enjoys better vision.

Wolff, Angelika. *Mom, I Need Glasses.* New York: Lion Press, 1970. Susan reads an eye chart, gets fitted for lenses, and learns about eyes (K–3).

9.4 CAN'T SWALLOW PILLS

All children must learn to swallow pills eventually, because most adult medications come in this form. Infants and toddlers get their medicine in liquid or chewable-tablet form, but older children are often expected to be able to handle a pill without trauma. No one is born knowing how to swallow pills, although some children do it more easily. Many times, the first occasion for taking a pill comes with an illness. If this is a particularly frightening experience, it can spell trouble for a long time. Here are some steps to prepare your child for this skill.

9.4-1 Teach the Child How to Do It.

Here's a logical sequence of events leading up to one pill "down the hatch."

• Be a role model. First, explain that pills are not candy and must never be taken without permission. Then let the child watch you take a pill:

"I'm putting the tablet on the middle of my tongue. See where it is?"

"Now I'm going to drink to wash the pill down. Oops! It didn't go down right away. I'll take another drink. All gone!"

• Have the child mimic you. Ask him to imagine taking the pill and then to pretend he's doing it. Have him point to where the pill goes on his tongue and then take a big slurp, pretending the pill is like Pinocchio being washed down into the whale's stomach.

• Practice. Now let him practice swallowing a tiny piece of cooked carrot or bread, a pea, or little piece of candy, making sure it's even smaller than the real pill he must take. Gradually work your way to a piece of food the size of the pill, encouraging him every step of the way. Some children require more practice than others.

• Try a pill-taking device, if necessary. Ask your doctor if you should get such a device, which is usually available in pharmacies, to help the child learn to swallow pills. Remember to use a piece of food no larger than a real pill.

• Practice on a chewable vitamin. Break the vitamin tablet in small pieces and ask the child to swallow them one by one. Then the next time he has a headache, break the chewable baby medication—baby aspirin or acetaminophen—into pieces and let him swallow each piece separately. You may be surprised by how well this may work.

9.5 FINICKY EATER

It's not easy to watch a child push food around his plate after you have prepared a good meal. All parents want their youngsters to eat healthily, and worry when they think they are not getting the proper nutrition. But remember that it is perfectly normal for a child's appetite to fluctuate from day to day, or month to month, and that some children are always finicky about their food. Many youngsters are so picky that they'll eat only the same foods over and over, while others who have been eating well suddenly get fussy.

Pediatricians will tell you that you can relax about day-to-day eating habits as long as the child's growth pattern is appropriate. Discuss your concerns with the child's doctor, who has kept information about the child's height and weight since birth. Plotted on a growth chart, this will let you see whether he is growing normally.

Though it's not wise to ignore what your child eats—or doesn't eat—it's also not wise to be too strict, because that leaves you open to the development of a power struggle.

Try recording your child's intake for two weeks, including all meals and snacks. Record the time as well as what he eats, including meals and snacks. Find out for yourself if he is consuming a well-balanced diet. Read about good nutrition, and ask your doctor for advice about what the child should be eating. You may be surprised to find his overall diet is fairly well balanced, and a vitamin tablet a day may be all that's needed to put you at ease.

The following solutions are ways to minimize the hassles that accompany mealtime in many households.

9.5-1 Limit the Snacks.

If you are concerned about what your child is *not* eating at mealtimes, look at your diary. You have probably given him special treats between meals to compensate for his skimpy appetite. Even though you may have given him healthy snacks such as peanut butter, nuts, fruit, carrots, raisins, and cheese, they may have become the major source of calories and it is not surprising that he's not hungry at dinnertime.

Try eliminating or restricting intake between meals. Cut back gradually, substituting less filling snacks, then giving fewer of them. Deal with complaints by using systematic ignoring and/or the broken record technique.

9.5-2 Make Mealtime Fun.

Meals should be a special family occasion, not a battleground. Refer to Section 3.5 if breakfast is the meal that interests your child least.

• Involve the child. Include your finicky eater in preparing the food. Let him help you shop, set the table, or help cook, so the meal will be more enticing. Four-year-old Jason never touched a green vegetable until he was given the chance to help Mom snap and prepare the beans. He was so proud of his part in making dinner that he made sure everybody else took small portions and left a lot of beans for him.

• Be a good role model. Here is one situation when you can set a good example for your child. Eat healthy foods and balanced meals, and everyone will benefit.

• Limit choices. Don't ask a child if he wants a vegetable. Instead, ask him if he wants spinach or squash. Give him fewer chances to say no.

• Add variety and appeal to meals. Both children and adults like food that is attractive and appetizing. One mother put an end to finickiness by making fancy vegetable flowers that her child loved to devour. Another put surprise stickers under her daughter's dish, to be seen only when the child cleaned her plate. Don't overload the child's plate, and arrange the food attractively. Think about color and presentation, as well as the mix of flavors. Milk doesn't taste great after grapefruit, for example.

9.5-3 Pay No Attention.

Very often, a child's resistance to food is maintained by the pressure and attention she gets for *not* eating. It's quite possible you can reverse this by systematically avoiding all references to food and eating for several weeks. Give the child small portions, and make no comments about what she eats or doesn't eat. If she eats it up, don't ask her if she wants more. If she asks for more, give it to her without comment. Be sure you have also limited her snacks so she will be hungry.

9.5-4 Shape and Reward Good Eating.

If ignoring doesn't work and you decide you want your child to eat more of certain foods, then use these methods:

• Apply the "No, thank you" rule. Make a rule that everyone at the table must take at least a "No, thank you" helping of each dish, even if she thinks she doesn't like it and especially if she has never tasted it before. The taste could be as tiny as one kernel of corn. That way, the child will experience more foods and will find more that she likes. When she's tasted, praise her and reward her with extra TV time, a small surprise from a grab bag, or a favorite dessert after dinner.

• Gradually increase the requirements. If the child has suggested she liked the taste of a "No, thank you" item, then after a week or so, increase the required taste to a slightly larger amount, such as two kernels of corn. Always reward the progress, and never go backward. If she hated the dish, simply maintain the status quo.

• Don't force, but stand firm. A child who doesn't sample the food doesn't earn his reward, whether it is a second helping of another dish or dessert. Soon the dessert will become more and more enticing. If necessary, put some surprise rewards in a mystery grab bag and offer them instead. Stick with it.

SUGGESTED BOOKS FOR PARENTS

Cohen, Stanley A., M.D. *Healthy Babies, Happy Kids.* New York: Delilah Books, 1981. Sound, sensible information on the role of nutrition in a child's life. Includes sections on finicky eaters and the underweight child.

Davis, Adelle. *Let's Have Healthy Children.* New York: New American Library, 1981. An expanded and updated version of the original guide for mothers, babies, and children.

9.6 UNFOUNDED PHYSICAL COMPLAINTS

All children use illness as an excuse occasionally, but some seem to go through periods when symptoms appear and then mysteriously vanish. Never ignore physical discomfort. Have repeated or unusual complaints checked out by a physician before assuming a course of action.

However, when a child seems to be becoming a little hypochondriac, with complaints tending to turn up just before a recital, on the first day of school, or on the morning of a test, then you must try to change the behavior. In this section you will find ways to ward off and set limits for the illnesses in your home.

9.6-1 Set Clear Criteria.

The child must know there are guidelines to determine whether he may stay home due to illness. Explain the rules to the child and then apply them consistently. For example, one rule may be that he may not stay home from school unless he has a temperature of over 100° F., is throwing up, or has some other observable symptom. Another may be if he's sick enough to miss school, then he is sick enough to miss soccer practice or ballet that day. Some schools set their own rules to limit communicable diseases. These will also provide criteria for you.

9.6-2 Model Healthy Behavior.

Little hypochrondriacs sometimes develop from emulating big ones. If you are always complaining about aches and pains, doctors and pills, your child will probably do the same. Be careful what you say in the child's presence, even when you're answering a simple question like "How are you?"

9.6-3 Avoid Overprotection.

If your child falls down and gets an abrasion, don't make a big deal out of it. Don't react to every sneeze with panic. Remember that all scratches don't require a bandage and, in fact, will heal more quickly exposed to the air. Don't ignore a small injury, but don't overreact. Offer sympathy, kiss the boo-boo, and assume the attitude that "the show must go on."

9.6-4 Teach the Child How to Deal with Stress.

For stomachaches, headaches, or other physical symptoms brought on by stress, use the techniques in Section 2.10 that are designed to defuse stress. Keep in mind that the symptoms are real, not imaginary, even though there is no "medical" cause for them.

9.6-5 Teach New Ways to Get Attention.

Some children use constant complaining to keep your attention focused on them. Try teaching more constructive ways.

• Comfort and explain. Tell the child you understand how she feels and explain what you think is happening. For example: "Every time I'm feeding the baby, you seem to get a new hurt. I know that sometimes it's hard to have a new baby brother, and you must feel jealous. I would. Let's have a secret signal. Whenever someone talks about how cute the baby is and you feel jealous, why don't you wink at me so I'll know."

• Role-play. Give the child five new positive ways to get your attention and then act them out together, such as, "Look, Mommy, look what I made!"

• Reward the child for using positive attention getters. Recognize the child's efforts to get your attention by helping you or being with you. Make time with her when she's not asking for it.

• Downplay or ignore inappropriate attention getters. When your child says he has a headache, suggest an aspirin or a short rest. Then go about your business. Don't show excessive concern unless there is a real need for it.

9.6-6 Reinforce Healthy Behavior.

To cure a child of unfounded physical complaints, it's important to praise and reward healthy behavior. Suppose she has butterflies before a recital, but instead of coming down with the flu, she talks to you about the funny feeling in her stomach, does her relaxation exercises, and then goes to the recital without a hassle. That's wonderful! Tell her so.

9.6-7 Deal with Out-and-Out Fakery.

If you are certain that your child is faking, then try overdoing your reaction. Become a sickeningly overconcerned nurse. Make life at home less pleasurable than the activity that's being missed. Play along with the "sickness," putting the child to bed and keeping him there. Feed him tea and toast because he's too sick for anything else. Turn off the television set because he must get a lot of sleep. He will be very glad when he's feeling well enough once again to go to school or tend to his other responsibilities.

SUGGESTED BOOKS FOR CHILDREN

Sharmat, Marjorie Weinmar. *Lucretia the Unbearable.* New York: Holiday House, 1981. Lucretia is so overly concerned with her health that no one wants to be with her. She learns that being sick and thinking she's sick are two different things (K–3).

9.7 HAS A WEIGHT PROBLEM

If you have turned to this section, you are worried that your child has a weight problem or has a tendency to put on too many pounds. This can be a difficult problem for an adult to deal with, and helping your child with it can be even more frustrating because there are no instant or even short-term solutions.

Crash diets are not healthy for anyone, especially children. They are appealing because they promise quick weight loss and the dieter feels he can then return to his normal eating habits. But they are medically dangerous, don't work for long, and tend to set up the child for a lifelong pattern of failure in weight control. Diets are negative and promote feelings of guilt and failure, because no one can stick with them. Your goal should be a healthy attitude toward eating and weight, not an instant cure.

A parent's eating style influences a child. In fact, obesity seems to run in families. Forty percent of children with one obese parent are also obese. Eighty percent of children of two obese parents are obese. On the other hand, average-weight parents have only a 7 percent chance of raising a fat child, according to Seymour Eisenberg in his book *Keep Your Child Thin*. It's been estimated that 16 to 33 percent of all children are obese. Of the children who are obese at ages ten to thirteen, 80 percent will be obese when they are twenty-six to thirty-five years of age.

This is an extremely weight-conscious society, and children who are overweight are generally less popular with their peers. Besides, they have a poorer self-image, do less well at sports, and are more prone to disease, including cardiovascular disease, later in life.

As parents, you have time to build good eating habits in your child and teach a lifelong healthy attitude toward food. Gradually, he will lose weight or grow into his present weight, while he learns not to use food as an emotional outlet.

Enlist the help of your doctor and perhaps a nutritionist to overcome this problem before it turns into a lifelong struggle that affects your child's health as well as his self-image.

9.7-1 Keep a Food-and-Activity Diary.

Many professionals believe that eating patterns are set before your child is a year old, so it's never too early to practice sound nutrition. Nor is it ever too late to initiate a healthy lifestyle.

• Keep a list of what the child eats for one week. Write down every bite your youngster takes, or let the child make a list himself, assuring him he may eat anything he wants as long as he records it accurately. Record, too, when and where the eating occurs and what he was doing or feeling at the time. This is especially useful for a child who is developing compensatory eating habits—eating to compensate for her feelings, happy or sad. It can also be a real eye-opener for a parent. With a toddler, a mother may find that she frequently uses cookies to stop tears or gives snacks when she's hungry herself.

• Write down activities, too. Record all exercise and physical activity during the week. Research has shown that many overweight children eat no more than their thin counterparts but get much less exercise.

Below is a sample food-and-activity diary:

Time	Foods	What You Were Doing	Exercise
8:30	2 eggs 1 toast 8 oz. milk	sitting at table	
9:30			basketball (20 minutes)
10:00	10 grapes	on the way upstairs	
11:30	banana	on the way outside	
12:00	hamburger chips pickle 3 choc. chip cookies	kitchen	

2:00	ice cream	watching TV	
3:30			playing with dog
4:30	chicken leg	watching TV	
6:30	salmon cro- quette rice green beans salad	dinner table	

9.7-2 Get Your Doctor's Help.

The first step is to assure yourself that your child is in good health. The next is to have the doctor determine the appropriate weight for your child. This doesn't mean simply looking up height and weight on a chart, but taking into consideration the child's growth pattern through the years. If your child, for example, has always been above the ninetieth percentile in both height and weight, then the fact that he weighs more than 90 percent of the children his age is not significant because it is normal for him.

• Determine a weight range rather than an ideal weight for a child. Weight varies slightly during the day and from one day to the next. There is no magic number of pounds that's best for any one person, and furthermore, a pound is not a pound. Muscle weighs more than fat tissue.

• With sound advice, determine whether the child should lose weight. Sometimes it's wise to help the child maintain his weight while he grows into suitable body proportions over time.

9.7-3 Plan a Healthy Eating Menu.

Remember that your goal is a healthy eating pattern—the proper balance of foods eaten in a healthy manner combined with appropriate expenditure of energy. Weight is maintained if you use up the same number of calories as you take in through food. If you eat more than your body needs to function, the extra calories are stored as fat. If we eat less than we need, the body uses up some of its reserves and weight is lost.

Based on the child's preferences, a healthy combination of foods, and the appropriate number of calories for a child of his age, size, and energy level, try to develop an eating plan. A few helpful books are listed at the end of this section. It's not simply a matter of omitting sugars or fats, so it is wise to get expert advice from your doctor or a nutritionist.

9.7-4 Develop a Healthy Eating Style.

Control of what is eaten is not the only issue. To acquire good eating habits, it may be necessary to change some well-established eating patterns.

• Examine the child's eating pattern. If your child is old enough, do it together. Using the food-and-activity diary and your own observations, look at the patterns with the help of these questions:

1. Does the child eat a balanced diet? Are each of the major nutrient food groups included? (These are milk and milk products, meats, poultry and fish, fruits and vegetables, breads and cereals.) Is the diet low in sugar? Low in fat? Is it high in fiber?

2. Does the child, on average, eat the correct amount of food based on his energy requirements? Review his intake over the week. Does he overload regularly or only periodically, on special occasions?

3. When does the child eat most? Does he get most of his food at meals or between meals? Does he eat all day long? Is there a relationship between when he eats and what he is doing? Is there a relationship between eating and emotions? Does he eat most of his food during the day or at night?

4. Where does the child eat? How often is he eating anywhere other than at the dining table?

5. How active is the child? Does your youngster engage in regu-

lar physical activities, or is most of the day spent in a sedentary manner?

9.7-5 Target Eating and Lifestyle Patterns to Be Changed.

After reviewing the diary, talking with your doctor, and gathering nutritional information, decide which habits and patterns need to be changed. List them in the order of their importance. For example, target "eating between meals" if the child tends to do considerable eating outside of regular mealtimes. Target "eating alone," "eating high-calorie/unnutritious foods," "overeating at meals," "eating when angry or bored," "exercising too little," or whatever other patterns you think must be altered.

Check the options that apply to your child and the order in which the child wishes to work on them.

_____ balanced diet
_____ healthier/lower caloric intake
_____ eating between meals
_____ eating alone
_____ eating when unhappy, bored, angry
_____ exercising more

9.7-6 Design a Plan.

Try to develop an eating plan that you and the child can live with, remembering the steps suggested in this book for all childhood problem areas.

• Think small. Don't expect all of the excess poundage to be lost in one week. Aim for changes to come about slowly but steadily. The goal may be to maintain weight or lose a fraction of a pound a week. You may choose to change eating habits before changing what is eaten.

• Take one step at a time. Using the order you've selected, work on one behavior at a time, and deal with that behavior day by day.

Ask the child to evaluate each day's progress and to plan what he's going to do the next day.

• With your child, define the new behavior clearly, laying out the rules to accomplish each change. Here are some examples:

1. Limit eating times. Make an agreement with the child to eat only at specific times. If he is used to snacking between meals, it may be appropriate to divide the day's menu into small meals throughout the day rather than restricting him to three big meals. But don't use extra meals as an excuse to eat more. Plan the menus the night before, making sure all the necessary nutrition is included. Take Jennifer: She agrees not to eat any food except at the usual three meals and at mini-meals that are scheduled for mid-morning and midafternoon. She and her mother design the foods and amounts to be included. She no longer has to "cheat," since legitimate snacks are included in her plan.

2. Limit eating places. If eating alone or on the run has been a contributing factor, then define rules to fit this target. For example: Jennifer may eat her three meals plus two snacks only when she sits down with others at the kitchen or dining room table. She must use appropriate utensils. Food is not allowed in other rooms.

3. Lengthen mealtimes. It takes about twenty minutes for the message signaling that you are full to travel from the stomach to the brain and back to the stomach. At the next meal, unobtrusively time how long it takes your child to eat his meal. At subsequent meals, use a kitchen timer to stretch the eating time by setting it a minute longer at each sitting. Tell your child to eat slowly, chewing each bite thoroughly, and putting his fork down between mouthfuls. Parents and siblings can practice too! Praise him for slowing his eating habits. Use mealtime to have conversations and discussions of the day's events.

4. Increase exercise and activity levels. What does your child like to do? What would he like to do? Investigate the programs available in your community. It doesn't matter what the activity is as long as it is done regularly. Current thought suggests that aerobic exercise provides the most benefits for the time spent. Walking, running, jogging, bicycling, skiing, dancing, skating, swimming,

and jumping rope are all forms of exercise that, performed appropriately and continuously for a certain number of minutes, will be aerobic. With some advice from your doctor, the school's physical education teacher, or another expert, design a program that will suit your child. Consult Section 9.9 for suggestions for beginning an exercise program.

9.7-7 Implement a Plan.

Losing or maintaining weight requires resolve on the child's part. Think about your own dieting experiences. You have to have a lot of will power to be successful. You can't provide that for your child, but you can give your support and reinforcement.

• Give support. The most powerful and successful support you can provide an overweight child is to join the effort. If you already have healthy eating habits, this will be easy. If not, then it's a good time for you to begin also. Eat along with the child, consuming the same healthy foods and eating them in the same healthy manner.

• Chart the progress. Keep track of daily and weekly progress on a calendar or a chart. Define the week's goals in terms of behaviors, record successful eating behavior daily, and record weight at the end of the week. Set next week's goals.

• Reward progress. Set up a reward system, based on the principles given in Chapter 2, to reinforce your child's efforts to change his eating habits. Making these changes is not easy for him, so let him know when you think he's doing well. Reward progress toward the goals every day and, later, every week to establish the new healthy lifestyle.

SUGGESTED BOOKS FOR PARENTS

Bailey, Covert. *Fit or Fat?* Boston: Houghton Mifflin, 1978.

Bailey, Covert. *The Fit-or-Fat Target Diet.* Boston: Houghton Mifflin, 1978. A pair of books that provide information and plans to develop a healthy lifestyle; not specifically for children.

Three books written for parents to understand their children's needs and eating patterns:

Eisenberg, Seymour. *Keep Your Kids Thin.* New York: St. Martin's, 1983.

Kamen, Betty and Si. *Kids Are What They Eat.* New York: Arco Publishing, 1983.

Silberstein, Warren and Lawrence Galton. *Helping Your Child Grow Slim.* New York: Simon and Schuster, 1983.

SUGGESTED BOOKS FOR CHILDREN

Bluestein, Bill and Enid. *Mom, How Come I'm Not Thin?* Minneapolis: CompCare Publishers, 1981. For children seven to eleven, the book offers reassurance and information about being overweight.

9.8 ANOREXIA/BULIMIA

Though anorexia nervosa and bulimia are usually associated with adolescence or young adulthood, the stage is set for these syndromes much earlier in life. Both conditions are physically devastating, and they are even life-threatening behavioral disorders. Therefore, we believe parents must be aware of them so that they may counteract the attitudes in our society that contribute to them and may also detect symptoms of impending problems.

Anorexia and bulimia, though different in symptoms and physical manifestations, are variations of a single theme: The person, usually a young girl, is consumed by an overwhelming concern with being fat. She is caught in a web of misperceptions, trapped in a distorted view of herself and the importance of food, weight, and body shape.

The anorectic's worry about fat leads her to give up food almost totally. She often starves herself, believing that every morsel is too much. She may develop elaborate eating rituals designed to limit intake. Or she may eat only certain foods. Meanwhile, her family goes to inordinate lengths to tempt her to eat.

It is important for parents to realize that the anorectic is attempting to control her life. The eating disorder is a defense mechanism, a means of dealing "successfully" with one small part of her existence. Anorectics especially may fear the passage of time and want to prevent separation from their parents. The bulimic, less worried about the future, has found a way to handle body needs without paying the usual consequences for overeating. These individuals often present a self-assured image, though their inner feelings are quite the opposite. While family problems may have some influence, the desire to be thin and the fear of weight gain remain the most frequently cited reasons for these eating patterns.

The anorectic strives to reach her ideal, pleased by her weight loss, and propelled by a distorted body image. No matter how many pounds she loses, she still sees herself as fat. She limits her nutrition and, at the same time, may increase exercise to burn up the "fat." She may even borrow some behaviors from bulimics, making herself throw up or eliminate what food she does consume.

The bulimic controls her weight gain and food intake through consuming vast quantities of food and then purging the body of its contents with laxatives, diuretics, and regurgitation. Usually not as thin as the anorectic, she may successfully hide her harmful habits until the side effects become apparent. These include dehydration, amenorrhea, intestinal disorders, loss of calcium, potassium, and sodium, and liver, lung, and heart disease. Other side effects include swollen parotid glands, loss of hair, tooth decay, broken blood vessels around the eyes and on the cheeks, and scars on the fingers.

Growing up is complicated enough. The preteen or adolescent goes through many stages as she reaches maturity. Overconcern with weight and looks, especially if it is promoted by parents who stress perfectionism and family interdependence, can affect a young girl's developing self-concept and predispose her to these eating patterns.

Eating disorders are not simple behavior problems. You can't talk your youngster out of them. Changes occur slowly, and the road back to good health is a very long one. Therefore, we will not attempt to provide solutions but only to point out warning signals. If you suspect your child has an eating disorder, you need professional help.

9.8-1 Be Alert to the Warning Signs.

The personality characteristics and appearance concerns of a developing anorectic or bulimic are common to many young people, but in these youngsters they are exaggerated beyond a normal degree. Although no one child will have all of them, you should consider seeking expert advice if you find several warning signs in your child.

• These aspects of the home environment may contribute to the development of eating disorders: family stresses such as divorce, illness, or death; parental overemphasis on weight and appearance; mother's lack of acceptance of her own body image or role; extreme closeness and interdependence between parents and child; abnormally high parental expectations of perfection.

• The following are some characteristics of youngsters that may contribute to susceptibility to eating disorders: the need to be the perfect child who causes no problems; intelligence, high achievement, and perfectionism; denial of feelings and frustrations; extreme desire to please others; overconcern with appearance, body shape, and weight.

• These changes in behavior and personality may signal other problems in the child: sudden shifts in mood; irrational and illogical behavior; unanticipated responses; inability to converse, laugh, and joke; a perfectionistic approach to life; an obsession with avoiding food and increasing exercise; ritualized eating patterns; fanatical attitude toward food preparation; swings between dependence and independence; an inordinate need for reassurance.

• These specific behaviors signal an eating disorder pattern in an individual: loss of weight up to 20 to 25 percent of her normal weight; eating very little or nothing; eating massive quantities of foods in a very short time; eating large quantities of food alone; vomiting after meals; overuse and overdoses of laxatives and diuretics; hidden stores of food; "midnight raids" on the kitchen, with noticeable quantities of food consumed; constant talk and fear of getting fat; distorted body image; dry skin, sunken eyes, yellow or gray complexion; sores on fingers or in creases of lips.

• The following behaviors may provide further confirmation of an eating disorder when they are associated with the above characteristics: shoplifting of food; stealing money to buy food or other items related to the abnormal eating patterns.

9.8-2 Expose the Problem.

If you believe your child has some of the above characteristics, the first step is to discuss the situation and your concern about health and body. Even if the behaviors you note are only part of a new fad diet, it is healthier to discuss your concerns than to ignore them. If there is a more serious agenda, then you will be closer to bringing it to the surface.

• Talk with your pediatrician or family doctor. Ask for advice for seeking further help. If your doctor is an old family friend and knowledgeable about eating disorders, he or she may be very helpful, not only suggesting a course of action but also outlining the health concerns and side effects after a physical examination.

• Discuss your concerns with your child. You may choose to do this alone or with the doctor. Don't be surprised if the child denies the problem.

• Don't be completely reassured by her assurance that she will change, eat more, become less irritable, stop taking laxatives, etc. The anorectic or bulimic means what she says at that moment but is compelled to continue the same behavior. She must learn to like and accept herself, to feel thirst and hunger, and to discover how to deal with those feelings in a healthy way.

9.8-3 Seek Professional Help.

If you are concerned about your child's eating behavior, don't waste time waiting for her to change. Get help from a professional who is experienced in treating these disorders. The problems seldom disappear on their own, and time is crucial.

• Ask for a referral to a mental-health professional with the proper experience. The American Anorexia/Bulimia Association, Inc., may help you locate individuals or groups in your area that have established programs for eating disorders. Also see Chapter 17.

• Make a proper match. Before beginning a therapeutic program, be sure you have asked these questions of the therapist:

1. How much experience have you had with eating disorders?
2. Would you consider this an area of expertise for you?
3. What is your success rate? How do you define success?
4. What therapeutic approach do you use? Do you think hospitalization is necessary? At what point?
5. How will the parents and other family members be involved in the therapy?
6. Will you inform us about the patient's problems and progress?
7. How much will the therapy cost?

• Continue to give the child your support. It's important that you understand that your support is even more essential now, because her guilt may be overwhelming at times. The recovery process may necessitate painful changes in family relationships. Talk about your feelings with an understanding person, or seek professional help yourself. Join a local support group—or if necessary, start one. Read about eating disorders.

SUGGESTED BOOKS FOR PARENTS AND CHILDREN

Bruch, Hilde. *The Golden Cage: The Enigma of Anorexia Nervosa.* Cambridge, Mass.: Harvard University Press, 1978. An interesting book based on a therapist's own case studies.

Claypool, Jane and Cheryl Diane Nelson. *Food Trips and Traps: Coping with Eating Disorders.* New York: Franklin Watts, 1983. An informational book about the characteristics of eating disorders and guides for coping with them.

Fonda, Jane. *Jane Fonda's Workout Book.* New York: Simon & Schuster, 1981. Information about exercise, of course, but Fonda also discusses her own early unhealthy eating attitudes.

Josephs, Rebecca. *Early Disorder.* New York: Farrar, Strauss & Giroux, 1980. A novel about a young girl caught in this trap.

Kinroy, Barbara P., in collaboration with Estelle Miller, John A. Atchely, and the Book Committee of the American Anorexia/Bulimia Association. *When Will We Laugh Again?* New York: Columbia University Press, 1984. An excellent book based on the experiences of individuals and their families.

Levenkron, Steven. *The Best Little Girl in the World.* New York: Contemporary Books, 1978. A fictionalized version of one child's story.

O'Neill, Cherry Boone. *Starving for Attention.* New York: Continuum Books, 1982. The writer tells her own life story and talks about her recovery from anorexia.

9.9 POOR POSTURE

If you are continually saying, "Jessica, sit up straight," or, "Andy, don't slump over like that. Pull your shoulders back," you're not at all unusual. Your child may even stand straighter for a moment or two, but then slump again. Occasionally, poor posture is the result of a physical problem such as scoliosis (curvature of the spine), the best known of these conditions. Approximately 2 percent of adolescents—four times as many girls as boys—have some structural spinal curvature, which should be checked by a specialist.

But usually, poor posture is simply habit or a reflection of a poor self-concept. When slumping and slouching indicate negative inner feelings, then nagging won't help, and continual comments make the child feel even worse. But when a child's poor posture has simply become a habit, then it must be treated as a behavior that needs to be changed. Try these solutions.

9.9-1 Check It Out.

Save your comments for a while and check out the situation first by observing your child.

• Observe her posture for a few days. Is her slumping an occasional occurrence, or does she carry herself like that most of the time? Do you notice the posture only when you're feeling irritable or angry with the child, or do you see it when things are cool?

• Look for signs of spinal curvature. While your child is wearing a swimsuit or a leotard, look at her from the front, sides, and rear while she is standing with arms up or bending forward with arms extended and hands touching. Look for unlevel shoulders, prominent shoulder blades, unlevel hips, or deviations of the spine. Asymmetry of the chest (a symptom of scoliosis) will be seen as a humped shoulder when she bends forward. An excessively rounded back (kyphosis) and swayback (hyperlordosis) are discernible from the side. If you suspect an abnormality, check it out with your doctor.

• Make a decision. If you do not suspect physical problems and if the poor posture is not as much of a habit as you thought it to be, decide whether you consider this a top priority. Try ignoring it— your constant comments may have perpetuated the slumping and slouching. Don't mention them, and instead, make occasional comments about how good the child looks when she stands up straight.

9.9-2 Try Habit Reversal.

This is a technique that is based on a series of steps designed to change habits. See Chapter 12 for details about this method.

• Help the child become aware of how he looks. No more nagging, no more comments. Take the child aside and talk about posture for a few moments. Then stand side by side in front of a mirror, asking him to stand as he usually does while you, it is hoped, provide an example of good posture. Take snapshots of him standing and sitting poorly and then properly, and let him compare them.

• Help him become aware of how good posture feels. Your goal is to have the child notice the difference in the way poor posture and good posture *feel*. Have him practice doing and undoing the undesirable posture ten times. Ask him to practice slouching and straightening his back ten times. Have him practice rolling and unrolling his shoulders ten times. Ask him to sit in a chair in front of the mirror and practice sitting stooped, then sitting up straight ten times.

• Have him list the reasons why good posture is desirable. Take out a sheet of paper and brainstorm all the reasons you and he think it would be good to stand straighter. How does he look when he stands properly? Do other people respond more favorably?

• Reward him for "catching" himself and realigning his body, and don't forget to praise and reward him when he stands or sits properly. Refer to Chapter 2 for a discussion of reward systems.

• Use habit reversal. If you see the child slumping or slouching, have him practice tightening the muscles that control good posture positions. If, for example, he rounds his shoulders, have him practice contracting the shoulder muscles to strenthen them, then relaxing them ten times.

9.9-3 Strengthen Posture Muscles.

The stronger the child's muscles, the easier it is to maintain good posture. Obviously, tight abdominal muscles hold the tummy in better and strong back muscles hold the back straighter. Talk with the child's doctor, the gym teacher, or perhaps a physical therapist for help in designing a program of muscle-strengthening exercises. Reinforce his efforts with praise and other rewards. Use the following guidelines to establish the program.

• Choose a few exercises for the child to do every day.
• Have the child keep a record of the exercises he does.
• Make a rule that the child must do at least one of the exercises every day.
• To provide motivation, reward his efforts with praise and rewards.

CHAPTER 10

Going Places

SOMETIMES it seems a lot easier to stay home! Taking a child on an outing can be exhausting. You must pack him up, buckle him in, get him to the right place at the right time, keep him entertained and well behaved. To complicate matters, he may act up in public because there's so much more to do and touch and many more ways to get into trouble when he's out of the confines of the house. Can you cope? Do you know what to do when your four-year-old throws a tantrum in the supermarket? How do you discipline your child when she throws the salt and pepper shakers at her little sister in the restaurant? What can you do about a toddler who won't wear his safety belt in the car?

This chapter is designed to help you set ground rules so you can enjoy going places with your child.

10.1 WON'T USE CAR SEAT OR SEAT BELT/ WON'T BEHAVE IN THE CAR

Automobile accidents claim more children's lives than any disease or other kind of mishap. We all know by this time that the risk of serious injury can be significantly decreased when children are restrained in sturdy car seats or by seat belts. But do we always buckle our children up? No, because it's often a big hassle. The child doesn't want to sit in his special seat or have the belt fastened around him, so he puts up such resistance that we give up. After all, we're just going "around the block" or to the mall.

It's most important, however, that despite the resistance, you insist that your child follow the safety rules. The facts prove it is worth whatever effort it takes. Perseverance may save your little one's life. The restraints will help keep him safe in case of an accident or fast braking and, as a fringe benefit, will improve his general car behavior as well.

10.1-1 Wear a Seat Belt Yourself.

Nothing works better with children than a good role model. By protecting your own safety, you are setting an example.

10.1-2 Start Young.

Teach your child from infancy that using a car seat or seat belt is a rule without exceptions.

- Choose a proper restraint. Be sure the one you choose is installed correctly and is manufactured in accordance with government regulations.
- Make it comfortable. When necessary, cover leather or plastic seats with covers or towels, because they do get hot and sticky. Be sure the straps are snug and secure but not so binding that they are annoying.
- Teach the child to buckle himself up. When your child is old enough, let buckling himself up become his own job. Then check to see that it's been done correctly. Tell him to give the signal when everyone in the car is also fastened in and ready to "take off."
- Explain the importance. Demonstrate to a child old enough to understand the reasons why seat belts are necessary. Show her what happens to an unrestrained doll when you make a sudden stop or go around a sharp corner.

10.1-3 Make It a Rule.

Never start the car until everyone is buckled up. Never.

• Announce the rule. If you're starting this strategy with a child who has never before been required to buckle up, plan an outing that excites her. Let her know she may go with you if she wears her seat belt from the moment the car starts until the moment it reaches its destination and you give permission to unbuckle.

• Write it. Display the safety-belt rule on the dashboard, so nobody will be tempted to forget it.

• Don't change the rules—even for short trips. Most accidents occur close to home. With that in mind, insist on the car seat or seat belt even if you are going one block. Being held by an adult is not an alternative; that is just as dangerous as total freedom in a car.

10.1-4 Plan Ahead.

Sitting still in one spot isn't easy for any child, so plan some diversions and give him ways to entertain himself during the trip.

• State the rules. Before leaving home, announce the rules of the road. Write them down and post them in the car. When the child learns them, he may be placed in charge of reciting them before each trip. If you are car pooling, meet with the other parents and write a set of rules that is announced to all the children. These may include wearing a seat belt, not distracting the driver, not throwing, etc.

• Plan car activities. Ask the child to choose a favorite toy to take along, one that's an appropriate companion inside a car. For infants, there are toys that attach to the car seat, and for toddlers, you may choose a special toy that's kept in the car. For long trips, take along a shoe bag and hang it from the back seat within the child's reach. Fill each pocket with a toy or a game that must be returned to its special niche before another may be removed. Tuck a boxed drink or a healthy snack in there, too.

• Play car games. Try rhyming words, seeing who can think of the most. Play counting games, assigning each person a specific car make or state license plate to look for out the window. Take along old magazines and a nonpermanent, nontoxic marker pen and show the child how to turn the people on the pages into monsters, clowns, or creatures from outer space. I Spy, Twenty Questions, and memory games are also good choices.

• Reward good behavior. Let your child know what a wonderful job he's doing by wearing his seat belt or behaving nicely in the car. When he stays buckled up for the entire trip in the car, reward him by stopping off for a snack on the way home. He could earn a special title or badge naming him Captain Car Seat or Sergeant Seat Belt. Children in a car pool could try to earn a daily or weekly sticker for good behavior. With a certain number of stickers, they stop for a drink on the way home from school. Choose a supercar star for each trip.

• Encourage the child to relax. Riding in an automobile puts some children to sleep! Take advantage of that possibility and encourage your youngster to make this a time for rest. Tell her to close her eyes and "dream" a scene of her favorite place to go. See Section 2.10 on teaching your child how to relax.

10.1-5 Take Action for Misbehavior.

If you've tried the positive approach but it doesn't work, take the following steps:

• The first time, make a fuss. Stop the car when the commotion or unbuckling occurs. Tell the child how upset you are about the way she's behaving. Do not start up again until she buckles up and sits cooperatively.

• Use time-out. If he misbehaves again, supervise and have him sit belted in the car at the end of the trip for one minute for every year of his age, up to ten minutes.

• Define the consequences. On the next trip, let him know the rules. Remind him that if he is still a problem, you will put him in time-out at the end of the ride and, in addition, you will leave him home on the next pleasure outing. Be sure to follow through. Consequences will certainly not work if you don't apply them.

• Initiate response cost. At the beginning of each week, all family members get a penny or a nickel per day. Every time someone is caught not wearing his seat belt or breaking one of the car rules, he must forfeit one of the coins and place it in the "car jar" made from a plastic container or a bank. The person who has managed to keep the most money by the end of the week gets the amount collected in the jar or a special treat.

10.2 CAN'T GIVE UP SECURITY BLANKET

Linus has carried that blue blanket around for years. Has it hurt his psyche? Does it matter? Should Sandra take her "blinkie" to school? Is it time to "lose" Mark's cherished shred of wool blanket? What about Ian's beloved monkey, which goes everywhere he does? It was cute when he was little, but recently, his parents find it embarrassing and annoying that they can't make a move without a stuffed monkey. Some children attach themselves to one object, while others change their allegiance frequently. Many suck their thumb, fondle the material, or practice another habit while clutching their beloved object.

It's ironic that the reason parents usually encourage a close relationship with a security object is to develop the child's independence. To make the youngster feel secure in his own bed, they give him a special friend. But in the end, this special object can be a source of insecurity for both child and parent. If the animal gets lost, then everything stops until the child and his shadow are reunited. One family bought backups of the stuffed animal their child carried around with him. When it got dirty, another one was substituted, in fear that the child couldn't sleep without it. Inadvertently, these parents bolstered his insecurity.

Obviously, the best solution for overdependence on a security object is never to let the habit get started. The next best solution is not to reinforce it. But if the child already has a close relationship with a security object, we offer solutions for remedying the situation. You may be surprised to find that your child becomes more secure and independent when he relies on himself rather than his security object.

10.2-1 Don't Start.

Be preventive when possible. Don't promote the habit.

• Vary the objects. Let the child carry around different objects, and don't create a dependency by focusing on one special favorite. Encourage their use as entertainment. When the child goes to bed or off on an outing, let him take one thing, but select different ones when possible.

• Establish rules. Set rules for a favorite animal or object by limiting it to the crib or bed. Restrict where it is allowed to go, and stand by your decision. This is especially effective for blankets. "Blankets stay in the crib. You may play with it there if you like. I'll put you back in the crib." The child may go into the crib to spend time with his blanket a few times, but soon, the phase will pass.

• Put limits on it. When you do allow the child to take an object with him, insist that it's an appropriate one. Based on where you are going, limit the number, size, or noisiness. A hand-held game, small doll, or book can be good choices. "Anything that fits in your pocket" is another criterion. Or, "Your monkey can go only in the car." Before you go anywhere, let the child know the object must stay in the car or that he, not you, is responsible for it. He may decide a big, heavy stuffed animal was not the best choice after he has carried it around the shopping center.

10.2-2 Stop the Habit.

Many experts suggest you never forcibly remove a security object from a child. We concur. Never play tug-of-war. If the child has become attached to a special object, there are several approaches you may try to discourage the dependency.

• Wean her gradually. Limit the places and times that the security object may tag along. Say, "It can stay in the house, but it can't go to school." Or, "The blanket is for nighttime only." Don't repair the object or even call attention to its unraveling or disintegration. Let the child carry a smaller and smaller piece of it, until there's nothing left.

• Provide alternatives. When you can, replace it with a more appropriate object. What's cute at one age is not so endearing when the child is older. For the preschooler, perhaps you can substitute a doll for the blanket, or an ID bracelet or a magic ring for a stuffed animal. Let the child choose something else that he may proudly take with him. Be careful, though, not to substitute one dependency for another even if you are providing age-appropriate alternatives.

• Choose D day and go cold turkey. With older children, sometimes the best approach is simply to quit. This is especially true when the object interferes with other activities. A new school year or a new activity is a perfect time to make this step toward maturity. "Ian, you're going to be a big boy now and go it alone. Monkeys are not allowed at school." Or select your own D day: "Starting Monday, Sassy Bear must stay in your bed. You may only play with it at home now." Build up to the big event beforehand, and prepare the child thoroughly. The first few days of the new ruling, divert her attention with activity so she won't have much time to yearn for her old friend.

10.2-3 Praise Her for Letting Go.

Applaud her efforts toward independence at every possible opportunity. Praise her for leaving the security object at home "like a big girl." Tell her she may help carry packages now that her hands are free. Reward her with a special gift for that big girl who no longer needs her blanket wherever she goes.

SUGGESTED READING

Cooney, Nancy Evans. *The Blanket That Had to Go.* New York: Putnam, 1981. Suzi must decide what to do with her favorite blanket when her mom says she may not take it to kindergarten (K–3).

Keller, Holly. *Geraldine's Blanket*. New York: Greenwillow, 1984. A picture book that tells how Geraldine ingeniously solves the problem of giving up her blanket (PS–2).

10.3 WANDERS AWAY

Children who are wanderers pose quite a problem to their family. Parents panic when suddenly their child is gone from their side, even though he's probably just "sightseeing" or investigating something interesting at the other end of the shopping mall. Obviously, wandering away is dangerous, and frightening to the child as well when he realizes he's "lost."

It is necessary for a child to know there are boundaries and rules that he must follow. The solutions for curing these disappearances during shopping trips range from planning ahead to training to keep your child at hand.

10.3-1 Teach Your Child How to Stay Close.

It's never too soon for the child to learn to stay with you. Here's how to teach him.

• Start early. From the child's first outings, train him to stay close to you even though you may not be holding his hand. Of course, you must never leave a child alone or out of your sight; and never assume he is right behind you. Keep close track of him at all times. For safety, both parents and child must do their part.

• State the rules. Each time you go out together, tell your child the rules and your expectations all over again. Teach her to stay within certain boundaries—and show her exactly where that means. For a very young child, that means holding your hand, or if that's impossible because you are carrying groceries or paying a bill, have the child hold on to your clothing so you'll know she's right there.

• Be realistic. Don't expect a young child to enjoy a long shopping excursion. She'll get restless, and if she's a born wanderer, she'll be likely to set out looking for a little diversion. Break up long stretches with a snack or perhaps the toy department. Wandering as well as resistance are frequently the result of just plain boredom.

• Praise her, and reinforce her positive behavior. Tell her what a big girl she is and how proud you are of her. Reward her for staying within bounds. For example, during a long wait, let her earn a finger up—"That's one!" When you have marked her good behavior with all five of your fingers, then she earns a surprise or an activity of her choice.

10.3-2 Plan Ahead.

If your child enjoys being with you, she won't be bored and restless and she'll be less likely to look around for fun.

• Give her a way to measure the passage of time. Help the child understand how long you will be out by explaining the sequence of events and the time limit. An older child, of course, can wear a watch. A small child might be told you'll be gone for three television shows or as long as it takes to go to and from Grandma's house. Make a checklist that the child can use to keep track of the excursion. Try including an unnamed mystery spot marked only by ? at the end of the tour. Then surprise your well-behaved companion with a cool drink or a swing in the park.

• Vary the experience. Reward good behavior, and keep the outing interesting by making a stop when possible or providing a break the child will enjoy. "If you stay with me here, then we'll go look at the toys." Just for fun, let the child window-shop and ask him to make up a wish list for his birthday.

• Take along something to do. Remember that shopping is usually most uninteresting to a child, so take along a toy or a puzzle saved just for shopping. Many toys fit on strollers for little children to enjoy, while older youngsters may want comic books or maybe a flashlight or a magnifying glass. With a pad and pencil, he can write down every object he spots that's bigger than his baby sister or begins with the letter *J*. Or get him to count everyone he sees wearing stripes or polka dots.

10.3-3 Train the Child to Stay Within Defined Boundaries.

These games will show her what you mean when you say, "Stay right here."

• Play Home Base. Tell the child you are home base. He may circle you, but he must stay within your reach or he's out. If he wanders outside the limits, put him in time-out right there in the store. Find him a place to sit and have him stay there for as many minutes as he is years old.

• Play the Shadow Game. Play a game at home for training, telling the child he must stay in your "shadow" or at an arm's reach. As you dodge around corners, see if he can follow you closely. Then, when you go to the store, let him show off his new skill of sticking right by you.

• Play Red Light. Red Light is another game that helps teach a child not to wander. If he goes too far from you, quietly recite, "One, two, three, four, five, six, seven, eight, nine, ten, red light!" If he can touch you before you say, "Red light!" he wins. Don't, of course, make this so much fun that he's encouraged to leave you so he can play the game.

10.3-4 Use Consequences.

If you've tried the positive approaches and they haven't done the job, then define the consequences for wandering away—and apply them when necessary.

• Use negative consequences. Let him stay home the next time you are going on a trip, making sure, of course, that it's a trip he'll be sorry to miss.

• Give him time-out. Take him to the restroom, a fitting room, a corner of the store, or perhaps out to the car, and have him sit there for a prescribed number of minutes—with your supervision.

• Use response cost. At the start of an outing, give her a specific number of points that are enough to buy a treat. To hang on to all the points, she must not wander away. It costs one point for every venture from your side, and if the number sinks below a specified amount, she loses privileges at home as well.

10.4 LEAVES THE YARD OR GOES INTO THE STREET

Some children are off and running as soon as they get outside. To them, it's one big playground. But even in the safest neighborhood, you must set boundaries and know where your child is at all times. Until he is mature enough to be responsible for himself, he must follow the rules.

10.4-1 Give Him Training.

When our children are very small, we constantly supervise them. They must learn to stay within the boundaries and then earn increasing independence.

• Supervise play near home. In your own yard or the nearby playground, help him learn how to play before you gradually retreat to the sidelines and watch the activity. Whether you're teaching him to pump the swing or play in the sand, you teach him how to do it first, then you watch.

• Define the boundaries clearly. With bright ribbons or visible landmarks, define the areas where he may go. Tie the ribbons— perhaps red for "stop"—on the mailbox or the tree at the edge of the yard. Tell the child he may go only as far as the ribbons or the big rock or the lilac bush.

• Ask the child to repeat your instructions. Tell her the rules: for example, "You may play on the swings or slides only." Then ask her to repeat what you said, and make sure she understands your meaning.

• Increase freedom gradually. When the child is old enough to understand, define the boundaries, but watch him from a distance. Give him a small area where he may play, and if you find that he follows your instructions, gradually enlarge the territory where he may go without your direct supervision.

10.4-2 Teach Safety Rules.

As the opportunities arise, use them to get across some important points.

• Define the rules clearly. Always try to make the rules positive, telling the child what he may do rather than what he may not do. Or combine the "don'ts" with the "do's." "Flowers are to look at and to smell but not to eat." "We build things with sticks, we don't throw them." "When you must cross the street, stop, look both ways, and listen for cars. Then if it's clear, you may go." The rules may seem cumbersome at first, but when the key words like *Stop, look,* and *listen* are combined with action, they will gain meaning.

• Make opportunities to use the rules. Role-play the rules at home and discuss them, but try to use them in real situations when you can. Every time you walk with the child, for example, remind her to "stop, look, and listen," before crossing the street. Exaggerate what you are doing when you reach the corner, then verbalize the rule as you follow it and, later, ask the child to say it to you.

• Show the consequences visually. Because some children can't understand how dangerous breaking safety rules may be until they see the results, prove your point by showing him a run-over can or a dead animal at the side of the road. Or stage a crash with a toy car and a doll. When the child is mature enough, discuss the reasons for the rules and have him help you set them.

10.4-3 Use Temptation Training.

It's usually not enough to teach a child to follow the rules when it's easy to do so. Teach her how to follow them even when decisions may be complicated by, for example, her new puppy running away down the path or a balloon flying over the fence. Train her what to do in more tempting circumstances.

- Play "what if." Let your child act out what he would do in these situations: What if a stranger wants to talk to you? What if your ball rolls into the street? What if you saw a piece of candy lying on the ground? What if your puppy runs away? What if you hurt yourself? Let her tell you what she would do, and then talk about your feelings and suggestions. Act out the scene.
- Reward with praise. Once the child exhibits the proper behavior, reward him with praise. Let him know how proud you are of him. Reinforce instances of safe behavior in both real and pretend incidents.
- Reward him with increased responsibilities and freedom. When the child is old enough, let him know you now trust him. "Johnny, you're playing so well in the yard, I am going to go inside to get a drink of water. Do you remember the rules? Tell me. Good. I'll get us both a drink." Of course, be sure to watch him secretly. Leave the yard for thirty seconds the first time, then a minute, in brief intervals. Then say, "Johnny, you did a good job staying in the yard by yourself."

10.4-4 Apply Consequences for Not Following Rules.

Let the child know that if she doesn't go by the rules, there will be consequences. Then be sure to follow through.

- Apply time-out. When you're outside, use a time-out seat. If the rules include not throwing rocks and Geraldine throws one, make her sit by your side for two minutes while you explain why it's so important not to throw rocks. If she walks outside the gate, which you have prohibited, have her come inside and sit for five minutes (or one minute for each year of age) and let her try again after she has acknowledged the boundaries.
- Decrease the boundaries. If she then doesn't stay within the parameters, narrow the boundaries. Return to earlier limits. You

may also have to supervise the child more closely or take away outdoor time for the rest of the day.

• Use positive practice. If Geraldine runs into the street after a ball, give her some practice waiting and then properly crossing the street ten times in a row. Supervise, of course.

• Use overcorrection. If the child ignores the boundaries, have her walk along them with you to prove to her that she knows what the limits are and where she must not go. Have her line up sticks to mark the yard space or use chalk to mark the pavement. Then let her earn outdoor time by being responsible.

10.5 WON'T TALK FOR SELF

Will says such cute things, but he refuses to say a word when you've got Aunt Jessie on the telephone long-distance. Your little ones hide behind your legs when the boss comes to dinner. Your seven-year-old refuses to acknowledge the presence of your next-door neighbor.

Remember that to a degree, a child's refusal to speak is quite normal. The world of small children is limited—what's natural to us may still be new to them. Besides, social graces often don't register. Not only are they uninterested in meeting your old college buddy, but they have no intention of saying hello to her. It's harder to understand the silence of older children, who obviously know how to speak for themselves—they talk incessantly the rest of the day.

Never explain your child's silence by labeling it shyness—even if the child is shy. You can make it a self-fulfilling prophecy, using that excuse until it comes true. Better to say: "Samantha has just met you. She'll feel like talking in a little while."

For children six to eighteen months, there is usually a period of stranger anxiety when they have identified the regulars in their lives and everyone else is suspect. Four-year-olds, on the other hand, often know no strangers and are friendly with everyone, while at seven they may become speechless with unfamiliar people once again.

You can't force a child to speak, nor should you. But there are things you can do to increase the probability that your youngster will speak for himself.

10.5-1 Plan Ahead.

Prepare the child for encounters with other people.

- Teach. Take the time to teach your child to speak to new people in new situations. Prepare by role-playing meeting someone and talking to that person. Have him practice saying hello, and talk about what he might say. Conversation starters can be as simple as sharing a favorite joke or riddle or asking new people a special question, such as, "Do you know my dog, Rover?" and "Do you know how old I am?"
- Don't put the child on the spot. You'll have less repetition of this behavior if you don't embarrass him or prompt him. The younger child needs time to warm up, and the fewer times you put him onstage, the better off you will both be.
- Reinforce the child for talking. When the child does talk for himself, praise him and let him know what a big boy you think he is, how grown-up he sounded, how proud you were of him, how much you liked what he said.
- Establish your expectations. Let the older child know you expect her to say something. Have a hello rule, and let the child know that even if she chooses not to talk, she must say hello and acknowledge the person.
- Don't talk for the older child. If the child doesn't answer and he's not extremely shy, do not talk for him. Let him know that if it happens again, there will be a consequence such as the loss of a privilege like telephone talking time. If he can't talk to people you want him to talk to, then he loses time talking to his friends.

10.5-2 Set Up a Specific System.

If the child refuses to speak to someone you often see, set up a system to help you in your efforts. Tell him that Aunt Sheila is coming over to see him and to have dessert. Set it up so he earns his dessert by saying hello and responding when he is spoken to. If he says, "Goodbye," and, "Thank you for coming," he earns a bedtime story that night. Let him know in advance what he will earn if he cooperates and what the consequences are if he doesn't.

10.6 WON'T BEHAVE IN PUBLIC

You may dress them up, but you can't take them anywhere! Though they may be good at home, they are transformed into little devils when they're out in public. The problem usually is that they have learned that the consequences for misbehavior are quite different away from home. Perhaps there aren't any at all. Either you are reluctant to apply them when other people are watching or the consequences may be too far removed ("I'll talk to you later at home!"). Sometimes someone else is caring for them and you aren't present.

The initial step to changing misbehavior in public is to ask yourself if you really have your child in control *at home*. If so, great—keep reading. If not, then you need to establish that control at home first. Read Chapter 2 once more and refer to other relevant sections in this book.

Here are ways to help you make taking your child out a more pleasant adventure.

10.6-1 Have Reasonable Expectations.

Don't expect a three-year-old to wait patiently in line at a restaurant for an hour without something to occupy her. Don't even imagine that a two-year-old will tolerate a lecture. Ask yourself if it's fair to take your youngster on an all-morning shopping trip. If you don't have options, plan ahead.

• Think it through. Don't impose a situation on the child that he cannot tolerate. Let the child know what you're about to do, how long you will be staying, and what you'll be doing afterward. Try to make the following activity enjoyable for him.

• Praise positive behavior. Often, parents tend not to say a word about the times their children are good. Remember to catch them being wonderful and tell them so. Tell Susan she behaved very nicely at Aunt Frieda's. Thank her for waiting so patiently while you shopped.

10.6-2 Use Preventive Measures.

A few ounces of prevention can head off a lot of unhappiness.

- Plan ahead. Take a toy or activity for diversion just in case there will be time when she has nothing to do. Have her choose a special possession to take along to show Uncle Jerry.
- Tell her the plan. Explain where you are going and what you will do. Let her know what to expect.
- Role-play the situation. Have your child pretend he has just arrived at the visit and let him tell you what he will say or do that will make you proud of him. Be sure to include role-playing good manners.
- State your expectations. Clearly inform the child what you expect of him and define what he is to do. Just before the activity, repeat your outline. Let him know too what will happen if he doesn't cooperate.
- Enlist help. Perhaps Grandpa has always interfered: "Let the boy have fun. Boys are like that." Or Uncle Doug roughhouses and then complains that Jeff is wild. Sit down with these people during a quiet moment and explain your feelings and how they may help. "Pop, Jeremy loves being with you. But you tickle him and throw him up in the air, and then you can't understand why he's all over you or gets wild at the dinner table. How about playing catch or trying a board game before dinner?"
- Set up a system for your absence. If you won't be there, you must set up a system for discipline. With the child right there, tell Grandma what the rules are. Then let the child know that you've told her: "Gerry, I have told Grandma you can play until seven-thirty. Then you must get ready for bed and go to sleep after one story. If you're good for Grandma, you may watch cartoons in the morning."

10.6-3 Be Sure to Follow Through.

In public, warn the child once and then, if he doesn't cooperate, you *must* follow through. Choose a consequence you can realistically apply. Your ultimate goal is to use soft reprimands, whispers to tell him you mean business, or that certain look that delivers your message. But until you achieve it, here is some help.

• Use time-out. In the diner, if you tell Leslie to stop throwing her fork and she continues, warn her: "Leslie, if you continue, you will have time-out in the car." Then, if necessary, swiftly remove her, even if you must carry her screaming from the premises. Of course you'll be embarrassed, but action now will mean fewer problems on future outings. In the car, tell her, "When you are ready to be quiet and behave, we will go back inside."

Then keep the faith. Sometimes you'll wonder if time-out is going to work this time, but be consistent. Alissa, two years old, commented to her mom as they sat in time-out outside a restaurant, "This is nice." But it was only a minute more before she said, "I be good now." Once you establish control with a toddler, then just a quiet "Do we need to leave?" will quiet her down.

• Take away a privilege. As a consequence for misbehavior in public, take away a privilege the child enjoys, such as a favorite television show. Always follow through. Do not make threats you won't carry out. If it is Pop's birthday, twenty relatives and friends are coming for the party, and Jeremy has a fit about getting dressed up, don't threaten him with, "None of Grandpa's birthday cake for you!" because you're sure not to follow through. Be realistic.

• Use response cost. Before setting out, tell the child she can earn a special reward if she cooperates. Give her five tokens and warn her that she will lose one each time she misbehaves. If she gets home with at least four of them, she will get a surprise.

10.6-4 Plan a Training Session.

If misbehavior in public has become a constant problem, enlist the help of a friend or relative and set up training sessions. Before you leave home, tell the child your expectations and the consequences for good behavior as well as misbehavior. Here is the plan of action:

Day 1: Go to Aunt Betty's house for dessert. If the child misbehaves, warn her, and if necessary, leave. Take her home and call the baby-sitter you've previously enlisted to be "on call." Tell the child why she had to come home and leave instructions for bedtime, etc. Then go back to the "party" at Aunt Betty's house.

Day 2: Go to Grandma's house (or any place the child really likes to go), but don't take her. Once again, she must stay home with the sitter. Explain why. Tell her she must earn the right to go places again.

Day 3: Try again. Take her again to a place she likes to go, repeating your expectations and the possible consequences. Be willing to follow through by taking her home again if necessary. If she is cooperative, however, praise her and let her choose another place to visit soon.

CHAPTER 11

School and
Learning Problems

IN our society, we all place great value on education and want our children to do well in school. But sometimes the process fails to go smoothly and problems come up that require solutions.

Your child's problems with school may be related to academics or behavior. They may range from talking in class to total defiance, from forgetting to do homework to severe learning difficulties, from refusing to go to school to utter frustration with the work load. How should you handle them? In this chapter, we suggest methods of assisting your child and working with his teachers to solve school-related problems.

11.1 DOESN'T WANT TO GO TO SCHOOL

For the third time this week, Josie has a stomachache *and* a headache and insists she doesn't feel well enough to go to school. Marty tries a different tactic—she is so anxious about leaving home that she's hiding under the bed so nobody can find her. Tim, ten, decides he isn't going to school anymore, period.

Parents are never sure whether making a child go to school is the right thing to do. They don't know if the youngster really does feel poorly or whether, like most children at some time in their young lives, they simply don't want to go. In households where going to school becomes a problem, the early morning hours are frequently filled with tears and arguments.

Most of the children whose parents bring them to us for help are motivated by very real reasons for this behavior, and a few develop intense fears about going to school. The emotions may range from separation anxiety to fear of the school bully. Children haven't learned how to deal with all the problems in the outside world, so they often choose to avoid them instead. Sometimes, though, the problems are right there at home. For example, the family is going through a stressful period and the child is afraid something will happen to a parent while he's at school. Or in another case, the child may subconsciously feel that if the family has him to focus on, the parents won't fight so much.

You can't make a child love school, but you can reassure him, help him work through his feelings, and guide him to a potential solution. In the same way, you can avoid or change behavior patterns that contribute to the problem.

11.1-1 Set Criteria for Staying Home.

Decide on the criteria for not going to school. For example: The child must have a temperature of 100° F and well-defined symptoms. He must stay in bed. If you find yourself at home with a child whose mysterious malady vanishes after the school bus passes, then make sure the day is not fun-and-games and snacks. Enforce a sickbed atmosphere: No friends to play with, in bed all day, only light, nourishing foods to eat.

11.1-2 Discover the Reason.

Find out what is bothering your youngster so much that he wants to avoid school.

• Have a talk. Encourage the child to tell you what is going on at school that makes her prefer not to go. Try asking her to list her favorite and least favorite things about it and give you reasons why. Look for clues that may tell you she's not afraid of school but, rather, afraid of leaving home. You may not be able to solve a problem, but you can help her deal with her feelings and reassure her with love and understanding.

• Talk with siblings and peers. Often you can gain insights into your child's feelings by asking others if they are aware of problems that contribute to this behavior. Sometimes a big brother or sister has special knowledge of the situation or can lend a hand.

• Talk with the teacher. Discuss the behavioral problem with the child's teacher. Whether the difficulty is academic or emotional, the teacher should be made aware of it and may possibly assist in finding solutions.

11.1-3 Bridge the Gap Between Home and School.

Try these ways to encourage willingness to attend school.

• Talk it up. Mark the calendar with special school events and encourage the child to look forward to them. "Next Friday is field day. Boy, that will be a lot of fun." Or, "Your class is going to the fire station this week. What do you think you'll see? Remember to tell me all about it."

• Use show and tell as a motivator. Help her find something special to take for show and tell, maybe a favorite book or a picture of her cat or an interesting gadget to share with the class. Help her plan ahead, using study units in social studies or other subjects as cues to the selection.

• Discuss what she likes about school. Ask the child to list everything she likes about school and then use this information as motivation: "Isn't today art day? You really like the teacher, Miss Angie, don't you? Today is Brownies, too. What a great day it's going to be."

• Encourage school friendships. Help your child make friends, and nurture the friendships that evolve, especially if he doesn't attend a neighborhood school and know lots of children who live nearby. Arrange for his friends to come over to play. Start an afternoon play group once a week, with parents taking turns as hosts. For older children, suggest ways to get together with friends:

"Sue, why don't you call Ellen and ask her to go to the movies with us tonight?"

11.1-4 Get the Child to School.

In most cases, your goal is to get the child back to school on a regular schedule, realizing there may be bouts of reluctance to attend, especially after vacations and illness. Whatever the reason or the strategy, get your child to school.

• Move the child quickly through the morning routine. Aim all your efforts at getting him ready and out. The more set your ritual is, the easier this will be. Make dressing and eating such a habit that he moves through the routine without thinking. If it has been working against you, change it. For example, Sharon is always so late that Daddy must drop her off at school; put an end to that, but let Sharon have breakfast with Daddy when she's ready on time.

• Ignore negative comments. Don't even respond to negative remarks about school. On the other hand, praise and reinforce positive comments and actions.

• Provide manual guidance if necessary. If you must, guide your child like a puppet through the morning routine and all the way to the classroom. Choose the least emotional parent to do the job. Put on a matter-of-fact but positive face, guide him through the motions, walk him to his classroom, and then leave promptly.

11.1-5 Phase the Child into Regular Attendance.

If the child hasn't attended school for a while or is especially resistant to going, it may be necessary to make special arrangements with the teacher and the school administrators. These suggestions have worked for several children.

• Arrange to have the child met at the door. Perhaps the teacher or another staff member will meet her at the entrance to the school and walk her to class. This must be done discreetly, of course, so other children won't notice or tease.

• Arrange for the child to spend time in a "safe" place. At the beginning of the school year, a child who is uncomfortable about going to a new classroom might be allowed to spend time with last year's teacher and slowly eased into the new environment.

• Go to school after school hours. Arrange to take the child to the school after school hours for a week; then she may be comfortable enough to try it when the other children are there.

• Arrange for part-time attendance. Have the child spend an hour at school, either in the morning or afternoon session, and then gradually spend more and more time there.

11.1-6 Reinforce Positive Attendance Behavior.

Let the child know you think it's grand that she goes to school. Praise every action that moves her toward attendance—getting ready, going, and staying there.

• Reward with your attention. If your youngster has been getting a lot of your time by *not* going to school, make a change. Have lunch with her after she goes to school for part of the day. Or pick her up after school for a special snack or outing.

• Set up a formal reward system. Let your child earn points for getting ready for school and then going to school and, later, for school attendance. Remember that in the beginning, the reinforcement must be stronger to get the behavior started. You may need to reactivate a reward system after vacations or illnesses. See Chapter 2 for details about charts and rewards.

11.1-7 Get Professional Help for School Phobia.

Some youngsters become extremely resistant to going to school, and if this is the case with your child, you will probably need help to get him past the problem. It is important to seek professional advice early, because many adults who suffer from agoraphobia were school phobics as youngsters. See Chapter 17 for information on finding the appropriate professional help.

11.2 WON'T DO HOMEWORK/STUDY

The purpose of homework is to reinforce what's learned during the day and to help the child learn to complete a task independently, budget time, and assume responsibility. It requires self-motivation, discipline, and the ability to utilize outside resources. It is one way a child discovers how to learn on his own.

No matter how much a child dislikes doing homework or studying, it still must be done. After a while, those endless excuses the teachers hear—"The dog ate my homework"; "We had company last night"; "My sister tore it up"—must be abandoned and the homework must be turned in. But how can you make studying outside the school environment a positive learning experience for your child and, at the same time, ease the pressure it places on the family?

Try these solutions.

11.2-1 Determine What Is Expected.

It's important for you to know what the school expects and to plan for it.

• Get information from the child. As the school year gets under way, you will start to get information from your child about homework and test schedules. Try to map this out with your child: math homework, Monday through Thursday; spelling test every Friday.

When you greet the child after school, ask what he did in school and what homework has been assigned. If he always replies, "I don't have any homework," or "I already did it," you may ask to see the books or the papers. This will help you monitor what he's doing and suggest nightly goals. Use this as an opportunity to let him know you are interested in what he's learning and that you realize his work is important. With some children, you may feel like a policeman for a while, but try not to act like one. Think of yourself as a facilitator: "Hi, Joey. How was school? It sounds like you really worked hard. Let's get you a snack and then figure out what you have to get done before TV time."

• Get information from the school. Meet with the teacher early in the school year and find out what's expected of your child that year. Ask about homework to be assigned nightly, and determine how long the average assignment should take. Are there any weekly tests? Book reports? Special projects? How will the student's work be graded? What role does the teacher wish the parents to play? This is your chance to get valuable insights into the school's and the teacher's policies and attitudes.

11.2-2 Develop a Homework Plan.

Together with the child, set up a homework and study plan that suits him. Remember that what works for one child doesn't always work for another. Some children need to have a break after school to burn off excess energy, while others do best getting their homework done before playing. Experiment at first, then be open to make changes if necessary.

The plan may be a formal one that's written as a contract, or it may be casual. With very responsible children, talking about homework and determining where it fits into the daily routine may be enough. For others, constant monitoring and parental support are required, at least initially, to get the child to persist. You may need to begin with more supervision, later phasing into more independent study. These guidelines will help you determine what works best in your case.

• Choose a specific time. Decide on a mutually agreeable time when homework will be done. The child must be involved in this decision so it will be a time he thinks he can live with. Tilt the odds in your favor by making sure you aren't competing with favorite TV programs or the child's need for physical activity. Acknowledge that the hour and length of time spent studying will vary when necessary.

• Create a place to work. Your child needs a personal place to study that is quiet, well lit, and equipped with a dictionary and other resources. Create a special niche and make sure you or other members of the family respect it. This will also help her learn how to organize and become responsible for her own school supplies and materials.

11.2-3 Monitor and Reinforce Study Behavior.

When your child isn't doing his homework or is having a problem with his schoolwork, then you must help him discover the cause and, when possible, change the task or the situation so he can achieve greater success.

• Isolate the problem. Try to establish some understanding of why the child doesn't want to do his homework or why he's having problems studying. Look for answers to these questions:

Is there one specific subject he doesn't want to tackle?
Is this an everyday problem, or does it occur only occasionally?
Does he understand the assignment?
Is he easily distracted?
Does he forget to do the work, or does he come home unprepared?
Is the material too difficult for him?
Is there outside interference that gets in the way?

• Change the schedule if necessary. Determine the need and redesign the plan. Freddy is easily distracted and he doesn't get any work done when he's alone in his room. Because he seems to need more supervision, it's agreed that he will do his homework at the kitchen table after dinner, with a parent close by. As for Linda, her homework takes more time than expected. She's getting to bed very late and is tired. Schedule the homework time for an earlier hour and find out if she needs extra help with the material.
• Use natural contingencies to reinforce study. For the child who plays when he's supposed to be doing homework, use playing or other fun activities as rewards for completing the homework assignment. Or alternate work and play periods: one assignment,

ten minutes of free time, another assignment, another ten free minutes, and so forth.

• Chart the study time. Set specific goals for the time spent studying, gradually increasing the length of time if necessary. Have the child time himself, stopping the clock when he takes a break. Try reinforcing the study of a specific subject or skill with rewards. Howard, for example, hasn't learned his math facts, so his homework problems are severe. Have him keep a record of how many minutes he studies his multiplication facts each day. Then on Fridays, give him a surprise, extra playtime, or later bedtime hours if he has increased his knowledge of the facts.

11.2-4 Teach Organization and Study Skills.

Organization doesn't come naturally to a child and neither does knowing how to study, so help him learn it.

• Check off completed assignments. Encourage the child to have a special place to record homework assignments and check off each assignment when it's completed.

• Segment assignments into manageable parts. If the child is constantly frustrated by not knowing how to begin, show him how to break a big assignment down into segments that are not so overwhelming. Have him ask himself, What should I do first for this assignment? What should I do next? What materials do I need? If he is easily frustrated, see Section 11.5.

• Teach the child how to allot time. Let him budget his time by planning ahead for extra study time when a test or special project is looming. Keep a monthly calendar to note upcoming tests and reports. Section 11.6 will give more helpful information about what to do if your child becomes very anxious about tests.

• Model how to plan ahead. Hold weekly family meetings to discuss everyone's special plans and needs for the coming week. Do your own planning so the child can observe you. Help her organize her week's activities. Perhaps Janine has a book report due on Friday. She decides that on Monday she will write an outline, on

Tuesday the first draft, on Thursday she will show it to her parents and then write the final copy.

For long-term projects, lead the child through her own schedule: "Here's the calendar. The science project is due after Thanksgiving. Let's break the job down into parts: 1. select the topic; 2. do special reading; 3. plan the project; 4. gather material; 5. do the experiment; etc. How long do you think each step will take you? Let's mark the calendar when you think you will have finished each task." Wendy has a book report due on Friday. How can you break the job down so you won't be up till one in the morning helping her finish it? Monday: outline. Tuesday: draft. Thursday: share with parents and write final report.

• Have homework checks. Show the child how to do a "homework check" every day before she leaves school to be sure she has the books and materials she will need. Encourage her to exchange telephone numbers with other children in the class in case she needs more information about the assignments.

11.2-5 Provide Additional Reinforcement.

As usual, praise, praise, praise, and when needed, use stronger reinforcement and rewards.

• Praise effort. Don't expect perfection. And remember to praise each and every step toward independence. Praise the child for remembering his assignment, then praise him for beginning it. If he then gets distracted, help him get back on track and set a new goal. If he is easily frustrated, praise him for working independently for a few minutes before asking for help.

• Be positive. When your child does his work well, tries hard, or shows patience doing a task, praise him. If he has difficulty in one subject, build confidence by commenting on his success with another assignment. Let him know mistakes are acceptable—everyone makes mistakes and can learn from them.

• Provide extra reinforcement when necessary. Some children need encouragement to build the homework habit, so try using a homework chart that rewards the child for getting the job done.

Allow her to earn a star for each day of completed work, with a certain number of stars redeemable for a special outing or activity in her honor. See Section 2.5 for more on charts.

11.2-6 Use Negative Consequences.

If the positive approach doesn't work in your case, try following the child's inaction by your action. Take away a favorite TV show, a special toy, or telephone time. Choose a consequence that occurs soon, so it will have an immediate effect.

11.2-7 Give Increasing Responsibility to the Child.

As your child matures, gradually give her the responsibility for homework and study. Rather than completing the assignment for her, do your best to facilitate her efforts. Many children become anxious when they can't complete an assignment the way the teacher did it at school. Sometimes, a leading question will get them back to work without giving away the answer.

• Phase yourself out. Though you may have to work directly with your child at first, try to decrease your direct supervisory role as quickly as possible. Move yourself to another area of the same room, but continue to be available for questions.

• Let the child take responsibility. Because homework is usually meant to reinforce what has already been learned in class, the child should be able to do it himself most of the time. Although you may have to reassure her or guide her, you shouldn't have to do the work for her, even for the youngest student. If she is consistently unable to do the assigned tasks independently, meet with the teacher for discussion. Perhaps additional classroom help or private tutoring is necessary.

11.3 TEACHER-STUDENT PROBLEMS

Sometimes your child will be assigned to a teacher he doesn't like. And sometimes the teacher doesn't seem to like him. Teachers come in all shapes and sizes, and somewhere along the line, the child is bound to come upon one who presents problems for him. As parents, it's important for you to determine the truth and the extent of the problem before jumping in with radical solutions. Often, the difficulties just fade away after a few weeks or the child adjusts to the teacher's personality and techniques.

Whether your child likes his teacher or not, you must help him find the way to perform well at school and to act appropriately. The negative feelings should not interfere with his schoolwork. You cannot make a child like someone, but you can teach behaviors to help him deal with his own feelings and gain the teacher's attention in positive ways.

11.3-1 Distinguish Between Fact and Fantasy.

Is there really a problem? Unless the situation seems truly alarming, we suggest that at first, you listen to the child's complaints without giving them undue attention.

• Start out ignoring the comments. Play down or even ignore the initial negative comments you hear from your child about her teacher. She may have heard from other children that the teacher is "mean" or "makes you work too hard." Reassure her that everything will work out just fine, and remind her that she didn't like last year's teacher for a while, either, but she loved her by the end of the first term. Tell her to give the teacher a chance before making a judgment.

• Decide if the problems are real and important. If the complaints continue, investigate whether the comments are justified. Is the information firsthand or more like "Susie said so"? Are there facts that lead you to believe there may be a problem in the classroom?

11.3-2 Talk with Your Child.

Let the child tell you how she feels about the teacher and the difficulties between them. Listen with understanding. But tell her firmly that she must learn to live with this teacher because all through life, she will meet people she doesn't like but must work with anyway.

11.3-3 Teach Teacher-Pleasing Behaviors.

Show the child how to be a more engaging student.

• Teach him to listen. Teachers want pupils to listen. If your child is a poor listener at home, then he may be the same way at school. Work on this by practicing listening skills: Say something to the child and then ask him to repeat what you have said. Show him how to listen with his eyes, too, so he will notice the teacher's reactions to his words and behavior.

• Teach him to follow directions. Following directions is one of the most important skills a student must acquire. If he doesn't "tune in" to the instructions, then he can't cooperate or learn in the classroom. Practice following simple directions, using games like Simon Says. When you issue directions at other times, have the child repeat them to be sure he has received them accurately. Point out key words, play games with prepositions, and *always* praise him when he attends to and follows directions correctly. For more suggestions, see sections 5.8 and 11.11.

• Be neat. Neatness shows the teacher that the child values his own efforts. Besides, his work will be easier to read and more pleasing to look at.

• Be courteous. Manners count in a class of thirty children. Everyone likes to feel appreciated and respected, teachers included. Teach your child to be polite, to say "Thank you" and "Please." And to smile!

11.3-4 Talk to the Teacher.

If the problems persist, ask for a conference with the teacher. Before you rush in ready to blame, remember that you know only one side of the story. Your purpose is to inquire if there are problems and, if so, to identify the specifics and come up with a solution.

Make an appointment with the teacher; don't just drop in for a talk when students may be waiting for her attention.

• Don't attack, use tact. You will accomplish more if you are diplomatic and understanding of the teacher's methods and approach. Tell her that you are concerned that your child thinks she doesn't like him or that the child's feelings about her are affecting his schoolwork. If the teacher comes up with specific problem areas, talk about how they can be overcome or ask the teacher to work with you to help the child deal with his feelings.

• Focus on the positive. Let the teacher know what you perceive to be the child's strengths and interests. Also discuss his weaknesses. The more a teacher knows about a child, the easier it will be for her to establish rapport and instruct the child. Similarly, the more you know about the teacher, the easier it will be to help the child understand her.

11.3-5 As a Last Resort, Talk with the School Administrators.

If the problem isn't resolved and if you believe there really is a serious personality conflict, make an appointment with an administrator of the school to discuss alternatives. The difficulties can probably be ironed out, though occasionally, the child should be switched to another class.

11.4 OVERACHIEVES OR UNDERACHIEVES

Such familiar words: "Do your best. As long as you do your best, that's fine with me." We're sure you've said them to your children, just as your parents said them to you. But what *is* your child's best? What can you realistically expect from him in academic accomplishment? If he brings home a C in math, how should you react? Or if he gets all A's with no studying, what do the grades mean?

Both overachievement and underachievement concern schoolwork that does not match the child's ability. The underachiever is not reaching his potential to learn, perhaps because of lack of motivation or lack of interest in the work. It's possible that emotional, behavioral, or learning problems temporarily prevent him from persevering, or maybe they are the beginning of a lifelong problem.

The overachiever is compelled to pursue goals that are unrealistic for him. When a child—or adult—relentlessly pushes himself to do better and better, he's likely to burn out eventually. He may be able to reach the same goal at a slower pace with energy to spare, a positive attitude, and the desire to continue.

Here is the information you will need to understand your child's learning power so your expectations for him can be realistic. If you discover he is an underachiever or overachiever, use the solutions we suggest.

11.4-1 Determine Realistic Expectations.

This requires gathering information about the child, much of which is available in school records. You may also want to request that the school psychologist, an educational specialist, or a private consultant do special testing and then review the records with you.

• Identify learning potential. Children are born with an inherent ability to learn. That ability, coupled with their environment, determines learning potential. Intelligence tests are designed to measure this characteristic by gathering information about the ability to solve certain types of problems, but whether they can do this accurately is questionable. Parents are usually mesmerized by IQ scores and place tremendous faith in the numbers. But the test score is simply a measure of how that child performed on a specific test on a specific day, and should be considered as an indicator and not an absolute measure. Though a child may never be able to do better than her best, she can surely do less than her best on occasion.

Group intelligence tests are designed to test masses of children and judge them according to whether their score is above or below a hundred, which is considered average. They are simple to administer, but the results are not as reliable or comprehensive as individual intelligence tests which are administered by a trained psychologist or psychometrist and are designed to give information on a wide range of very specific abilities. In a one-to-one setting, the tester observes the child's test-taking skills, his approach to problem solving, and his ability to deal with frustration.

• Discuss your child's intelligence score with a trained professional, asking him how best to interpret it. Some questions to consider are: What is the actual score? Is there a single score only, or is it the sum of subtest scores? In what category does your child's score fall: above average, average, or below average? Are there further classifications, such as superior, that might be appropriate? How does this score compare with the average for your child's school?

• Identify the actual level of achievement. Standardized achievement tests measure a child's academic performance against her peer group and assess her level of proficiency in basic skill areas such as math, reading, language, social studies, and science. The methods of scoring these tests—grade equivalent scores, stanines, or percentile ranks—have led to frequent abuse and misinterpretation. Parents are often totally confused by them.

Grade equivalents are based on the average score of a large number of children in a particular grade level. Because of the way achievement tests are constructed, a change of only a few points in raw score or number can make a large difference in the grade-equivalent score. Jenny may get only one more correct math answer than Alan and she can earn a grade-level equivalent of 3.5 while Alan receives 3.0.

The interpretation of scores is complicated when the national sample of scores doesn't relate to what is expected in a particular locality. At one school, most of the children in a class may be performing above the national norm. If your beginning fourth grader earns a 4.0 on the math subtest of an achievement test, he may be performing below the level of the rest of his classmates. Or if a third grader earns a 7.0 in reading on the achievement test, then he certainly has done well when compared nationally, but his local peers may have done just as well.

Therefore, in some communities, scoring at grade level puts the child at the top of his class while in other schools, that same score may mean he is functioning below the level of his peers.

Percentile ranks are helpful because they compare the performance of a child with his grade-level peers. Thus, if a second grader earns a grade-equivalent score of 2.8 in math and a percentile rank of 82, that means he scored as well or better than 82 percent of his peers. Again, you must compare your child's score with that of his peers at his school and not rely only on the national averages.

Stanines are scores that are not based on comparisons; instead, they are determined by the absolute performance on the test. Using a scale of 1 to 9: 9 is high; 1, 2, and 3 are considered below average; 4, 5, and 6 are average; and 7, 8, and 9 are above average.

Almost every school in the United States administers standardized achievement tests to its students once a year or more often. The California Achievement Tests, the Iowa Tests of Basic Skills, the Stanford Achievement Test, and the Metropolitan Achievement Tests are examples of standardized tests of academic performance and may be used in your area.

When you look at your child's achievement-test results, identify how they are scored and read the explanation of the scoring. Arrange a conference with the teacher or guidance counselor if you are confused or dismayed by the results.

• Compare the level of achievement with the learning potential to determine if the child is an overachiever, underachiever, or a student performing as you would expect. The chart below (Figure 7) will help you set some realistic expectations for his performance in school.

Fig. 7 The Achievement Matrix

	Achievement Test Scores		
	Low	**Average**	**High**
	Below grade level 1, 2, 3 Stanine 0–39% percentile	On grade level 4, 5, 6 Stanine 40–69% percentile	Above grade level 7, 8, 9 Stanine 70–99% percentile
Above Average IQ	Underachiever Bright child doing below-average work. Why?	Mild Underachiever Bright child doing average work. Why?	On target Bright child doing above-average work
Average IQ	Underachiever Average learner working below expected level. Why?	On Target Average learner functioning at average level.	Overachiever Average learner performing at above-average level.
Below Average IQ	On Target Slow learner performing appropriately.	Mild Overachiever Slow learner performing at a level higher than expected; will probably burn out.	Overachiever Slow learner pushed beyond expected level; will probably burn out.

The diagram is composed of two scales: The horizontal scale relates to achievement-test scores, while the vertical scale refers to intelligence scores. Compare the two to determine how your child is doing in relation to his ability. Grades are not used as a criterion since they vary from school to school. However, if your child's IQ and achievement test scores are average or above but he continues to earn poor grades, then he may also be considered an underachiever. Similarly, if your child's IQ score is below or near average and your child is earning very high grades, it is possible he is an overachiever. You will need to determine what the grading scale in your school means in terms of performance to make an adequate interpretation.

11.4-2 Help the Overachiever Work at a Comfortable Level.

You might ask, "What is wrong with overachieving? We've been taught that if you work hard, you will be successful. If you work harder, you will be even more successful." What's wrong is that some children push themselves so much that they become burned out or forget how to have fun. If a child works at a more comfortable level, he can reach his goal and still have enough energy and ambition left over to meet another one.

• Lower expectations, especially yours if you have been pushing your child too hard.

• Promote a well-rounded life. Grades aren't everything, and having fun is important, too. Think back to your own peers in school. Does there seem to be an exact correlation between A's and success in later life? Is the child modeling himself after a workaholic parent? Encourage your child to enjoy other activities besides goal-oriented work.

• Break perfectionistic habits. Studying until the small hours of the night or getting up before daybreak to complete more of the task is not a healthy habit. One little girl we know was so upset because she only got an A-minus on her science test that she couldn't fall asleep at night and insisted on studying long hours. Her parents had to enforce the rule that no studying was allowed after 9:30 P.M.

• Set realistic study goals. Discuss her strengths and weaknesses with the youngster, and help her decide on appropriate goals and the amount of study needed to meet them. Angela did well in social studies and science when she kept up with her homework and read the required material. She didn't need to read ten outside sources to understand the information. In spelling, she followed a weekly study plan provided by her teacher and could skip copying the words twenty times every night.

• Schedule fun activities. If your child tends to spend too much time working, insist that her schedule include more enjoyable activities. Help her find outside interests in sports and cultural areas, suggest inviting friends over to play, or take her on outings unrelated to schoolwork. If these activities haven't been part of her regular routine, you must actively promote them.

11.4-3 Help the Underachiever Reach Potential.

There are always reasons why a child's schoolwork isn't as good as it can be. Here's how to determine what they are.

• Determine the reasons for underachievement. Some children have learning problems, which interfere with their success in school, and may need special tutoring (see Section 11.14). Others may be overwhelmed by emotional problems that require professional treatment (see Chapter 17 for advice on seeking professional help).

Some children are simply late bloomers, immature and unmotivated until later in their young life. Zachary was brought to us at ten years of age because his parents felt he was not doing as well in school as he should. He walked into out office, sat down, and asked, "Is there any hope for me?" It turned out that he was a late bloomer like his parents, but they had overreacted. After determining that the boy did not have learning problems or an unhealthy attitude toward school, we helped the parents place the facts in the proper perspective.

• Lower the pressure. The underachiever has often been constantly berated and belittled for his lack of success. He is well aware that his performance is unacceptable. Stop demanding all A's or even B's and, instead, set realistic goals for each individual subject area. Get off his back. Don't demand the best in each course. Use reinforcement to motivate the child's improvement.

• Provide reassurance and support. Positive feedback does wonders and is much more effective than complaints and pressure. Always acknowledge the steps in the right direction, giving constant encouragement to persevere. Studies show that parents who make a practice of commenting on success do encourage achievement. So be supportive, letting him know what you expect every day, helping him feel good about his accomplishments, and communicating your interest in what he's doing.

SUGGESTED BOOKS FOR PARENTS AND CHILDREN
   Cohen, Miriam. *First Grade Takes a Test.* New York: Dell, 1980. Who's the best? Are grades all that count? For young elementary-school children (K–3).
   Kraus, Robert. *Leo the Late Bloomer.* New York: Windmill Books, 1981. Leo's parents are anxious waiting and watching him (PS–3).

11.5 IS EASILY FRUSTRATED/CAN'T HANDLE PRESSURE

"I can't do it!" Bang goes the book on the floor as the tears come to Brad's eyes. He responds with tears and tantrums when he can't do his math problems. Aileen expresses her frustration by retreating into herself, and Andre takes his out in fights after school. Bill crumples up the papers, one after another.

Tolerance to frustration grows with maturity. A two-year-old hasn't learned how to delay gratification, and when his efforts don't pay off, he has little perseverance. As he gets older, he learns to persist even when he's not immediately successful, and to figure out alternative approaches to problems. Some children, however, tend to give up too soon. When your child is frequently overwhelmed with frustration and pressure, then you must help defuse the situation. School should be a challenging place and learning should be a positive process, not a high-pressure affair. But when school expectations are out of sync with skills or when a child who usually copes well shows signs of frustration, then something is interfering with progress. Look to the causes and relieve them if you can. Then help the child learn new responses to his lack of success.

11.5-1 Pinpoint the Source of the Pressure.

Frustration indicates internal pressure to achieve a goal that is not being met. There are a number of questions you can ask to help you unearth the cause of the problem:

• Is the child overtired? Make sure she is getting enough rest. All children find life's obstacles and relationships more difficult when they are tired.

• Is the child overscheduled? We all get frustrated when we have too many responsibilities that pull us in different directions. Take a close look at your child's schedule to determine if it provides an appropriate amount of time for rest, study, and play. Drop some extracurricular activities if there are too many for her to cope with.

• Is the child a perfectionist? Some children have unreasonable expectations and unrealistic standards for themselves. Others don't know they can ask for help or are afraid to request it. In order to lessen the pressure, a child's perfectionistic tendencies may need to be curbed. Read the section on overachievement.

• Can the child label his frustration? If he doesn't understand what is bothering him, show him how to label his feelings and express himself appropriately.

• Does the pressure come from the outside? Are you expecting too much of your child? Do you demand that he do well in every school subject, as well as soccer, basketball, chorus, and the Boy Scouts? Does the teacher or the school demand too much of him? What unwritten messages are you giving your child? Do you need to let up?

• Does the child have opportunities to succeed? Your goal is to have your child feel good about herself and, at the same time, realize that trying hard has its rewards. Make sure she has enough positive experience to bolster her confidence and her ego. Talk with the teacher about drawing upon and playing up the child's strengths in class. Get her into outside activities at which she can succeed.

11.5-2 Teach New Responses to Frustration.

You can't possibly remove all the frustration and pressure from a child's world, and that means she must learn positive acceptable ways to deal with those feelings.

• **Teach relaxation skills.** We all deal better with the events of the day when we are relaxed. Help your youngster learn to raise her tolerance to frustration by helping her relax her body (see Section 2.10).

• **Teach labeling.** Show the young child how to identify the feeling by labeling it when it occurs: "Stewart, you are frustrated because you haven't matched your letter. Here is a letter A. Now find another one. Take your time." With an older child, do the same by discussing his feelings with him. Together, identify situations that are likely to be frustrating, then suggest alternative strategies for completing the task.

• **Teach positive self-talk.** Show the child how you talk to yourself in a positive way when you're in a difficult situation: "This is a very hard crossword puzzle. It's not worth crying over. I think I'll skip this clue. Oh, here's a word I know! Good! Now I'll get a dictionary to help me." Demonstrate the effectiveness of the old admonition "If at first you don't succeed, try, try again" by modeling how you deal with frustration, and praise the child when he does the same. For example, "I didn't get that stitch right again! I'm going to take it out and start all over. There! It's fine now."

• **Teach the child when to ask for help.** While some children are reluctant to ask for help, others always want help immediately. Teach the child to try to find a solution to his problem first (tell him to give it "my try"). Then, when he doesn't know what else to do, let him know it's okay to ask for help. When you notice that he's becoming frustrated with a task, intervene to teach this technique: "What could you say to yourself to help you do that? What could you do besides getting angry or giving up?"

• Role-play. At a relaxed moment, play a game with your youngster, acting out a frustrating situation. Pretend you are working on a jigsaw puzzle and can't find the piece that fits. Let the child act out being frustrated, then just the opposite. Encourage him to talk to himself positively and to choose a way to solve the problem. Take your turn at acting. Then discuss both responses with him.

• Reinforce the child for acting appropriately. Praise him for delaying his usual angry response to frustration, and praise him again when you see he's using a new appropriate strategy. Set up a reward system at home or in school to reinforce this maturing skill.

Danny was easily frustrated by oral directions. His parents worked with him at home, and his teacher set up a procedure in which she automatically came by his desk to check that he understood the instructions. Danny then earned points for persevering and working alone for longer periods of time.

11.5-3 Identify the Source of Frustration and Give Help.

This isn't a permanent solution, because frustrations will always occur. But when frustration is justified, remedying the cause is in order.

• Identify the problem and teach the skill. If a child is having difficulty performing a task she should be able to do or wants to do enormously, isolate the problem area and, if possible, teach her the skill she needs. Or arrange for help from the teacher or perhaps a tutor. Often it is the situation, not the skill, that is the problem. A child may panic when she faces a test or time pressure (see Section 11.6).

• Modify the task. Show the child an alternative way to accomplish the goal. When possible, break a big task into small component parts that can be conquered one at a time. Teach her how to outline notes or list the important vocabulary words. If a toy or game is too difficult for the child, put it away for a while until she is more mature, or change the rules so it is easier. If a child is frustrated by copying a book report without errors, relieve the pressure by letting her use an erasable pen.

• Be a role model. Set the example you want your child to follow. If she sees you slamming doors, cursing, or losing control, she'll have good reason to do the same.

11.6 SUFFERS ANXIETY AND PANIC OVER TESTS

Tests throw some children into a panic. They become so anxious and worried that they will fail or forget everything they ever knew that they may become paralyzed and do just that. It's critical to deal with these feelings early in your child's life, because they tend to grow with him, affecting him throughout his academic life. There are ways to help him learn to deal with and banish test anxiety.

11.6-1 Set Up an Atmosphere of Acceptance.

Create a supportive environment at home for the child.

• Be predictable. Can your child bring his poor papers as well as his good papers to you without fear of your reactions? Take pride in your child's accomplishments but not so much that there is no room for less than his best. Have realistic expectations, but don't overreact when you feel he's done less well than he should or could. Say, "Okay, let's look at this paper together. You made a C-minus. What made it difficult for you?" Make sure the child knows you are available for support and assistance as well as a pat on the back.

• Give praise. Praise the child for having studied hard even if the results of her efforts aren't reflected in good grades. Praise her for the behaviors that help diffuse the pressures of a test, such as preparing, relaxing, reviewing, and getting a good night's sleep.

11.6-2 Make Sure the Child Is Prepared.

To help the child deal with test panic and anxiety, make sure he's ready to take the test. For some children, this may mean overlearning the material before they feel comfortable.

• Help plan a study schedule. When a test is coming up, encourage the child to write out a study schedule that allows him to be prepared ahead of time. Break the content down into small amounts, and schedule one portion of it for each day.

• Help determine what to study. Make sure the child knows what material the test will cover. Ask her what kind of test is to be given, say, multiple choice or essay, and be sure she knows how to take that kind of test. Talk about how the type of test influences how she should study.

• Help the child learn study skills. After the child has studied the appropriate information for the test, show her how she can check what she has learned by questioning herself on the material. Teach her how to skim material for important points, take notes, or use a particular study technique. Teach her the study technique developed by Francis Robinson, SQ3R: Survey or look over the material; write Questions to use as a guide for study; Read the material to answer the questions; Recite the material to be sure you know the answers; and Review the material at a later time.

11.6-3 Teach Relaxation Skills.

Read Section 2.10 again, and help your child learn how to relax so she can combat the tension she generates before and during a test. After she has practiced the techniques, encourage her to say *relax* to herself as she exhales to associate the word cue for the relaxation response. When she is actually facing the test, she can then use the word with a mini-relaxation exercise to calm herself down. For the relaxation exercises to be effective at dissolving anxiety, practice is important.

11.6-4 Use Positive Self-Talk.

Replace the child's negative thoughts with positive ones.

• Make a list. Have the child list every negative thought he has before a test. For example: "I didn't study enough," "My mind will go blank," or "I will freeze." Next, have her make a list of positive counterstatements for each of the negatives: "I know the answers," "I studied enough and I will do fine," "My mind will be clear and I won't freeze."

• Talk to himself. Have the child practice saying these positive statements whenever he falls back into his old negative views. At first, have him say them aloud and later to himself.

11.6-5 Desensitize the Child to the Test Situation.

These steps will help the child become less bothered by the test.

• Have the child visualize what will happen. Guide her through all the feelings she is likely to have before it's time for the test. Have her imagine how she feels the night before, then going to sleep, waking up, going to school, having the test handed to her. Have her imagine coming upon a problem she can't do. Then have her imagine just the opposite, coping successfully and finishing the test with a flourish. At every step, have her imagine the negative possibilities and then the positive. Continue the visualizing sessions over several days, getting more and more detailed, and always ending with success.

• Have the child rate her feelings. Encourage her to rate on a scale of zero to ten the amount of anxiety she feels during the imagined experiences. Continue repeating the exercise until the ratings are on the low end of the scale. Let her know that a little anxiety is normal for everyone.

11.6-6 Give a Mock Test.

Several nights before the real test, give the child a pretend test.
Have her do her relaxation exercises first. Go over the test results
when she finishes, and help her review the areas in which she needs
greater confidence.

11.7 CHEATING

"Eyes on your own paper, please." Familiar words spoken by virtually every teacher during every test. It's been estimated that
more than a third of all students cheat at least once during their
school years. There are many reasons why children feel the need to
cheat on examinations. Small children are egocentric and want to
win, no matter how. Even the five-year-old feels the need to be
right, and he is not above cheating to get what he wants. Some
children who find it hard to accept defeat will cheat to win at
games and righteously accuse the other child of wrongdoing.

At school, a child may fear the repercussions of poor grades.
Unable to meet the mark, a child may not be able to resist looking
at someone else's paper. Especially in a competitive school, a child
who is unprepared or unable to achieve may cover up the deficit by
cheating. Others do it not because they need to, but because of peer
pressure. Even good students get caught up in the net by letting
others copy from them.

Repeated and frequent cheating and cheating that is one more
aspect of a general pattern of lying are different from occasional
departures from the path of righteousness. They can indicate more
serious emotional problems, and often require professional help to
work them out.

The following are some solutions to help you handle the situation no matter when it occurs.

11.7-1 Confront the Problem.

It helps to determine why the child has cheated and discuss it
openly.

• Look for the reason. Don't ask the child if he cheated when the act has been revealed. Calmly confront him with the proof. Some children will vehemently deny guilt, while others may fall apart, but don't come on as the enemy. Don't accuse, and don't berate. Try to find out why he has chosen to cheat. Was he unprepared for a test? Did he feel pressured to meet impossible standards?

• Express your disapproval. Let the child know, calmly and firmly, that cheating is not acceptable. Explain why cheating is not an acceptable option, and suggest alternate behaviors that could serve as solutions.

• Encourage honesty. Impress upon him the importance of making an honest effort. To do this, you must practice what you preach and set a proper example. Let the child know that how you play the game is what counts.

11.7-2 Have the Child Admit It and Make Amends.

Because it's important that he realize the consequences of his behavior, have him acknowledge his dishonest behavior and make amends for it. Even if this is the first time (perhaps especially because it is the first time), make a big deal of it. Discuss the behavior with the teacher, and depending on the situation and its seriousness, decide upon *appropriate* follow-up. Perhaps he will receive a failing grade on that exam and take a makeup test for no credit to prove he has learned the material. Or he may be required to do extra work on the subject. Sometimes the most effective consequence for repeated cheating is a public apology or an apology to the child from whom he stole the ideas. He should understand that it will take time for him to prove himself and regain the trust of the rest of the class.

11.7-3 Set Realistic Standards.

Now you must confront the reason that led the child to cheat. Are the goals you or the child have set unreasonable? If so, modify your expectations (see Section 11.4).

• Don't prompt cheating. Sometimes the tone set at home and school unintentionally encourages cheating. A competitive environment that emphasizes grades and winning increases the chances of cheating among the students.

• Set realistic goals. When expectations are too high, the child is more likely to cheat. When grades become more important than learning, the child is encouraged to cheat. When test scores and grades aren't kept private or are flaunted by peers, a child is tempted to cheat. To help your child avoid this inappropriate response to the pressure, have a conference with the teacher to discuss appropriate goals for your child and ask that the child not be labeled or made to feel inadequate. It's not only the child who is doing poorly who is likely to feel the need to maintain his average by any means. Discuss the child's concerns so that pressure can be alleviated. Request extra help when necessary to make up for deficits in skills or learning. Ask that the emphasis be placed on growth in skills and learning rather than on grades.

• Explain the meaning of honesty. Talk to your child in a calm and kind way about the meaning of honesty, and make sure he knows how to do his schoolwork appropriately. For example, explain the difference between copying from source books (plagiarism) and paraphrasing the material. Work with even the youngest student so he learns how to use reference sources appropriately.

11.7-4 Increase Study Time if Necessary.

When the source of the problem is the child's lack of commitment to her schoolwork, then another tactic may be needed. If she is always unprepared, she must be motivated to change her behavior. Positive as well as negative contingencies must be used to rectify the situation. Set weekly goals, then have the child keep a chart of the number of minutes spent studying. She may earn points to be exchanged for free time. Reinforce study behavior with television time or outdoor activities. See Section 11.2 for further suggestions.

11.7-5 Reinforce Honest Behavior.

After all of the solutions have been put into effect, then your job is to reinforce the child's efforts in school. Praise her for work well done, not merely for grades. Look for chances to praise her honesty (See Section 8.5), such as when other children cheat but she doesn't, when another child offers her answers but she refuses them, or when she writes a paper using references without copying the work of others.

11.8 MISBEHAVES IN SCHOOL

When you get a call from your child's teacher telling you Johnny is misbehaving in school, it's a bad moment. You worry that he will be labeled a problem child who will never fit into his environment. You may also feel you've failed as a parent. But remember that teachers rarely call to report the good things the children do, because they are busy people, and so you're likely to hear only the negatives. At the same time, don't underestimate the importance of the comments. Unless the problem is unusual, repeated, or severe, teachers usually like to handle school behavior themselves.

When the teacher says, "I'm afraid we have a problem," she may mean that Johnny gets into fights, or that Suzanne talks and passes notes. Perhaps the misbehavior is back talk or constant class disruption. Usually, there are discernible reasons for the child's uncooperative actions. He may be one of many in an out-of-control classroom, or the classroom may be just one more place where an out-of-control child is unmanageable.

Helping a child improve his behavior in school takes a united effort between home and school. The solutions we offer will help you identify the problem and develop a strategy to coordinate your efforts with the teacher's.

11.8-1 Gather Information.

The first step is to find out from all available sources exactly what is going on in the classroom.

• Talk with the child. At the first hint of a problem, have a serious discussion with your child about his behavior in school. Inform him that you are concerned and want to know what is happening from his point of view. Is he bored because the work is too easy? Why is he wandering in the halls? What happens when he doesn't complete his assigned work? What does he do after he's finished? Talk about the appropriate ways to behave and your expectations for him. Even a preschooler will understand when you say, "You must listen and do what your teacher says," or, "You must wait quietly for your turn."

• Arrange a conference with the teacher. Let the teacher know you place a high priority on learning and appropriate school behavior. Set up a meeting before or after school or during a free period—in person. A telephone conversation is rarely sufficient. Discuss the child's behavior, and ask about academic performance and general attitude. Ask how the teacher has been handling the problem thus far. Does the child misbehave in all his classes or only in one? Is it a recent problem or a recurring one? Do many of the children in the class behave poorly, or does your child stand out? If the child is very bright or has learning problems, how are his educational needs being met? Does she have suggestions? Express your expectations and let her know you are open to her ideas and feelings about your child.

• Observe your child in the classroom. Of course, the ideal way to observe your child in class is when she doesn't know you're there. Some schools have one-way mirrors for this purpose. If that's not possible, watch your child unobtrusively by becoming a volunteer aide in the class, at least for one day. Ask the teacher to put you to work so you can interact with the children and see the materials, activities, and daily routine. This will give you an opportunity to see your child and her classmates in action. How do most of the children act? Are most of them doing their work? Are they attentive and cooperative? If you can stay long enough or come to school repeatedly, your child will become comfortable with your presence.

• Use other sources of information. You may want additional information, depending on what you have observed. Is the child reacting to a new medication? If there is unusual stress at home, an emotional evaluation may be appropriate. If the teacher suggests that a learning problem may be the root of your child's acting out, it would be wise to have the child tested by a school psychologist or psychometrist (see sections 11.14 and 11.15). Ask for a meeting with the psychologist and the resource teacher for more feedback.

11.8-2 Identify the Problem.

Now you know what the child is doing in school that is considered out of line. There may be a series of behaviors involved, or perhaps it is a problem that occurs with only one of several teachers. Now you are familiar with the classroom situation and you know some of the background. It's time to go further.

• Define the behavior. Together with the teacher, define which behaviors need to be changed. Then work on one behavior at a time. Refresh your skills by rereading Chapter 2.

• Be objective. If your child behaves in a similar manner at home and at school, then management must start with you. If the child is out of control everywhere, you must back up and read the first chapters of this book, then set up a comprehensive course of action for your family. If, on the other hand, the problems are symptomatic of academic problems, you must begin with those.

11.8-3 Design a Plan to Change the Child's Behavior.

Get together with the teacher and plan the approach you will use to reach the goal. Sometimes a psychological or academic assessment will be needed before action can be planned. The following suggestions will provide for a continuous support system with feedback so you can monitor the school situation.

• Target the behavior. Outline what the child should do, preferably in positive terms. If she was annoying the other children and not getting her work done, her instructions will be: Stay with your task; complete assignments; remain at your work station. If she does those three things, she won't be able to bother her classmates. In other words, she keeps busy with academics, so she won't have time to get into trouble. Reinforcement and praise for good behavior make the strategy work even better.

• Coordinate efforts at school and home. Let the child know his teachers and parents agree about what is expected and that an information network will pass information back and forth. Perhaps the teacher will establish a program of independent study for the high achiever that will require learning to work alone. Both parents should be involved in the process, tailoring the plan according to the situation, and should agree on the plan, although the parent who is more effective or has more time may act as the major contact with the teacher.

• Set a timetable. For most problems, daily feedback is appropriate in the beginning, with longer intervals later. On-task behavior can be monitored subject by subject, cooperation with classmates can be noted hourly, and the results can be sent home every day on a prepared note. Or the flow of information could occur weekly or even monthly, depending on the problem. Be sure to schedule another conference with the teacher and to follow through with the plan. Many parents—and teachers—make a huge effort at the start of a project, then fade out. It's important to stay with it.

11.8-4 Link Home and School.

This series of techniques will help you link home and school so the child's behavior can be monitored.

• Use the "good-behavior letter." This an excellent technique because it allows the child to bring home only *good* news. Write a short letter describing the behavior that you desire from the child and make a number of copies for the teacher. Title the letter *Jesse's Good Work Letter,* or *Evelyn's Morning Work Report,* or whatever is appropriate. Have the teacher send a copy of the letter home with the child each day that the child's behavior matches the description.

By setting up clear guidelines, be sure the child knows how to earn the letter. Specify exactly what you expect, and settle on the consequences beforehand. The teacher must be consistent about sending the letters home when they are deserved. Keep in mind that this is not an all-or-nothing effort but a gradual way to shape the child's behavior toward the goal. Brent, for example, first earned letters for working independently during the morning, then later the requirement for letters increased to include all subject areas. His parents kept a record of the letters received, and Brent earned one star per note. Getting three out of five possible letters the first week earned him an extra point.

The letters may be traded for daily privileges or collected for a bigger reward. For example, Kelly was allowed to watch her favorite afternoon television show if she brought home the letter, but wasn't allowed if she didn't. If she collected four letters in a week, she could select something special to do with her dad on Saturday morning.

• Set up a self-recording system. After defining the expected behavior, let the child keep tabs on himself. Kevin knows he must do his work and keep his hands to himself. He may not hit, push, prod, or pinch anyone. If he does, he makes a mark on an index card. Each day that he brings home a blank card signed by him and his teacher, he earns a point. To start, the teacher keeps a count, too, signing Kevin's tally at the end of the day when they agree, and his accuracy is rewarded with an extra point. Later, he's all on his own.

Points are traded for predetermined items or activities. The number of points is slowly increased as the desired behavior becomes established. You may also want to have reports brought home every other day, then twice a week and, later, once a week. See Chapter 2 for detailed information about using reinforcement systems.

11.8-5 Use Negative Consequences.

Try a negative tactic when the positive approach seems to be going nowhere. The child may need extra practice to learn what he must not do.

• Use overcorrection. Help the child become aware that there is always a consequence for his actions. Have him overcorrect them. If he throws spitballs in class, then he must stay after school and clean them all up. Or perhaps he must sit in his seat after school to make up the time he lost while misbehaving.

• Use loss of privilege. Good behavior may earn extra privileges, such as extracurricular activities or special events, but poor behavior can lose them when the child doesn't earn the necessary points.

11.9 DAYDREAMS

Everybody daydreams, but for some children, daydreaming becomes a way of life that interferes with daily functioning. When it is used as an avoidance mechanism for not doing the tasks a child must do in school, then building castles in the air is a problem. Use these suggestions to help you determine whether it is a problem and what to do about it.

11.9-1 Determine if It's a Problem.

Ask yourself if the child is doing well in school, whether he gets all his work done, and manages to follow directions. If he is, then daydreaming isn't interfering with learning. But if the teacher still considers this habit bothersome, then it is a problem in the classroom.

11.9-2 Determine the Reasons.

There are many reasons why a child may prefer to daydream rather than participate in the world around him. Ask yourself these questions:

1. Is there a physical cause? Because dreaminess can occasionally be an indication of petit mal seizures, take the child to the doctor for a checkup if he hasn't had one recently.

2. Is it drugs? If you have any suspicions that your child may be using drugs, then check it out promptly, perhaps asking your child's physician to make an unscheduled urine analysis.

3. Is it emotional? Try to find out what the child's daydreams are about, because they may alert you to things that are bothering him. Daydreams are a way to escape from the real world. They are private fantasies, not easily shared, or a way to redesign unpleasant situations. To a degree this is quite normal, but when the child starts to prefer the dream world to the real one, it is time to be concerned.

4. Is it boredom? Perhaps his schoolwork isn't challenging enough, or maybe he isn't busy enough out of school. A two-pronged approach is needed: Make his life more interesting and teach him that participation is valued and rewarded by using these suggestions.

• Encourage relationships with peers. Make arrangements for her to be part of a play group. Invite other children over to play. And, especially for the child who is accustomed to and even prefers solitary activities, arrange participation in group activities.

• Reinforce participation in group activities. When the child comes home, ask him what he did so he knows you value and expect interaction with other people.

• If she spends too much time alone, set up activities in which she may join you. Little ones love to help with grown-up jobs. Choose those that she can do successfully, and praise her for her assistance and ability.

• Encourage constructive activities that involve the hands and the mind. Computer games, cards, crossword puzzles, and sports require an alert mind that's not on cloud nine. Find extracurricular activities that enrich his school experiences, and introduce him to new interests.

11.9-3 To Discourage Daydreaming, Set Time Limits for the Task.

Before the child begins his homework, for instance, ask him how long it should take him to finish it. Set a kitchen timer for that length of time and play Beat the Clock. Build routine activities, like setting the table or picking up toys, into games or races so that long trips into fantasy don't prolong the chores. Reward quick execution with a treat or free time.

11.9-4 Work with the Teacher.

Many children with academic difficulties spend a lot of time daydreaming to avoid what's going on. Others rely on daydreaming to fill their time because they get bored. Even if a child gets his work done, if the teacher thinks daydreaming is a problem, it is. Although you can't expect the teacher to set up a complicated motivation system just for your child, she will probably be willing to work with the parents using a simple system. Ask for a conference to plan a strategy to reinforce participation in academic activities.

• Ask the teacher to identify when the child daydreams. Choose that time period as your target time to reinforce involvement in academics. Define the expectations and behavior for the child: "Ross, Miss Lavin says you daydream during reading group. If you listen well and participate, she will give you a special note to bring home." The notes may then be exchanged for a predetermined set of points that accumulate and earn a special activity.

11.10 DOES SCHOOLWORK CARELESSLY

"Dena, you skipped three of the problems." "Jean, this is just carelessness. You know three plus five equals eight." "Calvin, why did you underline the verbs when the directions said to circle the pronouns?" Comments like these are often made by parents and teachers because they think the child is not doing his best simply out of carelessness. Of course, that's not the way the child hears them. She hears, "You dummy, wrong again!"

Learning to be careful is a big job for a child, and perfection is not the ultimate goal. The cure for carelessness is not nagging or constantly telling the child what she did wrong. Instead, it is teaching her to value being careful and assisting her in learning to accomplish the knack of it.

11.10-1 Define the Problem.

Review your child's work regularly, helping her find out what the problems are. If she understands the subject and the task, why does she make errors? Jean knew her math facts, but she turned her papers in without checking them. Calvin's problem was that he didn't read the directions on his work sheets because they all looked alike. Dena wanted to be the first one to turn in her test paper.

11.10-2 Check for Carefulness.

Nobody is a hundred percent careful, but if we have a method for trying to be, we come a lot closer to the goal.

• Use a cue. If reading the directions will overcome the problem, then use the instructions as a cue for the behavior. Have the child circle them after she has read them, or ask her to underline the key words that define the task.

• Check on checking. To be sure she has checked over her answers, have her underline or make a dot below each reread answer. Or ask her if she'd rather sign off each page with her signature after checking it—some children love to do that. Section 11.11 has more suggestions for helping your child follow directions.

11.10-3 Reinforce Carefulness.

Let the child know that being careful is important. Reinforce it.

• Praise the child. When she shows you work that has been carefully completed with few errors, tell her: "Lynn, this paper is very well done. I can tell you've checked the addition carefully." Or, "Boyd, these directions are really complicated, but you read them carefully and it shows."

• Use a chart, and reward the effort. Some children respond to a reinforcement system that tracks their new behavior. Again, define the rules before you begin. Natalie, who had been rushing through her daily work, was told she could earn points for carefully completing her papers with no more than one error per page. Read Chapter 2 again for the best ways to implement such a reward system.

• Display careful work. Make a special place to display your child's carefully completed work. Perhaps you could turn a bulletin board into the family "brag board." Or keep the work he's proud of in a special scrapbook. Encourage him to show it to visitors.

• Make being careful a priority. Let the child see that you think using care is important at home, too, and involve him in the effort. The older child could help you check the grocery receipts or read a letter you have written to make sure it is accurate. Discuss the importance of being careful in everyday situations. What would happen if you wrote the wrong time for a birthday party? What if the address is incorrect? What would be the result if you added four cups of water instead of two to the cookies you are baking?

11.10-4 Follow Through with Consequences.

After the child has acknowledged that she knows what it is to be careful, talk about the appropriate consequences for neglecting to use care. Remember, however, that carefulness can only be expected when she clearly understands the directions and can easily accomplish the task.

• Use overcorrection. The perfect follow-up for failing to check her work when she finishes a task is overchecking. "Gosh, Sally, you need to practice checking your work. I've found four mistakes in addition in this paper. You'll have to check all of the problems to find them." Or "Brad, you need more practice reading directions. I only looked at the first page and maybe there are more mistakes, so you'll have to go over everything, rereading the assignments to make sure you understood what you were supposed to do. Bring me the checked work when you finish."

• Have the child do the work again. If he rushes through an assignment, it may be appropriate to have him do the entire piece of work over again. Accentuate the solution without commenting on the careless nature of the work. For example, with sloppy handwriting, tell him the letters need to be carefully formed. If the story is skimpy, tell him the story needs more thinking to include more details. The child will soon learn that it's easier to do it carefully the first time than to do it all over again.

11.11 CAN'T FOLLOW DIRECTIONS

"Boys and girls, it is time to put away what you are doing. Put your work sheets in the tray on the left corner of my desk. Then go to your seat. Get out a sheet of paper and write your name and the date at the top right-hand corner. Title the page SPELLING and number from one to twenty-five. When you are ready, raise your hand." A child who hears those directions at school may be just as confused as the child who hears his mother say at home, "Jerry, go up to your room, change your clothes, wash your face and hands, and get your library books and your coat so we can take them back when we go to the store."

Parents and teachers are wordy when it comes to giving directions, and it's hard for children to remember all of them and then follow them. That's why adults should be careful not to overwhelm a child with a long sequence of directions, especially when they are given orally. But the truth is that success in the classroom depends on the ability to follow directions. You, as a parent, have many opportunities at home to observe your child's attempts to follow

directions. But you have little control over the kinds of directions
given in the classroom or to the child's response to them. To exe-
cute a set of directions successfully requires attention, understanding, and organization, and a problem at any point along the way
spells trouble. Some children don't even notice the directions,
while others don't understand or remember the tasks that are required. Some jump into the assignment before the teacher finishes
her instructions, while others can't seem to get started. With personal knowledge of your child's usual approach to directions and
whatever you can glean from the teacher, devise a plan to increase
his ability to follow directions.

11.11-1 Define the Problem.

As with any other childhood behavior, you must first determine
what particular problem affects your child's performance.

• Is this part of a larger learning problem? Sometimes the inability to follow directions is symptomatic of a learning disability.
The child may have difficulty deciding which is the important information in a set of directions so he can process the instructions
correctly. He may understand the words but seem not to hear
them. Or he may not be able to extrapolate from directions, continually taking you literally. For example, when you ask him to look
for something, does he look in only one place? When you say,
"Please take a bath," does he assume a shower is wrong?

Your child may have a hard time making transitions between the
tasks required in the classroom. Many children with learning disabilities have trouble hearing instructions and holding them in
mind long enough to follow them. If these patterns fit your child,
Section 11.14, on learning disabilities, may interest you.

• Is your child unable to tune in to the directions? Some children always jump into a task without waiting for the full directions. Others can't settle down and accomplish the job. If your
child follows a general behavior pattern of being unable to devote
his attention to one area of his environment at a time—his teacher's voice, a work sheet, a puzzle—and cannot focus on one activ-

ity or set of directions long enough to complete it, read Section 11.15, on attention deficit disorders. The child who is highly distractible often is receiving all information in his environment with equal intensity and can't filter out the unimportant material. Therefore, he can't focus on one thing at a time.

• Is the child not motivated to listen to instructions? There is a big difference between a child who doesn't follow directions because he can't and the one who doesn't follow them because he won't. The child with a learning disability may be unable to process the directions even though he is listening to them; and the child with an attention deficit can't attend to the directions because he's attending to everything. These children cannot follow directions until they learn how. But other children are simply not motivated to listen carefully. They know how to follow directions, but they don't. See Section 5.8 for suggestions on motivating your child.

• Does the child have the instructional skill? Maybe the language or the format used in the instructions are the cause of the problem. Test taking and mathematical word problems are special skills that must be acquired. If a child who normally follows directions well now develops problems, experience and a little help in interpreting these instructions will overcome the gap.

11.11-2 Improve the Child's Attention.

To learn and perform well in school, the child must know how to pay attention. Discuss the problem with the teacher and see if these suggestions will help.

• Move the child's seat. It may help tremendously for the child to be moved to a place in the classroom where she feels it will be easier for her to concentrate—maybe at the front of the class, nearer to the teacher's desk, or in a corner away from a noisy cluster of friends. Be sure this isn't done as a "punishment" but rather as a way to help the child succeed.

• Make eye contact. When he is receiving individual instructions, he should look directly at the person who is speaking. This may mean the teacher hesitates for a moment to ensure the child's attention before giving the directions.

• Develop a signal. Have the child give a silent signal when he has listened to the teacher's instructions. A nod or a finger on his nose will tell the teacher that the message has been received. For written instructions, the teacher and child may agree that the child will underline the key words in the directions.

• Give fewer directions in a series. Children are often given too many directions in a short period of time. A teacher can consciously slow down or include fewer instructions in each series. Evaluate the child's ability to follow a sequence and determine his best load by experimenting with series of two directions, three, then more at a time.

• Choose a study buddy. Ask that your child be given a buddy to whom he can repeat the teacher's instructions and with whom he can clarify what has been asked. This will remove some of the responsibility from the teacher and give the child another option for help.

• Have the child repeat oral directions. If the study-buddy suggestion is not feasible, have the child repeat the directions to herself or write them down immediately after they have been given. The teacher may then check them before the child starts the task.

• Reinforce the child for paying attention. Depending on the severity of the problem, at first it is helpful to reinforce the child simply for attending to the directions. A teacher can do this easily with comments like, "Phyllis is looking at me and listening as I tell you what to do next. She may lead the line." The teacher may praise the child for repeating instructions correctly or let him earn a point toward a reward for writing down the oral directions correctly.

At first, the child who has previously ignored directions should be reinforced for completing a task according to plan *even if the answers are not correct.* "Carl, I see you've read the directions because you circled the words that told you what to do. And you showed me you understood the directions because you circled the nouns in the first two sentences. Now, let's look at number three together . . ." Later, reinforcement can come when the child completes the task correctly.

11.11-3 Teach the Child Strategies.

In addition to explaining to your child that sitting in the front of the classroom, looking directly at the instruction giver, or circling written directions will all help him succeed at following directions, you can help him by showing *how* to follow directions.

• Teach him to plan ahead. Remind the child to read the instructions first before beginning a task. Have him assemble the necessary materials. If he must refer to pages in another book, have him flag the pages with paper clips.

• Identify significant words. Many subject areas have their own important terms. For example, social studies uses words like *list, contrast,* and *evaluate,* while math uses terms such as *altogether, sum,* and *area.* Without doing the problems for her, play a game in which the child must find all the key words in the directions to the math problems and discuss their meaning. Ask her what words clue a reader to the necessary steps.

• Review schoolwork weekly. Ask the teacher to send the child's work home each Friday. With the child, review the directions for the work and see how well they were followed.

• Devise a plan for coping with problem instructions. Take time to identify the tricky parts of directions. Discuss what makes the task difficult and decide how to break it into parts. For example, one child overcame a problem in learning vocabulary when she understood the meaning of the numbered definitions for dictionary entries.

• Use games and role-playing. Young children can often use practice in following directions. Try playing Follow the Leader or Simon Says to teach the skill. "Simon says, Put your hand on the left top corner of the page. Simon says, Fold your paper. Simon says, Look at me." Reverse your roles and let the child give the instructions and follow them exactly.

To help the older child to make eye contact, play the staring game to see who looks away first. Keep a record of how many times out of ten the child looks right at you when you give a direction. Time how many seconds it takes for her to "lock her radar" on to the person who is speaking to her. And of course, be sure to praise improvements.

• Give rewards for improvements. Reinforce the child for following one, then two, then three directions in a row. Start with the number she can already handle, then gradually increase it. Play a game: Tell her you have something you want her to do. Praise her for making eye contact, and have her repeat your directions. Encourage her to do what you ask quickly and carefully, following the sequence.

11.12 HAS TROUBLE FINISHING SCHOOLWORK

If your child seldom finishes his daily schoolwork in the time allotted by the teacher, submits papers half done or not at all, brings classwork home to finish, or uses up his recess time to complete assignments, you have plenty of company. This is one of the most common school problems presented to us by parents.

There are many reasons for this behavior problem. A child may be unmotivated to work to his potential. He may be sufficiently motivated but is so easily distracted that his attention is constantly diverted from the work at hand (see Section 11.15 for information and help on short attention span). He may be having difficulty with the subject matter, the thought processes involved, or the method for completing it. If he doesn't have the prerequisite skills, then there's no way he can finish the assignment correctly.

In some cases, a child will be slowed by problems with handwriting. Some children simply write more slowly than others and have difficulty shaping the letters. Another child may require more time to express ideas in words. Occasionally, a child is so concerned with personal or family problems that he can't concentrate on classroom assignments. Then there are children whose dawdling work habits are a cover-up for assignments they cannot or won't do. And finally, there are those who simply "goof off."

To reverse a pattern of not finishing schoolwork, the obstacles or the pattern of behavior must be changed. The solutions offered here should set parents and children in the right direction.

11.12-1 Determine if the Behavior Signals a Problem.

Although it's very easy to assume that the child is merely dillydallying, it's important to rule out other possible causes first.

• Talk to the child and the teacher. Just like any other school problem, this one should be discussed with the two major parties involved. With your child and his teacher, determine whether this is a recent or long-standing problem and whether it occurs in certain subject areas or in all of them. Get their ideas about the cause.
• Investigate the child's level of functioning. Determine whether the youngster's knowledge is equal to the teacher's expectations. Are there learning problems to be remedied? If necessary, ask for special testing by the school psychologist or psychometrist.

11.12-2 Adjust for Learning Discrepancies.

If the child is working with materials that are too hard for him, perhaps a change of level or additional support will make up the deficit. The teacher can make the needed changes. If, however, there are large deficits between the work requirements and the child's ability, specialized help may be required. The child with a learning disability, behavioral disorder, or attention deficit may need further adaptations in order to perform successfully.

• Change the requirements. Discuss with the teacher the possibility of moving the child to a lower reading or math group or helping her fill in the gaps in the needed skills.
• Provide tutoring. In the case of an isolated weakness, a little extra help from the teacher or a tutor may make all the difference. This is usually part of ongoing diagnostic teaching, but occasionally, a child needs more than that.
• Adjust time requirements. Many children can do the required

work but need more time to get it all done. Together, the teacher and child can set the amount of time they feel is appropriate for each task, which gives the youngster the feeling of completing assignments on time.

• Adjust the level of acceptability. For the children with handwriting difficulties that slow up their expression of ideas, more time can be allowed for completion of the assignment. But in addition, such children might be permitted to print, write in pencil, or when they don't already know it, be encouraged to learn cursive writing, which is faster once it is accomplished. Others whose handwriting is a handicap can learn to use the typewriter for long papers.

11.12-3 Give Special Support if Needed.

If a child has a learning disability, an attention deficit disorder, or an emotional problem that affects her schoolwork, then special support will help her function better in the classroom. For a learning disability, resource teachers or learning specialists can help overcome the deficiencies. The child with a short attention span or distractibility may respond to medication, moving her seat, and self-control training (see Sections 11.14 and 11.15).

11.12-4 Reinforce Staying With a Task.

Once the child is working on tasks and materials that are appropriate to his level of functioning, then he can benefit from a program designed to train him to finish assignments on time.

• Set time limits together. For the child who has trouble completing tasks with the rest of the class, a kitchen timer can help retrain this behavior. Together with the child, decide on a reasonable amount of time needed to complete an assignment easily. Write the time down, set the timer, and see how fast he can work. The ticking of the timer provides the motivation that helps him maintain the new behavior.

• Reinforce increasing ability to complete assignments. Allow the child to earn points for completing larger and larger percentages of the assignments in the designated time. Before long, the work load and the time frame should approach those of his classmates.

11.13 WON'T ASK OR ANSWER QUESTIONS

It can happen anywhere. You're in a large group of people and, though others actively participate, you don't express your opinion. No harm done, but in school that's not always true. If a child doesn't ask or answer questions in the classroom, the teacher finds it difficult to assess her knowledge and plan appropriate work. Not only that, but the child doesn't learn how to function as part of a group, which hinders her learning opportunities and perhaps her ability to complete assignments.

Sometimes the youngster is afraid of making wrong answers, of asking "silly" questions, or perhaps she feels it's a sign of weakness to ask for help. These feelings may be the precursors to a later fear of speaking in public. Whether social anxiety or the need for perfection causes the inability to participate, this is an important behavior to identify and change.

11.13-1 Identify the Problem.

If you believe your child is too timid to speak in a group even when it's small—in the car pool, perhaps, or at a Girl Scout meeting—determine whether it also hinders school performance.

• Look at the report card. Does the teacher comment on this?
• Discuss the subject with your child. Although Brian never seems to understand how to do his homework or what the task is, he shrugs his shoulders when his mother suggests asking the teacher to explain it. Probing further, she discovers that he's afraid to ask because he thinks he should know how to do it and that the other kids might laugh at him.
• Talk to the teacher. Air your concerns to the teacher, and try to identify whether the child is afraid to speak aloud in class in

general or whether he just doesn't want to look stupid by asking a question or answering incorrectly.

11.13-2 Treat the Behavior as a Fear.

If the child is afraid to speak out loud in a group, she must be desensitized to this fear.

• Talk to the child. Find out what she is afraid of. When does it happen? What constitutes a group? What results does she fear from speaking up?

• Have the child observe other children. Ask her what happens to other children who speak in class. What is the response of the class? How does the teacher respond? Have her keep notes about what occurs.

• Ask the teacher to talk to the child. In a private conversation, the teacher may alleviate some of the fears by suggesting she needs her help in finding out what the pupils need to know.

• Teach relaxation techniques. Turn back to Section 2.10 for instructions on teaching your child to relax. When she has mastered this skill, show her the mini-relaxation exercise, which she should practice when she's part of a group: Take a deep breath, exhale down to your toes, and say, *relax*.

• Simulate group and classroom situations at home. Role-play asking and answering questions in class. Prompt public conversation when the child is in a group. Use the car pool or large family groups as the setting for involvement.

• Formulate a plan for initiating class participation. Confer with the teacher, and come up with a program to encourage your child to speak up. At first, she may call on the child for simple yes or no answers that she is sure the youngster can answer correctly. Later, she may prompt discussion in a small group setting and reinforce it with positive comments: "That is a very good question, Larry. I'm glad you asked that because a lot of the other children probably were wondering the same thing."

• Record participation and reinforce efforts. The teacher may keep a daily tally of how many times the child speaks up in class each day and send the information home with the child. To make it easy, photocopy Figure 8 to rate the participation in each subject area.

Fig. 8 Melanie's Class Participation

Subject	Number of Times She Participated		Date:
	1	2	3
Mathematics			
Reading			
Science			
Social Studies			

The teacher records instances of Melanie's participation in class discussions.

11.13-3 Change the Belief.

If the child won't interact in class because he thinks he must be perfect in order to participate and is afraid to risk being wrong or laughable, then you must try to change these feelings.

• Talk to the child. Somewhere, he has received faulty information. Try to convince him the premise is false.

• Set an example. Make it a point to ask questions in public, clarify directions, or state an opinion. Show the child it's safe to speak out.

• Examine your reactions to the child's questions. Have you

inadvertently quashed questioning behavior or comments by making negative responses, being too busy to answer, or expecting silence? If so, it is your behavior that must change before the child feels safe enough to speak out.

• Prompt participation. Use the dinner table as a time for family sharing. Have each member tell about an event in his or her day. After listening to the news on the radio or TV, elicit your child's comments about what has happened. Prompt questions, and praise the new behavior. Your interest and good listening skills will encourage her.

• Reinforce self-confidence. Praise the child for whatever question she may ask, and be careful never to say things like, "Now, that's a silly question." Your goal is to make her feel comfortable even though she doesn't have all the answers.

11.14 HAS LEARNING DISABILITIES

Our goal in this section is different from the others because we will provide information on the most prevalent learning disabilities and some guidelines for recognizing a possible problem in your child. We will also offer suggestions to help families cope with a child with such disabilities, along with a list of suggested reference material. For additional information, contact your local chapter of the Association of Children With Learning Disabilities (ACLD).

A child may fail to learn in school for many reasons. The term *learning disability* does not mean mental retardation or emotional disturbance. In the 1970s, the term became a popular and powerful explanation for lack of achievement among children with average or above average intelligence, advantaged backgrounds, and the benefits of good schooling who should be just as able as other children but simply do not learn as naturally or easily. With the introduction of this label, however, the research and educational focus shifted from medical causes to the child's educational and behavioral characteristics.

In eight out of ten instances, the learning-disabled (LD) child is a boy. He is a child who may act younger than his age, may be quite impulsive and easily stimulated, as well as sensitive and intuitive. He baffles parents and teachers because he may readily learn a skill or concept one day and forget it by the next. He presents uneven, inconsistent, and unpredictable abilities.

This child has difficulty understanding and using the information he receives through his senses. The problem occurs in recognizing, selecting, or associating the incoming information and then linking it with previously learned material. He may not be able to hold items in his memory long enough to use them. He may perceive distinctly different forms or shapes as similar or identify letters incorrectly. The outward form of the learning disability varies from child to child, but there is always a distinct pattern of learning weakness that hinders accomplishments.

11.14-1 Early Characteristics of Learning Disability.

Children with a learning disability often have one or more of the following characteristics: Difficulty with speech, reading, writing, and math; difficulty in paying attention; confusion about time and space; impulsive behavior, difficulty remembering, poor physical coordination, poor self-concept, difficulty in organizing themselves for a task, difficulty making and keeping friends. Other common characteristics are discussed below, though every child has his own individual pattern of strengths and weaknesses that influence how he interacts with his environment.

Heredity and birth factors. Premature children, children who suffer from fetal alcohol syndrome, and those with a family history of learning problems are frequently found to have learning problems. On the other hand, a child with none of these characteristics may have the same problems, and a child who fits all of the characteristics may have an easy time in school.

General immaturity. These children have been described by many experts as immature or "unready," youngsters who don't quite have it all together. Sometimes they can "get their act together," and other times they can't.

Difficulty with abstract concepts and activities. Though an LD child may spend hours building elaborate structures, drawing complicated spacecraft, or playing with a favorite toy, at times he may be unable to stick with any activity. An abstract task may hold his attention for only a few minutes and he will become restless with written exercises. Copying shapes or letters is difficult. It's hard for him to find home in a maze game. He may use tools easily but finds holding a pencil difficult, grasping it improperly or bearing down too hard.

He may easily discriminate among jigsaw shapes to complete a picture puzzle, but he can't discriminate among the symbolic shapes of letters. He may be good at differentiating between bells and buzzers but be unable to discern the differences between similar words such as *beard* and *bread* or *pin* and *pen*. He may converse intelligently but be unable to follow a sequence of two instructions.

Language weakness. Early language problems are a warning sign for other learning difficulties, and LD children often have some form of linguistic weakness that results in reading disabilities. The child of three or four who does not speak at all or who can't follow a simple story line is at risk, as is the child who doesn't speak in simple sentences or shows little evidence of a growing vocabulary.

In general, a child from a literate environment who is developing normally should absorb some linguistic knowledge by the time he enters first grade. He should be a competent user of language, and if stories have been read to him regularly, he should show some interest in books and written words.

11.14-2 Diagnosing a Learning Disability.

Learning disabilities are often a hidden handicap, so if you suspect them, have the child diagnosed by a trained professional. Early diagnosis, proper remediation, and support can make an enormous difference in how well a child copes with his problem.

• Identification requires information from many sources. Multiple criteria, including observation of behavior in normal settings, informal task analysis, and standardized testing, are required for an adequate diagnosis.

• Identification of specific strengths and weaknesses are needed.

Every child's difficulties are different, and it is essential to know your youngster's individual pattern in order to determine what to do about it. Many children have a weakness in the receptive sphere, so perception of incoming information is distorted. When integration is a problem, the child has difficulty relating the new information to what he already knows. This may show up in inability to remember, to sequence, or to differentiate important facts from details. Other children have a problem relating to the expression of information, whether it is written or oral, and may have a hard time communicating thoughts or acting appropriately.

• Request a staffing at school. Every child in the United States is entitled to a free and appropriate education, though children often fall through the cracks because federal and state funding cannot meet their needs. A staffing is a formal meeting of people, which includes the teachers, other resource people, and the parents, convened to identify the child's problem and designate a remediation plan. Service provided by public schools includes, when appropriate, an Individual Education Prescription (IEP), a formal plan of instruction and, perhaps, special support services, to be monitored by school personnel.

Together with the school team, explore other options that will help the child succeed and feel good about himself, such as a teacher who has experience with such children and is flexible enough to adapt assignments to the child's abilities. Questions to ask include:

1. What are my child's learning strengths and weaknesses?
2. How will this pattern translate into academic behavior and everyday skills?
3. Is further testing or referral to other specialists advised?
4. Does my child need special help? What are the priorities?
5. How do I explain this to the child, and what is my appropriate role?

• Get adequate help for the child. Sometimes private tutoring is advisable, especially when the child does not meet eligibility criteria for special services or is in a private school. Always choose a tutor who specializes in LD children, discussing her methods and techniques as well as her coordination with the school and parents. Appropriate questions might include:

1. What are realistic goals for my child at this time?
2. What support activities can we provide at home to reinforce what he is learning?

Occasionally, a school that specializes in LD children is your best choice, perhaps only temporarily, until he learns to work successfully in a regular classroom environment.

11.14-3 Discuss the Learning Disability with the Child and Family.

The way you accept and respond to your child's learning disabilities is extremely important to his self-concept and the attitudes of other family members.

• Speak openly. Often, a school-age child with a learning disability has already decided she is stupid, and it's essential to give her information that dispels her notions of inadequacy. Help her understand her strengths and weaknesses, and teach her coping strategies. Encourage questions and responses. Let her know she is an intelligent person with certain problems that can be dealt with. Help her understand that even though she has a learning disability, she can cope successfully by using new strategies.

• Speak openly to the family members. A sibling's learning disability is a fact of life that affects the other children, so be frank with them. They may feel guilty or afraid to do their best in school for fear they will surpass an older sister or brother; they may be embarrassed by a sibling who acts out or doesn't do well in school. Or they may be too protective. Give them information so they can understand what is going on and perhaps even help their brother or sister.

11.14-4 Develop Realistic Coping Strategies.

A learning disability is not a problem that will vanish overnight. You will probably have to teach an LD child many of the skills you take for granted, because he seems to view the world from a completely different perspective. When you understand his strengths and weaknesses, you will see he is not being purposely uncooperative. Then you can work together to find coping strategies.

• Identify your goals. When you discover a behavior that is particularly difficult for your child, identify it as a problem needing a plan to overcome it. Use an especially trying day as an opportunity to determine how the child's disabilities affect his actions and feelings.

• Devise a strategy. Whatever the difficulty, try to devise a plan to overcome it. For example, if the child has difficulty remembering what she must do, teach her to make lists and plan ahead. If she has a sequencing problem and short-term memory weakness, give her only one or two directions at a time. Perhaps her teacher will allow her to do one math homework problem at school, so she will have a model for the rest of the work. Use the appropriate sections of this book to work with particular weaknesses and promote organizational skills.

11.14-5 Emphasize the Child's Strengths.

Look for ways to let the child succeed and feel good about herself. Praise her for the things she does well. She may have trouble with addition, but she may be a very good artist, a kind big sister, and a responsible pet owner. She may be very conscientious and determined. And she should hear about all of these wonderful characteristics.

Help the child find extracurricular activities that she enjoys. Ask her teachers to use the child's strengths. If, for example, she speaks well but has difficulty writing, perhaps she can give her reports orally. Maybe she would love the drama club or the debating team.

11.14-6 Help the Child Develop Social Skills.

Because many LD children have problems with social relationships, try these suggestions:

• Encourage friendships. Invite children over to play, or involve your child in supervised play situations. When necessary, teach her the correct responses and have her practice them with you.

• Model and teach social skills. LD children often act impulsively, speaking out of turn or behaving inappropriately. Role-play social situations and show him how to interact with other people. Suggest that he watch what his friends do in social settings and then copy their actions.

11.14-7 Don't Look for Miracles.

There is no cure for a learning disability; there are only coping strategies that compensate for weaknesses. Don't be fooled into putting your efforts into unsubstantiated remedies through diet, vitamins, or elaborate patterning routines. Remember that many people who were LD children report that elementary school was the most difficult time for them, and as they grew older, they learned to use their strengths. This takes time and endless effort, but it can pay off handsomely. Just look at Albert Einstein, Nelson Rockefeller, and Thomas Edison, all of whom had learning disabilities.

SUGGESTED BOOKS FOR PARENTS AND CHILDREN

Blue, Rose. *Me and Einstein.* New York: Human Sciences Press, Inc., 1979. Having tried for years to hide the fact that he couldn't read, a nine-year-old finally learns why (Gr. 2–6).

Farnham-Diggory, Sylvia. *Learning Disabilities.* Cambridge, Mass.: Harvard University Press, 1978. Informative overview on the topic.

McWhirter, J. Jeffries. *The Learning Disabled Child: A School and Family Concern.* Champaign, Ill.: Research Press Co., 1977.

Written by a parent of a learning-disabled child, this book presents a personal and professional view.

Osman, Betty B. *Learning Disabilities: A Family Affair.* New York: Random House, 1979. Highlights the practical aspects of living with a learning-disabled child.

Osman, Betty B. in association with Henriette Blinder. *No One To Play With: The Social Side of Learning Disabilities.* New York: Random House, 1982. Explores the social interactions of many learning-disabled children.

Smith, Sally L. *No Easy Answers.* Toronto: Bantam Books, 1980. Good description of characteristics of the learning-disabled child, with suggestions of how to live with him and teach him.

MONTHLY MAGAZINES

ACLD Newsbriefs, from the Association for Children and Adults with Learning Disabilities, Pittsburgh, Pa. 15234.

Their World, by the Foundation for Children with Learning Disabilities, Box 2929, Grand Central Station, NY, NY 10163

11.15 HAS ATTENTION DEFICIT DISORDER WITH OR WITHOUT HYPERACTIVITY

"He is really hyper today," we often hear. The term *hyperactivity* has become so much a part of our language today that many people not only abbreviate it, they also confuse its meaning. Having an attention deficit disorder (ADD) is not the same as being overactive or hyperactive. In fact, ADD children may or may not be hyperactive. Some are quiet and well behaved, though they are unable to focus their attention for very long. Others may also display high energy and movement, have difficulty following rules and sleeping through the night, and generally cause havoc wherever they go.

Before we go on, let's make one point clear: Not every child who is a perpetual-motion machine, constantly on the move, and into everything is "hyperactive." Sometimes, this child has been allowed to become unmanageable. Take Mrs. Ambrose, who came to us about her sons, Craig and Alvin, whom she described as so active that they wrecked the house and even ran up and down over parked cars in the neighborhood.

When we consulted their teachers, we found that the boys were not disruptive in school, nor were they when we tested them in our offices. They were quite capable of settling down and persisting at a task when the rules required it. When we watched them with their mother, however, we saw them turn wild, disobedient, and unruly. These were normally active children who were not well managed.

Even children who are truly hyperactive don't necessarily run, jump, and move more than their peers. They do, however, have trouble controlling their movement in situations that require it. They may find it nearly impossible to stay in their seat at school or at the dinner table, and end up being called "a wiggle worm" or "hyper."

Although overactivity is the most commonly recognized characteristic and the earliest to be identified by parents, it is not the primary source of difficulty for these children. There are youngsters who do not display excess energy. They are able to remain still, yet they are highly distractible. They cannot focus attention as long as their classmates can. Many of the superactive children become less "hyper" as they pass through puberty, but unfortunately, they don't always lose their inability to focus attention and concentrate. Because of this differentiation, the American Psychiatric Association adopted the new classification of attention deficit disorder (ADD) with or without hyperactivity.

The major problem for these children is the inability to maintain attention. A high activity level may then complicate their situation. With or without hyperactivity, ADD children and their families may develop lasting problems because these children have a lower self-concept, more academic and behavioral difficulties in school, and more conflicts at home. They usually lag behind their peers scholastically, and about 70 percent of them also have other learning disabilities that influence their ability to acquire specific skills.

Although diagnosis does not automatically lead to immediate relief for families with children with hyperactivity or attention deficit disorder, it is the first step. Parents often feel guilty and confused because their child is hard to control, or they wonder if they could have better prepared him for school. Conflict, frustration, and depression are frequent emotions among them.

Because several professionals are needed to make the diagnosis of ADD, the parents must be the ones to coordinate the effort. There is no cure for these problems, but it is possible to cope successfully with them so that the whole family feels good. This section will describe the diagnostic process and discuss strategies for coping.

11.15-1 Identify the ADD/Hyperactive Child.

If you suspect that your child has these problems, discuss your concerns with your pediatrician or family doctor, who may refer you to other specialists.

1. Rule out medical causes. Occasionally, this kind of behavior is caused by such medical conditions as anemia, thyroid malfunction, or neurological problems. Be sure your doctor rules these out.

2. Review both the child's and the family histories with your doctor or trained professional. ADD/hyperactivity is a persistent condition present at birth. It shows itself before the age of six unless it is caused by an accident to the central nervous system at a later age. A child is not hyperactive one year and calm the next. Scientific studies and our own interviews with parents have shown that up to 35 percent of the fathers of hyperactive children had a similar behavior pattern in childhood.

3. Ask teachers, past and present, to rate behavior. It is particularly important to get the teachers' judgments about the child's behavior. Keith Conners has developed an effective rating scale to be used by teachers and parents. The scores will yield a highly reliable index for determining whether a child's behavior is truly hyperactive. Your pediatrician can provide this questionnaire and help interpret it.

4. Complete a parent rating form. When you work with a psychologist or psychiatrist, you will probably be asked to use a formal questionnaire to evaluate your thoughts about your child and

assess his behavior. Your ratings will then be compared with those of the teachers.

The doctor will also use the diagnostic criteria categorized by the 1980 Diagnostic and Statistical Manual of the American Psychiatric Association to make his evaluation. Some of the characteristics he will use in the assessment include:

1. often fails to finish activities
2. often doesn't listen
3. is easily distracted
4. can't seem to concentrate on a task for long periods
5. can't stick to a task
6. often acts before thinking
7. changes activities frequently
8. has difficulty "getting organized"
9. needs a lot of monitoring
10. interrupts or calls out in class
11. has trouble waiting for his turn
12. runs or climbs constantly
13. can't seem to sit still
14. is "a perpetual-motion machine"

5. Have a professional observe the child in school. A learning-disability specialist or behavior-disorders teacher should observe the child in the classroom setting to evaluate class norms and expectations and compare your child's behavior to that of his peers.

6. Arrange for testing by a psychologist or psychometrist. Tests, usually one-to-one, will assess the child's performance under optimal conditions, yielding valuable information about his strengths and weaknesses as well as his motivation to perform in the educational setting. His behavior may be a cover for a learning problem or may be produced by anxiety or boredom. However, testing alone is not enough to make a diagnosis of ADD or to rule out the condition, either.

7. Review all information. With your doctor and the other professionals, review the material. Because there is no single test for ADD/hyperactivity, the diagnosis for ADD or ADD/hyperactiv-

ity will be based on a pattern of behavior. It is also possible that these conditions will be ruled out by the data and another problem will be discovered.

11.15-2 Coping with ADD/Hyperactivity to Minimize Problems.

This condition can affect your child's actions, perceptions, and self-concept throughout his childhood and, probably, adolescence. There is no cure for ADD/hyperactivity; therefore, coping is the key. Don't blame yourself or your child. On the other hand, don't allow the condition to become an excuse for your child to misbehave. Use the techniques in this book, realizing that with each behavior it may take more patience, planning, reinforcement and consequences to build and maintain desirable behavior. The most effective treatment is a multimodal approach that includes behavior management, classroom intervention, self-control training and, for some youngsters, medication.

11.15-3 Use Medication Correctly.

Many ADD/hyperactive children get remarkable results from appropriate medications, which are usually central nervous system stimulants. Here are some facts about the drugs.

• The stimulants affect the part of the brain that controls the ability to pay attention to one thing at a time. Like a deer who hears a twig break in the forest, the rest of us focus our attention on the sound until we discover its cause, but ADD/hyperactive children have difficulty doing this. Their attention moves on to something else too quickly. This is not the result of lack of interest. The child starts to look for the source, then hears the water, turns to the clouds drifting by and then to the birds singing. His attention flits across the scene.

Medication allows the child to focus on the sound, ignoring the birds, the water, and the clouds. With better concentration, he appears less active and can tend to the activity at hand. In school, the effects are often quickly apparent in handwriting and the ability to follow directions and stay with a task.

• Ritalin (methylphenidate) is the prescribed medication in about 82 percent of the cases. It is fast-acting like Dexedrine (dextroamphetamine), another choice, with its effects apparent in fifteen to thirty minutes and lasting three to four hours. Time-release capsules, which extend the effects for as long as eight hours, are sometimes prescribed for children who resist taking medication or have a poor reaction to repeated doses.

Cylert (magnesium pemoline), the newest drug, is given in a spanule, or slow-release capsule, and its effects build over time, taking up to three or four weeks to reach peak potential. When correctly adjusted, one dose will influence a child's behavior for a good part of a day.

Children who do not respond to the most frequently prescribed drugs may respond to others. Tofranil, an antidepressant, is often effective with youngsters who are especially distracted by their own thoughts. Tranquilizers, such as Mellaril (thioridazine) or Thorazine (chlorpromazine), will reduce activity level, although they also reduce motor skills and do not increase the attention span.

• No major side effects have been reported for Ritalin, in use since 1956, or Dexedrine, in use even longer; nor is there correlation between reliance on these medications and later drug abuse. Minor side effects, many of which disappear after a few days or weeks, include stomachaches, insomnia, decreased appetite, and headaches. Because it's possible for poor appetite to retard growth slightly, many professionals recommend that children take the medication after meals or early enough before meals so that appetite is not affected, or that they are given "drug holidays."

• Dosages are best determined by trial and error with professional guidance, using the following steps:

1. Get preratings of the child's behavior with the form in Figure 9 or using the completed Conners rating forms as a base for later comparison.

Fig. 9 Behavior Rating Form

Activity Level:	**Very high**	**Average**	**Low**
Work Completion:	**All**	**Most**	**Little**
Attention:	**Long**	**Average**	**Short**
Comments:			

Ask the child's teacher to complete a weekly behavior rating form to assess the effects of medication.

2. Try a double-blind test. Without informing the teacher or the child (tell him it's a new vitamin), give a daily morning dose of the medication selected by the physician for one week.

3. At the end of a week, ask the teacher to rate the child's behavior again, giving her a copy of the chart in Figure 9. Compare her judgments with yours.

4. Discuss the results with the doctor or other professional. If there were no noticeable changes in the child, ask for a slightly higher dose of the medication and start the new dose in midweek, so the teacher will not know when the switch occurs. After a week, evaluate the child's behavior again. Keep in mind that undermedicating will produce little change, while overmedicating can make the child lethargic and even less able to concentrate.

11.15-4 Restructure the Classroom Environment.

Now that the medication has been regulated, or if you are not using medication, talk to the teacher and the school administrators about changes in the school routine that may help the child. Many ADD/hyperactive children already lag behind in academic skills by the time the diagnosis is made and are likely to have other learning disabilities as well. Be sure your child's academic level is tested so that appropriate plans may be made.

Some of the classroom needs include:

• Structured classroom. Because his attention is easily diverted, this child concentrates best in a small class in a room with few visual distractions. Color and clutter can pull his focus from his tasks. He will do best in a quiet, well-controlled classroom with tasks and requirements that are clearly structured. The teacher should be firm, though not so strict that the child has trouble following her rules.

• Small work units. The child will probably learn well when the teacher provides materials at the proper academic level, gives clear instructions, divides the work into small units, and reinforces him for staying with one task for an appropriate length of time. The behavior-disorders or learning-disabilities specialist in the school should help the teacher set up the program.

• Home/school network. To link home and school support systems, arrange for a report to come home with the child every day (see Section 11.8). With regular information on his school performance, you can reinforce his achievements by praising and rewarding him first for bringing home the report and later for his increased ability to complete work and stay with his tasks.

11.15-5 Structure the Home Environment.

The ADD/hyperactive child can cause tremendous problems within a family because his impulsive nature makes it hard for him to follow rules. Medication or success at school will help, but you must make changes at home, too.

• Give clear and consistent directions. This is extremely important with all children, but it is even more essential with ADD/hyperactive youngsters. There must be a set of rules that everyone in the household knows and follows. Write the rules down and post them in a prominent place. When you speak to the child, make sure he looks directly at you. Outline the consequences for failure to follow the rules and carry them out when necessary. Read Chapter 2 again and see sections 5.7, 5.8, and 11.8.

• Provide structure. This child performs best within the confines of routine and structure. Plan each day ahead, and write out a schedule for the family. Although you may not stick with it totally, it will help the child know what is expected and when. The more set the routine, the more signals it will give him to help him control his behavior.

• Simplify the environment. Your child is easily distracted and overstimulated, so it is best to do just one thing at a time. For example, when you want him to eat his breakfast, turn off the television set. At playtime, take out only one or two toys at a time. Control the noise level in the house.

11.15-6 Teach Self-Control.

The ADD/hyperactive child has difficulty controlling his impulses. When he's required to behave in a certain way, his attention wanders and impulse takes over. Medication will improve some of this behavior, but it is not the only answer. Teach him to assume increasing responsibility for himself.

• Teach him to maintain eye contact. A common problem shared by these children is difficulty maintaining eye contact or orienting themselves toward a speaker. If you can overcome this one stumbling block, you may see dramatic results. Use these games to develop the skill (and check Section 5.8 as well):

Look Away Game: Challenge the child to a staring contest. Time the seconds he can maintain eye contact, keeping a chart of increasing "world's records."

Radar: After staring has been mastered, challenge the child to "zoom" his attention to whoever is talking and to "lock in his radar" on that person until he stops talking. At mealtime, each parent can purposely alternate speaking so the child must really pay attention, earning points for focusing correctly on the speaker for longer and longer periods of time. When the skill has been learned, he can continue to earn points for focusing on his parents whenever they speak to him.

• Decrease distractions with "zapping." Timothy was a seven-year-old who could hardly make it to his bedroom because he was distracted by every noise, toy, and light switch along the way. When he did get there, he would forget why he had gone. We taught Timothy to "zap" each thing that tried to get his attention with his handy imaginary finger gun, and his parents rewarded him for finishing whatever task he set out to do. After a few weeks, he reported that he could hang up his gun because he could zap things with his mind.

• Teach him to ignore distractions. Play a game in which you try to distract him as he works at a school assignment. Make noises. Walk softly around the room. Reward the child when he persists at his work and ignores the happenings.

• Use the timer. Read Section 5.7 for suggestions about using a kitchen timer to lengthen the time a child can sit still. Play Beat the Clock, gradually teaching him to sit at a desk, the dinner table, or wherever else sitting still is required.

After showing him how to use the kitchen timer and time himself sitting still, teach him to use it to control his own behavior. If he would like to finish his homework in a shorter time, ask him to set a goal. For example, he will read his assignment for three minutes. He sets the timer and makes himself sit still reading for three minutes. With each success, he can set another goal and gradually increase his study time. If he estimates that his math homework will take twenty minutes, he can set the timer for two ten-minute periods with a break between. This technique can also help him stop rushing and lengthen the time it takes him to do jobs or eat meals.

Of course, you will praise him as he gains control in many situations. You may also design a reinforcement system, with points for each goal met. These points can be traded in for coveted rewards.

. A variation is to have the child keep a tally of his behavior. If, for instance, he always gets out of his seat in school when he should be sitting down: With the teacher's cooperation, have him count the number of times he gets up. The next day, set a goal of fewer occasions of getting out of his seat, with points or privileges earned when the goal is met.

• Teach relaxation techniques. We all perform better when we're not anxious, and this is especially true of the ADD/hyperactive child. When he learns to relax himself at will, he can then use this skill whenever he needs it to calm himself or think things through. See Section 2.10.

• Teach cognitive self-control. Train the child to control his behavior with verbalized thoughts. Start a task with him and talk out loud to yourself: "I must keep my mind on what I'm doing. I'll try another way." Teach the child to copy your behavior whenever he's doing something that requires perseverance, first aloud and later silently. See the suggested-readings section at the end of this chapter for the titles of some books that will explain this technique.

11.15-7 Join a Support Group.

In a group of parents of ADD/hyperactive children, you will learn how others cope with their problem children. The Association for Children with Learning Problems can tell you the group nearest you.

11.15-8 Seek Professional Help.

A skilled professional will work with the child and the family to speed success in managing the problems of daily living.

SUGGESTED BOOKS FOR PARENTS AND CHILDREN

Barkley, R. *Hyperactive Children: A Handbook for Diagnosis and Treatment.* New York: B. Guilford Press, 1981. A comprehensive view of assessment and treatment procedures. Designed primarily for professionals; may also be of interest to parents.

Kendall, Philip C. and Lauren Braswell. *Cognitive Behavior Therapy for Impulsive Children.* New York: B. Guilford Press,

1985. Describes a new treatment approach using cognitive/behavioral techniques.

O'Leary, Daniel K. *Mommy, I Can't Sit Still.* New York: New Horizon Press, 1984. Written for parents and professionals, the book presents a discussion of diagnosis and treatment of hyperactive and aggressive children.

CHAPTER 12

Nervous Habits

MOST children, at some time in their young life, develop a "nervous habit" that helps them release tension and reduce anxiety or frustration. They suck their thumb, bite their nails, pull out hair, grind their teeth, or find some other habit for the times when they are tired or pressured. They become less dependent on these behaviors as anxiety decreases or they learn better ways to cope with everyday stress.

Sometimes, however, the behavior becomes an ingrained habit that continues even when the child isn't fatigued or tense. One child twists his hair and sucks his thumb whenever he watches television. A little girl started biting her nails when she was taken on long car trips and now bites them constantly. When nervous habits are repeated enough, they develop a life of their own, often persisting into adolescence or adulthood. In the dark of the night, there are even a few college students quietly sucking their thumbs.

But don't overreact. Don't feel pressured to put an immediate stop to your child's habits for fear that he will walk down the aisle sucking his thumb, twirling his hair, and dragging his blanket. Most children quit them on their own if you stay calm and don't pay too much attention to their particular habit. On the other hand, you should not ignore habits that last beyond the typical age or are so intense that they lead to social rejection or have physical consequences.

The suggestions in this chapter can greatly reduce or completely banish nervous habits before they become a permanent fixture. Although the details of the solutions vary, there are common techniques to be applied. Read and understand these basic steps before you begin. Some of them originate with Drs. Nathan Azrin and R. Gregory Nunn, who describe them in their book *Habit Control in a Day*. New York: (Pocket Books, 1977), an excellent source for further information.

The basic principles are:

Relaxation.

The first step to overcoming your child's nervous habit is teaching her how to relax—no one can be relaxed and nervous at the same time. Furthermore, a relaxed state will make her more receptive to suggestions and better able to change her behavior. To help her reach a relaxed mood at will, the general relaxation techniques described in Section 2.10 should be followed carefully and consistently for several weeks, until the child has mastered them. Younger children will need shorter training sessions and more rewards to keep on practicing. A back rub at bedtime and other quiet activities such as sharing feelings or listening to soothing music can also promote a calm mood.

Sometimes all you have to do to reduce the frequency of the nervous habit is teach the child to be more relaxed. But focusing on relaxing the specific part of the body involved in the habit can lead to even better results. If the child sucks her thumb, emphasize relaxing the hands, arms, and of course the mouth, since that's where the thumb ends up.

Awareness.

Most habits become so automatic that the child is no longer aware he's engaging in them, and friends and relatives become so used to them that they no longer bother to comment. Parents often get upset over a habit, but only now and then. The child will suck his thumb, holding on to his blanket, for a few days and incur no comment and then, suddenly, Mom will fuss at him to stop or Dad will tire of dragging that blanket everywhere. Accustomed to occasional criticism, the child makes a feeble attempt to quit and then pops the thumb back into his mouth.

Scattered nagging isn't an effective way to change a habit. Instead, the key to stopping a nervous habit is to make the child constantly aware of what he's doing, minute to minute every single day, during the time when you are working on this problem. In each section in this chapter, you will find specific techniques to heighten the child's awareness in a consistent and noncritical way. They require special effort on your part.

Change in situation or association.

Many nervous habits occur only in specific situations or places. One little boy, for example, sucked his thumb while stroking his blanket and watching TV. Breaking the habit was much easier when he was no longer allowed to hold his blanket while he watched. Another child banged her head whenever she sat in a favorite easy chair. She quit when a wooden chair was substituted. Later, she was allowed to use the comfortable cushioned chair again, but only if she didn't bang her head. Head banging led to time-out from that chair and the television set.

Try to identify when and where the habit is used so that these associations can be changed.

Alternatives.

Often, a child resorts to a nervous habit because it's the best available thing to do at the moment. It's hard to do two things at once, so teach the child an alternative behavior that competes with the habit and won't allow it to occur. For example, the child might use tensing and relaxing his hands whenever he feels the urge to put his thumb in his mouth. Or he could squeeze a ball or stroke a rabbit-foot.

Motivation.

Reinforcement often gives children a little extra push to try to break a habit. See sections 2.4 and 2.5 for details about setting up charts and rewards to motivate your child. Be sure to praise her every time you see her using an alternative to the habit or simply avoiding the old behavior. Catch the child doing well. If he doesn't twirl his hair whenever he sits in the back seat of the car anymore, give him recognition. At the beginning, you may have to praise and/or reward him every few minutes or every time he does not engage in the habit in the usual situations. But once the habit is on its way out, you can decrease the rewards and the recognition.

Practice.

Whenever the child engages in the habit, have him practice the alternative behavior for at least three minutes. This not only interrupts the habit and heightens awareness, it also increases the motivation not to use the habit. Soon the child will start catching himself when he resorts to the habit. When he notices his hand halfway up to his mouth and uses the alternative instead, be sure to give him extra praise and rewards and shorten the practice time.

Specific alternatives and corrective actions are described for each of the nervous habits—use these as well as those you invent yourself. One mother had her child work on a three-dimensional puzzle block when he watched TV or sat in the car. It helped him break the association of hair pulling within these settings and was an acceptable substitute action for him. He not only succeeded at breaking his habit, but he became the house champion of 3-D puzzles.

12.1 THUMB-SUCKING

Many children are born thumb-suckers. That thumb finds it way up to the mouth early in life and just stays there. This doesn't mean the baby is insecure or anxious but, rather, that the habit satisfies her need to suck. Some infants have a strong sucking response.

The chances are fifty-fifty that a natural thumb-sucker will quit on her own before she's five years old. Of those who continue, most quit before they are eight. Though you may worry all you want about thumb-sucking, we believe that there are just two valid reasons to change the habit. One is social and the other dental.

Young children today must interact with many people much more often than they did in years past, because they go to day-care or preschool programs at earlier ages. If thumb-sucking is considered unacceptable by parents, teachers, or peers or if it interferes with a child's involvement with others or performance in school, then it may be appropriate to help him change the habit. In addition, thumb-sucking may possibly affect the alignment of the child's teeth when his permanent teeth start to erupt.

If you decide to change your child's thumb-sucking habit, use the general approach to eliminating a nervous habit and add the other solutions specifically designed for this particular activity.

12.1-1 Pacify the Infant's Sucking Reflex.

To discourage the development of the thumb-sucking habit in an infant with a strong sucking response, give him more sucking time. A bottle with a slow-flowing nipple or a pacifier may help satisfy his need. Many pediatricians believe that most of the babies who use pacifiers for the first few months of life never become thumb-suckers. And often those who become dependent on the pacifier give it up sooner than they would have given up the thumb.

12.1-2 Use Systematic Ignoring.

Since the chances are pretty good that your child will quit sucking his thumb all on his own before he's in first grade, you could just ignore the whole thing. And in fact, it's better not to call attention to the habit constantly. Check back with Chapter 2 for a discussion of the basic technique of systematic ignoring.

Remember that elimination of this habit won't come overnight.

It requires patience and perseverance on your part. But if you are consistent in your ignoring, it will gradually decrease. Here's how it works.

• Do not comment negatively or positively about thumb-sucking. Avoid *any* comments of any kind. Avoid conversation and eye contact with the child when she is sucking her thumb.

• Do not offer comfort through physical contact or closeness when she is sucking her thumb.

• But when she *stops* sucking her thumb, touch and hug her and give her a lot of love. Except for the oppositional child, positive feedback at this time may be helpful: "Oh, I like the way you look without your thumb in your mouth!" Or, "You look like such a big girl without your thumb!" On the other hand, if your comments seem to increase the sucking, then go back to totally ignoring the habit, resuming normal contact without any comment when she stops doing it.

12.1-3 Devise a Well-Planned Program.

Encourage the child to give up the habit by using the six essential basic steps outlined at the beginning of this chapter.

1. Encourage the child to relax. Most people, especially children, fall into old habits when they are tired or stressed. Learning to relax will help the child avoid those habits and learn to use a valuable new one. Use the techniques described in Chapter 2. For an older child, once he's relaxed, encourage him to focus on his hands (see Section 12.4, on nail-biting).

2. Make the child aware. Encourage her to be aware of her thumb-sucking by tactfully pointing out to her what her thumb looks like after it's been sucked. Have her look at herself in the mirror while she's busy doing it, and talk about how she looks. Suck your own thumb and ask her what she thinks. Point out other children when they are sucking their thumb.

3. Give the child a "thumb sub." If the thumb is soothing, then a less noticeable substitute may satisfy her. A rabbit-foot or a small

furry stuffed animal may do it. Sometimes, hand squeezing will give her enough satisfaction. Remember to encourage her to use relaxation skills when she feels the need to suck.

4. Change the situation/break the association. For very young children, try to reduce the time spent sucking rather than eliminating it altogether.

• Place restrictions on where he may suck his thumb. Keep a record for several days of where and when he sucks. Choose one place or time and tell him that it is no longer acceptable to suck his thumb in that place or at that time. Be sure to choose a place and time when you will be there for several consecutive days. You must be present to monitor the situation, remind, reinforce, and reward the child for changing his behavior.

• Apply a natural consequence. Choose a natural consequence to follow if the child does suck his thumb in the forbidden place. If watching television is selected, turn off the set for five minutes when he sucks his thumb. After the five minutes—with no TV or thumb-sucking—he may resume watching. Other negative consequences might be no dessert if mealtime is the restricted time or a five-minute time-out if playing outside is the time. Be sure to inform the child beforehand of the consequences. Observe him and consistently administer the consequences if necessary. But remember to deliver praise when he is successful.

• Chart the behavior and reward efforts. A reward chart increases the chances that a child will practice a new behavior. Tell her she may "print" her thumb on a thumbprint chart like the one in Figure 10 every time she is successful in the restricted place or time. Use nontoxic vegetable dye, of course.

Fig. 10 Thumbprints for Success

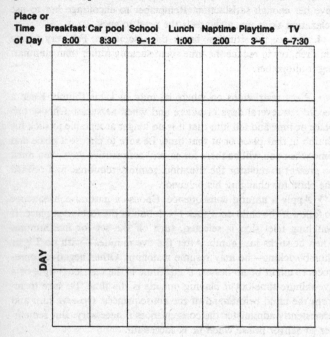

Child collects her own thumbprints on a reward chart as she practices her new behavior.

For each time the child watches television without sucking her thumb for example, she earns a thumbprint. Begin with a time frame you are fairly certain she can manage easily. Choose an appropriate reward for a specific number of thumbprints. Gradually increase the length of time required to earn a thumbprint. Thus: The first day, the child may earn a thumbprint for not sucking her thumb for five minutes while watching TV. Later in the day or the next, she may need to watch successfully for fifteen minutes per thumbprint.

4. Begin the process again. When sucking is successfully eliminated at one place or time, start again in another place.

To eliminate the habit at school, you must work with the teacher. Tell her what you are doing at home. Let the child know she can earn a thumbprint at home by not sucking in school for a certain amount of the day. Decide whether it should be the entire day, all day except naptime, for an hour after arrival, or whenever. Each day that the child is successful at school, have the teacher send home a thumbs-up letter like this one (give the teacher a supply of notes):

Dear Mom and Dad,
    Hi! Guess what? I didn't suck my thumb at school today! Thumbs up!

                                                          Love,

12.1-4 Use Intensive Therapy for Older Children.

For the older child or the rare adolescent who still sucks his thumb, you may need a more systematic and intensive procedure. Try habit reversal, described in detail in the Azrin and Nunn book *Habit Control in a Day* (New York: Pocket Books, 1977). In a technique called intense awareness, the child is taught to "catch" himself as the thumb moves toward the mouth and to practice hand isometrics as a consequence to thumb-sucking.

A dental appliance prescribed and fitted by a dentist works for some older children who want to quit their habit. The most effective device is one that is painful to both thumb and palate when the thumb goes into the mouth.

12.2 GRITS AND GRINDS TEETH

When a child continually grits and grinds his teeth, a habit known as bruxism, it should be considered more than just an annoying habit. Continual tooth grinding can seriously affect the teeth and jaws.

The youngster who grinds his teeth at night usually clenches them during the day. To break this habit, start first with inhibiting the daytime activity.

12.2-1 Teach Relaxation.

When a child is anxious and tense, the facial muscles contract and the jaw tightens. He grits his teeth. For some youngsters, the gritting turns into grinding and continues even when the tension is relieved—it has become a habit.

- Teach the child to relax. Though he is suffering from facial tension, he must learn how to relax his whole body. See Section 2.10.
- Emphasize facial relaxation exercises. When whole-body relaxation has been mastered, focus on the facial muscles. Have the child practice relaxing his face several times a day until the response is well learned.
- Teach mini-relaxation. The brief exercise outlined in Section 2.10 will help him keep himself relaxed throughout the day. The child smiles to himself, grits his teeth a little, and takes two deep breaths. When he exhales the second time, he drops his mouth open and thinks, Relax, relax, relax.

12.2-2 Consult the Dentist.

Take the child to the dentist and discuss the bruxism. The dentist will check the alignment of the temporomandibular joint to see if it is contributing to the problem. Depending on the child's age and the extent of damage to his tooth enamel, the dentist may prescribe a plastic guard for him to wear at night.

12.2-3 Teach Awareness.

These exercises will heighten consciousness of tooth grinding.

- Mirror feedback. Have the child look at himself in the mirror and observe how his face looks and feels as he grits and grinds his teeth. Ask him to practice a mini-relaxation exercise. Does his face look different now? Have him practice the two activities until he is aware of the look and the feel of it.

• Practice. Have the child practice the two activities around the house until he becomes conscious of his habit of tightening his jaws when it occurs during the day.

12.2-4 Provide Motivation.

Sit down with your child and make a list of reasons why she should stop grinding her teeth. The dentist will supply some during your consultation, the mirror will supply others, and you can help by giving the child rewards for overcoming the habit.

12.2-5 Reward No Gritting/Grinding.

Choose a time, perhaps a weekend, when you will be with your child for an extended period. Tell the child she will be rewarded for each period of time she does not clench her teeth. Using a kitchen timer, begin with fifteen-minute periods for the young child and thirty minutes for the older child. Increase the time by small increments until the reward period is doubled. For each successful period, the child may earn a check or a point; these will accumulate and earn a reward. As she makes progress, gradually increase the cost of the rewards so she will earn them less often.

12.2-6 Teach Open-Mouth Breathing.

Whenever you see the child clenching or grinding her teeth, have her practice this exercise: Breathe slowly through her open mouth for three minutes. When she begins catching herself and practicing on her own, she'll be on her way to breaking the habit. Be sure to praise her frequently.

12.2-7 Now Work on Nighttime Grinding.

After the child has learned to control gritting and clenching in the daytime, begin working on the night grinding. Have her practice the relaxation exercises just before going to sleep—every night. Have her check every morning to see if her jaw and teeth feel like they have been tense during the night. Keep a chart to monitor improvement.

12.3 STUTTERING

Stuttering is a perplexing and frustrating problem for speaker and listener. The symptoms of stuttering include swift repetitions of beginning consonant or vowel sounds, elongated medial vowel sounds, and complete blocks on words. S-s-s-s-stuttering sounds like-like-like this! A sound, syllable, word, or even a phrase may be repeated. Approximately 1 percent of the population of the Western countries stutters, and the stutterer is usually a male.

Stuttering is usually a temporary developmental occurrence among children two to five years of age, disappearing as the child becomes fluent in the use of language. It may increase when the child is upset, tired, or excited. Of those who stutter after this age, four out of five stop by the end of adolescence.

Along with the stuttering, a child beyond preschool age may develop accompaniments to his struggle to speak, such as facial contortions, eye blinking, arm swinging, irregular breathing, or other movements designed to propel him beyond the interruptions. Most stutterers know in advance which words are likely to cause trouble, and the anticipation often contributes to the problem. Stutterers do not stutter all the time. Some can converse easily with children, sing without difficulty, speak fluently in a foreign language, or talk in chorus without a hitch.

Once it has begun, stuttering, like other habits, becomes the normal pattern of behavior. In this case, the habit is built upon an involuntarily learned set of behaviors related to speech and breathing.

Some of our suggestions will be helpful to parents of young

children who stutter, alerting you to what to look for and how to respond. Other suggestions are for the parents of older children who have been stuttering for a long time. They require diligent and patient efforts, because overcoming stuttering is not simple.

12.3-1 Ignore Early Stuttering.

Your reaction to your child's attempts to communicate are important factors in developing fluency. Speak correctly to the child, but don't expect his language to be as mature as yours. Listen with patience and tolerance as he practices his emerging language skills.

• Don't finish the child's sentences. Give your child your calm attention when he speaks. If he has trouble getting a word out or finishing a sentence, wait patiently. Don't interrupt him, and don't speak for him. When you do answer, use the correct word form and expand the language with new words.

• Maintain a relaxed atmosphere. During times when the family gathers for conversation, at dinner perhaps, establish a calm, un-hurried atmosphere and give each child a chance to speak. Let each one know that you want to hear what she has to share.

• Speak in a relaxed manner yourself, but do not tell the child to slow down. Don't call attention to your child's stuttering in any way. You want her to feel comfortable speaking to you, so be to-tally accepting. Speak to her at a natural, relaxed pace without obviously slowing down. Use shorter and clearer sentences so she will feel free to do the same.

• Do not comment on stuttering. Do not label her a stutterer. The more self-conscious a child is made to feel about her stuttering, the more likely it is that the problem will get worse. Try to imagine how you would feel if you had to worry that every word was correct.

12.3-2 Teach Relaxation When Speaking.

Stuttering often increases as the child learns to worry about speaking fluently. When the stuttering is met with a negative reaction or comment that calls attention to it, the worry may turn into fear. With fear, the vocal cords tighten and breathing becomes constricted, making speaking naturally even more difficult.

• Teach the child to relax his throat, shoulders, chest, and abdomen. Use the techniques in Section 2.10 to teach the child the relaxation response. When he learns general relaxation, focus the training on the muscles involved in speaking. Have him practice the exercises several times a day until he can readily relax those parts of his body.

12.3-3 Teach the Stutterer to Regulate Breathing.

Speech requires airflow across the vocal cords, and the child's breathing pattern affects the way he speaks. Many stutterers breathe in short gasps and actually run out of air when they talk.

• Teach regular deep breathing through the mouth. Have the child place one hand on his chest and the other on his stomach. As he inhales, his stomach should fill up and move more than his chest. Tell him to repeat the word *relax* to himself as he breathes out slowly and naturally and his stomach deflates. He should practice this every day, so he will become increasingly skilled at noticing his own tensed breathing.

• Teach him to inhale before speaking and exhale as he speaks. Making sounds requires a flow of air across the vocal cords, so begin by having the child practice breathing correctly when saying short sentences. You may have him write out a set of short sentences or phrases to use for the exercises: "Inhale before speaking. Think *relax* and exhale as you speak." Inhaling by phrases will naturally slow down his speech.

• Have the child stop speaking when he starts to stutter. Rather than attempt to push past the interruption, the child should pause, take a breath, and then start to speak again as he exhales.

• Have the child speak softly. A stutterer, like any other person under stress, naturally raises his voice. A louder voice requires more air, increasing the tension in the vocal region. A modulated voice will help reduce the stuttering.

12.3-4 Desensitize the Child to Stutter-Inducing Situations.

Fear increases the probability that the child will stutter, and anticipation of difficulty getting the words out makes it worse. Use the following steps and the information in Chapter 14 to desensitize him to the fear.

1. Make a list of the feared situations and words. Have the child identify the occasions when he often has speaking problems. List the words that frequently cause him to stutter.

2. Practice the relaxation exercises. The child will be more receptive to these exercises if he is relaxed.

3. Have her imagine herself speaking fluently in one of the feared situations. Suppose she has difficulty saying her own name, as many children do. Ask her to close her eyes. Lead her through a detailed description of the imaginary situation, anticipating sitting in class on the first day of school as the teacher calls the roll. Have her imagine how she feels waiting for her name, then have the teacher call her name, and she answers, "I am Sharon," without stuttering.

4. Rate the anxiety level. Ask your child to rate her distress in the above situation on a scale of one to ten. Repeat the imaginary exercise until the rating afterward falls to a comfortable level. Do the same with other imaginary scenarios.

5. Simulate situations when the child usually stutters. When she has become comfortable with the imaginary situation, simulate or role-play other experiences. Pretend you are the teacher. Ask the child who she is. When she can respond successfully, go on to other situations. Be sure to remind her to use her breathing and relaxation techniques.

6. Provide practice in planned situations. Set up real situations in which the child can practice her new skill. Invite friends over to play, or take her on outings so she can practice speaking where she

would have stuttered. Have her rehearse beforehand, imagining what will happen and seeing herself coping successfully.

7. Support efforts to speak in unplanned situations. Before she goes out in public, remind the child to practice the exercises that have helped her be successful. Be supportive and praise her efforts. If she stutters, say nothing. Simply continue with the plan of action.

12.3-5 Try "Pair" Speaking.

Many stutterers can speak normally when they speak in unison with someone else or in time with a beat.

- Practice speaking in unison. Recite prepared readings with the child. Speak naturally, using material the child can easily read. After repeating this several times, gradually fade out your own voice until he is speaking alone. Have him visualize speaking in unison when he's on his own.

- Use a metronome. Set the metronome at a very slow speed. Have the child regulate his speaking (see Section 12.3–3) and then read the material to the beat. When he can do it without stuttering, simulate other speaking situations with the metronome marking the timing of the words or syllables.

12.3-6 Seek Professional Help.

If the stuttering is severe or is not improved by your efforts, get outside help. Ask the school, health services, your physician, other parents, etc., for special speech programs designed to help stutterers.

SUGGESTED BOOKS FOR PARENTS

Azrin, Nathan H. and R. Gregory Nunn. *Habit Control in a Day*. New York: Pocket Books, 1977. Complete step-by-step guide to eliminating nervous habits.

Jonas, Gerald. *Stuttering: The Disorder of Many Theories*. New

York: Farrar, Straus & Giroux, 1977. Discussion of various theories about stuttering and the means to overcome it.

Schwartz, Martin F. *Stuttering Solved.* Philadelphia: J. Lippincott, 1976. Planned approach discussed to solve stuttering.

12.4 NAIL-BITING

Biting and picking at fingernails is a habit for many people, children and adults. Of all nervous habits, nail-biting is the most common and the one that is most likely to follow a child into adolescence or adulthood if left untreated. It's been estimated that up to a third of elementary-school children and about half of adolescent children bite their nails. About a quarter of college students bite their nails.

A less conspicuous version of nail-biting is picking at them. This can be done in your lap or behind your back and isn't as obvious as biting. But the result is the same. Both versions result in most unattractive hands.

To help your child give up this habit (and you, too, if you bite your nails), refer to the general information at the beginning of this chapter and then follow these steps.

12.4-1 Teach Relaxation.

The first step is to teach the child the relaxation response outlined in Section 2.10. Then focus the training on the fingers and the mouth.

• Relaxing the hands. Have the child tense her hands by making fists and holding them tightly closed for a count of fifteen, then releasing suddenly. She should feel a warm, tingling sensation. Repeat until the hands are relaxed, warm, and heavy.

• Relaxing the mouth and jaw. Give the child these instructions: Press your lips together, grit your teeth lightly, and smile a broad clown smile with your mouth closed. Take a long, deep breath through your nose. As you exhale, relax your mouth suddenly, letting it drop open about an inch. Repeat the exercise until your face feels relaxed.

• **Practicing.** Have the child practice both exercises several times a day for a week or more, until she begins to recognize the tenseness in her face and hands that leads her to bite her nails. The relaxation exercises can then be used to counteract the tension.

12.4-2. Teach Awareness.

It's important to make the child aware of the negative aspects of nail-biting and nail-picking.

• **Use comparison.** Have the child compare her hands with a parent who doesn't have the habit. Ask her to look for pictures of attractive hands in magazines and paste them in a scrapbook or tape them to a mirror. Comment when you see people with nice hands. Stress the good points about your child's hands, suggesting how great her unbitten nails will look.

• **Encourage awareness of how he looks.** Have the child sit in front of the mirror and watch himself biting his nails. You'd be surprised by the impression this makes on some youngsters. Analyze his technique: Decide if he chews all ten nails or just two, if he nibbles at the cuticles too, if he bites them down to the quick or only "straightens them out."

• **Encourage awareness of when and where he bites.** Once more, analyze this activity, this time discussing the times of day and the particular situations in which he engages in this habit. Melanie bites her nails when she's watching television or reading, but never when she has something in her hands, like a pencil. Jerry bites his at school or when he's doing his homework. Camille feels compelled to pick or bite rough spots or jagged edges.

• **Keep a tally on the habit.** Make a list of the times and places when you and the child realize she's biting her nails. If you see her start to bite or pick, give her a signal. Remember, however, that you must not be hostile or punitive. You are teaching awareness that may decrease the frequency of the occurrences.

12.4-3 Change the Situation/Break the Association.

By now, your child should be very aware of his habit. Now, make changes.

• Provide an alternative. Many children bite, scrape, or pick at their nails when their hands are idle. Give your child something better to do! Give her an object small enough to take anywhere unnoticed—a smooth stone, a rubber ball, a bit of clay, a rabbit-foot—and encourage her to play with it when she gets the urge to bite her nails.

Older children will enjoy learning a skill that requires two hands, such as knitting, needlepoint, jigsaw puzzles, or making model airplanes. Though we're not enthusiastic about letting a child chew on anything as a substitute for her nails, she could satisfy her oral needs with a plastic straw if she is old enough to do this safely.

• Change or avoid situations associated with the habit. We've already told you that Melanie bites her nails when she is watching television. Now, the rule is that she may watch only if she keeps her hands busy and does not bite her nails. She earns additional TV time by refraining from the habit for specific time periods.

12.4-4 Teach an Interruption to Nail-biting.

In addition to providing some alternate activities, teach a "competing" action.

• Substitute a gesture. Have the child practice making a fist, squeezing a ball, or grasping the arm of the chair for three minutes or until the urge to bite her nails passes. Then she should release the tension suddenly. Or have her sit on her hands, feeling the pressure of her palms against her legs.

Remind her that the relaxation exercises are another way to free herself from the urge.

• Have the child practice. When you catch the child biting or picking his nails, have him practice the alternative he's learned, such as clenching his fist for three minutes. If he catches himself, he practices for a shorter time, perhaps two minutes. If he refuses to practice, stop the activity he's engaged in and have him go to time-out until he cooperates.

12.4-5 Reinforce and Motivate.

Always remember to catch the child using alternatives to biting, and let her know how wonderful you think it is that she's beating her habit.

• Praise and point out progress. Show the child how her fingers are less red and raw and how her nails are growing longer. Give her a mini-manicure to eliminate rough spots, which might be tempting to an experienced nail biter. The older child will eventually note her own progress.

• Use positive motivation. The important thing is to find something the child wants to work toward. Motivate a young girl with juvenile nail polish, fancy gloves, or rings. Boys could get stickers, secret rings, or nail clippers on a chain. Toys like finger puppets, magnifying glasses for examining nails, fingerprint kits, clay, and finger paints are appropriate rewards. Take pictures now and then to show the big improvement.

• Teach care of the nails. A proper manicure will teach nail care and is a nice, healthy luxury.

12.5 TWITCHES AND TICS

Little twitches or tics—irregular repetitive involuntary movements —are a nervous habit that tends to occur most often in children, mainly boys, between the ages of six and twelve. They include eye blinking, shoulder jerking, tongue clicking, grimacing, and head shaking, with a lot of other variations. Sometimes the tic develops as a reaction to an especially stressful period of life, but often, these isolated habitual motions result from the normal stresses of growing up. One young man we treated developed a new tic every time his teacher introduced a new math level.

Usually, a stress-provoked tic disappears within a few weeks. Nagging and critical remarks do not speed up the process. On rare occasions, however, the tic perseveres beyond a few weeks. If it persists and interferes with social interaction or causes embarrassment, it should be dealt with directly through a series of planned interventions such as we suggest below.

Severe tics or a series of them may be a matter for more concern. When they are accompanied by strange sounds or curse words, they may be symptoms of a neurological disorder called Gilles de la Tourette syndrome. If there is any reason to suspect that a tic may be symptomatic of a more serious emotional or physical problem, an examination by a physician is in order immediately.

12.5-1 Reduce Stress/Teach Relaxation.

Because a tic is usually a response to stress, try to reduce the stress level in your child's life by cutting down on overscheduling, getting help for academic problems, helping with social difficulties, or doing anything else that might help to relieve the tension. And, of course, add the relaxation response to the child's repertoire of coping skills. Teach him the techniques described in Section 2.10. Try to build self-confidence and a good self-concept so that he can withstand the stresses of life.

12.5-2 Teach Awareness.

Have the child watch himself in the mirror, and ask him to describe what the tic looks like and exactly how it occurs. If he is a shoulder jerker, the pattern of motion may be that the muscle tightens before the jerk occurs. The shoulder rises about two inches, pauses there for a second, then returns to its normal position. The jerking is repeated three times in a row. Help the child draw up a list of situations when the tic most often occurs, plus the social drawbacks of the habit.

12.5-3 Teach an Alternative.

The key to overcoming a twitch is to substitute a counteracting motion, as described in Drs. Azrin and Nunn's book *Habit Control in a Day*. This motion should tense those muscles that are in direct opposition to those involved in the tic. To stop a shoulder jerk, pull the shoulder downward and hold it down for several minutes. Similarly, the counter to eye blinking is to raise the eyebrows and open the eyes wide for several minutes. For trembling arms and hands, tense, then relax the fist as described in the relaxation section. Use the exercises discussed in Section 2.10 to help you identify the appropriate alternate motion, experimenting with your child in front of a mirror until you recognize it.

12.5-4 Praise/Practice.

Consistent practice and use of the counteracting movement is most important in overcoming a tic. Praise the child for practicing it, and reward him for catching himself as the tic starts or earlier in the cycle, when he feels the muscles tighten.

12.5-5 Give Negative Practice.

If the techniques already described do not seem to be effective, add sessions of negative practice. Have the child practice the tic so much that the muscles that produce it become exhausted. For example, with eye blinking, the child should blink his eyes rapidly until they are tired. An arm jerker would repeat the jerk of the arm to the point of true fatigue, though not until the muscle is strained or overworked. The purpose of this exercise is not to punish the child, but to discourage the tic through overuse of the muscles.

12.6 OBSESSED WITH CLEANLINESS

Most parents struggle to get their children to wash their faces or clean up their rooms. But there are children who are so obsessed with cleanliness that it becomes a real problem. If you have a child who is fanatical about being sure every perfume bottle on the dresser is perfectly aligned or goes wild if he thinks a germ is on his hands, then you know this mania can rule the entire household. Besides, if these tendencies continue, they can cause the child tremendous emotional distress.

Some people, adolescents and adults, wash their hands fifty times a day but still do not feel clean. The more anxious they become, the more zealous they are about washing. One boy who was brought to us for a consultation spent at least an hour a day straightening his toys. Every soldier and truck had to be lined up in the right spot or he could not go to sleep. Then he would follow his father through the house checking doors and windows before he could go to sleep at night.

Young children are comforted by regularity and routine, and a healthy respect for neatness and cleanliness is fine. But their appreciation of these attributes must remain at a manageable level.

If your child seems to be in a quest for perfection, the following suggestions are for you.

12.6-1 Explain the Reasons for the Obsession.

In a manner that is appropriate to his age, explain to the child why he's so concerned with germs or keeping everything in its place.

• For the young child, use a story in which the hero cleans whenever he feels nervous or can't control the events in his life. The hero spends so much time cleaning or straightening that he misses all the fun or gets into big trouble. Try this one:

Once upon a time, there was a white knight. He was very proud to be Sir Kleen, but he was a little worried, too. What if he wasn't up to the job? He wanted to look his best, so he began cleaning his armor. The king called to the knights, alerting them that the battle was about to begin. Sir Kleen started buffing his armor even harder. He rubbed and shined, telling himself how important it was to get every spot out. He was so busy cleaning that he missed the herald's call to battle. This made him so upset that he started cleaning his quarters. He spent all his time straightening and polishing and didn't have any time to do anything else. He even missed the king's big party . . .

• Discuss the behavior with the older child. Make the connection between his concern for cleanliness or neatness and how anxious or worried he is. Though he may deny his stress, over time, he will start to notice that he cleans and straightens more before tests or other stressful events.

If you have similar tendencies, admit to him how you sometimes clean the closets or check the doors when you're anxious. Explain that both of you are being superstitious and perhaps you should try to change together. Try to identify other examples of superstitious behavior among people you know. Aunt Bella always walks around her car before getting into it. Bowlers sometimes make special hand movements, trying to control the ball after it leaves their hand.

12.6-2 Teach Relaxation Skills.

Generalized relaxation and anxiety control are especially important for children with this type of nervous habit (see Section 2.10). Be sure the child associates a cue word, such as *relax*, with the calm feeling, because this will help him block obsessive thoughts.

12.6-3 Change Thought Patterns.

The obsessive child usually has many misconceptions, repeating them to herself as she works.

• Correct the misconceptions. Ask the child why she thinks it's so important to have every object on her desk in a straight line. It may take many attempts before she is comfortable enough to share this private feeling. It's likely that she believes she possesses inside information crucial to her success that is very hard to give up. She may think that if the items on the desk are not in place, she will do poorly on the math test. Point out that this doesn't always hold true by reminding her of the times the desk was in order but her math grade was not perfect.

• Combat her ideas. In a series of discussions, have the child list his thoughts about cleanliness and orderliness. Help him understand that all these thoughts are not exactly true. Together, compose a set of positive statements to counteract the wrong ones and have the child repeat them to himself. For example: "A little dirt won't hurt me. I can wash my hands later." Or, "There's no relationship between how neat my room is and whether I get to school safely."

• Practice the counteracting statements. Encourage the child to practice saying the positive counteracting statements, first out loud and then silently, whenever he feels the urge to clean or straighten. Perhaps it would go like this: "I have studied hard for this test and I know the material. I have done well on the last four tests. Straightening my desk has nothing to do with my grade."

12.6-4 Practice the Dirty Dozen.

The real secret to overcoming obsessive habits is to practice *not* overwashing, *not* overstraightening, and even messing up more. Though the child may think this is funny at first, it will probably be very difficult for him to accomplish. Your goal is to help him feel more comfortable and less driven.

• Make a list of actions you wish the child to do *less* frequently, such as not putting all the freshly sharpened pencils in a neat row on the desk or not changing clothes twelve times a day.

• Make a list of actions you wish the child to do *more* frequently. The list could include moving everything on the desk out of place, getting his clothes purposely dirty and not changing them immediately. Increase the list gradually to twelve actions the child should continue doing until they no longer bother him.

12.6-5 Develop a Reasonable Compromise.

When you see that the child is more relaxed and less obsessive, praise and reward her for her new attitude. Formulate a list of behaviors that are healthy and reasonable: i.e., reorganizing her room twice a week rather than twice a day; washing up before meals instead of every time before she goes outside.

12.6-6 Seek Professional Help.

If the habit persists or gets worse, you need professional help (see Chapter 17). Obsessive cleanliness and neatness may be a sign of more serious emotional problems.

12.7 PULLS OUT HAIR

Sometimes, an active child finds his hair a quiet focus for extra energy, pulling at it, twirling strands around his finger, or picking at his scalp. What starts as an innocent occupation sometimes progresses to a more unfortunate habit known as tricholomania. One four-year-old boy who pulled his hair out in clumps looked like Friar Tuck by the time we met him. A twelve-year-old girl who continued tugging ended up with bald spots the size of a half dollar all over her head. Obviously, when such a habit reaches this stage, it must be stopped immediately.

12.7-1 Consult with Your Physician.

Check with the doctor to rule out scalp conditions that may foster the habit. If the child is hyperactive, medication may help curb the excessive activity that may lead to such actions.

12.7-2 Teach Relaxation.

Learning to relax is the first step in breaking the cycle of any habitual act. Refer to Section 2.10 and help the child learn this skill. When she has gained mastery over it, teach her to focus on relaxing the hands.

Sometimes, however, a child pulls or twirls her hair when she is relaxed. If this is true with your child, then the relaxation training will probably not help curb the habit.

12.7-3 Develop Awareness.

If this is a frequent activity, the child may not be aware she is doing it. She must be taught to be aware and to notice the motions involved.

- Point out the habit. Have the child watch herself in a mirror and play with her hair. Have her play with a few strands, tugging until she pulls out some of them. Show her exactly what she does and how it looks.
- Examine the effects. Have her study her head, looking for bald spots or skimpy hair. Or if the bare spots are in the back, take a picture. Compare her hair with the models' hair in a magazine.
- Make a list. Where and when does your child pull her hair? What is she doing at the time? Isolate and list the situations when she does it the most.

12.7-4 Change the Habit.

Examine the way the child spends his time, and try to improve it. Try to make changes when you have a few days to spend.

- Keep the child's hands away from his face. In the beginning, you must keep him very busy, perhaps playing board games or going outside to swing. During quiet times, have him keep his hands busy with a lump of clay or a small ball, a card game, or a puzzle. When he reads or watches television, have him sit on his hands. Encourage him to hold a pencil when he studies.
- Give him a hat. Let the child choose a hat, or a number of different hats, to wear around the house when he's likely to want to pull his hair.

• Cut her hair. By cutting it short, make the hair harder to grab. Or rearrange it with a barrette, or make a ponytail to discourage tugging and hide bald spots.

• Keep the child busy. This is a top priority. Make sure she has enough constructive activities to fill up her time while you supervise and reinforce her efforts to resist pulling.

• Practice a corrective action. If the child does pull his hair, have him stop immediately, make a fist, and hold it tight for several minutes before relaxing. If possible, catch him as he reaches for his hair and stop the action.

12.7-5 Praise and Reward.

The only way to break this habit is to monitor, intervene, and reinforce success, especially with a very young child.

• Praise the child. Be bountiful in your praise of her involvement in activities that keep her hands away from her hair. When she practices the substitute activities, like twirling a pencil when she's studying, tell her you appreciate her effort and self-control. As you see changes in her hair growth, comment on how good her hair is looking.

• Reward the child. Let her earn small rewards or points toward a reward for specific periods of no hair pulling. At first, ten minutes without pulling should be enough for a reward. Later, fifteen minutes may be required. Play a game with the child, read her a story, or allow her to watch television only as long as she refrains from pulling. As her new behavior becomes more established, slowly stretch the reward periods to hours, then days, as discussed in Chapter 2.

• Monitor success with pictures. Keep a set of before-and-after pictures, comparing the length of the hair and the size of the bald spots. A trip to the beauty salon for a little girl could be the perfect finishing touch.

12.8 NOSE PICKING

Nose picking begins as an innocent but efficient solution to an obvious problem, and small children can't understand why Mommy disapproves of it. Unfortunately, however, it is unattractive and therefore socially unacceptable, which means that it is another behavior that must be conquered.

Nose picking, just like any other habit, can be effectively discouraged without constant nagging. Here are the suggested procedures.

12.8-1 Encourage Awareness.

A child who picks his nose doesn't think he's doing anything wrong. To him, this is simply a natural behavior, like scratching his stomach when it itches. So let him know how it looks.

- Have the child observe himself. Ask the child to sit in front of a mirror and watch himself pick his nose. Or if he won't cooperate or feels too silly, show him how it looks yourself. Tell him why other people think this is a disgusting habit and do not like to watch it.
- Give the child information. Explain how the cilia and mucus are designed to catch foreign matter and protect the nose; constant picking can injure the sensitive lining and make it bleed.

12.8-2 Teach the Child Alternatives.

Show him more acceptable ways to clear his nose.

- Be preventive. Keep the child's nose from becoming excessively dry and thus tempting to pick. Noses have evolved with cilia, which work effectively to clear the nose. However, heated homes have a drying effect on the mucus. Consult your doctor about the use of a humidifier and other preventive measures.
- Teach nose blowing. Children frequently pick their nose when it is stuffy or feels like it is crusty. Show your youngster how you

blow your nose, mouth closed, holding one nostril closed while you blow air through the other. To get the knack, have him try to blow bits of tissue from his palm. Then show him how to use a tissue to catch the mucus. Give him tissues or a colorful handkerchief to encourage him to practice by himself.

12.8-3 Identify the Times and Places the Child Picks His Nose.

Observe him for several days and make a list of the times and places you have seen him picking his nose. When you have determined when and where he's most likely to spend time doing it, be sure he has his hands occupied with other activities at those times. Drew picked as he sat in his favorite chair watching television, so he was encouraged to color or play with his ball and jacks when he sat in the TV room. Laura kept her hands in her pockets when she rode in the car.

12.8-4 Use Praise and Rewards.

When the child exhibits good nose manners, then be sure to praise him for his efforts and awareness. Let him know how proud you are that he has chosen a healthy and mannerly way to care for himself. If the problem persists, reinforce his abstention from the habit for certain periods of time with points and rewards, beginning this project when you have enough free time to monitor the behavior. Gradually increase the time required to earn points, letting the older child keep a private tally of the number of occasions when he catches himself about to pick his nose. Then reward his self-control.

12.9 HEAD BANGING/BODY ROCKING

There are few parents who can watch their child bang her head against the wall or continually rock back and forth without great alarm. They worry not only that she will hurt herself badly but that perhaps she is emotionally disturbed. A child may rock so strenuously that the crib moves across the room, or bang his head so hard that it is always full of lumps and bruises.

First, let us give you some reassurance if your child is a rocker or a banger: Children rarely hurt themselves physically with their banging or rocking. They may use these activities as tension relievers, soothers, or relaxers, especially at the end of the day or when they are tired or stressed. Many infants take up these disturbing habits as early as two or three months of age, but in most cases, they quit them by the time they are three years old. On the other hand, rocking and banging do need to be controlled if they persist longer than that.

12.9-1 Use Systematic Ignoring.

The attention these behaviors get from parents in their attempt to curb them only serves to increase them. Why quit something when it gets you what you want? So ignore these behaviors, especially during the daytime hours. Make up your mind that they will elicit no attention or comment from you. Don't try to comfort the child or show affection until he stops rocking or banging; then move closer and demonstrate your love (see Section 2.2).

12.9-2 Change the Environment.

Rearrange the room so injury is more unlikely and the noise level is decreased. Move the crib or bed away from the wall. Put brakes on the bed wheels. Pad the headboard or put proper bumpers around the crib or mattress. Sometimes when the thumping or rocking makes less noise, the child is less likely to persist at it.

12.9-3 Help the Child Relax.

Many children who engage in these habits during the day need a way to relax.

• Alternate the activities. Find appropriate ways for the child to spend some of his energy. Dancing, sports, and active games can be outlets. Alternate these active periods with quiet activities like coloring, reading, playing card games, unless the child is one who is more likely to bang or rock during sedentary activities.

• Teach the infant or toddler to relax. Until he is old enough to learn the relaxation techniques, try back rubs and soothing music. Walk him through imaginary peaceful scenes as he lies with his eyes closed.

• Have a quiet period before bedtime. Play quiet music and read the child a story. Don't roughhouse or play games. Create a relaxing routine to help him wind down before bed.

• Teach relaxation techniques. When the child is about five, he is quite capable of learning the relaxation skills outlined in Section 2.10. Emphasize the whole-body relaxation exercises and make a chart so the child can keep a record of his training sessions, which should occur before peak head-banging times.

12.9-4 Provide Rocking Time.

Some children need the relaxing motion of rocking, so sit in a rocking chair to feed the infant or read to the older baby or toddler. For the older child, agree to rock her for a set number of minutes if she will promise not to rock herself or bang her head.

12.9-5 Limit the Situation.

If a child rocks or bangs at certain times or places, permit these activities only when she abstains. "Jill, you may watch television as long as you don't bang your head. If you start to rock, I will turn it off." "Gary, if you're going to rock, you may not sit on the couch." Reward the child's self-control with additional television time or another favorite activity—and some hugs and kisses.

12.9-6 Provide Before-Sleep Supervision.

If your child rocks and bangs her head when she's trying to fall asleep, spend this time with her. Sit next to the crib or on the edge of the bed and give her a back rub or tell a story. Listen to music or a story tape together. Give her a comforting sleep toy. Practice relaxation techniques. Your goal is to lull the child to sleep without rocking, providing intervention so she will learn to fall asleep in a new way.

12.9-7 Seek Professional Help.

If head banging or rocking continues or becomes severe, seek advice from a professional. These behaviors can be indicative of more serious problems.

12.10 CRACKING KNUCKLES

Snap, crack, and pop may be okay for cereal, but when it comes to fingers, these noises are very annoying and possibly harmful. Although some children may be born thumb-suckers, no child is born knowing how to crack his knuckles. He picks it up by watching somebody do it, and then the habit is reinforced by the frowns of his parents and the admiring looks of his peers.

Don't contribute to setting this habit by making comments like, "That's gross." At best, nagging leads to a temporary pause, and at worst, to defiance. But there are ways to help the child stop this annoying habit.

12.10-1 Encourage Relaxation.

Have the child practice the relaxation techniques described in Section 2.10.

• Focus on the hands. When the child has mastered the general technique, encourage him to concentrate on relaxing his hands. Have him practice making a fist and then relaxing it whenever he has the urge to crack his knuckles.

• Intervene with a tense/relaxed fist. If the child starts pulling on his fingers, have him make the fist for a full three minutes to interrupt the habit.

12.10-2 Teach Awareness.

Let the child know how this habit looks and affects other people.

• Have the child observe himself and others. Sit him in front of the mirror and watch himself cracking his fingers. Record the sound it makes, and let him listen to it over and over. Use pictures or a skeletal model of the hand to teach him how the joints work and what happens each time he cracks his knuckles. Point out other people who crack their knuckles. Discuss how the habit looks and feels to him. Help him become aware of the other movements involved, such as pulling at the fingers.

• Discuss your feelings. Tell the child honestly why you want him to stop cracking his knuckles. Remind him that it gets easier for the joints to crack the longer he keeps doing it and that this means they are getting worn and loose, perhaps leading to problems later in life. Tell him that the longer he continues doing it, the harder it will be to quit. (If you also crack your knuckles, now is the time to give it up together!)

Explore other ways he can impress his peers or get their attention. And let him know you'd like to find an alternative to nagging to help him stop, such as a special signal the two of you can devise.

• Make a list. Write down all the situations in which he's most likely to crack his knuckles and let him decide where he wants to stop doing it first.

12.10-3 Teach Alternatives.

Give the child a motion that can take the place of cracking. Perhaps sitting on his hands will do it, or playing with worry beads, puzzles, or other objects. The key to the cure is to devise an action the child will use even when you're not around to watch him. When he cracks his knuckles, have him make a fist and squeeze for a full three minutes to counteract the habit.

12.10-4 Motivate.

Praise the child for not cracking his knuckles and for practicing alternate behaviors. Reward him for eliminating the habit in each of the places he has agreed upon. Let him earn points for refraining for a specific period of time, gradually increasing their cost as he becomes successful, and exchange them for rewards. Make the rewards appropriate—for example, a ring, baseball glove, a manicure, balls, exercise grips, etc.

12.11 MAKING NOISES

Smacking lips, clearing the throat, clicking teeth, and snorting are only a few of the strange sounds children sometimes adopt as coping skills. Like many other nervous habits, making sounds often begins during a time of stress and then becomes a constant companion whenever the going gets tough. One little boy always clicked his teeth when he felt uncertain, and another constantly sniffed his surroundings. Both of them were totally unaware that they were doing this.

If your child continues to make a special sound for longer than a month or switches from one nervous sound to another, then you need to help him overcome this pattern before it becomes ingrained.

Note: Noises made together with uncontrolled verbal outbursts or unexplained movements may indicate a neurological problem that must be treated by a physician.

12.11-1 Make the Child Aware.

Though she may have been corrected by adults and teased by peers for making her special noises, it does not necessarily mean she is completely aware of when, where, and how often she does it.

• Have the child make the sound. Have the child watch herself in a mirror and make the sound. Then ask her to describe all of the movements involved. A tongue clicker may see that she places her tongue on her palate, takes a breath, and then snaps the tongue down onto her lower teeth. A throat clearer will tighten his chest, open his lips, and expel air. Label the steps. Make a tape of the noise and play it back to the child.

• Keep a tally. Have the child keep a daily record of every time he makes the sound, noting the time and setting. Reward him for keeping accurate records and analyze them with him: "You seem to smack your lips the most when you're doing your schoolwork." Sometimes, the simple act of counting the occurrences will help him quit.

12.11-2 Teach Relaxation.

Teach the child the general relaxation skills described in Section 2.10, then help him work on relaxing his face, jaw, and throat. Be sure he knows how to use the mini-relaxation and slow-breathing techniques. This child will benefit tremendously from relaxation techniques and should be encouraged to practice them even after the habit has been abandoned.

12.11-3 Teach Countering Actions.

After analyzing the steps involved in making the noise, invent an alternative action to interrupt the habit. For example, you and the child will realize that it is impossible to make a clicking noise if he keeps his tongue away from the roof of his mouth. Have him practice pressing his tongue against his lower teeth for thirty seconds whenever he feels the urge to click. In the same way, if he tends to make sniffing noises, have him breathe slowly through his mouth for one minute when he feels he's going to sniff.

12.11-4 Reward the Child.

Be generous with your praise and rewards for practicing the relaxation skills, using countermeasures, or for not making the noise in specific situations. Praise instantly and profusely at first, gradually requiring longer noise-free periods to earn the rewards. At the start, let him earn points redeemable for a reward after a few soundless minutes. Increase the ante as he becomes more successful, so it gradually takes longer to earn points and rewards. See sections 2.4 and 2.5 for complete information about reinforcement.

CHAPTER 13

Problems With Peers
and Siblings

ALL parents want their children to have friends and feel accepted, to form close bonds that will last through the years, and to get along famously with siblings. But that usually doesn't happen without some help from the parents, who must teach their children social skills and nurture the qualities that make them likable. A two-year-old doesn't naturally relinquish a coveted toy to a friend or a sister, because she has no concept of the value of sharing. A five-year-old who wants to act big may bully other children to get his way, and a six-year-old little-leaguer may have a tough time accepting defeat in the season's opener. But all of them can be helped to get along in this world.

13.1 ARGUING AND FIGHTING

If a child is going to grow into an independent, self-motivated person, then he is not going to agree with everyone around him all the time. Dissent is a normal part of life. Some children, however, seem prone to confrontations. It's almost as if arguments seem to find them, and often, the arguments lead to fights.

Some children who scrap a lot are displacing their frustrations with situations at home to school or vice versa. Others lack social skills and don't know how to interact with peers without arguing or fighting. While some youngsters use aggression as a way to establish dominance in a group, others are copying what they've seen or been subjected to at home.

Parents should model and teach their children the appropriate skills and encourage them to use them, whenever possible, to settle their own disputes. However, excessive arguing and fighting require intervention.

13.1-1 Label Acceptable and Unacceptable Methods.

Let the child know right from the start what you consider acceptable and unacceptable methods of resolving disagreements. And of course, set a good example.

• Provide feedback. Describe the behavior you expect from a toddler as an acceptable resolution of disputes: "Jessie, we don't hit. It is Alan's turn. Next it will be your turn to play with the ball." Praise her for finding nonaggressive ways to deal with a friend.

• Generate a list of acceptable ways to end disputes. With an older child, get together at a calm moment to discuss the possible solutions for avoiding or resolving conflict. Be very specific. List situations that often occur in the household, and for each one, write down the possible solutions, like this:

Situation	Poor Solution	Good Solution
Dispute over turns on swings	Push other child away	Take turns
Argument over who won the game	Call opponent bad names	Look at scorecard, present both sides, ask someone to referee

13.1-2 Teach Alternate Solutions to Conflicts.

Using the examples you have generated and any new incidents that have occurred, role-play better ways of solving conflicts.

- Demonstrate. Play the child's peer in several situations, asking your child to provoke an incident. Show him how you would avoid escalation of the dispute. Then switch roles, letting the child play the calm resolver.
- Teach a calm attitude. When arguments arise, have each party to the dispute step back and take a deep breath. Ask each child to define the nature of the argument in a quiet voice without name-calling. Then ask each one to suggest a solution. A child may need to learn to count to ten and take two deep breaths, or use the other mini-relaxation exercises, in order to think clearly. But resolutions are usually close at hand when the participants cool down.
- Discuss when you should walk away from an argument. Sometimes the best response to a conflict is to walk away or even give in. The argument may not be worth the effort.
- Provide praise and feedback. Praise your child when she uses her new skills to resolve a conflict or avoid an argument. Give her recognition when she finds solutions to problems rather than fighting or arguing over them.

13.1-3 Keep a Tally of Fights and Arguments.

Devise a system to record the positive resolutions to disagreements, arguments, or serious fights.

- Make two lists—one of the arguments or fights you observe and another of those the child reports to you. Post the lists in a prominent place.
- Review the lists every couple of days, and praise the child's progress with sincerity: "Congratulations, it's been three days since you've had a fight." Or, "You're really improving. You had seven arguments last week and only two this week." Or, "You calmed yourself down and tried what we practiced twice this week."

13.1-4 Reward the Progress.

To make your feedback system more effective, use rewards for less frequent arguing and fighting (see Chapter 2 for details about rewards). Set a reasonable goal for fewer fights, and promise logical consequences for better behavior. For example, if your child and his friend have fewer arguments, take the two of them to a movie. If two brothers diminish their fighting over television programs, let them earn the right to stay up later than usual and watch a special show.

13.1-5 Use Negative Consequences if Necessary.

Inform the child beforehand that you will invoke certain negative consequences for future fighting.

• Restrict privileges. If two boys fight over TV programs, forbid television for the rest of the day. If children fight over where they will sit in the car, leave them home with a baby-sitter or have them lose the right to choose their seats on the next two trips.

• Use time-out. Remove the child from the situation for a specified length of time if the fighting continues. If your son gets into a fistfight during a baseball game, restrict him from playing for the rest of the day. Explain that if he fights again, he will be timed-out for two days. If two good friends fight while playing together, separate them into separate time-out corners and say to them, "If you can't cooperate, then you won't be allowed to play together." After timing them out for the appropriate number of minutes (see Section 2.7), let them try again.

SUGGESTED BOOKS FOR PARENTS AND CHILDREN

O'Brien, Anne Sibley. *I Want That.* New York: Holt, Rinehart and Winston, 1985. Part of a series of board books about daily issues (PS–2).

Wilt, Joy. *Handling Your Disagreements.* Waco, Texas: Educational Products Division Word, Inc., 1980. A book for the child to work through to learn how to resolve conflict (elementary).

13.2 SPITTING, HITTING, AND BITING

These are all immature behaviors indulged in by many children around the ages of two, three, and four—and sometimes even after that—as the response to frustration or excitement. Your job is to catch these behaviors before they get out of hand. If they continue, your child will not be very popular or acceptable in social situations.

13.2-1 Confront First-Timers.

Express your disapproval the very first time your little one uses these responses.

• Discuss and label. If the child doesn't talk yet, label his actions by saying, "No biting," "No spitting," or "No hitting." Use a stern voice to let him know what he did was wrong, but don't get angry. If the child is old enough to understand, tell him clearly that these behaviors are not acceptable.

• Define the consequences. Make sure the child knows what the result will be if he continues to hit his sister. Perhaps it will be time-out or loss of a privilege.

13.2-2 Teach Alternative Behaviors.

Prepare the child with alternative ways to respond to the urge to hit or bite.

• Identify when the behavior happens. Notice the times and situations in which the child resorts to hitting and biting, and use this information to avoid or change them. If the child tends to bite when he's tired, skip the play group if he has missed his nap.

• Teach alternatives. One small boy bit other children when they wanted the toys he was playing with. His parents showed him a different way to respond. He was taught to say, "It's your turn and then it will be my turn, okay?" and to ask an adult for help if necessary. When he shared, he was praised to encourage his new behavior. Another toddler was persuaded to walk away and say she's not playing anymore instead of hitting.

13.2-3 Use Preventive Measures.

Set the limits before young children play together. Make simple rules, like taking turns and letting company go first. Encourage the children to be buddies and to think how the other person feels. Monitor and supervise them during play, perhaps structuring the play periods to cut down the opportunities to get into trouble. Give incentives to cooperate, such as cookies and milk if they play nicely for twenty minutes. Always be sure, of course, to define what you mean by "playing nicely."

13.2-4 Use Negative Consequences.

When positive measures don't do the job, there are other routes to take.

• Limit opportunities. Often, the best tactic is to eliminate the situations that are likely to incite hitting, biting, or spitting. If the child bites to fend off competitors for the swing set, then make the swing set off limits until he understands that he may play on it only if he controls himself. If he tends to do his hitting when he's in a large group, arrange playtime with just one child at a time.

• Use overcorrection. Have the child remedy what she's done in a way that impresses her. A little girl who spit at other people was required to brush her teeth, gargle with mouthwash (never soap!), and wipe up the floor where she had spit. It was explained that spitting spreads germs and so the cleaning of both her mouth and the floor was necessary. This method stopped the objectionable behavior very quickly. The approach for biting could include the oral hygiene, washing the site of the bite on the other person, and making amends by giving the other child a special toy to play with.

13.2-5 Give Training in Self-control.

Have your child pretend he's about to slap, bite, or spit, and then stop himself before he does it. At the same time, have him make a positive statement such as, "We only bite food, not people." Praise and reward him whenever he stops himself in real-life situations.

13.2-6 Reinforce the Child for Good Control.

To keep the appropriate behaviors in use, be sure to let the child know how proud of her you are for her self-control.

- Praise and reward her for not biting, hitting, or spitting.
- Chart the progress. Keep a chart of the no biting, no hitting, no spitting days. Set up a good-behavior letter if the problems have been occurring at school, and arrange with the teacher to send a note home every successful day (see Section 11.8).

13.2-7 Seek Professional Help for Severe and Persistent Biting.

When a conscientious effort to control biting is not successful and the child is hurting others, it is time to get professional help (see Chapter 17).

13.3 CHILD WHO IS PICKED ON OR IS OVERSENSITIVE

Some children seem to be wearing a sign on their back that says, "Tease me. Pick on me." Somehow, they let other children know that they are good victims, people to make fun of or annoy. Their Achilles heel is highly visible, and everyone knows they are very sensitive. Wherever they go, the affliction follows them, because their skin is too thin and their reactions are too strong. Children can be very cruel to other children.

For children who tend to be picked on, the remedy lies in teaching them new ways to respond to teasing.

13.3-1 Analyze the Happenings.

You can help the child recognize how ridiculous most of the teasing is. For those comments that hurt, discussion is needed.

• Identify the verbal labels that tormentors use. List all the teases the child remembers and then add a few you can recall. Keep a record for a few days.

• Categorize the epithets or remarks. Some comments or names are so silly or obviously untrue that the two of you can laugh about them. "Your head's on upside down." "Your mother wears combat boots." Explain to the child that she needn't feel it's necessary to defend herself or her family, that such remarks are meaningless and not worth a response. If other children's comments ring true, however—"Your feet smell," or "Your nose is as big as a lemon"— the child must learn to respond in a manner that discourages the ridicule. It may mean a change in behavior or growing a layer of thick skin.

13.3-2 Desensitize the Child to the Teasing.

Teach the child to respond to teasing by not responding at all.

• Role-play the situation. Let the child be the teaser and the parent be the victim. Have the child tease the parent with the same slurs that have been used against him. This will help him get used to hearing them, and it also provides an opportunity for a lesson in ignoring them. Model how you do not react to the words, but simply turn your head or walk away.

• Practice. Now, have the child play the victim. Taunt her with a few mild labels or remarks and have her rehearse ignoring them. Work your way down the list, with the most derogatory remarks at the end. Your goal is for the child to become so accustomed to them that she won't be tempted to respond. Give her positive feedback. If she shows an emotional reaction, stop the session or go back to an easier-to-take taunt.

• Teach relaxation. Be sure to teach the child the relaxation techniques outlined in Chapter 2, and remind her to use them to help her remain calm.

13.3-3 Teach a New Response.

Enlarge her repertoire of responses, and practice possible alternatives.

• Role-play. Pretend once more that you are the victim and your child is teasing you. Try a variety of responses, including those her peers have used. Laugh: "That's ridiculous, my mother doesn't have any boots." "Of course my mother has hair on her legs, doesn't yours?" Or try the mature approach: "I know what you're trying to do and it won't work. I'm not going to get upset."

We have found another technique that often stops the teasers in their tracks: asking the other child why he is teasing. "What is your motivation for saying that?" one eight-year-old asked. The teaser stared at him and then said, "I don't know." That old jingle "Sticks and stones may break my bones, but words will never hurt me" has worked for many children for many years.

Sometimes, a child's best defense is a good offense. A quick tongue can be an effective tool. Help the child come up with appropriate responses and then practice using them.

• Simulate the situation. Using the taunts you have listed, have the child practice the responses with you, starting with the choices that are easiest for the child to handle.

• Practice with a confederate. A sibling or good friend may be willing to help. Let them improvise situations. They may have a lot of fun.

• For practice, tease the child gently and unexpectedly. Do it affectionately when the opportunity presents itself so she can rehearse her response and toughen up a little more.

13.3-4 Report the Real-Life Response.

Have the child share the real situations with you and tell you how she handled them. How did she feel? How did the teaser react to this new response?

• Suggest ignoring. Warn the child that a playmate may try very hard to rile her now, when she sees that her tactics aren't working anymore. Explain that she must stand firm and *ignore* the taunts. Soon, her tormentor will give up.

• Suggest an alternative. Help the child choose the most effective response to the teasing and to evaluate which one seems to work best for her. The goal is not only to deflect taunts, but to reduce their frequency.

13.3-5 Reinforce the Child's Efforts.

When she finds a method that works, support it. Encourage her. Suppose she always ran from the dinner table when her brother teased her and now she stoically sits there and eats. That's a step in the right direction. Tell her so. Suppose she reports that she walked away from Sally Sue when she teased her about her frizzy hair. Acknowledge how difficult that must have been and how proud you are that she did it. Then have an afternoon snack together.

13.4 BULLYING AND TEASING

If your child repeatedly bullies or teases other children, you must take action before this behavior becomes his customary way of dealing with other people. Teasing is fun if you're doing the teasing, and many older youngsters have been known to push smaller kids around. You can't follow your youngster around the playground to be sure he's nice to everybody, nor should you expect saintly behavior. But bullying and frequent teasing are cruel and must be stopped.

13.4-1 Identify the Reasons.

Try to determine why your child is acting this way. Ask yourself these questions:

1. Is the child overcompensating? It's possible the child feels insecure, weak, and left out and therefore puts up a front of being tough.

2. Has the behavior been prompted? Sometimes, a child has been encouraged to tease and act the bully because it seemed cute. Adults often use teasing as a playful way to interact with a child and the child may try to do the same with his peers. He may have been teased or bullied by an older sibling (or perhaps you) and then takes out his frustrations on other children. Make sure you are neither prompting nor encouraging this kind of activity.

3. Is the child larger and more dominant than his peers? If he is, the teasing and bullying may be an attempt at leadership.

13.4-2 Model Appropriate Behavior.

Set a good example of the behaviors you want your child to emulate. Quit the teasing. Examine your sense of humor, your ideas of fun, even your methods of discipline, to be sure they are behaviors you'd be pleased to see in your child. If the child is emulating siblings or peers, put the pressure on them to change and on this child not to follow.

13.4-3 Teach Positive Leadership Skills and Alternatives.

Make sure the child knows there are better ways to act, and assure her that she will be better liked if she chooses them.

• Discuss the bullying and teasing. Talk to your child about what is acceptable and what isn't. Help her identify situations when she starts to tease or when others act like bullies.
• Use role-playing. Take turns being the aggressor and the underdog. Ask the child how it feels when she is the victim. Create

situations to model leadership skills, like praising others for good ideas or agreeable actions. Role-play and practice the art of ignoring others who aren't acting as she might like. Have her practice using persuasion and reasoning to get her point across rather than resorting to bullying tactics.

• Point out good and bad behavior. Point out characters on television or in books who exemplify both the desirable and undesirable ways of treating other people. Ask the child how these characters are perceived by the world. Would she enjoy being their friend or victim?

• Praise the child. Let her know how great you think it is when she uses these techniques. Comment on appropriate actions, and ask the child her feelings about them.

13.4-4 Switch Play Settings.

Sometimes, changing play groups or day-care settings will change a bully into a more restrained child, especially if the group is composed of mixed ages and has children larger than him. For the older child, try a scout troop or club program with leaders who practice and teach good behavior. A team sport with a conscientious coaching staff can also provide positive peer pressure.

13.4-5 Use Negative Consequences.

Let the child know that there will be consequences if he continues to bully. The consequences may include time-out from the group, loss of a toy or piece of equipment being used during the incident, or loss of privileges. Overcorrection is an effective consequence, "undoing" the damage by having the child apologize to the other person on the telephone or in a note.

13.4-6 Reinforce and Praise Positive Behavior.

Always give positive feedback to the behavior you want your child to continue. Every day that he doesn't tease or bully, let him earn a star or a point to go on a daily chart. As he changes for the better, give him appropriate rewards, like going to a special event with a friend.

SUGGESTED BOOKS FOR PARENTS AND CHILDREN

Alexander, Martha. *Move Over, Twerp.* New York: Dial, 1981. A young boy finds a solution to being teased about being small (K–3).

Sharmat, Marjorie W. *Bartholomew the Bossy.* New York: Macmillan, 1984. A picture book in which the president of the club learns about being bossy (PS–3).

13.5 TROUBLE MAKING AND KEEPING FRIENDS

"Brigette didn't want to play with me today. She just wants to talk to Samantha." Sound familiar? Kids are best friends today and best enemies tomorrow, and whoever is coming home with them after school is the pal of the moment. Clubs and cliques form and re-form constantly.

Some children have a large circle of friends who come and go, others have a couple of close buddies who they are inseparable from. There are natural loners, who prefer their own company and their own interests, and shy children, who wish for more friends but can't achieve their goal. Then there are children who are isolated, purposefully excluded by the group. These children are the outsiders, who may then withdraw socially and avoid interaction with other children.

Parents feel so helpless when their child has trouble making and keeping friends. Every youngster needs a few good friends or a small group to call his own. It's one good way to learn about himself.

The parents' role in helping the child form friendships is very important, especially for the youngster who is having trouble in this area. So many social situations can be difficult for a child who doesn't know how to act or can't find the right words to use.

13.5-1 Pave the Way for Friendships.

Provide early experiences with children of all ages—a little child cannot learn how to behave socially if she doesn't have the chance for interaction. Teach her the social skills she will need, and support her when she feels awkward or a friendship ends.

• Plan playtime for toddlers and preschoolers. Make sure your little one has plenty of opportunities to get together with other children. If you don't live where others are readily handy, invite children over to play. Limit the time and the situation until the relationships are well established and the adults as well as the children know each other. Supervise the early experiences and be ready to pitch in and facilitate their play.

• Engage in family activities. Group get-togethers with other families provide a good opportunity to immerse your child in social situations with children of mixed ages. They give her a chance to try out her social skills and watch you interact with other people. Family outings also build strong bonds within the household that will pay off later, when your child must withstand peer pressure.

• Take the pressure off. Don't put the child on the spot in front of other people: "Can't you say hello to Aunt Eleanor?" "Sing your ABCs for everybody." The more self-conscious your child is in social settings, the more difficult it will be for her to feel comfortable.

• Don't label the child. Describing your child as shy, as a loner, reticent, or unfriendly can be a self-fulfilling prophecy. You are walking down the street and you meet an acquaintance. Two-year-old Michelle is reluctant to say hello or even look at the stranger. You explain her response by saying, "She's shy." But by labeling her, you reinforce that behavior. Similarly, when you label the child as a loner or one who finds it hard to make friends, you can promote antisocial behaviors.

You can encourage him to be more social by saying, "He's just met you. It will take him a few moments to warm up," rather than, "He's like that. He doesn't talk to other people."

13.5-2 Look for the Reasons for the Problem.

If your child seems to have difficulty making and keeping friends, try to find out why. Is she so sensitive that she loses friends because her feelings always get hurt? Is she quiet and reluctant to interact with others? Is he bossy and aggressive so that other children don't want to be with him? Does she lack social skills? Does he lack the skills for being a loyal friend?

13.5-3 Talk to the Child.

If the child is old enough, sit down and discuss the situation with him. Choose an event you have observed as the subject for discussion. Kathleen's mother overheard Kathleen bossing a guest around. She called her daughter out of the room and quietly suggested she allow the guest to select the next activity. Later that evening they talked again, and her mother praised her changed behavior.

• Be specific. Discuss the behaviors you have observed and how they may affect relationships.

• Discuss friendship. If the child is hurt by an ending friendship, talk about the nature of friendships and how she will have many friends over the years, some for the long term and some for only a little while. Point out that people have many kinds of friends —sports friends, study buddies, and a few trusted cohorts.

• List the characteristics of a good friend. Ask the child to name a classmate everyone likes. Discuss the reasons why she is liked. How does she act? What does she do? What are the qualities of a good friend? Which of these characteristics would your youngster like to develop?

13.5-4 Set Friendship Goals.

Decide together what social skills the child needs to develop and the friendships he would like to make. Most children can readily supply the names of children they'd like to have as friends.

13.5-5 Set a Good Example.

Your child will try to be just like you, so remember that you are modeling social interaction skills for her when she sees you greet people, talk on the telephone, shop, play games, or do anything else with other people. She will probably also emulate your shyness if that is one of your characteristics, so you may wish to work to overcome it.

Remember that there may be other social skills you are teaching your children that you'd prefer they not learn. If your only social interactions occur with a drink in your hand or when sharing drugs, then that will be the model for them.

13.5-6 Teach by Role Playing.

This provides you with an excellent opportunity to model the appropriate ways to interact with other people and gives your child a chance to try out his budding skills safely. Create simple pretend situations at first and then make them more complicated. The situations could include inviting a friend to play, turning down an invitation, talking on the telephone, disagreeing agreeably, greeting adult guests, making conversation with children and adults, and being a good sport. Alternate the roles between you. Refer to sections 13.1, 13.3, and 13.9.

• Teach conversation skills. Practice saying hello, introducing yourself, asking open-ended questions to keep a conversation going, answering other people's questions, and so forth.

• Teach skills to make the child liked by others. Well-liked people make others feel they are interested in them. They make their friends feel special. They remember names and ask questions about the other person. They give compliments that are true, and they listen to what the other person has to say. Explain these attributes to your child and then practice them together. Afterward, point them out in other people, and praise the child for trying them himself.

• Teach name repetition. Role-play introductions and tell the child to repeat the other person's name so that he will be sure to remember it. Besides, the person will be flattered that the child cared enough to make sure to get it right. Teach the child, too, that it is acceptable to ask to have a name repeated after an introduction.

13.5-7 Offer Opportunities for Practice.

Give the child the chance to use his new skills. Without pushing, encourage him to invite friends over to play. Suggest he invite one potential friend from his list, and be available for providing transportation.

• Structure first play situations. It will be easier for the child if you organize the occasion. Suggest a movie, or invite a friend to have a hamburger and then go to football practice together.
• Move to longer, less-structured situations. Gradually increase the time the children spend together, perhaps inviting a friend over to play after school or to spend the night. At first, suggest some special activities to fill the time, like baking cookies with you or going to the park. Later, phase yourself out, but be ready to take up slack time with a good suggestion: "How about painting or playing a game of checkers?"
• Invite a few children over to play. Children who are uncomfortable in large groups may be quite at ease in small gatherings. Though three can be a difficult number, try inviting several children to spend the night or watch a movie or make ice cream.

13.5-8 Observe and Give Feedback.

Let your child know how she's doing, not by giving test grades, but by telling her.

• Use praise. Say a few admiring words about the way your child offered to share with her friend, talked to the guests, or has become more resilient in social situations.
• Identify problems and suggest solutions. Each negative situa-

tion can be an opportunity to teach new behaviors. If your child is rude to a guest, ask her if you may see her for a moment. Identify the behavior: "You are not being nice to your friend. You must let her have a turn on the swing." If she says she's tired or in a bad mood, say, "That may be true, but it's your responsibility to be nice. Let's decide how you can do that." This gives her a chance to change.

If the child has difficulty making conversation, suggest a few possibilities or suggest talking about a common interest. Perhaps she can develop a special expertise that will interest others.

• Give reassurance. Sometimes, friendships don't last and the relationship may not be in your child's complete control. Reassure her that this will happen now and then but that she will find other more lasting friends.

13.5-9 Try and Try Again.

Long-lasting friendships aren't made in a day but require repeated interactions, shared experiences, and interests. Let the children get together consistently, and do your best to encourage good times.

SUGGESTED BOOKS FOR PARENTS AND CHILDREN

Cohen, Miriam. *Best Friends.*: Collier, 1971. The ups and downs of friendship are explored. For children ages eight to ten.

Naylor, Phyllis Reynolds. *Getting Along With Friends.* Nashville, TN.: Abingdon, 1980. For children nine to twelve, this is a book that explores quarreling, sharing, and being yourself with friends.

Wilt, Joy. *A Kid's Guide to Making Friends.* Waco, Texas: Word Inc., 1979. Teaches social skills by having the child read to personalize the concepts (elementary).

Zimbardo, Philip G. and Shirley L. Radl. *The Shy Child.* New York: Doubleday, 1982. Written for parents, a guide to preventing and overcoming shyness in individuals of all ages.

13.6 SIBLING RIVALRY

Big brothers and sisters often fantasize about how much fun the new baby will be. And most parents have a romanticized and idealized view of the wonderful times their children are going to have together. They'll be best friends, back each other up, tell each other their secrets, and always be there for one another. But the truth is that siblings don't always get along well, at least in their younger years, and that they usually spend a lot of their time arguing and fighting. Sibling rivalry is natural and is influenced by age difference, personalities, and personal interests. That doesn't mean, however, that you can't help your youngsters form strong bonds with one another and get along more peacefully.

Sibling rivalry is promoted by three basic drives:

To get the parents' attention: Each child wants all of your attention, or at least more of it than his brother or sister gets. A younger child often regresses after a new baby arrives—if only to gain the same attention the infant receives—by sucking his thumb, drinking from a bottle, and wetting his pants.

To gain power: There is a pecking order in any group. The older child in a family tries to maintain a position of power through size, age, and first arrival, while a younger sibling vies for that position by being smarter, more athletic, prettier, or whatever other advantage she can muster up. When there are more than two children, coalitions may form; perhaps the oldest and youngest combine forces, or it's the boys against the girls.

To gain ownership: Fights over possessions or friends are often part of the effort to gain parental love and approval. They may reflect the ongoing power struggle within the family. "That's mine!" is a familiar call to battle. You can't eliminate sibling rivalry, but you can promote a healthy relationship between siblings and, in the process, keep the household turmoil down to a bearable level.

13.6-1 Prepare for an Addition to the Family.

If you have only one child, that child is the focus of your attention and you are the primary focus of his world, at least until he's about three years old. When you are expecting a new baby, your child's life will change and you must help him prepare for an additional family member with whom he's going to have to share you.

In general, the shorter the span between siblings, the more difficult this transition is likely to be. If the span is three years or more, the older sibling has become quite self-sufficient and attuned to activities outside the home. He plays with other children and has developed some peer relationships.

But whatever the first child's age, his world is going to change dramatically when the new baby arrives in your home. That's why we suggest you try to provide a smooth transition into this next phase of family life.

• Tell the child about the new baby. Involve your child as much as possible in your preparations, and share the experience of waiting for the new arrival. Let him listen to the baby's heartbeat, help decorate the nursery, tape pictures to the crib.

• Include siblings in the arrival. Some parents today want to share the birth experience with the whole family. If you choose to do this, you must carefully educate the older child (or children), letting him know what will happen, so he will not be frightened. After the delivery, have the siblings come to the hospital to visit the new brother or sister and, if the hospital allows it, let them hold the baby. Enroll them in the special big-brother-and-sister classes now available in some hospitals.

• Let siblings help with the baby. Siblings will be eager to help with the new baby, at least in the first few weeks. Let them do what they can, always with constant supervision. This will help build a bond between them. On the other hand, don't make a servant of the older child—one big sister told us she often felt like Cinderella when her little brother was born.

• Save time for the older children. To them, it will seem that you are always busy with the baby, and they will be jealous and perhaps angry with you or the baby. They may try to get your attention through acting out, acting perfect, or even reverting to babyish behavior. Try to give each child some special attention every day. Arrange days when you and your older child or children spend much of the day together without the baby.

• Involve older siblings in outside activities. If your child now spends most of his day with you, plan ahead. Before the baby arrives, organize some activities that don't involve you—perhaps a play group or a mother's-morning-out program. He will learn how to separate and feel comfortable without you.

13.6-2 Don't Compare Children.

Some comparisons are inevitable. If you never voice them, Auntie Evie will or the children will recognize the differences themselves. But remember that while it's tempting to make comparisons among children in order to control or motivate youngsters, they are harmful to young egos. A child who feels she isn't as good as the other children isn't motivated to try harder; instead, she feels the situation is hopeless. Comparisons intensify rivalries and increase reprisals and guerilla warfare within the family. Try to value each of your children as an individual, enjoying them separately and together. Help them build their strengths and cope with their weaknesses.

• Use praise instead. Praise can be an excellent motivator when it's used correctly and not as an obvious method of comparing two children. If you tell Seth he's doing well, the other child will get the idea without feeling put down: "Seth, I like the way you came in from school and started your homework right away. When you're finished, let's go hit a few balls."

• Acknowledge all achievements. Recognize whatever each child accomplishes, letting the children feel comfortable with and proud of one another. WRONG: "Why don't you sit up like your brother does? See how good he is?" or "Your sister got all A's and B's. Why don't you study more?" RIGHT: "Jeremy, your grades are really improving. You came up from a C to a B in math. I'm really proud of you. Let's talk about what else we can do to help." Or "Brent, you brought home an excellent report card. I have two fine boys who are working hard and doing well."

13.6-3 Avoid the Fairness Trap.

Though, of course, you must not play favorites, it is unrealistic to expect that you will treat each child the same all the time. It is impossible to do that, because each is different in age and personality. Don't fall into the trap of feeling that you must do something for one child every time you do something for the other. Your obvious balancing act will prompt the rivalry you are trying to avoid.

• Set rules, and give privileges according to age, sex, and accomplishments. Two children shouldn't have everything alike. Lisa is two years older than her sister Laura, so she should be able to stay up later. Everybody gets presents for his own birthday. Janice earned a reward for not sucking her thumb, but other family members who didn't accomplish such a wonderful feat don't get rewards just because she did.

• Encourage individual interests. Just because it is easier for you, don't insist that a younger child follow along with an older sibling. Let each one follow his own pursuits and schedules.

• Don't encourage contests. Do not get drawn into explanations when your child says, "Billy got new basketball shoes and I didn't," or, "It's not fair! Billy gets to stay up later than me!" If you do, there will be a never-ending contest between them for privileges and attention.

• Ignore tattling. It's an aggravating hassle, so don't get involved. React only to your own observations or respond to tattling with, "To play together, you must cooperate." Follow through with time-out from each other if it seems necessary.

13.6-4 Set Rules.

Whatever your children's ages, they must know the rules of the household.

• Define acceptable behaviors with a new baby. Let the older siblings know exactly what is acceptable and what is not in their relationship with a new infant. Deal with attention-provoking and negative behaviors, like tantrums, immediately (see Chapter 8). Be sure to explain to the older child that an infant will need time to learn the rules. Praise and even reward him when he responds patiently to the baby who messes up his toys, and encourage big brother or big sister behaviors.

• Write out the rules for older children. You can decrease sibling problems by posting the rules that you have defined together. One family composed these:

Don't	Do
Hit or push brother or sister	Try to solve problems
Call names	Walk away from arguments
Enter another child's room without permission	Ask parents to help if all else fails
Borrow possessions without permission	Ask for permission

• Designate responsibilities. Identify the chores for which each child is responsible. Design a rotating system based on a weekly rotation, age, or seniority, so that no child feels he is getting unfair treatment. See Section 5.1 for a discussion of chores.

• Don't expect perfection. No child is going to do everything right, just as you don't. Allow for mistakes and remember that the rules are goals to work toward.

13.6-5 Teach Children How to Handle Conflicts.

Rules aren't enough. Children must have the skills to be able to follow them.

• Model the behaviors. You parents are your child's best teachers, the people she is most likely to imitate. So look to your own conflict-resolving skills and make sure you set the example you'd like the child to follow.

• Hold family meetings. When real problems arise, call everyone together, not for a gripe session, but to generate solutions for conflicts.

• Use role-playing. Discuss the conflict with each child separately and role-play the solutions. Continue until approved strategies for resolving a dispute are clear.

You can use role-playing in a group, too. Take the part of one child, while another is the aggressor who takes away a toy, changes the television channel, or bothers a sibling when a friend is visiting. Respond in ways you would like the children to resolve conflicts, such as ignoring, walking away, reasoning, or sharing. Reverse the roles and act as the aggressor while the children practice the skills you have demonstrated.

13.6-6 Reinforce Cooperation.

Your goal should be to "catch" your children being good and praise them for cooperating. Don't sit back saying nothing until the fights begin and then step in with criticism and rules.

• Praise the behavior you want. When things are peaceful, check on what's happening. If Allie and Cassie are curled up on the sofa watching television, say something like, "It's so nice seeing you together, enjoying quiet time with each other." If the boys cleaned up the kitchen after dinner, tell them, "You cleaned up so nicely, and doing it together made it take less time than usual." Throw in a reward, too, sometimes: "Let me make you some popcorn to eat while you play Monopoly."

• Count cooperative times. For a day or a week, keep a record of the times your children cooperate rather than fight, letting them try to beat their previous record or work toward a special treat. A fun family activity is a perfect reward for learning to play together. See Section 13.7 for suggestions for teaching children to share.

13.6-7 Force Constructive Solutions.

Don't always be the mediator. Let the children learn how to solve conflicts.

• Use systematic ignoring. Totally ignore minor disputes (see Section 2.2), because often it is your attention that the children are looking for. Step back out of the conflict, or even out of the room. Later, if necessary, talk about the problem.

• Give the children the responsibility. When your children ask you to resolve a dispute, give them some breathing space to effect their own solution. If James says, "Mommy, Terry won't let me use his crayon," respond with, "What else could you do?" This gives the child a chance to use the alternatives he practiced in role-playing.

13.6-8 Use Time-out for Battles.

If fights and arguments continue after you have tried the other solutions, then use "one, two, three, time-out" (see Section 13.1 for other suggestions on using time-out).

• Treat the children as a unit. Don't try to be judge and jury and select the guilty party. They were unable to resolve their conflict, so give them all the same treatment.

• Separate them from each other and/or the situation. Give the two fighting siblings time-out from one another. Or remove them from the scene of the crime. The scenario might go like this: The children have been going at it for a few minutes. You say, "Kids, that's one. Find a solution." The fuss continues, or they try to enlist your aid. You say, "That's two. If you can't settle this yourselves, it will be three." The battle continues. "Okay, that's three. Go to time-out until the buzzer rings."

• Skip to three. For major battles, move right to three. Unacceptable behaviors require immediate consequences. A fist in the stomach is three, no question about it.

13.6-9 Use Overcorrection.

You should save this solution for the times when the others haven't been effective. See Section 2.8 for information about this technique, which has the children practice positive actions many times before allowing them to play together again or to engage in the activity that provoked the dispute.

• Overcorrect the guilty party. If you have personally seen one child break his sister's toy purposefully, you state the rule: "The child who breaks a toy must buy his sibling two toys." If the child has no money, then he must give up a toy of his own, do services for the other child, or perform extra chores that will earn him money to buy a toy.

• Overcorrect both children for fighting. Make them both remedy the situation by writing "I will not fight" ten times. Or have them each do three nice things for the other one. Or set up a role-playing session and have the children choose an appropriate way to end the conflict, and role-play this alternative ten times.

• Use overcorrection for name-calling. The natural consequence could include saying pleasant things to one another ten times, writing "I will not call my brother a bad name," and then apologizing.

SUGGESTED READING FOR PARENTS AND CHILDREN

Bank, Stephen and Michael D. Kahn. *The Sibling Bond.* New York: Basic, 1982. A comprehensive discussion of the sibling bond, including examples of famous siblings. For parents.

Blume, Judy. *The Pain and the Great One.* New York: Dell 1974. Depicts the ups and downs of relationships between brothers and sisters (K–12).

Carlson, Nancy. *Harriet and Walt.* London: Puffin, 1982.

Harriet is angry because she has to take her little brother with her, but she's the first to defend him when he is picked on (K–3).

Frankel, Alona. *The Family of Tiny White Elephants*. Woodbury: Barrons, 1980. A picture book for young children about a new baby sister and a jealous brother (PS–3).

Ginsburg, Ben. *The Sibling Rivalry Monster*. Trumansburg: Crossing Press, 1985. Siblings learn to work together and fight the monster that makes them argue (Gr.1–3).

Hoopes, Lynn Littlefield. *When I Was Little*. New York: Dutton, 1983. A mother answers her daughter's questions and reassures her of her love, even though there's a new baby brother (PS–3).

Lakin, Patricia. *Don't Touch My Room*. Boston: Little, Brown, 1985. New room, new toys, new baby. Antipathy turns to protectiveness, and siblings learn to share (PS–3).

Szasz, Susan and Elizabeth Taleporos. *Sisters, Brothers, and Others*. New York: Norton, 1984. The sibling relationship is depicted in photographs and text for parents and older children to read together.

13.7 WON'T SHARE

"It's mine!" "No, it's mine!" "Mommy, Jonathan won't let me play with my truck!" Sound familiar? It's quite normal for small children to resent sharing, and very little ones usually consider everything within reach to be their very own, not to be touched by the other children. But they also love to please adults, and if they are taught to do so, they will learn to share material things, tasks, and turns. By the time they are five or six, they are usually able to play cooperatively together—most of the time.

13.7-1 Teach the Need for Sharing.

Some parents try to avoid sharing problems by buying identical toys for each child, but that's impossible for most of us to do.

Besides, it doesn't teach the children the concept of ownership and the value of cooperation.

• Teach ownership. Let the child know what is his, and label the personal items with his name. Let him keep them in a special storage place. See Section 15.1.

• Identify family items. Let the child know that some of the toys belong to everyone in the family and so everyone may play with them, but sometimes they must be shared. Use natural opportunities with the family television set, the car, or the stereo to point out that adults must share and take turns, too.

13.7-2 Teach Sharing Skills.

Sharing isn't automatic, so you must teach your child how to do it.

• Experiment with cooperation. Show the child the benefits of working together and sharing tasks. The payoff for cooking together is a natural. Make cookies or a cake with two children and let them take turns stirring and adding ingredients. After they have shared the work, then they may share some of the results.

Or tell two children they may have a treat but that they must share it. Ask them how they can share a bag of candy or a cupcake. When they come up with a workable solution, let them use it and eat the treat. Suggest an activity like making paper chains or a collage, but give them only one pair of scissors. Before they start, ask them to plan how they will share the scissors.

• Tell them they must share. Children don't think the way you do, so let them know in advance when they must share something: "Danny and Mark, we're going outside to play. You'll have to share the tricycle by taking turns." Many children love to share at someone else's house, but at their own, they are not so willing. If this is the case, before the guest arrives, let your child select a few toys she is willing to share and tell her she may instruct the guest how to play with the toys if she is worried that they will get broken. This gives her some control over the experience while she's learning to share unconditionally.

• Identify the means of sharing. When your child comes to you and says, "I want to play with the ball, but Donny has it," suggest she ask him if they may share it or take turns.

• Set ground rules. Make the rules for the children to diminish the chances of arguing. You might say, for example, "A toy is yours while you are playing with it and have it in your hands. When you stop playing with it and put it down, then it's fine for someone else to have a turn with it." Another rule might be: "If you grab it, you lose it." If children are having difficulty accomplishing a task, show them how they can divide the effort to accomplish the goal. Christopher and his sister were wrapping packages for a holiday and arguing over the scissors. Finally, they decided that one of them would cut all the paper and ribbon and the other would do the wrapping.

With very young children, be sure to clarify how each child will have a turn: "Shane, it's your turn to sit next to me. On the way home, it will be Shelly's turn."

• Don't expect too much. Though children may learn to share, this is a difficult concept for young ones. Be sure your child has enough time playing with her own toy before she's asked to share it. Acknowledging a child's ownership may make her feel that sharing is under her control and it will seem like a good deed to share it rather than surrender to a demand. Then be sure she gets her possession back.

• Be preventive. If sharing has been a constant problem for your child, plan ahead for situations when sharing will be expected. Think about possible activities and the material that will be needed so you can anticipate and avoid problems. The parents of a group of two-year-olds discovered their children were more willing to share when each brought one toy with him. The child was proud of his own toy but more excited about taking a turn with another youngster's toy. The turns were timed, and when the bell rang, the toys were traded. The game became a favorite. Another mother set up the playroom with the toys laid out and numbered. The children drew numbers and then went to the appropriate toy first.

13.7-3 Praise and Reward.

Sharing is a big accomplishment for a little one, so let your child know you appreciate it.

• Praise the child for each instance of sharing behavior. When she offers to share a toy, take turns, or cooperate as a solution to a problem, praise her: "I'm so proud of you for letting Jeanie play with your doll. That way, you both had a nice time."
• Reward sharing behavior. Do something pleasurable for your children when they behave appropriately. When they take turns choosing the TV shows, bring in a bowl of popcorn for them to enjoy. Surprise a child who let a friend look at his sticker collection with a new sticker. Design a chart (see Section 2.5) to record sharing. To get the behavior established, every time you notice your child sharing, let him earn points toward a shared treat like two tickets to a movie (one for him, one for a friend or sibling), two ice cream cones, or any other surprise he can share with somebody else.

13.7-4 Use Natural Consequences.

Make non-sharing more unpleasant than sharing by applying a negative consequence.

• Use overcorrection. When your child won't take turns, let the other child have two turns in a row, with your supervision. When it's your child's turn again, let him play but remind him he must take turns if he wants to continue playing.
• Time-out the toy. If your child refuses to share a toy, warn him that he will lose it for a specific amount of time. First his friend will get a chance to play with it, then you will keep it for the rest of the afternoon.

SUGGESTED BOOKS FOR PARENTS AND CHILDREN

Lionni, Leo. *It's Mine!* New York: Knopf, 1985. Picture book with a delightful story about a little frog who fights about what's his until he learns about "ours" (K–3).

Wilt, Joy. *Mine and Yours.* Waco, Texas: Word, Inc., 1979. For children four to eight. A series of discussions about rights and responsibilities, including ownership, privacy, and sharing.

13.8 GIVES IN TO PEER PRESSURE

All children are influenced by peer pressure. They want to do certain things because "everybody" is doing them. Surely, you can remember being the same way. Never underestimate the power of peer groups—it's not easy be different or to stand up to the majority. Some children are more likely to be influenced by peers than others, and all children gain understanding of themselves by relating and comparing themselves to their companions.

The child who is secure and clear about his academic abilities, his sex role, and his ability to relate to other people has less need to rely on others for his sense of self. But when a child is uncertain of himself, he has a more difficult time constructing a consistent self-image and so he relies more heavily on the reactions and opinions of others. He may be more likely to adopt a ready-made image offered by his peers.

As parents, you can't immunize your child from peer pressure or hold open auditions for his friends. You can, however, build a strong relationship with him and attempt to head off the worst aspects of this common behavior.

13.8-1 Build Your Relationship with Your Child.

Your most effective defense against the power of peer pressure is a close family relationship. Restrictions and reprimands will not control the child who doesn't care what you think or feel.

• Remember that communication must be mutual. Talk to your child and listen to him. Take the time to find out what he's doing and feeling. Beginning with the earliest school experiences, be a person in whom your child wants to confide. You may not always agree with him, but you always listen (see Section 2.9, which gives valuable information on building two-way communication with your child). Remember, both quality and quantity of time count, so make sure to nurture the relationship. The payoff will come for the rest of your life.

• Build a history of family experiences and shared interests. Parents who develop common interests and activities with their children throughout childhood and into adolescence have a much better chance of countering peer pressure. Start early. Find hobbies and skills to share. Share adventures—like hiking, rafting, and camping—in which trust is built. Spending plenty of time doing things together gives you a natural opportunity to get to know one another as individuals.

• Be a parent, not a pal. Don't make the common error of trying to be your child's best friend. If you like and respect each other, the relationship you seek will grow. He needs a parent, not another friend. You are not just another kid on the block, but his mother or father. Unless there are special circumstances, as in blended families, it is better not to allow your child to call you by your first name.

13.8-2 Build Self-esteem.

The comments you often make to your child are the ones he will say to himself. Criticism demolishes a child's positive feelings about herself. Praise, on the other hand, builds them. The stronger your relationship with the child, the more important your opinions and comments become. Section 13.10-7 gives specific suggestions for building self-esteem.

13.8-3 Help Establish Positive Friendships.

As your child grows older, you have less influence over the people she meets and chooses as her friends. While she's small, encourage healthy relationships by inviting congenial children to play and discouraging invitations to others. Attaining the Miss Popularity Title is not the goal, but every child needs a few good friends (see Section 13.5).

• Get to know your children's friends. Volunteer at school, coach games, drive for field trips, offer your home as the meeting place, make your house the place where your children and their friends like to be. Take time to talk to the friends and get to know them.

• Know what the children are doing. When your child and her peers play in your home, supervise, be directly involved, or monitor from a distance. Get to know the parents of friends so you know you share compatible values and feel comfortable when your child visits.

• Don't get involved in peer politics. Friendships are fragile at best, especially for children. Kids are always fighting and making up later. In general, it's best not to get involved in these interactions. Be sympathetic and perhaps offer some suggestions, but don't attempt to solve the problems.

• Don't criticize the child's friends. The older the child, the less effective this is. It's better to focus on actions: "I notice that when you've played with Suzanne for a while, you use bad language." Let the child know that consequences will be applied if this continues.

• Encourage many groups of friends. Try to get your youngster involved in a variety of activities. She will meet many children and make friends who have different interests and ideas. This will encourage her individuality and independence from any one peer group.

13.8-4 Teach Assertiveness to Combat Group Control.

If you have taught your child sound values in his first dozen or so years, then you must try to trust his judgments. But you must also teach him how to follow his own mind. Some children are naturally assertive and can say no with confidence. Those who are more prone to give in to peers must learn how to say no and stick with it.

• Explore the reason. Talk to your child about why it is difficult to differ from the group. Most youngsters are afraid of being ridiculed, losing their friends, or being left out of the group. Talk about what is likely to happen if he disagrees with his peers, and help him understand that though his friends may give him a hard time for a while, eventually they will admire his strength. Besides, the children he may lose aren't true friends anyway.

• Role-play saying no. Give the child a chance to practice saying no or convincing his peers of his position. Let's suppose some children suggest building a fire in the backyard, starting the car, or trying a cigarette. Play the part of your child, then reverse roles, showing him how to suggest alternative activities instead. Then, if the group doesn't go along, act out the possible endings in which your child is not coerced to follow the leader.

13.8-5 Praise and Reward Assertiveness.

When your child asserts himself or expresses an unpopular opinion, praise him. Let him know how wonderful you think it is that when all his friends wanted to swim in the pool, he said they couldn't because there were no adults to supervise. Don't turn into a policeman for other children, however. Correct them if necessary, but don't report the incident to their parents unless you feel they must know, and in that case do it privately, making the other parents promise not to inform their children of the source.

13.8-6 Use Consequences for Following Peers into Trouble.

Lectures are not enough when your child elects to follow the group into trouble. It's important to give him rational reasons for why the behavior is unacceptable, but then you must act.

• Restrict privileges. When your child demonstrates that he is not behaving responsibly, restrict him. If he rides his bicycle across the street because the other children were doing it, tell him he is not responsible enough to ride his bike. Take it away for a few days, then allow him to ride it with your supervision for another few days, until he has earned the right to ride it alone again.

• Time-out from the group. If the child has given in to group demands, limit the amount of time she may spend with the group. Depending on the offense, you may ground her for a few days and then allow her to be with those friends as long as no other incidents occur. Or as an alternative, discuss the situation with other parents in the play group and mutually decide whether to decrease the time the children spend together. In extreme situations, you may have to time-out your child for a longer period to weaken the bonds. It's best to do this naturally. In other words, don't simply ban the group, but try to replace it with camp or a new activity or other children in other settings.

• Use overcorrection. Have your child undo the offense. If, for example, the children have thrown eggs at a neighbor's house, have him clean the soiled area, then do extra chores to earn the money to pay for the eggs. If he asks why he must pay for what the group did, tell him it is because you are *his* parent, not the other children's.

SUGGESTED BOOKS FOR PARENTS AND CHILDREN

Elkind, David. *The Hurried Child.* Reading, Mass.: Addison-Wesley, 1981. For parents, an excellent book that offers insights and advice about the stresses on children.

Wilt, Joy. *You're One-of-a-Kind.* Waco, Texas: Word, Inc., 1979. One of a series of books for young children designed to teach the child about his uniqueness (K–5).

13.9 BAD WINNERS/BAD LOSERS

Winning and losing are daily occurrences in everyone's life, and being a poor sport is not endearing. Do you feel like playing another game of checkers with a child who's just shoved the board off the table? Would classmates vote for Joe the next time he is a candidate if when he loses one election he berates his peers for not voting for him? What if he won and bragged about the accomplishment? Do other children enjoy playing with Gloria, who always cries when she loses, or Fred, who is overbearingly triumphant when he wins a game?

Learning to be a good sport doesn't happen overnight. Most children go through their early elementary-school years having a difficult time losing. But if you provide a model of good sportsmanship and accept nothing less from your child, then the youngster will learn how to be a good loser and a good winner, too.

13.9-1 Explain Sportsmanship.

When the subject comes up naturally, explain to the child the meaning of gracious winning and losing. Use the terms *good sport* or *gamesman* frequently, and describe situations when the people don't gloat, pout, throw tantrums, brag, or berate.

13.9-2 Demonstrate Good Sportsmanship.

Children learn from what they see, especially from what they see you doing.

• Set a good example. Be a good sport yourself, winning graciously and losing with dignity. The child will learn to do the same and copy your actions when he finds himself in a difficult situation.

• React appropriately to the child's wins and losses. Be a good sport here, too. Many parents behave worse than their children after a contest. Isn't the adage ". . . it's how you play the game" still true?

13.9-3 Practice Manners.

Give children chances to practice their fledgling responses. For little ones, it's appropriate to give them chances to practice winning and losing.

• Play one-on-one games with the child. Whether you are playing Old Maid or tossing coins, don't pass up the chance of reinforcing desirable behavior or explaining why certain responses are appropriate or inappropriate. As you play, make comments to teach the child how to react: "Hey, you really did a good job! You're beating me three to one. I'm going to have to try harder this time." Or, "Okay, I got you that round, but you were a strong opponent. I don't know if I can do that again."

Practice gamesmanship repeatedly in natural and private situations so it's safe for the child to display a quivering lip while learning to smile. Most children will catch on quickly and learn to control their reactions.

• Role-play what a winner can say. Before a game, talk about what the child might say if he wins the match or beats an opponent: "Your backhand was really good. I had a hard time beating you." "You really put up a good fight. I hope you'll work with me on the class council."

• Role-play what a loser can say. Suggest appropriate comments and reactions, like shaking hands and saying, "Congratulations. You did a great job." Or, "Now I can't wait for a rematch."

• Watch the pros. When you watch televised games or matches or attend sporting events, talk about the way professional athletes handle themselves in both winning and losing situations. Praise the good sports. When you see other adults or children win or lose, discuss their sports manners. What else could the winners have done or said? What about the losers? What made them seem like good sports?

13.9-4 Do Not Accept Poor-Sport Behavior.

If your child acts like a poor sport, let her know this is unacceptable. If Janet throws the cards down when she loses, refuse to play another hand with her or exclude her from the game until she proves herself a better sport. If the poor sportsmanship occurs in a team endeavor, talk with the coach or warn the child she will be taken out of the next game if this happens again. Then follow through.

13.9-5 Reinforce Good Sportsmanship.

Recognize and praise the child's efforts to act like a winner no matter what the score. Comment, too, when she recognizes good conduct in other players.

13.10 BOASTING AND BRAGGING

"I got ninety-eight on the social studies test and you only got seventy-six." "My Dad's stronger than yours." "I can hit five home runs! I'm the best baseball player in the school."

Your child may see boasting as a way to win friends or influence enemies, but in truth, nobody likes a braggart. That's particularly unfortunate because the child who boasts and brags repeatedly usually does so out of insecurity. He uses it as compensation for a poor self-image.

Our solutions focus first, therefore, on decreasing this inappropriate behavior and then on building self-esteem.

13.10-1 Ignore Minor Boasting.

It's normal and natural for anyone to blow his own horn occasionally. If the child's friends and siblings get tired of it, they will give a clear signal and you won't have to.

13.10-2 Label the Bragging.

When bragging becomes a problem, then label it clearly. Don't call it lying. "Bill, you've carried on all afternoon about how well you played in the game. Now you are bragging. We're proud of you, but that's enough now."

13.10-3 Explore the Reasons.

When you see a bragging pattern developing, discuss it with your child. Why does he find it necessary to brag?

• Point out how bragging often backfires. If the child is trying to impress people, ask him what he thinks when he hears other children telling how wonderful they are. What do his friends say when he brags?

• Let the child hear himself. Act out a recent situation when you heard your child bragging. You play the child, then reverse roles, and tell him your reactions.

13.10-4 Teach Alternate Ways to Make a Good Impression.

Assure your child that it's fine to want people to think well of her, but there are better ways to accomplish this. Here are some ways to do it.

• Teach the child to give compliments. Everybody likes to be noticed and praised. Role-play situations in which your child can learn how to give compliments naturally.

• Help the child develop skills. When you boast, you are really asking others to notice you. If your child feels comfortable with herself, she won't require so much feedback. Help her develop her skills so she will receive recognition without asking for it.

• Teach the child to be a good winner or loser. See Section 13.9 for suggestions for showing the child how to win or lose graciously. Other children like those who have fun ideas or know how to be good followers when *they* have the bright ideas.

13.10-5 Be a Good Role Model.

Check your own behavior and notice if you talk about your possessions and your accomplishments. Is it possible that you're seeing yourself in your child? If so, try to change your own behavior so that you become an admirable example for her to emulate.

13.10-6 Praise Nonboasting Behavior.

Make positive comments when you notice the child bragging less often or practicing new behaviors. "You know, it's been several days since I heard you brag. That's terrific." Or, "I really must pat you on the back. You were so modest about your new bike. You let your friends give you compliments without boasting once."

13.10-7 Build Self-esteem.

If your child has adequate self-esteem, he won't have to flaunt his accomplishments and possessions.

• Give the child unconditional love. Your child must know for sure that you love him for who he is, not for what he does. Tell him you love him. Tell him you are proud he's your child (see Section 2.1).

• Help your child find skills, interests, and activities. A child who has skills and interests has more information and experiences to share. In addition, he feels better about himself because he has special knowledge and abilities.

• Solve school problems. If your child has difficulty learning, then much of her day is an awful struggle. A child who experiences constant failures can't feel smart or able. Get help for her so she can feel good at school (see Chapter 11 for suggestions on focusing your efforts).

• Help your child make friends. Friendship is one of the most important ways a child learns about herself and builds self-esteem. A child who has difficulty making friends or is excluded from social groups can develop a negative self-image. Being on the outside is not fun, especially when other children let you know you are not wanted. See Section 13.5 for steps in teaching your child how to make friends.

• Generate positive lists. This technique is very effective, though children with a poor self-concept may find it difficult. Have your child list everything he likes about himself. You make your own list of his good traits. Ask him to record compliments he receives or qualities that other people like about him.

• Keep a "good book." Make an anecdotal record of everything your child does that you appreciate. Review the book together regularly. Your child may be surprised by all his good qualities.

• Be consistent. Self-esteem isn't built quickly, so make sure you make this a long-term effort that is applied every single day. Always try to increase the positive comments, while keeping the criticism to an absolute minimum.

13.10-8 Apply Negative Consequences.

If your child continues to brag, then you will need negative means to change the behavior.

• Take away a privilege. "You bragged about what a great diver you are, so we're not going to the pool tomorrow."

• Take away an object. "You bragged so much about the new bike you were going to get that we have decided to postpone buying it. We'll wait a few weeks until you can show us you are able to talk with your friends without bragging."

• Limit playmates. "Whenever you play with Billy, you seem to compete with him by bragging, so you may not play with him for the rest of the week."

CHAPTER 14

Fears

SOME children sail fearlessly through each day. Others encounter a never-ending series of frightening experiences. They are scared of strangers, the dark, animals, storms, toilets, vanishing parents, and just about anything new or different. Many children grow in and out of fears, and some fears become particularly pronounced at certain ages and stages.

Two-year-olds, for example, tend to be frightened by loud noises. This is generally a joyful time, but it is also a time when he is increasingly aware of his place and size in a big world. There are new things to be afraid of—big things like trains and loud things like vacuum cleaners and sirens. There are strange things like animals, toilets, and weather. And this is a time to be afraid of parents leaving.

As the child gains experience in the environment, he will lose some of these fears but replace them with others. Some three- and four-year-olds may be especially fearful of loud noises or the dark and the unknown. The five-year-old is more worldly, knowing about fire engines and trains, common animals and "bogeymen." But he may be apprehensive about dark places and more worried about falling down and hurting himself. He may still be afraid that Mommy might leave and not come back.

For many children, six is a fearsome age. Noise fears may return.

Fear of witches and goblins is high on the list, as is the fear of getting lost or sleeping alone. The child is often scared of elements like wind and fire, which are so strong; she may be brave about big hurts but frightened of splinters or scratches. Again, she may be very fearful that something might happen to Mommy or Daddy.

The seven-year-old is a thinker and an interpreter. Shadows are monsters. Basements are filled with scary creatures. He fears what might happen under his bed or late at night, or what will happen if his country goes to war. He worries about everyday occurrences like not being liked, being late, or Mother not coming home at all.

When a child turns eight or nine, she has fewer fears, although personal failure and ridicule can be major worries. At ten, she may begin to express more confidence.

Nevertheless, it is a mistake to assume that all fears vanish with increasing age. Children of all ages have their fears—highly ranked today are being hit by a car, not being able to breathe, fire, death, war, poor grades, arguing parents, looking foolish, heights, and burglars—and so do adults. A 1985 study by Ollendick and his colleagues found that the only difference between children's fears today and those many of their parents experienced when they were children is that now burglars and height have crept into the top-ten list.

Many intense fears that still haunt people after they have grown up stem from childhood experiences. Social fears like the fear of public speaking may have grown from a series of early incidents, and agoraphobia may have sprung from separation anxiety and school phobia. Your goal is to help your child pass through many fears as he develops skill and confidence in his own abilities, and to prevent intense fears from developing into phobic reactions.

Using the following guidelines, you can help your child minimize and overcome fears.

GENERAL GUIDELINES TO PREVENTING FEARS FROM GROWING OUT OF HAND

Determine if the fear is age-appropriate.

Each fear has its characteristic age and pattern. In each section, you will find information to help you decide whether the anxiety your child is experiencing is appropriate for his age and how long you can expect the feelings to last. You will also learn the various forms the fear can take.

But even if the fear is typical, it needn't be ignored. Intervention is needed when the child's apprehension is so intense that it hinders his ability to function. Many young children of three, four, or five are afraid of the dark, but if your child can't get a good night's sleep, then it is appropriate to intervene.

Don't overreact to the child's fears.

Never ignore the fears or overreact to them, but do be aware that your response can help prevent a fear from growing. Teasing, anger, and criticism will increase the anxiety, as will statements like, "Don't be such a baby," or, "That little kitten can't hurt you." The child may hide his alarm to please you, but it's unlikely that she'll give up the foreboding. The more anger you display when, say, a child is afraid to go upstairs alone, the more panicked she may become.

On the other hand, don't be too sympathetic or attentive, either. Don't hold, soothe, and baby her every time she is frightened because then she may assume there really is danger. A grown man who still feared cats had never had the chance to develop an appreciation for the animals. His parents would pick him up as one neared, saying, "Don't worry! You're safe! See, the cat can't get to you!" This convinced the little boy that cats were definitely dangerous.

Be calmly supportive.

Quite matter-of-factly, support your child as she confronts her fear. If she's afraid there is a monster under the bed or in the closet, assure her there isn't. Encourage her to look for herself as you stand by. Then continue with the bedtime routine. It is not necessary to persuade her with a long discussion that monsters are imaginary or to repeatedly search the room yourself. If the child is nervous about a strange dog, model how you study the dog to see if it looks friendly, then quietly hold out your palm for the dog to sniff. Let the child repeat the actions with you.

Reinforce coping behaviors.
The key to helping children become less fearful is to praise and reward coping behaviors. When she leaves your side to greet a new animal or situation, be positive. Serve as home base, but let her venture out, returning many times for reassurance. Don't hold her tightly or push her away. Instead, make positive comments about how well she handled the situation and follow with a quick hug and a smile. The child will be more likely to try again another time.

GUIDELINES FOR OVERCOMING FEARS AND PHOBIAS
When a child's fear lasts longer than expected or is so intense that it disrupts his life, then you must attempt to reduce it so it does not become a true phobia. Professional help may be the ultimate solution, especially for the child who repeatedly develops new intense fears, but there are steps you can take to help the child overcome his problems. Based on the work of Dr. Joseph Wolpe, desensitization is a successful approach to reducing fears.

Pinpoint the fear.
Is the child afraid of all dogs or only small black dogs? Is it the lightning or the thunder that bothers him? Talk to the child and observe his responses in frightening situations to gain insight into his exact fear.

Teach the child to rate the fear.
There are many degrees of fearfulness, and knowing how anxious the child is will help you control her exposure to frightening situations and help her recognize her own decreasing terror. For older children, we like to use a zero-to-ten scale, with ten at the top. For young children who can't use numbers easily, hand signals will

work. Have the child practice moving his hands far apart to signify a lot of fear and close together to mean very little.

Make a fear list.

Once the child can measure fear using the scale, you can begin to divide the fear into manageable segments. At the bottom of the list, identify the least threatening fears and work up to the major anxieties. For fear of dogs, the least frightening activity may be simply looking at illustrations of puppies. A little more disconcerting might be examining photographs of larger dogs, and still farther up the scale would be looking at a real dog. Finally, it would be petting a dog.

Identify and teach ways to counteract anxiety.

As you help the child overcome his fears, be sure he maintains a low anxiety level for two reasons: First, if the fear accelerates rapidly, he will want to escape before he has learned that his fear will decrease if he stays with it a little longer. Second, with a high fear level, he won't have the opportunity to associate the situation with feelings of less fear. So explore ways to counter anxiety before you begin desensitizing the child to his fears.

Relaxation is one of the best ways to confront anxiety because it is physically impossible to be relaxed and scared at the same time. See Section 2.10 for details on teaching the relaxation response. Teach general relaxation and also how to link the relaxed feelings to a cue word like *relax*. The child can become adept at calming himself by inhaling deeply and saying the cue word to himself. Use relaxation skills before, during, and after practice sessions to control anxiety.

Your presence is also a source of support as the child confronts a feared object or situation. Your physical closeness or touch and soft reassurances will help him feel more secure and encourage him to continue when he might prefer to retreat.

Other methods of countering anxiety include listening to music, eating a treat, or counting numbers or objects to distract the child from the fear. One child listened to her favorite music during thunderstorms. Another counted the squares on the dentist's ceiling, while still another ate ice cream while a small dog was brought closer to him. Use whatever works to help your child stay calm.

Each section in this chapter includes specific ways to overcome a specific fear. You will recognize the general principles, though, as the desensitization steps you have just learned.

SUGGESTED BOOKS FOR PARENTS

Morris, J. Richard and Thomas R. Kratochwill. *Treating Children's Fears and Phobias.* New York: Pergamon Press, 1985. A comprehensive text written primarily for professionals that clearly presents current views.

14.1 FEAR OF ANIMALS

Some children love animals from the start and others view them as monsters. A wariness of animals normally surfaces between the ages of two and three, when the child is old enough to realize that some animals are threats but not knowledgeable enough to discriminate among them. But unless she is particularly fearful or has had a bad experience with an animal, she usually loses her fear by the time she is five or six.

Many commonly feared animals are avoidable—interaction with snakes, rodents, and large animals is controllable—but common pets are not and a child who fears them can be immobilized. There are many things you can do to minimize your child's fear so she may comfortably coexist with animals.

14.1-1 Ignore or Downplay Initial Signs of Fear.

At the beginning, it is best to ignore the child's responses. Show her through consistent actions rather than discussion that you are not afraid of the animal. When the two of you come upon a dog, for example, don't refer to the child's obvious concern. Just go up to the dog and pat it or play with it normally. Do not insist that the child do the same, but model your positive feelings for the animal.

14.1-2 Determine What the Child Fears.

Find out what frightens her, eliciting as many details as you can. She may be scared that the cat will scratch her or that the puppy may jump on her.

14.1-3 Show Pictures of the Feared Animal.

First, make your own renditions of the animal, then use drawings in books and magazines. Study the pictures with the child. What does the animal look like? How does he usually stand or hold his head when he is happy? Now use photographs of the animal, leaving them around the house where the child can look at them whenever she likes.

14.1-4 Read Books About the Animal.

Select stories that depict the animal in a friendly, unfrightening way. Read articles and nonfiction books to increase the child's information. Discuss the meaning of the animal's seemingly threatening behavior. It would be helpful for the child to learn that a dog wags its tail, barks, and puts his ears down when he feels friendly but is afraid of you.

14.1-5 Watch TV Programs and Movies About the Animal.

Check the listings to find positive media presentations about the animal the child fears, preferably with a child actor interacting with the animal.

14.1-6 Observe Animals from a Distance.

Don't force the child to interact directly with the feared animal, but have him watch other children doing it. Enlist the help of friends or neighbors with children so the two of you may watch another child playing with the animal. Have the animal on a leash when that's appropriate. You may wish to start by watching from indoors; then later, you can walk outdoors but keep a safe distance. As the child becomes more comfortable, edge a little nearer, but never force the child to get close. Be patient. Even small steps closer may require a few days to accomplish. Point out the animal's behavior that you have discussed earlier.

14.1-7 Set a Good Example.

With the child maintaining a comfortable distance or standing with a friend, show the child how you interact with the animal, explaining aloud what you are doing. "See how I am holding out my hand for the dog to sniff? I am scratching behind his ears. See how Fido is wagging his tail? He likes that."

14.1-8 Role-play Approaching an Animal.

In the safety of your home, talk with the child about how you played with the animal. Talk about what he would do if he were going to approach it. Pretend to be the animal, and give the child feedback about what you are doing and how the child is handling you. If you are a dog, bark, wag your tail, and sniff the child's hand or feet, saying, "See, I am wagging my tail because I want to be your friend. I am sniffing because I am a little afraid of you. I want to make sure you are friendly." For fun, reverse roles and let the child pretend to be the dog.

14.1-9 Approach the Animal Together.

Try to find the smallest, calmest, and friendliest possible example of the animal. Praise the child for getting closer and closer, walking by your side or holding your hand. Remind the child to practice his breathing and relaxation skills.

• Teach positive self-talk. Have the child repeat a list of positive statements such as, "I am okay. This is a nice doggy."
• Use fear ratings to guide movement toward the animal. Ask

the child to rate her fear from one to ten and to give you frequent
readings as she gets closer to the animal. If her fear gets to too high
a level, pause right where you are until the level decreases. If the
child panics, retreat and try again later. Move back and forth if it
seems wise, perhaps two steps forward and one step back, until
you're able to reach touching distance.

14.1-10 Provide More Experiences with the Animal.

You can look for opportunities to expose the child to the animal
that worries her.

• Play with the animal longer as fear decreases. The major accomplishment comes when the child touches the animal. Gradually, she will be able to touch or stroke it if it is a domestic animal.
Be sure to show her the right way to do this. When she is comfortable, move away a few steps and encourage her to continue. With
her permission, continue to distance yourself as long as she feels in
control.

• Play with bigger and friskier specimens. Up to this point, you
have chosen a small, quiet animal for your training sessions. Now,
provide other experiences with friends' pets. Teach the child the
characteristics of the many kinds of animals.

• Teach the child how to meet strange animals. Be sure the
child is aware of the body signals animals use to indicate friendli-
ness or aggression. Show him how to get a strange dog to approach
quietly or a mean dog to stay away. Model the behaviors with
strange animals to show him what you mean.

14.1-11 Talk About Getting a Family Pet.

When the child has overcome her fear and the family would like a
pet, then discuss this possibility. The child may love his own pet,
while remaining wary of others. Arrange a visit to a family with a
pet like the one you are considering. Don't get a pet simply to
vanquish your child's fears because this won't be a happy experience unless the animal fits your family. Make sure you are pre-

pared for this step and feel confident you can handle it as a positive experience for the family and the animal.

SUGGESTED BOOKS FOR PARENTS AND CHILDREN

There are many children's books centered around animals. A few are:

Brown, Margaret Wise. *When the Wind Blew.* New York: Harper & Row, 1937. About an old woman and her comforting cats (PS–3).

Ets, Marie Hall. *Play With Me.* New York: Viking, 1955. A picture book about the wariness of forest creatures (PS–2).

Schick, Eleanor. *Jeanie Goes Riding.* New York: Macmillan, 1968. About a little girl who loves horses and loses her fear as she gains skill (K–3).

Zion, Gene. *Harry the Dirty Dog.* New York: Harper & Row, 1956. Harry is a family pet who loves to have fun but also takes care of the family (K–3).

MAGAZINES

World, published monthly by the National Geographic Society. Excellent source of information and photographs.

14.2 FEAR OF INSECTS

Not very many people really like insects, but you don't want your child to become unreasonably fearful of them, because it will be difficult to change his mind. Depending on the child's personality and the family's feelings about insects, a normal aversion can turn into real fear that, ingrained, complicates life in the great outdoors. We have worked with children, and adults as well, who could not go into the backyard without great anxiety.

14.2-1 Prevent the Fear.

Your feelings about insects will shape your child's views. A calm and firm approach will teach the child, without frightening her, what not to touch.

• Set a good example. When your child's responses to insects are first being formulated, don't show too much fear yourself. If insects scare you, make an attempt to overcome it or hide it.

• Don't overreact. Don't panic if the child picks up insects. React as you would with any object you would prefer the child not to touch, speaking clearly and firmly without communicating alarm.

• Educate the child. Insects are fascinating. Talk about the balance of nature and the important jobs insects perform in the environment. Spend time watching ants carry bits of food or a spider spinning a web. Share books about insects to instill a healthy respect for these creatures.

• Teach the child how to control insects. Teach him how to dispose properly of insects, whether it's swatting a fly or carrying a caterpillar outdoors on a piece of paper. Make a game of stepping over worms on the sidewalk. Show the child how to stand very still until a bee moves on.

14.2-2 Help the Child Overcome Fear.

If the child is already fearful, try the following suggestions.

• Isolate the fear. Determine which insects the child fears most and list them in order. Show her pictures and help her identify them.

• Discuss the fear. Talk to the child about what scares him about the insect. Correct misconceptions. Talk about which insects are harmless and how they may be helpful.

• Desensitize to the fear. Using the list, select one of the least feared insects you can easily find. Capture a specimen and place it in a clear container. Place the captured insect about ten feet from the child and approach it together. Have the child rate his anxiety on a scale of one to ten. If his fear increases, stay in the same spot for a while, then gradually move closer to the insect. Have the child use his relaxation skills and repeat positive statements like, "The bug is locked in the jar and it can't get out. I can handle it."

• Provide experiences with the insect. Encourage the child to hold the jar, reassuring him that he is quite safe. Then insert a stick through the lid so he can play with the insect. The next step is to remove the lid and let the insect crawl but not escape.

Repeat the experience within wider boundaries. Let the insect run free in an enclosed area. Demonstrate how to get it outside or kill it with a flyswatter or long-handled broom. Let the child do it several times over a week, until he can do it by himself.

Repeat the whole process with different kinds of insects until the child feels competent to deal with any insect he may encounter.

14.2-3　Use Praise.

Praise the child for ignoring or controlling the insects. Remind him it's not always necessary to kill them but that when it is necessary, he knows how to do the job. Use natural rewards for overcoming the fear, like a picnic. When he can eat his favorite cookies with the insects flying and the ants marching, that's success.

SUGGESTED BOOKS FOR PARENTS AND CHILDREN

Carle, Eric. *The Very Busy Spider.* New York: Philomel, 1985. Farm animals try to divert a spider from producing a beautiful and useful web (multisensory). (PS–2).

Carle, Eric. *The Very Hungry Caterpillar.* New York: Philomel Books, 1979. A hungry caterpillar eats through the garden, spins his cocoon, and becomes a butterfly (PS–2).

Graham, Margaret Bloy. *Be Nice to Spiders.* New York: Harper & Row, 1967. A spider spins her web, using it to help the zoo animals (K–3).

14.3　FEAR OF THUNDER, LIGHTNING, AND OTHER WEATHER

A black sky, bolts of lightning, and howling winds can be very frightening to children, and many adults as well. Fear of violent weather peaks when a child is three or four and again perhaps at nine or ten, but children differ. Some are intrepid weather lovers, relishing a good storm. Others hide under the bed at the first crack of thunder, and some are literally obsessed and controlled by the weather.

If your child's fear of weather is intense or lasts for months, we suggest you begin the following program so that the fear does not follow her into adulthood. If your feelings are contributing factors, you must control your reactions to weather, too.

14.3-1 Teach Relaxation.

Help the child relax by using the techniques described in Section 2.10. When he can relax, he'll be more receptive to working through his fear.

14.3-2 Desensitize to the Fear.

This process will help the child gain control over the fear.

1. Identify the fear. Find out what aspects of the weather are more frightening and make a list of them, ranking them from one to ten.

2. Correct misconceptions. Explain and correct inaccurate ideas about the weather. Jason believed the wind could pick him up, and Linda thought the lightning was sent by witches.

3. Teach useful facts about weather. Choose age-appropriate books about weather and read them together. To explain weather, conduct simple science experiments, such as estimating the distance of lightning by counting in seconds the delay between seeing the flash and hearing the thunder (each second represents about one mile).

4. List positive coping statements. Make up a list of reassuring statements the child can use to comfort himself when he is afraid of the weather. Examples: "A tornado hasn't hit this town in years"; "Lightning hits the highest object, and I am not up on the roof or in a tree"; "The wind is only going fifteen miles an hour, not seventy-five miles an hour like the hurricane on television"; "The thunder is only noise. It can't hurt me."

5. Re-create the fear. Make videotapes and sound recordings of

feared weather from television shows or real storms. Sound-effects records of storms can be ordered through most record shops. Play the videotapes repeatedly without sound. Then gradually increase the volume as the child becomes comfortable viewing the scenes. Now have him listen to the tape with his eyes closed, imagining a small storm and progressing to more intense storms while he copes with his fear and nothing bad happens. At the end of each sequence, describe the end of the storm with the sun coming out.

6. Use real experiences. Now, when a real storm blows up, play your child's favorite records or tapes as buffers to block the sounds of the weather. Start with the volume fairly high while you watch the storm through the window, but from across the room. Decrease the volume slightly and edge closer to the window.

During the first few storms, do something that's fun, like making popcorn or playing a game, so it will be easier for the child to keep calm.

As his fear decreases, lower the volume of the music.

14.3-3 Use Praise and Reinforcers.

Tell the child you think it's wonderful that he is overcoming his fears and learning so much about weather. Praise his efforts at every step. If the fear has been the wind, reinforce his new courage by flying kites on a nice windy day. Take him on a visit to the local weather station. Let him pick out a new raincoat and an umbrella.

SUGGESTED BOOKS FOR PARENTS AND CHILDREN
   Yashima, Taro. *Umbrella*. New York: Viking, 1958. A little girl anticipates playing on rainy days (PS–2).

14.4 FEAR OF THE DARK

Almost every child is afraid of the dark at least for a while, with the fear first making an appearance when he's about two or three years old. The particular fears vary among children and change over time. One day the child may worry about monsters in the closet, another night it's a burglar. Handled with concern and care, this fear of the dark need not grow to the point where it affects her life. Usually, a little reassurance is all that's required to keep the fear from becoming so intense and persistent that it lasts into later life, but sometimes it can endure. The suggestions below should help you overcome it.

14.4-1 Discuss the Fear.

Never dismiss the fear, but acknowledge it—because to the child, it is very real. Reassure her that you believe there's nothing to be afraid of, but do not ridicule her feelings as silly or babyish. Find out what she imagines is happening in the dark, using a picture book for the very young child who can't easily express herself. Sit in her darkened room with her to encourage her to show and tell you about what she fears.

14.4-2 Play Games to Desensitize the Child to the Fear.

A series of games can help you accustom the child to dark places so she will no longer fear them. Choose as many as you need.

• Play Follow the Leader. Be the leader and have your child follow you in and out of dark places, keeping her busy with arm movements as she goes. At first, dart in and out of the dark, then slowly increase the time both leader and follower spend in the dark. When the child is willing, exchange roles and let her go first.

• Play Count Up. Go into a dark place with the child for the "count of . . ." At first, stay there for a count of three, then five, and so on, until the child can stay there with you for sixty seconds. Praise her profusely. When she is comfortable as you count out loud, start counting silently for the sixty-second period. For an older child, extend the time to several minutes.

• Play a game of tag in the dark. Alternate being the one who is It, and sing or make happy noises to keep the mood light.

• Make a secret playhouse. Turn a card table into a secret playhouse or fort by placing an old blanket over the table and letting the child decorate it with doors and windows. This new place then becomes the perfect space for the child to practice playing in the dark.

• Share a scare. Sit with the child in her dark room, watching for shadows and listening for noises that scare her. Explain them, turning on the light to identify the sources if necessary. Let the child try to scare you by making noises in the dark—be a ham and let her succeed.

• Play Scavenger Hunt. Hide the clues in dark places, such as closets, and award a point for every object that she finds.

14.4-3 Reassure the Child About the Dark.

Take some practical steps to help her feel comfortable and safe.

• Make nightly security checks together. If the child fears intruders, have him accompany you on your nightly check of doors and windows. Explain that burglars rarely break into occupied homes, but also tell him what you would do if the event were to occur. Buy a wireless intercom for the child's room so he knows he can call you at any time. Additional safety features like window locks, pins and rods across sliding doors, or an alarm system will also help dampen the fear.

• Add a dimmer switch. Connect a dimmer switch to the lamp next to the child's bed and show him how to use it. Agree on an initial nighttime setting. Every few nights, set the dimmer a tiny bit lower, until the child is sleeping in the dark.

• Make a courageous kit. Make your child a special kit with supplies for staying alone in the dark. Include a small flashlight, a safe snack, or a boxed drink with a straw. The first night, give him the kit with an elaborate presentation. Sitting together in the dark, show him how to use the flashlight, then, while he eats the snack, play a game of I Spy with the flashlight so he will become adept at lighting sections of the room.

• Teach the child to use positive talk. He can imagine himself being brave in the dark when he uses brave words: "I am not afraid. Nothing can really hurt me."

14.4-4 Use Reinforcers.

As the child seems less fearful, encourage his success, and don't forget to praise all his efforts.

• Make a braveness chart. When the child can stay in the dark quite comfortably with an adult, introduce a braveness chart. Explain that bravery means accomplishing the task or deed even when you are scared. Use the courageous kit and the dimmer switch to make the goal more possible to achieve. Set the criteria for earning a feather on the chart at four minutes the first night, five minutes the second, and more each night, until the child is comfortable in his bed before he falls asleep. The feathers may be redeemed for a special prize. See sections 2.4 and 2.5.

14.4-5 Give a Special Reward.

When the child has shown that he is building a tolerance for staying in the dark, reward him by letting him choose a movie to see in a theater. If necessary, it's fine to let a young child hold a toy or your hand for reassurance. And don't forget the popcorn!

SUGGESTED READING FOR CHILDREN

Bonsall, Crosby. *Who's Afraid of the Dark?* New York: Harper & Row, 1980. A small boy gives advice to his dog, who is afraid of the dark (PS–2).

Strand, Mark. *The Night Book*. New York: Clarkson N. Potter, 1985. A book about a little girl who is shown by the moon why she doesn't need to be afraid at night (PS–2).

14.5 FEAR OF LOUD NOISES

Around the ages of two and three, it's common for children to react strongly to loud noises like sirens, thunder, or even doorbells. Though most children become accustomed to these sounds by the time they are four or five, some continue to experience intense fear responses to them.

When this happens, you should start to work on helping the child overcome the problem. First, of course, have the child checked over medically, because it's possible she is extremely sensitive to certain sound frequencies.

14.5-1 Teach Relaxation.

Refer to Section 2.10 and teach the child relaxation skills, practicing until she can relax completely and calm herself with a key word or phrase.

14.5-2 Desensitize to the Fear.

Now, begin the desensitization process. See the introduction to this chapter for an explanation of this technique.

1. Determine what sounds the child fears. Discuss sounds with the child and try to determine why they scare her. Isolate the noises and make a list of them in order of the fearfulness they provoke.

2. Re-create the sounds. Make tape recordings of the noises she fears. Be sure to record them as clearly and loudly as possible.

3. Prepare the child. Explain that you're going to help her stop being scared of noises by using the recordings. Tell her she can start and stop the tapes and may control the volume herself.

4. Play the tapes. With the child very relaxed, turn on the tape at a very low level and ask her to repeat the relaxation cues to herself to remain calm. Ask her to rate her anxiety from one to ten. Play the tape at this level until the anxiety remains low, then increase the sound slightly, or let her do it herself. Keep going until she can listen to the recording at a very loud level with little reaction for longer periods of time. Don't forget to praise her for her progress.

5. Use real experiences. Switch to real sounds, telling the child to cover her ears if she likes or to move farther away. Pop a balloon, shoot a cap gun, hammer a nail. Now, try it closer to the child and let her do the popping or the hammering.

When she has become comfortable with these sounds, visit a firehouse or a police station. Explain what you are doing, and the officers will probably cooperate with you. One five-year-old who was terrified by sirens overcame his fear when he was allowed to control the sound himself. His reward for controlling his feelings when he heard sirens after that was a trip to the fire station to visit his new friends.

14.6 FEAR OF HEIGHTS

Many weak-kneed parents have wished their children were more fearful of heights when they've found them waving from treetops or climbing on the roof. Like many basic fears, the fear of heights seems to be inborn and to have its own timetable. Infants have little fear because of their immature depth perception, but a three-year-old can be terrified just stepping across the threshold of an elevator or climbing steps with open risers.

Many youngsters are so afraid of heights that they won't climb jungle gyms or slides, and Ferris wheels are out of the question. A fear of heights can deprive a child of a lot of fun, it can provoke teasing and ridiculing from peers, and it can follow the child all his life. In fact, Agras and Oliveau report that 35 percent of adults have this fear. All sufferers, at whatever age, report the same symptoms: dizziness, imbalance and, often, a feeling that a magnet is pulling them toward the edge. Now, that's frightening, so follow our suggestions to help rid your child of this fear at an early age.

14.6-1 Prevent the Fear.

When a two- or three-year-old demonstrates this fear, you may feel fairly sure it will pass before long. To help prevent it from becoming more permanent, do not overreact or pressure the child.

• Give quiet support. Hold the child's hand or let her hold your finger when she exposes herself to new heights. She needs time to develop confidence.

• Let the child observe. Give her the chance to see other children playing on slides and jungle gyms. If she indicates that she'd like to give it a try, give your smiling approval and applaud her efforts, even if she makes it only halfway up the ladder. Say, "Next time you'll go higher," to underline your confidence, and never make comments like, "Don't be a baby, go ahead!" or even, "I'm so glad you're getting over your fear of heights." Nonverbal cues can reinforce the child's fears, so don't anticipate that she will be afraid today because she was afraid yesterday.

• Shield the child from teasing or pressure. Be careful not to communicate your own fear of heights, and be especially careful not to make fun of the child or push him into doing something he doesn't want to do. If he climbs up and is afraid to come down, give him a free ride. Climbing is fun, not a test of bravery. Do not allow other people to apply pressure, either.

14.6-2 Teach Coping Skills.

If a child's fear continues past the age of about four, start teaching him skills that will lessen his anxiety. Perhaps he starts breathing rapidly and shallowly when he's confronted with his fear; this can cause the dizzy feelings that will increase the fear of falling. Explain this to the child and teach him to take slow relaxing breaths. Teach him the relaxation techniques described in Section 2.10.

14.6-3 Use the Ladder Technique.

One of the best ways to desensitize your child to this fear is to have him learn to climb a ladder.

1. Find the first rung of fear. Have the child climb up one step and then another step, until he's frightened. Have him signal his feelings, using the one-to-ten scale or simply a verbal description. When he reaches the step that really scares him, have him come back down.

2. Shape confidence. Beginning with the lowest feared step, have the child step up and stay there for a few seconds, perhaps holding your hand. Do it again and let him stay there longer, until he can stand comfortably without holding on to you. Let him climb up

one step at a time and master each level before going to another. Stop at the height you deem appropriate.

3. Use praise. Although it may take days, weeks, or even months to develop the child's new sureness, keep on praising his efforts. Don't be put off by setbacks or slow progress.

14.6-4 Use Real Experiences.

As your child progresses up the ladder, use real situations in a similar way.

• Desensitize the child to the fear of heights. If, say, the child is anxious about climbing on a jungle gym, play together on the bottom rungs while you hold hands. Then unobtrusively stop holding her and let her play on her own. Stay at each level until the fear subsides before tackling the next.

With slides, start with the smallest slide you can locate. Go down with her a few times until she wants to go by herself. If you are frightened of such experiences yourself, get someone else to work with the child.

Find a hotel with a glass elevator and work your way up one floor at a time. At first, the child may only be able to walk into the elevator cab for a few seconds. She will progress and ride to higher levels, but make sure to return to the lobby and rest each time before going higher.

If the following job isn't for you, find a volunteer who loves amusement rides to help with this project: You or the volunteer must go to the park and let the child identify the rides she'd like to go on someday. Then, starting with the least frightening one, stand and watch for a while; when the child is willing, take the ride together until she is comfortable. The key to success is to monitor the anxiety rating with each experience, then to repeat the activity until the fear subsides.

14.7 FEAR OF ENCLOSED PLACES

The fear of small, enclosed spaces, claustrophobia, is a common adult phobia that is often traced back to childhood experiences. Sometimes those experiences include obvious causes, such as being trapped in an elevator for several hours or being strapped onto an operating table, but usually it's an accumulation of minor happenings that seem to precipitate the fear.

Be alert to the early signs of claustrophobia in your child, and keep the small fears from growing into something larger and more permanent. Precursors may include anxiety in elevators, sitting in the backseat of a car or bus, being left in a closed room, being held down in play, and wearing a mask, among others. There are many ways to prevent these worries from expanding.

14.7-1 Recognize and Discuss the Feelings.

If your youngster seems anxious in small or confined places, ask him what he is feeling. Don't put words in his mouth or feelings into his mind, but simply find out if he feels dizzy, trapped, panicked, clammy, smothered, tearful, or whatever. Explain that his feelings are symptoms of his fear, and make sure he doesn't think he has a medical problem.

14.7-2 Teach Coping Skills.

Begin with teaching relaxation techniques (see Section 2.10), then teach other ways to counteract the response.

• Teach countering actions. Show the child how to cool off if the small space makes her feel hot and sweaty. Tell her she may loosen or remove some of her clothes, open a window, fan herself, or wash her face. If she feels she can't breathe freely, show her how to breathe slowly and deeply with her mouth slightly open, holding the breath, and then slowly exhaling. Purposeful controlled breathing (see Section 2.10) will convince her that she's not smothering.

• Teach imagery. Have the child close her eyes and pretend she is at the seashore, in a flower-filled meadow, or even at a birthday party. Let her think about what she is doing there, so she can block the feelings of being trapped. This technique works best if the child has practiced imagery earlier.

14.7-3 Practice in Real Situations.

Now, using the new coping skills, begin to break down the fear in actual settings.

• Start in a large space. If the child is claustrophobic about a small space, start with a large room with the door open, then with the door closed, and later move to a smaller room. Eventually, the child will probably tolerate a tiny room or even a closet for very brief periods of time. Always progress very slowly, even in a place with plenty of light and air, and never go beyond the point at which the child feels comfortable.

• Increase the population. Another way to effect the same results is to maintain the room size but gradually increase the number of people occupying the space. At first, let the child have the whole backseat of the car to himself. As his anxiety lessens, let another person sit back there with him, and later, a third, with the fearful child in the middle.

The same plan will work with a fear of elevators. Go to an office building or a hotel during a slack time and ride with the child in a large elevator that's empty or almost empty. Glass elevators are an excellent starting point. Then progress to smaller, more crowded elevators. Remind the child to practice his relaxing, countering, and cooling skills during the practice sessions.

14.7-4 Teach the Child to Control Feelings.

If the child is afraid of being restrained or of smothering, design a series of steps to overcome the fear.

• Practice covering the child's face. Together, make a list of face coverings that he thinks he could tolerate. Start with sunglasses or goggles, work up to Halloween masks, diving masks, or any other object he wants to use. Let him control how long he keeps the coverings on his face, and praise the progress.

• Anxiety about dental procedures often begins as a fear of gagging. If this bothers your child, include it in your home training. Buy a dental mirror and have the child examine his own teeth first, then hold his mouth open while you look inside. A flexible straw under his tongue can be a pretend mouth drain. Tell him to practice talking with his mouth open or with the dental tools in place, so he will see that he can still communicate. Work out some hand signals to signify that he's doing fine or wants a break.

Dentists are accustomed to dealing with this fear, so discuss it with yours and schedule some get-acquainted visits before the child requires a real session.

• Play games to overcome fear of restraint. Many children can't bear being held down or physically controlled. Do a little wrestling together and let the child pin you down before reversing the roles and holding him *very briefly.* Increase the time gradually over a few days or weeks, until the child can tolerate being held down for a few minutes without panic. Always explain why you are doing this. You are not tormenting him, only trying to help him overcome a problem. Later, shift to play situations where the child's arm might have to be restrained for a blood-pressure test or he may have to stand perfectly still for an eye exam.

14.8 FEAR OF DEATH OR DYING

This is a common fear among children and may manifest itself in extreme separation anxiety, an inability to go to sleep, or constant talk about dying. One family came to us recently, concerned about their three-year-old daughter, Denise. The child's great-grandmother and two puppies had recently died within weeks of each other and the child was obviously upset. The parents wanted reassurance that they were handling the situation correctly. They were. They told the child the truth, answered her questions at her level, and did not replace the lost pets too quickly. In time, the fear diminished.

Around the age of five or six, most children start asking questions about death, but they have only a rudimentary understanding of the cycle of life, associating dying with old age, which excludes them from the danger. By seven, they may suspect that they too will die someday, and their questions may focus on the physical aspects of disease and dying. By nine or ten, most children are ready for direct and complete answers to all their questions.

We cannot and should not protect our children from reality by avoiding unpleasant subjects such as death. They will experience their own losses, whether of a pet or a distant relative or a neighbor, and see plenty of destruction on television and in the movies. They must be allowed to talk about it, air their fears, ask their questions, and get real answers.

The suggestions here provide a guide for introducing the subject in a natural way and for dealing with difficult events.

14.8-1 Answer Honestly and Lovingly.

It may be easier to use half-truths, but it is not better. Children need answers if they are to handle abstract concepts.

• Answer questions at their own level. When your four-year-old asks you, "Where did Rover go when he died?" give her simple but concrete answers. Complicated answers will only confuse her. A simple explanation consistent with your religious beliefs, that you can accept yourself, is quite appropriate. Or you might try to explain the cycle of life, using flowers or the seasons as examples.

• Use appropriate words. Don't avoid words like *kill, die,* or *dead.* The children already know and use these words.

• Avoid half-truths and fairy tales. Don't tell the child Grandpa has gone away on a trip; the child may interpret that to mean his grandpa doesn't love him or will come back any minute. Let him know Grandpa loved him very much but cannot come back. Don't equate death with sleep because the child may then fear going to sleep himself. Don't say Aunt Tilly died because she was very sick, because you don't want your child to fear that every illness, his or yours, may end in death. Let him know most people get well again.

• Focus on life. After you have talked about death honestly and given the child a chance to discuss his feelings and fears about it, then focus on life. Talk about living in a healthy way so we will live a long life—eating properly, having medical checkups, exercising, and so forth. This gives the child some feeling of control over his body.

14.8-2 Teach the Child About the Cycle of Life.

The best way to learn about death is to know about life. As early as your child can help, let her plant a garden, and watch and discuss the phases of nature. Have pets that will teach her about love, life, and responsibility as well as death. When a pet dies, have a funeral and bury it, but do not decide to replace it immediately.

14.8-3 Discuss Serious Illness.

When a close relative or friend is seriously ill, children are often excluded from the conversation and left to guess what is going on. Give them information, depending on their age, personality, and situation.

• Include the children. Children need to know when someone close is very ill, although they may not necessarily be told immediately if the illness is terminal. A young child can be told the person is very sick but that the doctors are trying to help her get well, then that the doctors haven't been able to help her yet, and so forth. Children need opportunities to talk about the situation before a crisis occurs. If they are not given the information, they may reach erroneous conclusions, perhaps blaming themselves for the death. They may remember they once wished their brother would die. Or they think this wouldn't have happened if they had prayed more or had been very good or hadn't been angry with the loved person for being sick and unavailable to them. If you keep the child up-to-date, you can talk about his feelings along the way.

14.8-4 Allow the Child to Express Emotions.

Your child will have many feelings when he knows someone is very sick or has died. He will feel denial, anger, despair, guilt, and fear that the same will happen to him or other people he loves. Let him talk about his feelings, and don't deny them to him but simply reassure and support him. Later, let him know that it is normal and acceptable to feel better after a while. Tell him it takes a long time to get over being unhappy (this is especially true with the death of a parent). He will always miss the person very much, but he will feel better eventually.

On the other hand, a child may feel guilty because he doesn't feel sad that second cousin Lou has died. He must be told that you are sad because you grew up with cousin Lou but you recognize that he never really knew him.

14.8-5 Prepare the Child for Rituals.

You must make your own decision about whether your child should attend a funeral, depending again on her age, personality, and situation.

• Make an individual decision. Many experts suggest that a funeral is not an emotionally helpful experience for a child below the age of five or six. Nor is it helpful for an older but very sensitive child to attend a funeral you know will be a very emotional occasion. If the child feels strongly that she prefers not to attend, respect her wishes without denigrating them.

• Explain the rituals. Before the event, explain just what will happen at the funeral home, the church or synagogue, the cemetery, or at home. Explain how people will act and what the child will see and hear.

BOOKS FOR PARENTS AND CHILDREN

Clifton, Lucille. *Everett Anderson's Goodbye.* New York: Holt, Rinehart and Winston, 1983. A story of a young boy who is trying to accept his father's death.

Krementz, Jill. *How It Feels When a Parent Dies.* New York: Knopf, 1981. Children who have experienced the death of a parent share their stories and feelings.

Kübler-Ross, Elisabeth. *On Death and Dying.* New York: Macmillan, 1969. The respected expert discusses stages of acceptance and emotions that accompany death. For adults.

Kübler-Ross, Elisabeth. *Remember the Secret.* Berkeley: Celestial Arts, 1982. Kübler-Ross's first book on love and loss written for young people.

Kushner, Harold S. *When Bad Things Happen to Good People.* New York: Schocken Books, 1981. This book was written to help those hurt by life come to terms with their emotions and beliefs. For adults.

Rofes, Eric E. and The Unit at Fayer Weather Street School. *The Kid's Book about Death and Dying.* Written by students eleven to fourteen years old as they explore the subject together.

Stein, Sara Bonnett. *About Dying.* New York: Walker, 1974. A book for parents and children to read together, with text for both.

Viorst, Judith. *The Tenth Good Thing About Barney.* New York: Atheneum, 1984. Everyone is sad after Barney the cat dies, but the children feel better remembering him (K–4).

14.9 FEAR OF SHOTS, NEEDLES, BLOOD, DOCTORS, HOSPITALS

It's no fun to get a shot. Blood can be scary. And so can doctors and hospitals. You can help your child be more relaxed about medical treatment and accept it patiently without trauma. It's important that he doesn't continue to be inordinately frightened, because it makes medical treatment more difficult and the fear can follow him into adulthood.

The following suggestions should help you and the doctor work through many problems before they become permanent.

14.9-1 Correct Misconceptions.

We are always amazed at the ideas children have about medical treatment, but simple explanations will usually alleviate the concerns.

• Provide the facts. Children don't necessarily know that their blood will clot and that they won't bleed to death from a shot. Tell your child she has four quarts of blood and that it circulates through the body, carrying the medication in the injection to the sick parts of the body. When blood must be drawn for tests, explain why and show how little will be taken. Tell her that even so, she will make more.

• Explain a shot and demonstrate the procedure. One little fellow was convinced that getting a shot was the same as being stabbed. He relaxed when he saw how short the needle was, and a demonstration using an orange showed him the needle would reach only below the skin.

• Tell the child how long the shot will take. Because most children think a shot will go on forever, give them a time frame. A simple counting system often is enough to make "eternity" quite manageable.

14.9-2 Teach Coping Skills.

The experience will be less unpleasant when the child knows ways to control his responses.

• Teach ways to stay calm. Relaxation skills are the key. Explain that a relaxed muscle hurts less during and after an injection. Teach the child the relaxation skills described in Section 2.10. Have him repeat his cue word *(relax)* before, during, and after the shot as he takes a deep breath and exhales very slowly.

• Teach distraction. Although many doctors and nurses are experts at distracting children while they give them shots, they won't mind if they get a little help from you. After explaining to the child what you want to accomplish, remind him how, when he is deeply involved in a TV show, he is so distracted that he's not so likely to hear you calling or notice the telephone ringing. Suggest that the same principle can work at the doctor's office.

Never try to trick the child, because you want him to trust you next time. Distraction will work best if the child is involved in the search for a solution to his fear. Give him some suggestions of both visual or auditory distractions. Looking away from the injection and studying the doctor's office can help. Reading a book, listening to a music tape through earphones, counting the tiles on the ceiling, or thinking about a math problem have worked for many children. We remember one little boy who practiced thumping out the Morse code with his free hand.

14.9-3 Desensitize the Child to the Fear of Shots.

If the child continues to be extremely fearful, then it's time to begin a program of desensitization. Before starting, teach the child the rating system discussed in the beginning of this chapter.

1. Use pictures and props to create a series of experiences. Find pictures related to the child's fear—shots, needles, blood, arms, nurses. Search through library books or medical pamphlets and first-aid manuals or shoot your own series of photographs of a friend or you receiving a shot. Arrange the pictures from the least fearful to the most.

2. Have the child look at the pictures while she is relaxed. Ask her to look at the least fearful picture for a few seconds and then rate her discomfort. If the anxiety level isn't too high, let the child look at it repeatedly until the level drops. Then proceed to the next picture, working your way through all of them over a number of sessions until the child can look at each of them comfortably.

3. Show the child the real equipment. After she has mastered pictures, gradually expose her to medical material such as sealed, sterile syringes or blood-test kits. Begin by showing it at a distance, and when the fear ratings decrease, allow the child to move slightly closer.

Greg was terrified of shots when we met him. He would scream all the way to the doctor's office, not even knowing if he would be getting a shot. In our practice sessions, Greg was uncomfortable when the unopened boxed syringe was brought into the room. But when he could tolerate the carton on the table, we opened it. Fear ratings controlled our actions. Gradually, we moved the material closer to Greg, and eventually, he could hold it and allowed us to pretend to give him a shot. The desensitization allowed him to go to the doctor without panic.

4. Observe real situations. For many children, examination of the materials and an understanding of the procedures will allay their fear so they can tolerate shots and tests. When this doesn't happen, however, then gradual exposure to real situations is needed. Have the child watch other children or adults who are not frightened getting shots—you can arrange this with the doctor. Or visit a bloodmobile. If you explain your goal to the officials before the event, they will probably be cooperative and allow the child to observe the procedure.

If your child feels faint, let him lie down while he watches. As he gets more comfortable, he can raise his head gradually. Don't use the relaxation techniques beforehand with this child, however, because the exercises may lower his blood pressure and actually promote faintness.

5. Involve the child in real experiences. When he is comfortable seeing others getting a shot or a blood test, talk to the doctor and plan a gradual exposure program. Make a list of the procedures the child must eventually learn to tolerate—finger pricks for blood tests, immunization shots, physical examinations, etc. Visit the doctor's office when it's not busy, bringing distracters, and arriving early for the appointment so the child can become accustomed to the surroundings. Introduce him to the nurses and the doctor and remind him to use his coping skills. Set up rewards for the child's cooperation and progress. Above all, don't expect perfection. Gradual improvement is your goal.

14.9-4 Promote Good Feelings About Doctors and
         Hospitals.

Fear of doctors and hospitals usually stems from real experiences.
Generalize the child's new confidence to other situations by planning ahead. When possible, especially with new doctors or procedures, arrange orientation and get-acquainted visits in advance of
any real need of medical treatment, so the child will feel more
comfortable when the time comes.

• Schedule checkups and well-baby visits. If you visit the doctor
regularly for examinations, the child will understand that the doctor takes care of us even when we are well. Ask the doctor to give
the child a reward (which you may provide) to make her feel good
about her cooperation.

• Visit hospitals. Always acquaint the child with the local hospital before she needs to go there, because you may not have the
time to do so in case of an emergency. If it is allowed, take her with
you to visit a new baby or a sick friend or take her to a local health
fair. When she is scheduled to be hospitalized, take her for a tour
and inquire if children's classes, to familiarize the youngsters with
their upcoming environment, are given.

• Tell the child where she's going and why. Let her know why
she must be hospitalized, what will happen, and how long she will
stay there. Telling her it won't hurt or making other promises that
can't be kept won't help. Be sure she visits the hospital at least a
few days before her scheduled hospitalization, and arrange for her
to talk with her doctor so she can ask questions.

• Involve the child in the preparations. When the time approaches for a hospitalization, let the child choose some things she
would like to take with her—a stuffed animal, a few toys, pictures,
a special blanket—for extra comfort and security.

SUGGESTED READING FOR CHILDREN
    Howe, James. *The Hospital Book.* New York: Crown, 1981. A
guide, with photos, to staying in the hospital (Gr. 2–4).
    Rodgers, Fred. *Going to the Doctor.* New York: Putnam, 1986.

Honest talk about visiting the doctor, illustrated with colorful photographs of the procedures, including shots and weighing (PS–2).

14.10 FEAR OF RIDING IN CARS OR PLANES

Most children love riding in cars and going up in airplanes, but if such events make your child apprehensive and anxious, you must alleviate her fears. You don't want her to join the twenty-five million American adults who won't fly or the millions who won't drive on highways, over bridges, or on surface streets.

Usually brought on by a bad experience or accident or triggered by stress, the fear can grow. If the child is already afraid or shows early signs of strong fear, then the steps below will help you help your child overcome the apprehension.

14.10-1 Set a Good Example.

Don't pass your fears on to your child. If riding in cars or planes makes you very anxious, use these steps yourself or join a phobia group.

14.10-2 Desensitize the Child to Fear of Flying.

A parent who isn't frightened by planes should work through these steps with the child. You will find a complete discussion of the desensitization process in the introduction to this chapter.

1. Talk about the fear. Find out just what the child is afraid of and let him vocalize his anxieties. If his underlying fear is of heights or being confined in a small space, check out sections 14.6 and 14.7. Stress the safety precautions taken by airlines and airplane crews.

2. Familiarize the child with planes. Using pictures, stories, toys, and home experiences, give the child some experiences with planes before flying in one. Fly paper airplanes. Build model planes. When you drive in the car, play Tower to Pilot or Pilot and Co-

pilot, talking yourselves to your destination. Read books together about airplanes and flying.

3. Take the child to the airport. On the first visit, just watch the planes take off and land. If you know someone who's leaving on a trip, see him off and watch others depart. If you see any tearful partings, be sure to point out that the people are sad to leave each other.

• Take the child on a stationary airplane. Call the airport or an airline and explain your child's concerns. Ask if they are conducting fear-of-flying classes or if you and your child may visit a plane on the ground. If a real plane is not available, there may be a replica on exhibit at the local museum to use as the next step. Have the child walk around the plane and look inside. On the plane, have him sit down and buckle up. Explore the cockpit. Find the restrooms. Walk around.

• Make preparations for a plane trip. When the child has progressed comfortably through these steps, he's ready to take a ride. It's best if you can make his first trip a short one on a clear day. A rough flight may undo your good work. Make sure the child has practiced the relaxation exercises taught in Section 2.10 so he can use them to calm himself if he feels anxious.

Take along a flight bag full of activities to keep the child busy during the flight, a treat, and some gum to chew to keep his ears from popping, and be sure to ask your pediatrician for appropriate medication if there's a possibility that motion sickness may become a problem.

Get to the airport early and ask that the child be allowed to meet the pilots and flight attendants on the plane.

Keep up a running conversation, explaining what is happening at all times until the plane is in the air. Be sure to give explanations for all unfamiliar noises and sensations, such as the revving of the engines and the bumps when the wheels are folded.

Play games during the flight, find pictures in the clouds, listen to music or taped stories, or watch the movie.

14.10-3 Desensitize the Child to Fear of Riding in Cars.

Most children who fear cars are afraid they will be in an accident. These steps will help them work through the apprehension. Take anxiety ratings at each step (see the chapter introduction) and proceed to the next step only when the child is comfortable.

1. Discuss the fear. Try to find out exactly what frightens the child, and discuss her emotions openly. If she or a relative was involved in an accident, talk about it but also discuss how safe automobiles are.

2. Take safety precautions. Sit in the car without turning on the engine. Show the child how the seat belt works and explain why it is helpful (see Section 10.1 on seat belts). Demonstrate the directional signals and the brake lights and inform the child that their purpose is to advise the drivers behind you that you will be turning or stopping.

3. Take a short ride. When the child has become comfortable sitting in the car, suggest a short ride around the neighborhood. Use a lightly traveled road and avoid expressways. Have the child practice her relaxation skills. Drive slowly and carefully, telling the child what you are doing and where you are going. Play games like Bug, where the child looks for a certain kind of car. The winner is the one who sees, for example, the most blue cars during the ride. Drive to a place that interests her, like the ice cream parlor or the movie theater.

4. Increase the driving time. Gradually, take the child on more trips to more places, playing the games, driving at a more normal speed and on your customary highways.

14.11 FEAR OF BURGLARS AND KIDNAPPERS

Pictures of lost and missing children appear on television, in the newspapers, on milk cartons and grocery bags, and are posted on walls of supermarkets, so it's not surprising that children today are often extremely fearful that they, too, will be spirited away. Not only that, but children today are constantly cautioned to lock the doors and beware of strangers or, for that matter, anyone who gives them that "oh-oh" feeling.

For some youngsters, however, caution has turned into such tremendous fear that they can't engage in the simplest activity without worrying. Melissa, an eight-year-old, was afraid to play outside by herself. Penny would play only on the door stoop while her mother remained nearby. Seven-year-old Mickey was sure that every creak was a burglar trying to break into the house. He dreamed of ladders at his window and kidnappers taking him away while he slept. Night after night, he would creep into his parents' room and sleep at the foot of their bed.

It's important to teach children safety rules and to caution them against known dangers, but when they become so fearful that they cannot function normally, you must help them become more realistic. The suggestions below focus on ways to decrease the fears while maintaining a healthy awareness of potential danger.

14.11-1 Don't Be Overprotective.

There is a difference between being safety conscious and overprotective, and you may not be aware of the messages you are sending your child. If you hold the reins too tightly, you send two inhibiting messages: One, the world is so dangerous that I must protect you at all times; and two, you are incapable to playing alone or doing even small things for yourself. Neither message is healthy for your child.

14.11-2 Limit the Child's Exposure to Crime News.

Television news programs constantly reveal the horrors of the day in living color. Adults become hardened to most of them, but children do not. Limit your child's exposure to the gruesome crimes that seem to happen all around him. Watch the news when he's not around, turn off the set during dinner, avoid discussing crimes when he is present.

14.11-3 Explain When Necessary.

The child is going to hear about crime even when you try to control her exposure. Suzanne will see the headlines when she brings the newspaper in for you in the morning. When Jim pours the milk, he will notice the photographs on the carton. Answer their questions factually and matter-of-factly and in minimum detail. Explain that missing children are usually taken away by parents, not strangers, and that many of the older children are runaways.

14.11-4 Teach Safety Precautions.

Be sure your child knows how to behave and what to do under certain circumstances. Tell her the rules as she gets older and as the information becomes relevant. Do not frighten her—you want her to know that most people are nice and that only a very few would harm children. Teach, role-play, repeat the discussions, and read books together until you feel that she really knows the rules.

• Have the child memorize the facts. Teach the child her full name, address—including city and state—and telephone number—including the area code. You will be amazed how much information some two-year-olds can proudly learn.

• Teach the child to use the telephone. Make sure she knows how to call a neighbor, a relative, the police, and 911 for help. Tell her what to expect if she dials an emergency number and how to respond to questions. Role-playing is a good way to do this. Remember to set limits on when to use the telephone.

• Teach the child how to answer the phone. Tell her never to inform an unknown caller that she is home alone, and many parents prefer that the child not tell her name, first or last, to a stranger on the telephone. When a caller asks, "What number is this?" teach her to respond, "What number are you calling?" When the caller gives the number, she can say, "I'm sorry, you have the wrong number," and then hang up. Decide how you prefer the phone to be answered, then teach the skill.

• Teach the child not to answer the door. A child must never answer the door when she is home alone or you are not nearby. Act out this situation and show her what to do if someone comes to the door.

• Teach the child what to do if lost. Explain how to behave in stores or public places to prevent problems (see sections 10.3 and 10.4), and discuss what she should do if she is ever lost. As you enter a crowded place together, tell her where to meet you if you become separated accidentally, suggesting a familiar location or pointing out how to identify store personnel so she can ask them to have you paged. Remind the child never to leave the area with *anyone,* but if someone should try to force him to go, he must drop to the floor and scream, "This is not my mother [or father]!"

• Inform the school or day-care center about who may pick up your child. Let the teachers and administrators know the people with whom the child may leave the premises. Teach the child a prearranged secret code word to be used as a signal if an unfamiliar adult, such as a neighbor, must pick her up. Be sure to check occasionally that the child remembers the secret word.

• Teach the child how to say no to an adult. If an adult asks him to do something that he knows he shouldn't do or that makes him feel uncomfortable, then it is best to say no and quickly leave. Tell the child that no, under those circumstances, is a good enough response and he doesn't have to have an answer for "Why not?" Role-play scenarios so you are sure he understands.

• Teach the child to respect her "gut reaction." Tell the child that if she has any feeling that things are not right, then she must take action. For example, if she lets herself into the house and it doesn't "look right," then she should follow her instincts and leave immediately, going to a neighbor for help. Explain that she must not worry about seeming to be rude when she refuses to approach a stranger in a car who asks her a question. Role-play responses, including ignoring the person, pointing directions, and walking by quickly.

14.11-5 Now Teach Ways to Counter Unfounded Fears.

You do not want your child to go through life frightened of what's going to happen. Once the child has learned how to behave cautiously, then teach him to think positively and act confidently. This will make him happier and less likely to be a victim of crime as well. Teach him to think rational thoughts that counteract the fear: "The dog would bark if someone were trying to break in." Or, "I don't go off with strangers." Or, "I am safe at home. Mommy and Daddy will hear me if I call them."

14.11-6 Allay Fears with Safety Practice.

Here are the ways to reassure a child who is extremely fearful of danger at home (also see Section 14.4 on fear of the dark).

• Have a safety check made. In many communities, the police will come to your home upon request and discuss crime prevention measures. If the suggestions they make are suitable, follow them. These may include special locks on doors or windows, outdoor lighting, alarm systems, window coverings, and so forth.
• Set up a communication system. Many children's fears center on being alone in a room at night when everybody is asleep. When the child knows his parents can hear his noises while they are in their room, his fears subside. Install a simple intercom or arrange a special signal for the child to use if he needs you.

14.11-7 Teach Relaxation Skills.

Most of the time, of course, a child's fear of kidnapping and burglary are unrealistic. The anxiety about them, however, is quite real. Teach him to use the relaxation techniques in Chapter 2 to counteract those anxious feelings.

SUGGESTED READING FOR PARENTS AND CHILDREN
    Ebert, Jeanne. *What Would You Do If . . . ? A Safety Game for Your Child.* Boston: Houghton Mifflin, 1985. A workbook

for children to work through, learning how to respond to various situations.

Lenett, Robin, with Bob Crane. *It's O.K. to Say No!* New York: Tom Doherty Associates, 1985. A manual for parents, with text for children, that teaches safety skills.

14.12 FEAR OF PUBLIC SPEAKING

For some children, speaking in public is an opportunity to show off what they know. But for others it is total stress. Eight-year-old Michael slouches into his chair, hoping the teacher won't call on him. He knows the answer, but the idea of saying it in front of the whole class puts him into a state of panic. He forgets the answer, or his heart pounds and his mouth goes dry. The prospect of making a mistake or a little giggling from classmates is all it takes to cause trauma.

Many adults can empathize with Michael's feelings. This fear can become so intense that it turns into a true phobia if it's allowed to continue. The fear of public speaking is one of the most common anxieties among children and adults. It usually begins in elementary school, when youngsters are called upon to read aloud or give reports and they have a few bad experiences. We know teenagers who position themselves in the back of the classroom or sit behind the tallest person to avoid being called on, and we worked with a college student who almost didn't graduate because of the required public speaking course she had been avoiding.

Because this fear can cause so much distress and may well carry over into later life, it is important to help your child overcome it as early as possible.

14.12-1 Teach Relaxation.

The first step in overcoming the fear of speaking is for the child to learn an effective relaxation response so he can deflate his anxiety at will. Section 2.10 provides the information you will need to teach this technique. Emphasize the breathing skills and the mini-relaxation technique. Then have him practice saying his cue word, breathing slowly, and relaxing his body while he stands up in front of you without having yet to speak.

14.12-2 Identify the Fear.

Try to find out what it is that bothers the child. Is it fear of making a mistake, of looking foolish or nervous?

• Determine what frightens the child. Some children are most fearful when they must read aloud, while for others it's when they must talk without having the information written down for reference. Often, the size of the group makes a difference. Many youngsters can function well in a small reading group but freeze in a large classroom. Sometimes, especially in adolescence, the fear involves speaking to children of the opposite sex or talking when adults are present.

• Make observations. Observe the child in many different situations, and talk to his teachers when that is appropriate. Like many actors, the child may feel extremely apprehensive but never show it. Other times, the fear may be quite devastating. See Section 10.5 for helpful suggestions if your child won't answer or speak for himself in everyday situations.

14.12-3 Teach the Skill of Speaking in Public.

Help the child overcome his fear by building his confidence and increasing his competence.

• Give the child opportunities to speak. From an early age, give the child chances to talk in front of groups without forcing him or putting him on the spot. Encourage him to speak up at the dinner table or family gatherings, feeling that his thoughts are important, too. Most little ones love to show off, so take advantage of that. When natural opportunities present themselves, let him sing a song or put on a skit for the family, remembering that the experiences build confidence only if they are fun for him.

• Prepare the child for speaking in public. If the child is already fearful, teach him the basic skills. Encourage him to choose a topic that interests him and that he knows something about. Talk about what makes a speech or report interesting to the audience. Make sure he knows exactly what he is going to say, and help him plan the steps to prepare the presentation. This may include gathering information and writing the speech out first and then practicing it many times. Maybe an outline or cue cards will provide a safety net.

• Prepare him for snags. Discuss what he can do if he forgets what he's saying, gets upset, or is distracted. The solutions could be to take a deep breath and repeat the last idea, to refer to his note cards or outline, and then keep going. He might admit he's lost his place momentarily, or joke, "I always was afraid of public speaking!" This will gain him the empathy of his audience, but then, of course, he must continue. Role-play a number of situations.

14.12-4 Desensitize to the Fear and Practice.

Help the child overcome his fear by having him practice the situation in a supportive environment. Reread the introduction of this chapter for the steps for desensitization.

1. Make a list. Compile a list of the situations that frighten the child, rating them from least to most scary. Then start working from the bottom. Start with the least feared situation and create a hierarchy of practice sessions. For example, if your child is afraid of reading aloud, design a series of experiences around that skill, such as reading to his baby brother, then to you, then to two family members, then to the whole family.

2. Hold practice sessions. Before starting, have the child do the relaxation exercises and let you know when his anxiety level is near zero. As he practices in each circumstance, have him rate his discomfort. When the discomfort is high, abandon the practice, suggest relaxation, and have the child imagine himself participating successfully. For example, have him imagine himself speaking in a relaxed situation and gradually move into a more intense situation. If his major fear is giving a report in class, have him imagine

presenting it to his teacher alone, then to his teacher plus one student, then two students, and so on. Remind him to use his cue relaxation word while imagining the scene for about twenty seconds. Rate the anxiety and move on when it remains low.

3. Use pretend situations. When the child can imagine the most fearsome scenes with less anxiety, start simulating real situations. Give him ten questions from his homework to study, then pretend you are the teacher calling his name. Ask the child to stand and answer the question. Tape-record his answer and let him listen to it several times before going on to another question. Videotaping can add another dimension to the pretend situations.

When this procedure rates low on the anxiety scale, go on to speeches, book reports, or whatever has been bothering him, until he no longer experiences intense anxiety. Remind the child before each situation to repeat his cue word in order to relax. Tape-record everything and play it all back many times.

4. Be positive and patient. Encourage the child to focus on the solutions, and do not respond to negative statements like, "I will never be able to do this." Ignore them, or say, "I know it's difficult," and then continue to provide practical, positive suggestions. Do not criticize, ridicule or discount the child's feelings in words, expressions, or gestures. Do not pressure him, but do help him gain confidence.

14.12-5 Practice Mistakes.

When the child can imagine and simulate public speaking with less anxiety, turn your attention to desensitizing him to mistakes. Let the child know most people are afraid of looking foolish or stupid but that everybody—including his parents and the president of the United States—makes mistakes.

• Notice the mistakes of others. Share some of your own experiences, and have the child pay attention to other people, including teachers, relatives, television personalities, and other children, when they speak and notice the mistakes they make. Make mock speeches and deliberately make mistakes that the child can catch.

• Practice the presentation with mistakes. If the child fears that his voice will crack or his hands will shake, have him talk before an imaginary class or group and exaggerate these happenings. Then have him imagine remaining relaxed and finishing the reading or speech. Make up positive statements he can say to himself when he needs them: "Everybody makes mistakes," or, "People will still like me even if I make mistakes or my hands shake." Teach him to use the old standby "I just wanted to see if you were paying attention" if he does fumble.

Have him practice saying his positive statements out loud and then silently, so he will learn them well enough to think of them whenever he needs them during the practice sessions.

14.12-6 Practice in Real Situations.

Now it's time to tackle real life. Explain to the teacher that you are trying to help your youngster overcome his fear of speaking and would like her help in planning the right approach. Ask her if she would start him off in small steps, perhaps answering a question or reading aloud from a short prepared text rather than making a talk until he is more comfortable. Talk to the teacher and make a plan. You may decide to let the child choose a favorite toy to talk about in Show and Tell. If the class is studying a special topic like a foreign country, he might take an interesting souvenir from that place and practice one sentence to say about it. Or he could tape-record his book report and present it to the class before doing it live the next time.

14.13 FEAR OF SLEEPING AWAY FROM HOME

Children today are expected to function well away from home, sleeping over at Grandma's house or going away to camp or spending the night at a friend's home. But many children find this an awesome feat to accomplish because of many possible fears.

These steps are designed to help you find an appropriate solution to overcome your child's apprehensions.

14.13-1 Identify the Fear.

Sit down and talk with your child about what is frightening her, and share your own experiences if you once felt the same way as a youngster. Perhaps she fears new situations, the dark, wetting the bed, being kidnapped. Maybe she has trouble sleeping sometimes and worries that she'd be awake in a strange house or that she might get sick. If you find that the fear relates to one that has already been discussed in this book, refer to the relevant section before taking any other action. For example, if your child wets the bed, then you must not pressure her to sleep over at a friend's home before this problem has been solved.

14.13-2 Make a List of Acceptable Hosts.

Ask the child which relatives and friends she would like to spend the night with. Rank the names from the ones with whom she feels most comfortable to the ones with whom she is most anxious.

14.13-3 Prepare for a Practice Session.

Starting with the person with whom she feels most comfortable, explain your goal. Set up a series of practice sessions when the child will stay with her host until 7 P.M., 8 P.M., 9 P.M., 10 P.M., and so forth, but be available to pick the child up earlier if necessary. There may be times when you have to get your child at 1 A.M. or later, but most children will fall asleep much earlier than that.

14.13-4 Prepare the Child.

Let the child decide how late she would like to stay with her host at each stage. Talk about strategies she may use to feel comfortable away from home.

• Tell the child she may call you "just to talk" because you will be home for the evening.
• Allow the child to make preparations. Let her take a favorite

belonging, like a toy or book. Let her plan the evening with the host, perhaps even deciding what to have for dinner or a snack.

• Teach relaxation. Be sure the child knows the techniques (Section 2.10), and remind her to repeat her cue word and to breathe slowly if she ever feels frightened.

• Make a list of positive statements. Help the child compile several positive thoughts, such as, "I am safe here," "Mommy and Daddy are fine," "I am having a good time and Aunt Susan will play with me." Tell the child to repeat the good thoughts to herself if she is uncomfortable.

14.13-5 Design a Reward System.

Rewards to mark the child's progress will help her become more independent.

• Reward progress. No matter how early your child wants to come home from her first practice session, reward her for spending time away from home. Tell her how wonderful it is that she did it so well. Later, give rewards for longer stays. Eventually, tell her that when she decides to fall asleep there and stay for the night, she will earn a very big reward.

• Use natural consequences. The logical rewarding consequences might include a special breakfast at a restaurant the morning after or a movie that afternoon. Let the child invite a friend to stay overnight or have a spend-the-night party at your house after she has successfully spent the evening out herself.

14.13-6 Now Include Other Homes.

When the child feels comfortable sleeping over at the "easy" home, start arranging visits to others, using the same gradual approach. She may not require all of the trial runs now and soon may need none. Continue to reward success, and alternate evenings out with inviting friends to your house.

14.13-7 Extend the Plan to Camp.

When your child is ready for camping experiences, start with day camp and family camping trips. The key is to move along slowly. When he is spending the night happily with friends, he will be ready to think about camping away from home.

• Have cookouts and picnics and graduate to camping out in wilderness areas or parks. Include only family or close friends who are experienced campers.

• Enlist the child in day camp. Let the child get accustomed to camp life during the day. Most day camps will have late-night cookouts for young campers, progressing to a sleep-out experience when the children are older. If your child is fearful, inform the counselor and ask for his or her help.

• Select sleep-away camps carefully. Begin with weekend camp, progressing to a week and then longer. Choose carefully, and look for a camp that specializes in younger novice campers. Talk with the staff before signing on, and ask questions about their experience and the methods of dealing with children. Ask how they cope with homesickness. Take a tour of the camp with the child if possible. Or attend a presentation in your community so the child may see pictures, meet staff members, and talk with other potential campers.

SUGGESTED BOOKS FOR PARENTS AND CHILDREN

Waber, Bernard. *Ira Sleeps Over.* Boston: Houghton Mifflin, 1972. A little boy who sleeps over at his friend's house can't decide whether to take his teddy bear (K–3).

14.14 FEAR OF PARTIES AND SOCIAL GATHERINGS

Most children and adults enjoy parties, but sometimes social activities cause anxiety. What should you do if your child gets frightened when an invitation to a party arrives in the mail? How should you handle it if she clings and won't let you go home when you get to the scene? Can you cope when the child hovers by the door begging to go home while everyone else is having fun? This is a fear that won't be cured overnight, but you can set a plan into action that will gradually decrease her anxiety and eventually lead to joyful times.

14.14-1 Identify the Fear.

When you can, find out what it is that frightens her about the social situation.

• Talk to the child. When you are both relaxed, sit down and discuss what it is that bothers her about a party or gathering. Maybe it's the noise, the singing, the costumes, or being without you. Perhaps she suffers from separation anxiety or doesn't know what to talk about. If these are her problems, refer to the appropriate sections of this book.

14.14-2 Have Pretend Parties.

Expose the child gradually to a series of little parties in your own home.

• Start slowly, and make it fun. Begin with a pretend tea party with just one guest. Later, you can invite more. Have an ice cream party, a movie party, or a birthday party for the cat.
• Involve the child in the plans. Let her help by making cupcakes, writing the invitations, decorating, planning games.

14.14-3 Desensitize the Child to the Fear.

When she is comfortable with the mock parties in your own environment, it's time to try parties away from home.

• Rate the worries. Compile a list of the child's fears for the party and rate them in order of their intensity. Use the list, beginning with the least threatening experience, to design a series of steps to overcome the anxiety. For the first party, have her simply drop off the gift. The next time, she may want to take the gift and stay for a few minutes. Always move at the child's pace, never pushing or forcing her to attend or stay and always praising her at every sign of progress.

Here is a sample plan for gradually exposing your child to parties. Choose the steps that are appropriate for you, and always make sure the child agrees to try them and is ready for the experience.

1. Go to the party very early or late.
2. Walk to the door and leave the gift.
3. Stay five or ten minutes, or longer. Or arrive at cake time.
4. Stay close to the child throughout the party.
5. Stay in the room, but not so close.
6. Stay at the party, but in another room.
7. Leave the party for five, ten, and then fifteen minutes.

14.14-4 Use Praise and Rewards.

Every step of the way, tell the child you think she is great and you are proud of her. In addition, set rewards to encourage her: "Lauren, if you stay for the cutting of the cake, there will be a special gift waiting for you in the car on the way home."

14.14-5 Keep on Practicing.

Practice is essential. A fearful child needs plenty of chances to practice her social skills because if the real parties are too infrequent, she may revert to her old ways. Plan for at least one party a month, maybe something as simple as a lunch outing with another child or a new neighbor. Make an occasion out of holidays and birthdays or use group events like Girl Scout meetings or fashion shows.

14.15 FEAR OF WATER

There are a lot of skills you want your child to learn, and swimming is surely one of them—if not for the enjoyment, then because it is safer to know how to swim. The opportunity to swim is readily available to most children at community, neighborhood, or family pools.

Most children learn to swim with a few tears. But some children are so frightened by water, they can't stand to get the stuff on their face in the shower. Often, the child's fear follows a previous mishap, reflects the parent's fear of water, or stems from the child's lack of experience.

If your child is afraid of water, then the solutions below create a series of experiences for her to overcome this fear.

14.15-1 Prevent a Fear of Water.

Provide early experiences with water so the child can naturally become accustomed to it and maybe learn to enjoy it.

• Don't overreact. The most important suggestion we can make is not to overreact if your child should slip in the tub or get water on his face. Take care of the situation without screaming, "Oh my gosh! Oh no!" Your infant doesn't necessarily understand the situation, but your reaction can cause him to become concerned.

• Make getting wet fun. Water routines like bathing and shampooing should be a fun time for everyone. Section 9.1 offers suggestions for making it so. Don't make comments like, "We have to keep the water out of your eyes!" At some point, to become a competent swimmer or be drown-proofed, the child will have to get water in his eyes and up his nose. Avoid getting stinging soap in the eyes; don't try to avoid getting water in the eyes.

• Learn how to play with your child in a pool. There are many classes for teaching babies how to swim. The most important skill learned through such instruction might be your ability to work and play comfortably with your child in the water. Whether or not you believe in formal swimming classes for infants, don't assume that you know the best way to drown-proof your child or teach her to swim. Get the information and help you need to assure it.

14.15-2 Discover What Frightens Your Child.

If your child is scared of water, identify the elements and situations that particularly frighten her. If the child is anxious in the tub, then his list might begin with putting a wet washcloth over his face, slipping in the tub, putting his head under the faucet, and so forth. Another child's fears may center on larger bodies of water—pools, lakes, and the ocean. Her list might include the depth of the water, its temperature, climbing into the pool, not being able to touch bottom or a previous frightening experience. Rank your child's list, starting with the ones that make her the least frightened.

4.15-3 Gradually Expose Your Child to Experiences with Water.

Desensitize your child to his fear of the water by gradually exposing him to the situations you have listed together, beginning with the least frightening one. Throughout the process and afterward, always supervise your child in the water.

• Keep the pace comfortable. Design a series of small experiences, proceeding to the next one only when the child reports a low fear rating on a scale of one to ten. A set of activities for the child who is scared of bathing and washing could begin with holding a wet cloth to his eyes, pouring spoonfuls of water on his body, gradually progressing to cupfuls and larger containers. The child might then work through the series, pouring water over his head with his eyes open, closed, and then with you doing the pouring.

• Increase the depth of the water. In a bathtub or pool, start with very shallow water. Repeat the experiences in gradually deeper water, making sure the child is comfortable at each step. This is easy to control in the tub. With a pool, begin with a wading pool before going to the shallow end of a larger pool. A pool with steps rather than a ladder entry will provide less threatening exposure to the water.

14.15-4 Teach Your Child to Swim.

A competent swimming teacher knows how to handle children in the water. He or she is confident in the situation, and the child will feel it. Group instruction can work to the child's benefit when she sees her peers happily swimming.

• There is no right age to learn to swim. Be aware of the controversy about teaching infants to swim. There is some concern about forced submersion, through which the infant or child is likely to swallow a lot of water. Of course, if your child is going to be exposed to water early, then you will want him to be safe. And the earlier he is independent in the water, the more fun both of you will have.

• Select a teacher carefully. You must be confident of the instructor's approach and rapport with children so you can support his efforts to teach your child to swim. Observe a teacher before signing up for a class. Watch him interact with students at various skill levels. Discuss the fears your child has had. Be wary of techniques that include forced submersion or throwing children in the pool. It's true your child will have to put his head under water to learn to swim, but the approach must be carefully planned so the child can achieve success at every step.

• Praise the child's success in the water. Be supportive, but do not be overly sympathetic to tears and pleas. Reinforce cooperation in the water and praise every success, letting the child know how excited and proud you are of his efforts.

• Provide incentives. Add a little extra motivation. Have the child earn a star for his super-star chart for following the teacher's instructions. Stars can be traded for special rewards like swim fins, goggles, and aquatic toys. Other natural consequences might include swimming parties, water games and, of course, trips to the pool or beach when the child knows how to swim.

CHAPTER 15

Special Behavior Problems

THIS chapter discusses four special problems that are especially upsetting to parents. What do you do when you get a note from the teacher telling you that five-year-old Vanessa offered to exchange a peek at her vagina for a look at a little boy's penis? How should you deal with a child who seems to enjoy being rough with animals? If your youngster takes a toy from a friend, does that mean he is destined to be a thief? If he is fascinated by matches, will he be a pyromaniac?

Often, these behaviors are just as manageable as the other common problems we have included in this book, but some, like purposely setting fires or torturing animals, may signal serious emotional problems that require professional help. This chapter focuses on solutions to unusual problems a parent can manage and provides essential information for finding specialized support when it is needed.

15.1 STEALING

No matter how minor the incident and how well they remember doing the very same thing, most parents are horrified when their child steals something that doesn't belong to her. They promptly visualize visits to the county jail in their future.

The best approach is to take specific steps to teach honesty and correct the misdeed. Do not overreact or underreact to stealing. Passing it off as borrowing is just as bad as labeling the child a thief.

15.1-1 Teach Ownership.

Little children are egocentric and territorial. Not only do they tend to scream, "That's mine!" if anyone dares reach for one of their possessions, but their "territory" often extends to things they *want* as well as things they already have. Many parents have been embarrassed to discover candy bars from the check-out stand or a friend's toy stuffed in their child's pocket.

• Explain purchases. Let the child know you have had to pay for everything in your house. Discuss what it means to receive a gift. When you go to the store, show the child how you pay for the items you take. When she is old enough to receive an allowance or earn money for chores, start teaching respect for the value of objects. Allow her to buy items for herself, and urge her to save money for gifts.

• Teach the meaning of ownership. Play a game that will help the child identify what's his and what isn't. Let him go through the house and claim his possessions by pointing out what belongs to him. Label his items and point out that everybody else in the family has personal possessions that may not be taken or used without permission. Role-play borrowing and returning things.

• Discuss the child's actions. If a small child takes something that is not his, talk to him about how he would feel if somebody took one of his possessions. Have him return it, but because apologies are difficult for young children, don't expect him to give one the first time. Explain that "I'm sorry" will be required next time. Teach him that when he sees something he wants, he must first ask you or someone else if he may take it. If he has difficulty accepting no for an answer, see Section 8.7.

• Work toward apologies. Apologies don't come easily to toddlers—or many older children, either. Practice using the skill yourself when it's called for, and role-play with the child for practice. If the child continues to take things that belong to other people, insist that now he must return it and apologize.

15.1-2 Teach Impulse Control.

All children must learn to control their impulses to take anything they want. When you approach the supermarket check-out line with your child, point out all the items nearby. Tell the child they do not belong to him and that he must not touch them. When he doesn't touch them, be sure to praise his control. You may wish to reinforce the self-restraint by letting him choose one item to buy.

15.1-3 Label the Action for What It Is.

When a child takes something that is not his, confront him quickly, just as soon as you get a chance to talk to him privately. Tell him he must return the item to its rightful owner. An older child, who clearly understands the difference between ownership and taking something not his own, should be told that he is stealing. Don't ask him if he took the object you found in his pocket. Don't ask why, but in a calm yet serious tone, simply say, "You stole that," as soon as you discover the act. It's important not to be accusatory, hostile, or disdainful in this situation, but to speak calmly and coolly without giving the impression that the child is bad. It's the action that's wrong.

15.1-4 Apply Negative Consequences.

Yelling, accusing, and giving long lectures are not the correct approaches to this behavior. Real consequences are required for children to learn that stealing is a serious offense.

• Undo the act. Ask the older child what she thinks should be done to undo the deed. Make your own suggestions and come to an agreement, then return together to the scene of the crime. At the very least, the child should face the person from whom he took the item even if she doesn't utter a word. If possible, she should apologize as well.

• Add a natural consequence. To make a lasting impression, a natural consequence should also follow. The older child should have to do extra chores to pay for the stolen item, even if it has been returned. The child who takes a candy bar from a store might lose all sweets for a reasonable period of time (a few days for a small child, a week for an older child). If she took a toy from a sibling or friend, she can use her money to buy another for him or lose one of her own to make up for the moral damage. Perhaps she could perform services for the wronged party, like the little boy who washed the blackboard and dusted the erasers after school for a week when he stole money from the teacher's desk.

15.1-5 Reward Honest Behavior.

It is equally or more important to reinforce honesty consistently as it is to make restitution for lack of it. Praise the child for walking past the candy counter without reaching for anything; give support to the youngster who finds and returns lost items to other people. Point out items in the newspaper or stories on television that illustrate honesty. If a child has previously taken money or other items from family members, don't hide your money or other tempting things. Behave normally, and as he shows his new trustworthiness, praise his honesty lavishly.

15.1-6 Provide Supervision.

Stealing often occurs when children are unsupervised and subjected to peer pressure. The solution is to keep an eye on your children's activities.

• Share responsibility with others. Get together with other parents, and be sure the children are not left alone. If you go to work before the school bus comes, for example, arrange for your child to wait with a neighbor in the morning. Perhaps one parent can keep neighborhood children in the morning while another does it in the afternoons after school.

If the stealing has been a group activity, talk to the parents of the other children who were involved. One group of parents agreed to keep all their boys from playing outside for a week, then they were allowed to play together again on "test" days. When no further problems occurred, they were permitted to play regularly with the understanding that if any one boy stole again, all the boys would lose the privilege of playing together for several weeks. The parents also helped the youngsters start a football team coached by a teenager, who was paid to supervise the practice.

• Enroll the child in an after-school program. Many school systems have started such programs, so check out the possibilities. Along with supervision, your child will have fun and will learn new skills besides.

• Supervise the latchkey child. If your youngster comes home before you do, call him soon after he should get there and then randomly to let him know you care and will be checking, not as a policeman but as a concerned parent. Leave your telephone number as well as other safety numbers. Before you leave home, discuss how he will be spending his time. Set clear and reasonable expectations—homework, snack, television, chores, etc. When you get home, check it out and praise him for following the plan.

15.2 SETTING FIRES

Setting fires is a rare behavior for a child, but when it occurs, the results can be disastrous. Most fire setters are boys around the age of six or seven, but both sexes and all ages may be culprits. Usually, playing with fire occurs only once, with firm parental reaction and explanations of possible results preventing other incidents, but sometimes children persist in setting fires and this may be a sign of a more serious emotional problem.

There are many things you can do to prevent or overcome fire setting.

15.2-1 Teach Fire Safety and Awareness.

Let the child learn to respect the power of fire.

• Teach fire-safety procedures. Even if your child has never set a fire or never plays with matches, you must teach him fire safety. Explain what could happen if a fire got started in the wrong place. Let him observe or help you put water on the campfire. Never leave matches or lighters where he might find them and be tempted to try them. Reward and praise him for bringing lost matches and lighters to you. If you smoke, show him how carefully you extinguish your cigarettes. Visit the firehouse. Hold fire drills in the house to teach the proper escape plans. Your goal is to teach a healthy respect for fire.

• React appropriately to playing with matches. If the child plays with matches, seems especially fascinated by fire, or has accidentally set a fire, let him see that you are angry but also very frightened about what could happen as a result. Maybe he was only playing scientist, but he must know that his little experiment could cause the curtains to ignite and then the walls. Tell him that the whole house could burn down and everyone in it would be hurt or killed. Show him pictures of serious fires and burn victims.

15.2-2 Increase Supervision and Precautions.

If a fire has been set, immediately increase the level of supervision for that child, especially after school and on weekends. If you won't be home yourself, enroll the child in an after-school program or hire someone to be with him when you are not there. Get rid of the matches and lighters or lock them up.

15.2-3 Deal with the Desire to Light Fires.

Many children go through periods when they are fascinated with fire, and no amount of supervision or punishment extinguishes the interest. So teach them how to handle fire safely. Camping and scouting experiences give opportunities to build and enjoy fires and, at the same time, instill respect.

• Teach fire rules. Show the child how to light matches the safe way, with the cover back in place. Discuss the appropriate occasions for matches and explain that they may be used only with supervision. Allow her to start the fire in the fireplace or to light the candles for the table in your presence. Praise her for heeding the rules about not lighting matches at any other time.

• Satiate the child's interest. In extreme cases, some children have shed this fascination with fire by having to light matches repeatedly for an hour or more at a time in supervised practice sessions over a number of days. This, of course, must be done with extreme care. Important: If you try this tactic and see that the child is becoming even more obsessed with fire, stop the experiment and seek professional help immediately.

15.2-4 Test Safety Behavior.

Under most circumstances, testing a child is not recommended. However, you must be sure your child understands the safety rules. Neutralize a pack of matches by wetting them, then place these decoys where the child will easily find them. Be alert. If the child doesn't bring the matches to you immediately or tries to light them, reprimand him and apply negative consequences. If he does bring them to you, be lavish with your praise and rewards. Be sure to reinforce other fire safety behaviors, like staying a safe distance from fireplaces and turning off burners.

15.2-5 Seek Professional Help if Necessary.

If your child intentionally arranges materials to burn and purposely sets fires or seems inordinately fascinated by fire, it would be best to have him evaluated and perhaps treated by a therapist. See Chapter 17 for help in finding professional services.

15.3 HURTS ANIMALS

All children get too rough with animals occasionally, usually because of excitement or lack of awareness. Some youngsters are overly impulsive, active, or aggressive or get carried away with teasing or wrestling, some are too young to realize the effects of their actions, while others are influenced to show off their toughness in a group, though they would never hurt an animal when they are alone.

Information, instruction, and supervision are the keys to avoiding this unintentional harmful behavior. But when the abuse is intentional or you suspect that it is, then you must get professional help as quickly as possible. Such behavior signals a serious emotional problem.

To prevent or overcome unintentional acts, try these steps:

15.3-1 Teach Appropriate Play with Animals.

Show the child the right way to treat a pet.

• Teach the child how to care for a pet. Teach him very specifically what to do and what not to do with an animal. Show him how to control it and what to do if the animal jumps on him or scratches him. The younger child shouldn't be told to discipline the animal himself but to come to you when he cannot control it. If you can, have the child be the one to work with a dog in an obedience class, where the dog will be taught to behave and the child to manage the animal.

• Teach the child how to play with a pet. Tell the child that the pet will love him when he is gentle and kind. Remind him that just like him, the animal will be unhappy if it is treated roughly and may even strike back. Supervise him when he is with the animal until you are sure he knows the rules. Teach him other ways to play together.

When Pete was a toddler, he loved to pull his dog's tail, ears, and clumps of fur, and Lightning was a pretty good sport about it.

But Pete's parents showed him how to play fetch with Lightning and they both enjoyed themselves more.

15.3-2 Use Time-out from the Pet.

At the first sign of aggressive play or the first sign of distress from the pet, apply time-out from the animal (see Section 2.7). Start with having the child go into the time-out location for the pre-scribed number of minutes. If this isn't effective, restrict the child from being with the animal for the rest of the day.

15.3-3 Use Overcorrection.

If stronger action seems necessary, apply overcorrection (see Section 2.8) and have the child undo the harm she has done or make amends for her behavior. Have a very young child practice "making nice" to the animal for several minutes. Have an older child make up by brushing the dog, taking him for a long walk, or buying him a special snack from her allowance. Or have her clean up after a pet or change its water several times as a consequence for being too rough. One child had to give up twenty-five cents of his allowance for each incident of throwing the cat. The money was used first for a new collar and then for cat treats, until finally this behavior became too expensive for him to continue.

When you use overcorrection, be sure the child understands that he's attempting to make amends for hurting the animal.

15.3-4 Reinforce Appropriate Behavior.

Be sure to praise and reward your child when she plays nicely with the animal. One parent gave the dog a biscuit and the child a poker chip every time he caught them playing together appropriately. The child earned extra chips for grooming and exercising the dog and traded them all in for a reward (see Section 2.4).

15.3-5 Seek Professional Help.

If intentional abuse continues, if animals repeatedly disappear without apparent reason, or if you have other reasons to be uneasy about the child's behavior with animals, have the youngster evaluated and treated by a trained professional (see Chapter 17).

15.4 MASTURBATING IN PUBLIC/SEX PLAY

Sex is a subject that makes most parents uncomfortable. Talking to children about sexuality is usually so difficult for them that many parents don't get around to it until their child has learned some twisted facts from friends and is loaded with misconceptions. Some parents never really come to grips with teaching their children about sex.

Children begin to learn about their sexual nature much earlier than you might expect. Before six months of age, many infants have discovered their genitalia, exploring that area just as they do the rest of their body. Later, their early experiences with sexual stimulation usually occur accidentally, too. Once children discover this pleasure, they often pursue the activity. They will masturbate deliberately or find pleasure rubbing against a bed or a tricycle.

Masturbation is normal at any age, and it should be of concern to you only when it is excessive or is done in public. Remember that all children are naturally interested in their own body, as well as those of others, and like to do things that cause them pleasure. Also recognize that your little boy isn't always masturbating when he touches himself. Sometimes all that hopping and touching means he has an urgent need to urinate!

Your sex education goals should be to teach appropriate behavior, to help your child understand sexuality, and to accept his or her body.

15.4-1 Don't Overreact.

When you discover your child masturbating, keep cool. If you are uncomfortable with this activity, take care not to shame the child. Remember that masturbation is not bad. It is normal.

15.4-2 Start Sex Education Early.

Many parents believe that their responsibility for teaching their children about sex begins when they are nearing puberty. That's far from the truth. Sexuality concerns much more than sexual intercourse. It concerns the way we think about ourselves and our bodies, our feelings about intimacy, touching, and being touched.

Children are interested in bodies just as soon as they notice them. They want to know how men and women differ. The way you answer your child's questions is just as important as the information you give, so provide answers that are appropriate to his age and level of understanding. If you are uncomfortable with your own sexuality, be careful not to transmit this attitude to the child. He needs to feel good about his body, his gender, and his ability to make sexual decisions.

• Discuss sexuality at a level appropriate to your child. You may worry that giving too much information as the child is growing up will encourage sexual curiosity and activity. The opposite is true. Studies reported by Marty Klein in the February 1986 issue of *Parents* magazine indicate that children growing up in families where sex is openly discussed tend to postpone having intercourse and are more likely to use contraception.

• Give your child the facts early. The earlier you begin, the more natural the attitude toward sexuality will be in your home. When your three-year-old son pulls on his penis and says it gets long, don't respond with, "Don't touch that!" Instead: "Your penis does get longer sometimes." There's no need for a detailed discussion of erections now, although a five-year-old may require more information.

Do the best you can to understand what your child is asking, then provide a truthful answer. We've all heard stories about the little girl who asks her mother, "Where did I come from?" and the mother takes a deep breath before explaining the facts of life, only to be told, "No, Barbara was born in City Hospital. Where was I born?"

Rudimentary facts are better than myths like "Babies come from a vegetable garden." There are many excellent books for parents and children that will help you find a comfortable way to give the child the information he should have.

If you open the lines of communication early, your child will feel free to come to you with his questions and worries later. Five- and six-year-olds are very interested in their own and other people's bodies. They may have many questions and may use words that embarrass you if they have discovered the topic bothers you. From eight on, girls and boys should be well informed about the changes their bodies will undergo in the next few years. You must provide information, reassurance, and an ear.

• Label body parts with correct names. Starting at about age two, children become interested in body parts. Just as you teach them the names for arm, stomach, and foot, why not teach them vagina, penis, and breasts? When the names are used naturally, they won't become the high-impact words you fear.

• Explain about private parts of the body. Teach your child that certain parts of the body are private and personal: "We don't touch each other's private parts, and we don't let anyone else see or touch them." Begin very early to let your child wash himself, including his genitals, even if you must supervise. Clearly advise your child that no one has the right to touch him in these private areas or in any way that makes him feel uncomfortable and that he should never feel ashamed to discuss such events with you (see Section 14.11–4).

15.4-3 Model Modest/Private Behavior.

The very best way to teach modesty and a respect for privacy is to model them with your own behavior. Don't parade around nude, and respect his privacy. Teach the child to close the bathroom door and do the same yourself. Encourage him to dress appropriately.

15.4-4 Redirect Behavior to Private Places.

Don't be surprised if you find your son or daughter masturbating. When you see the child touching himself, don't tell him that's a bad thing to do. Tell him, "It's fine to touch yourself, but you do it in private when no one is around to see you."

When you find your young child engaged in innocent sex play, even in mutual masturbation, don't punish him. Simply say, "We don't touch each other's private parts," and redirect their interest to another activity. After all, "playing doctor" is a universal pastime for little children. If you have not yet discussed sexuality with the child, use this occasion as an indication that he wants more information.

15.4-5 Teach Tension Reduction.

Sometimes frequent masturbation is used to relieve tension or stress. If you find your child uses it as an outlet, teach her other ways to relax. The relaxation skills described in Section 2.10 will be helpful, but also try to discover what problems or worries are causing the anxiety, and find solutions together.

15.4-6 Use Habit-Reversal Techniques.

If the child masturbates frequently in public, then you must intervene. Have the teacher help if it occurs in school. Use these solutions and check out the habit-reversal procedures outlined in Chapter 12 as well.

• Set a goal. Don't criticize or shame the child. Instead, tell her she must not touch her private parts except when she is in the privacy of her bedroom.

• Call attention to it. Often, the masturbation has become such a habit that the child is unaware he's doing it. Use a silent signal or a hand on the shoulder to heighten his awareness.

• Provide an alternate object to fondle. When the child uses masturbation as a tension reliever, give him something else to handle, such as a rabbit-foot.

• Apply corrective action. When the child touches himself this way in public, have him make a fist and hold the fist tight for three minutes. Chapter 12 provides more information on this technique.

15.4-7 Provide Consequences.

If the child continues to show her private parts or touch herself in public, you must provide consequences for this behavior. Repeat the reasons why her actions are inappropriate and tell her what the consequences will be if she keeps them up.

• Limit unsupervised activities. Eliminate the opportunities for the sex play to occur. Don't allow your child to go to the bathroom with a friend or to play unsupervised with friends for long periods of time.

• Set a positive goal. Decide with the child that he will not expose or touch himself in public for x number of days, then praise and reward him for his positive behavior.

• Use overcorrection. When the older child exposes or touches himself publicly, have him make a public apology for embarrassing others and invading their sense of privacy.

15.4-8 Seek Professional Guidance.

If an older child exposes himself repeatedly or attempts to interact inappropriately with other children, seek professional advice and perhaps counseling to help him with problems that cause him to act out in this way.

SUGGESTED BOOKS FOR PARENTS AND CHILDREN

Andry, Andrew and Steven Schepp. *How Babies Are Made.* Boston: Little, Brown, 1968. An introductory book, for children from three to ten, on the basic facts of sexuality.

Cole, Joanne. *How You Were Born.* New York: Morrow, 1984. A fluent explanation of human conception suitable for young children.

Madras, Lynda. *What's Happening to My Body?* New York: Newmarket Press, 1983. An excellent source for preteens and adolescents about body changes and sexuality as a natural part of life.

Waxman, Stephanie. *Growing Up, Feeling Good: A Child's Introduction to Sexuality.* Los Angeles: Panjandrum, 1979. For ages five to eight, photographs and text talk about different kinds of love and sexual development.

CHAPTER 16

Problems a Book Can't Solve

SOME childhood behavior problems can't be solved by parents with the help of this or any other book. They require the direct intervention of professionals because they are long lasting, dangerous, or indicative of serious emotional disorders. In this chapter, we will talk about these problems and how to know when you must quit trying to deal with them yourself. Chapter 17 will tell you how to get the help you need.

16.1 SELF-DESTRUCTIVE BEHAVIORS

These behaviors can lead to injury or even death and should never be ignored. If you are concerned that your child will hurt himself, you must seek specialized guidance immediately.

16.1-1 Suicidal Talk or Gestures.

Children often make remarks like, "Oh, I wish I were dead!" in moments of frustration or anger, sometimes to get back at parents or to manipulate them into giving them something they want. An isolated statement like this doesn't mean your child is suicidal; nor does it mean he is not. Repeated verbal threats alone or together with other signals are warnings that should be taken absolutely seriously.

The possibility of suicide must be taken so seriously because this is the eighth leading cause of death among boys from five to four-teen and is the third leading cause of death among teenagers. About four or five times as many boys as girls commit suicide, though girls make more unsuccessful attempts. While it is rarer among children under the age of ten, suicide does occur at young ages.

The warning signs of a potential suicide by a child include:

1. A sudden change in personality
2. Prolonged sadness, including crying for no apparent reason
3. Loss of interest in his/her world
4. Loss of appetite
5. Sleep disturbances, either insomnia or excessive sleeping
6. No animation (flat affect) in voice or actions
7. Negative statements about himself such as "I am no good," and feelings of hopelessness
8. Threats such as "You will be sorry when I kill myself." Be concerned by these statements even if the child threatens suicide as a way to get back at you, and be especially concerned if he de-scribes the way he will kill himself, for example, "I am going to take those pills in the bathroom cabinet," or "I will get a gun and shoot myself."
9. Suicidal gestures or preparations. Climbing out a window onto a ledge, for example, should not be taken lightly. Neither should signals such as collecting pills or other potentially danger-ous substances, walking heedlessly across busy streets, running away on an extremely cold night and, especially, writing suicidal notes.
10. Chronic depression or other serious emotional problems, es-pecially if there is a family history of suicide.

These warning signs are not always crystal clear, and some chil-dren have committed suicide without any warning. There have been many reports of several suicides within a school or community, sometimes seemingly triggered by the suicide of another youth. Anytime your child has been exposed to a suicide through the media or personal experience, discuss the incident and his feelings with him. Keep the lines of communication open (see Section 2.9), and occasionally ask your child, "How's it going for you?" Although you may believe you are totally in touch with his problems, it is true that most suicides are triggered by real-life events like school failures, family problems, or not making the team.

If you have any question about whether your child is at risk for suicidal acting out, promptly consult a professional who is an expert in this special field.

16.1-2 Excessively Impulsive Out-of-Bounds Behaviors.

Some children are so active and impulsive that they engage in potentially self-destructive behavior that could easily result in disaster. Such out-of-bounds behavior as darting into the street without looking, constant wandering away from home or parents, climbing to dangerous heights, and inserting objects into electrical outlets must be brought under control. If you cannot prevent your child from acting out, then you must seek help.

16.1-3 Self-mutilation.

If your child harms his own body by hitting, biting, banging, scratching, or cutting himself, this can lead to permanent damage and must be stopped. Get professional help.

16.2 BEHAVIORS DESTRUCTIVE TO OTHERS

If you recognize these problems in your child, remember that they can be dangerous to you or others and will leave you legally liable for any harm that is caused by them.

16.2-1 Extreme Aggression.

You must intervene if your child repeatedly hurts other people. Some children lose control in a fight and can't seem to stop themselves, while others act purposefully to inflict damage on others. Either way, they can cause serious harm and must be controlled. Get professional help.

16.2-2 Fire Setting.

Continual playing with matches or actually setting fires is obviously dangerous to the child and to everyone around him. If this behavior occurs in any but its most innocent forms (see Section 15.2), get professional help.

16.2-3 Torment of Animals.

This behavior may be a sign of very serious emotional problems, and you must not ignore incidents or dismiss them as "accidents." Very small children may not have learned better (see Section 15.3), but older children are doing this for a reason and the problem is beyond the ability of most parents to resolve. Get professional help.

16.2-4 Drug Use or Alcoholism.

In recent years, the age when drug and alcohol problems tend to begin has been dropping steadily; drug pushers and addicts have been found even among elementary-school students. More dangerously, alcohol and drug use is accepted as a normal phenomenon for many youth. The National Institute on Drug Abuse reported in 1985 that 93 percent of American high school students have drunk alcohol, 57 percent have at least tried marijuana, and more than 5 percent use these drugs on a daily basis.

Prevention and early intervention with young children is very important. Many schools have begun drug-awareness programs; if yours has not, encourage the administrators to do so. If you see signs of drug use by your child, find drug-related material, or see sudden changes in behavior and loss of interest in previously engaging activities and friends, you must act without delay. Get professional help.

16.3 LONG-LASTING PROBLEM BEHAVIORS

Some behaviors are age-related and will almost always disappear over time whether or not you take a stand. But if your child continues to manifest a difficult behavior far past the age when his peers have outgrown it, it may be wise to seek advice.

Other behaviors, which may not seem unusual or serious problems in childhood, may become difficult to handle later in life if they are allowed to persist into adulthood. Such behaviors include extreme fears and phobias, nervous habits, learning difficulties and disabilities, attention deficit with or without hyperactivity, stress reactions, eating disorders, extreme shyness, and so forth. Your child's life will be happier if you deal with these difficulties early. Get professional help if the solutions we suggest do not make a real improvement.

16.4 BIZARRE BEHAVIORS

There are certain behaviors that are so strange or unusual that you must make every attempt to deal with them as early as possible. These include seeing hallucinations, hearing voices, consistent dressing in the clothes of the opposite gender or wishing to be the opposite sex, feces smearing, urinating publicly or inappropriately around the house, eating plaster, engaging in fetishes or strange sexual behaviors, or any other behavior you are uncomfortable with. Get professional help.

16.5 OTHER REASONS TO SEEK HELP

The behaviors we have discussed above are compelling reasons to get counseling from an expert, but there are other reasons why you may want professional help in your efforts to raise a healthy and happy child. You may simply look for reassurance that your decisions are the best in your individual circumstances, or you may want new ideas for improving your family life. Many couples want to interact more effectively with their children, and some are seeking to head off potential problems. Your family may have experienced severe stress as in a death or a divorce and seek to ease the children's emotional response.

If your child engages in behaviors that make her constantly difficult to manage, if you and your spouse differ greatly in child-rearing theories or how to handle a specific situation, if you find yourself constantly yelling and punishing and locked into criticism instead of enjoying your children and helping them feel happy about themselves, then you should get help in changing your approach.

The willingness to look for and accept help when you need it will lead to happier healthier children and families.

SUGGESTED BOOKS FOR PARENTS AND CHILDREN

Dupont, Jr., Robert L., M.D. *Getting Tough on Gateway Drugs —A Guide for the Family.* Washington, D.C.: American Psychiatric Press, 1984. An excellent source of information and help for families.

Gardner, Richard, M.D. *The Boys' and Girls' Book About Divorce.* New York: Bantam, 1970. An excellent book to read to younger children or for older children to read by themselves. Also available: *The Parents' Book About Divorce* and *The Boys' and Girls' Book About One-Parent Families.*

Krementz, Jill. *How It Feels When Parents Divorce.* New York: Knopf, 1984. Photos and words of children ages seven to sixteen.

Rofes, Eric (editor). *The Kids' Book of Divorce.* New York: Vintage Books, 1982. Written by and for children about their experiences (Gr. 4–6).

Seixas, Judith. *Alcohol—What It Is, What It Does.* New York: Greenwillow, 1977. Easy-to-read introductory book about the effects of alcohol.

Shyder, Anne. *Kids and Drinking.* Minneapolis, Mn.: Comp-

Care, 1977. Written for preteens and adolescents; presents three stories to help young alcoholics.

  Tobias, Ann. *Pot—What It Is, What It Does.* New York: Greenwillow, 1979. An introduction to the basic facts about marijuana. Easy reading.

CHAPTER 17

How to Find
Professional Help

A professional can help you change undesirable behaviors and resolve conflicts in the family and can provide a hopeful outlook for what seem to be overwhelming problems.

Finding and choosing a professional, however, can be bewildering because there are so many kinds of specialists—psychologists, psychiatrists, social workers, family therapists, and counselors, all with their own individual orientation to therapy. And there are more: Educational consultants, reading and learning-disabilities specialists, and other special educators will diagnose, tutor, and counsel to help you conquer childhood problems.

In this chapter, we will give you short descriptions of the many categories of specialists among whom you may choose a person to work with your family. We will also show you how to select the best possible person for you and your child. Each of the therapists will have a subspecialty or favorite problems with which he or she works best, and each has an individual personality and approach. It is important to choose a therapist who has the ability and expertise to help you and who you and your child will trust and like.

17.1 THERAPISTS: WHAT KINDS ARE THERE?

Here are short descriptions of some of the therapists available to help parents today.

17.1-1 Psychologist.

A psychologist has earned a four-year college degree, has attended graduate school for approximately five years, and may have completed an internship for a Doctor of Philosophy (Ph.D) degree. Others have a Doctor of Psychology (Psy.D.) degree instead, usually indicating that they have completed the same requirements as the Ph.D but have not written an original piece of research, called a dissertation.

In some states, experienced psychologists with only a master's degrees (M.S. for Master of Science or M.A. for Master of Arts) may practice privately. If you have questions about the qualifications of a psychologist, ask about his or her degree or contact the local chapter of the American Psychological Association for information.

Although once psychologists were primarily academicians and limited in the amount of private practice they did, today they do everything psychiatrists do except prescribe medication. In many states, they may admit patients for hospitalization.

17.1-2 Psychiatrist.

After a college degree, four years of medical school and earning a M.D. degree, and a one-year internship in general medicine, the psychiatrist has then taken a two- to three-year residency in psychiatry. The residency is usually spent in a hospital setting, treating severely ill patients. Psychiatrists study medications in detail, and thus, some specialize in treating problems that respond to drug treatment. Like other therapists, psychiatrists differ in their orientations and approaches to therapy.

17.1-3 Social Worker.

A clinical or psychiatric social worker has a four-year college degree, a Master of Social Work (M.S.W.) degree, and has completed an internship. Some social workers also have a Ph.D. They may practice privately, seeing patients individually or in groups, and may specialize in one of many areas, including marriage and family therapy.

Other social workers have only a bachelor or master's level degree, work in organizations or social services agencies, and usually have not trained to see patients for counseling.

17.1-4 Marriage and Family Therapists.

Several kinds of specialists may be qualified to be marriage and family therapists. Those who may use this title include psychologists, psychiatrists, social workers, and others who have completed the training requirements of the American Association of Marriage and Family Therapists. They work primarily with family groups or couples rather than individuals.

17.1-5 Counselors.

There is a large number of people with various backgrounds who call themselves counselors and do therapy. Some have a bachelor's degree, while others have a master of education degree (M. Ed.) in counseling. Many work in elementary or secondary schools, while a growing number work in private practice.

In addition, there are those who have a Ph.D. in counseling. Most are counseling psychologists who work in private practice or at college counseling centers.

17.2 HOW TO CHOOSE A THERAPIST

This is a complex choice and a hard one to make. If your child clearly requires medication that your pediatrician or family doctor doesn't feel comfortable prescribing, then you should consult a psychiatrist. If not, then you may select from any of the specialists we have discussed.

The key factor in selecting a therapist is your child's problem. Your goal must be to make a match between your needs and the expertise of the therapist.

• Ask your doctor for suggestions. Request the names of three possible candidates whose work your pediatrician or family doctor knows and respects. If he doesn't know three, ask if he or she will research the question with colleagues or talk with a potential therapist to judge the person's qualifications and appropriateness in this situation.

• Talk to friends. Although they may not have talked about it openly, friends who have consulted therapists for help with their children are a good source of information. Find out how they feel about their therapist and how he or she worked with them.

• Ask your school principal and/or counselor. Most principals and counselors have had experience with many therapists, and while they may be reluctant to suggest that your child see a specialist, they may be willing to discuss therapists with you. Ask them to offer three names. Stress that you will not hold them responsible for recommending therapy or for the work of the person you choose. Let them know you will get names from other sources, too, and will interview the therapists yourself before making your final decision.

• Check the phone book under the heading of psychologists, psychiatrists, psychotherapists, social workers, marriage and family therapists, and mental-health clinics. Look for people who specialize in working with children, adolescents, or families. Remember that the telephone company that lists the names is not responsible for verifying or establishing credentials. Don't forget to consider location in your choice. Convenience is very important for maintaining the relationship.

• Call your local college or university. Ask for the department of psychology, special education, or social work. Or ask for the counseling center. If the institution has a medical school, ask for the department of psychiatry or child psychiatry, and speak with the chairperson or a faculty member. Explain your problem with this professional and ask for suggestions of experts or services offered at the institution or in the community.

• Check with state and national associations. Lists of members, by location and sometimes specialty, are kept by all the professional associations. Contact your local chapter of the American Psychological Association, the American Psychiatric Association, the American Association of Clinical Social Workers, the American Association of Marriage and Family Therapists, the Association for the Advancement of Behavior Therapists, the Association for Children with Learning Disabilities, or others listed in the resources for this book. Your state information office should be able to advise you of the boards in your state that regulate these professions, and may have a current list of practitioners as well.

17.3 CONSIDER THE POSSIBILITIES

Review the lists of potential therapists and decide on three to five names, taking into consideration the number of recommendations each has received, which ones were recommended most enthusiastically, which therapists specialize in your child's problem, and the location of their offices.

• Call each therapist and ask him as many of the following questions as seem appropriate in your case. Don't be shy. Most therapists understand how difficult your decision is. Some, however, may not be willing to talk at length—or at all—on the telephone and you may have to make an appointment, for which you must pay.

Here are some suggested questions:

1. How much experience and training have you had dealing with children?
2. How much experience and training have you had dealing with this particular problem?
3. How do you usually work—with the child alone, with parents

and child separately, with parents and child together, or with the entire family?

4. Would you explain your approach or theoretical orientation?

5. How long is each session?

6. How often do you usually meet—once a week, every other week, several times a week?

7. Can you estimate how long the therapy will take? (The therapist may be reluctant to make an estimate until after he has met with you and/or your child several times, but he may tell you how long similar cases have taken. He may also estimate the number of sessions needed to assess your situation.)

8. When can you schedule our appointments? Do you work evenings or weekends? Do you have enough time to see us regularly if necessary? (Although the appointments may require missing time from work or school, finding the right therapist must be your paramount concern. If the initial appointments are at an inconvenient time, the therapist may be able to schedule a different hour later, when another time slot opens up.)

9. What is the cost per session? Will it be covered by our insurance? Will you accept payment directly from the insurance company and the difference from us? If not, what arrangements can be made?

17.4 CHOOSE A THERAPIST AND BEGIN THERAPY

Speak to as many therapists as you like, though not so many that you cannot make a decision among them. Choose on the basis of their answers to your questions and the rapport you felt as you spoke to them. It is extremely important that you trust and respect the therapist as a person. After you have made a decision, make an appointment immediately. Do not wait for the next crisis.

17.5 GIVE THE THERAPY A CHANCE

Once you start, stick with it. The results will not be immediate or miraculous. Don't set unrealistic goals for progress, but expect small steps forward. Therapy is hard work and you must be active participants in the process. The therapist will probably advise you about what to do or not to do each week. Be open to these suggestions and follow them closely. Discuss your concerns and ask questions, even if this means you require additional sessions.

If you feel, after a number of initial sessions, that sufficient progress has not been made, tell this to the therapist and ask for her assessment of the situation. She may feel more time is needed or that consultations with other experts are required. She may suggest cotherapy with another therapist or with other members of the family.

17.6 DON'T BE A DROPOUT

Many people decide to discontinue treatment as soon as they see a little improvement. Don't make this mistake. If you stop prematurely, the gain may not be permanent and you won't have solved your problems.

When real progress has been made, the therapist may suggest fewer visits and will eventually cut back the appointments to monthly or occasional follow-up sessions. These are usually essential for preventing relapses, and they give the child an opportunity to touch base with an understanding and helpful friend who recognizes his needs and his ability to change.

Afterword

WHEN you became a parent, you knew it was a long-term job. Raising a child takes years. Disciplining a child is an ongoing process. As you see him grow and learn, as you develop your parenting skills, your confidence increases so you can teach your child what he needs to know. *Good Behavior* is a source book to turn to through the years. Incorporating its techniques into daily family interactions, you will act with confidence and authority.

When your child behaves well, feel comfortable telling her so, and when a behavior crops up that is inappropriate or annoying, act to change it. Alternative solutions for most of the behaviors you will meet are presented in *Good Behavior,* but along the way you will adopt the tools and create your own. Based on sound principles, your solutions can be successfully applied. When you find an effective solution, share it with us. We will be happy to hear of your success. Please write to us at:

Good Behavior
The Behavioral Institute of Atlanta
The Medical Quarters
5555 Peachtree Dunwoody Road
Suite 106
Atlanta, GA 30342

Effective parents combine discipline with unconditional love. Don't be afraid to show your love for your child or reluctant to clearly define unacceptable behaviors. To make your disapproval effective, combine it with reinforcement for the correct behavior. Praise the positive efforts of your child. You both will feel better and learn from the experience. When there is a problem, make a plan. Take it one step at a time. Select a solution, then recognize progress and welcome it with praise. Teaching good behavior is a continuous process. It is discipline at its best. Your willingness to train and guide your child with positive expectations, love, and understanding sets the foundation.

Parent Resources

The following associations and organizations are listed for your reference. We recommend that you include a self-addressed, stamped envelope in any correspondence.

ALCOHOL PROBLEMS:
Alcoholics Anonymous
P.O. Box 459
Grand Central Station
New York, N.Y. 10163

BEREAVED PARENTS:
Compassionate Friends
P.O. Box 3696
Oak Brook, Ill. 60522–3696

CAR SAFETY:
U.S. Department of Transportation Inc.
National Highway Traffic Safety Administration
400 Seventh Street, S.W.
Washington, D.C. 20590

CHILD ABUSE:
Parents Anonymous
7120 Franklin Avenue
Los Angeles, Cal. 90046

Child Find, Inc.
7 Innis Avenue
New Paltz, N.Y. 12561

DENTAL HEALTH:
American Dental Association
211 East Chicago Avenue
Chicago, Ill. 60611

DIVORCE:
American Arbitration Association
140 West 51st St.
New York, N.Y. 10020–1203

EARLY CHILDHOOD:
National Association for the Education of Young Children
1834 Connecticut Avenue, N.W.
Washington, D.C. 20009–5786

EATING DISORDERS:
American Anorexia/Bulimia Association, Inc.
133 Cedar Lane
Teaneck, N.J. 07666

HANDICAPPED CHILDREN:
The National Information Center for the Handicapped
P.O. Box 1492
Washington, D.C. 20013

National Society to Prevent Blindness
79 Madison Avenue
New York, N.Y. 10016

HEALTH CARE:
American Academy of Pediatrics
141 Northwest Point Road
P.O. Box 927
Elk Grove Village, Ill. 60007

LEARNING DISABILITIES:
Association for Children and Adults with Learning Disabilities
4156 Library Road
Pittsburgh, Pa. 15234

MENTAL RETARDATION:
Mental Retardation Association of America, Inc.
211 East 300 South
Suite #212
Salt Lake City, Ut. 84111

SINGLE PARENTS:
Parents Without Partners
7910 Woodmont Avenue
Bethesda, Md. 20814

SLEEP DISORDERS:
The Association of Sleep Disorders Center
604 Second Street S.W.
Rochester, Minn. 55902

SOCIAL WORKERS:
National Association of Social Workers
NASW Building
7981 Eastern Avenue
Silver Spring, Md. 20910

STEPPARENTS:
Step Family Association of America, Inc.
28 Allegheny Avenue
Suite 1307
Baltimore, Md. 21204

TWINS:
National Organization of Mothers of Twins Clubs, Inc.
5402 Amberwood Ln.
Rockville, Md. 20853

References

Agras, Steward, M.D. *Panic: Facing Fears, Phobias, and Anxiety.* Stanford: Stanford Alumni Association, 1985.

Agras, Sylvester D., and D. Oliveau. "The Epidemiology of Common Fear and Phobia." *Comprehensive Psychiatry,* Vol. 10 (1965), pp. 151–156.

Ainsworth, Mary. "Patterns of Attachment Behavior Shown by the Infant in Interaction with the Mother." *Merrill-Palmer Quarterly,* Vol. 10 (1964), pp. 51–58.

Anders, Thomas F. "Night-Walking in Infants during the First Year of Life." *Pediatrics,* Vol. 63 (June 1979), pp. 860–864.

Applebee, Arthur. *The Child's Concept of Story: Ages Two to Seventeen.* Chicago: The University of Chicago Press, 1978.

Ayllon, T., D. Layman, and H. Kandel. "A Behavioral-Educational Alternative to Drug Control of Hyperactive Children." *Journal of Applied Behavior Analysis,* Vol. 8 (1975), pp. 137–146.

Azrin, N.H., and V.A. Besalel. *A Parent's Guide to Bed-wetting Control, A Step-by-Step Method.* New York: Simon and Schuster, 1979.

Azrin, Nathan, and V.A. Besalel. *How to Use Overcorrection.* Lawrence, Ks.: H & H Enterprises, Inc., 1980.

Azrin, Nathan, Ph.D., and Gregory R. Nunn, Ph.D. *Habit Control in a Day.* New York: Pocket Books, 1977.

Azrin, Nathan H., Ph.D., and Richard M. Foxx, Ph.D. *Toilet Training In Less Than a Day.* New York: Pocket Books, 1976.

Baily, Covert. *Fit or Fat?* Boston: Houghton Mifflin, 1978.

Bank, Stephen P., and Michael D. Kahn. *The Sibling Bond.* New York: Basic Books, Inc., 1982.

Becker, Wesley, Siegfried Engelmann, and Don Thomas. *Teachers: A Course In Applied Psychology.* Chicago: Science Research Associates, 1971.

Behrstock, Barry. *The Parent's When Not to Worry Book.* New York: Harper & Row, 1981.

Bellman, M. "Studies of Encropresis." *Acta Paediatrica Scandinavica,* Supplement No. 70 (1966).

Benson, Herbert. *The Relaxation Response.* New York: William Morrow, 1975.

Bernstein, Joanne E. *Loss and How to Cope with It.* New York: Seabury Press, 1977.

Bernstein, Joanne E., and Stephen V. Gullo. *When People Die.* New York: E.P. Dutton, 1977.

Brazelton, T. Berry, M.D. *Toddlers and Parents.* New York: Dell, 1974.

Caplan, Frank. *The Parenting Advisor.* The Princeton Center for Infancy. New York: Anchor Books/Doubleday, 1978.

Cohen, Stanley A., M.D. *Healthy Babies,Happy Kids.* New York: Delilah Books, 1982.

Cole, Joanna. *Parent's Book Of Toilet Training.* New York: Ballantine, 1983.

Conners, C.A. "A Teacher Rating Scale for Use in Drug Studies with Children." *American Journal of Psychiatry,* Vol. 126 (1969), pp. 884–888.

Corder-Bolz, C. "Mediation: The Role of Significant Others." *Journal of Communication,* Vol. 30 (1980), pp. 106–118.

Cuthbertson, Joanne and Susie Schevill. *Helping Your Child Sleep Through the Night.* Garden City: Doubleday, 1985.

De Hirsch, Katrina. "Unready Children." In *Language and Learning Disabilities,* edited by Adele Gerber and Diane N. Bryen, pp. 61–74. Baltimore: University Park Press, 1981.

Eisenberg, Seymour. *Keep Your Kids Thin.* New York: St. Martin's, 1982.

Elkind, David. *The Hurried Child.* Reading, Massachusetts: Addison-Wesley, 1981.

Frederick, Calvin. "Self Destructive Behavior Among Younger Age Groups." (ADM 77-365). Department of Health, Education and Welfare. Rockville, Md.: 1977.

Gerber, Adele. "Historical Trends in the Field of Learning Disabilities: An Overview." In *Language and Learning Disabilities,* edited by Adele Gerber and Diane N. Bryen. Baltimore: University Park Press, 1981.

Ginott, Haim. *Between Parent and Child.* New York: Avon, 1969.

Gordon, Thomas. *Parent Effectiveness Training.* New York: Peter H. Wyden, 1970.

Greenfield, Patricia Marks. *Mind and Media.* Cambridge, Mass.: Harvard University Press, 1984.

Greenfield, Patricia. *Mind and Media: The Effects of Television, Video Games and Computers.* Cambridge, Mass.: Harvard University Press, 1984.

Grollman, Earl A., ed. *Concerning Death: A Practical Guide For The Living.* Boston: Beacon Books, 1974.

Gurian, Anita, and Ruth Formanek. *The Socially Competent Child.* Boston: Houghton Mifflin Company, 1983.

Hall, R. Vance, Ph.D., and Marilyn C. Hall, Ed.D. *How to Use Time Out.* Kansas: H & H Enterprises, Inc., 1980.

Haslam, David. *Sleepless Children: A Handbook For Parents.* New York: Long Shadow Books, 1984.

Ilg, Frances. L., M.D., Louise Bates Ames, M.D., and Bakers, M.D. *Child Behavior.* New York: Barnes and Noble Books, 1981.

Jacobson, Edmund, Ph.D. *You Must Relax.* New York: McGraw-Hill, 1934.

Johnson, Otto, ed. *Information Please Almanac* (1985). Boston: Houghton Mifflin, 1984.

Jonas, Gerald. *Stuttering. The Disorder of Many Theories.* New York: Farrar, Straus & Giroux, 1977.

Kaye, Evelyn. *The ACT Guide to Children's Television.* Boston: Beacon Press, 1979.

Kenny, Thomas J., Ph.D., and Raymond L. Clemmoens, M.D. *Behavior Pediatrics and Child Development.* Baltimore: Williams and Wilkins, 1975.

Klein, Marty. "Talking to Your Kids About Sex." *Parents,* Vol. 61, No. 2 (1986), pp. 70–74.

Krementz, Jill. *How It Feels When A Parent Dies.* New York: Knopf, 1981.

Kübler-Ross, Elisabeth, M.D. *On Death and Dying.* New York: Macmillan, 1969.

Lapouse, R. and M. Monk. "Fears and Worries in a Representative Sample of Children." *Journal of Orthopsychiatry.* Vol. 29: 803–818.

Lerer, R.J., P.M. Lerer, and J. Artner. "The Effects of Methylphnidate on the Handwriting of Children with Minimal Brain Dysfunction." *Journal of Pediatrics,* Vol. 91 (19), pp. 127–132.

Lesser, Gerald. *Children and Television: Lessons from Sesame Street.* New York: Random House, 1974.

Meichenbaum, D. and J. Goodman. "Training Impulsive Children to Talk Themselves: A Means Of Developing Self-Control." *Journal of Abnormal Psychology,* Vol. 77 (1971), pp. 115–126.

Merlingoff, L. "A Story: The Influence of the Medium on Children's Apprehension of Stories." *Journal of Educational Psychology,* Vol. 72 (1980), pp. 240–249.

Moore, T., and L. Ucko. "Night Walking in Early Infancy." Cited in *Helping Your Child Sleep Through the Night,* by Cuthbertson, Joanne and Susie Schevill. Garden City: Doubleday, 1985.

Morris, Richard J. and Thomas Kratochwill. *Treating Children's Fears and Phobias.* New York: Pergamon Press, 1983.

National Institute on Drug Abuse. "Drugs in American High School Students." *Psychiatry Letter,* Vol. 4 (May 1985) p. 26.

O'Leary, Daniel. *Mommy, I Can't Sit Still.* New York: New Horizon Press, 1984.

Ollendick, T.H., J.L. Matson, and W.J. Heisel. "Fears in Children and Adolescents: Normative. *Behavior Research and Therapy,* Vol. 23 (1985), pp. 465–467.

Post, Elizabeth. *Please, Say Please.* Boston: Little, Brown, 1972.

Pringle, Laurence. *Death Is Natural.* New York: Four Winds Press, 1977.

Robinson, Francis P. "Study Skills for Superior Students in Secondary School." *The Reading Teacher,* Vol. 15 (1961), pp. 29–33.

Rogers, Carl. *Client-Centered Therapy.* Boston, 1972. Houghton Mifflin, 1951.

Rosen, Gerald M. *The Relaxation Book: An Illustrated Self-help Program.* Englewood Cliffs: Prentice-Hall, 1977.

Rutter, M., J. Tizard, and K. Whitmore. *Education, Health, and Behavior.* London: Longman, 1970.

Salk, Lee, M.D. *What Every Child Would Like His Parents to Know to Help Him with the Emotional Problems of Everyday Life.* New York: Simon and Schuster, 1983.

Safer, Daniel, and Richard P. Allen. *Hyperactive Children.* Baltimore: University Park Press, 1976.

Schaefer, Charles E., Ph.D. and Howard L. Millman, Ph.D. *How To Help Children with Common Problems.* New York: Van Nostrand Reinhold, 1981.

Spitzer, R., ed. *Diagnostic and Statistical Manual of Mental Disorders.* Washington, D.C.: American Psychiatric Association Press, 1980.

Spock, Benjamin. *Baby and Child Care.* New York: Pocket Books, 1976.

Stroebel, Charles F., M.D., Ph.D. *The Quieting Response.* Manual and Audio Cassette Program. New York: BMA Publications, 1978.

White, Burton L. *The First Three Years of Life.* New York: Avon, 1975.

Wolpe, Joseph. *The Practice of Behavior Therapy.* New York: Pergamon Press, 1973.

Zimbardo, Phillip, and Shirley L. Radl. *The Shy Child.* Garden City: Doubleday, 1982.

INDEX

541

About The Authors

STEPHEN W. GARBER, Ph.D., is a clinical behavioral psychologist in private practice. He is a consultant to hospitals, juvenile courts, schools and other child care institutions. He has worked with children with various learning and behavior problems and has consulted with parents, teachers, pediatricians and other specialists.

As director of the Behavioral Institute of Atlanta, he has developed and now conducts programs for children and adults for overcoming specific problems ranging from attention deficit disorders/hyperactivity to phobias. He serves as consulting psychologist to Scottish Rite Hospital. A past chairman of Georgia Psychological Association Divison of Licensed Psychologists, Dr. Garber has published many articles in professional journals, was quoted in *Newsweek* magazine and is nationally known for his work on fears and phobias. He is an active speaker to PTAs, professional groups and organizations.

MARIANNE DANIELS GARBER, PH.D., is director of research and development of the Behavioral Institute of Atlanta and an educational consultant in private practice with her husband. She serves as co-director of the Atlanta Hyperactivity Clinic. Dr. Garber has taught at the primary, college and graduate levels and has held positions as reading specialist, supervisor and research assistant with the Atlanta public schools and was a grant specialist for Georgia State University. She has presented her research on children's language and reading development at professional conferences around the United States. The Garbers appear regularly as the *Noonday* counseling team for NBC-affiliate WXIA-TV and live in Atlanta, Georgia, with their three children.

ROBYN FREEDMAN SPIZMAN has published twenty-five books and numerous articles for parents and teachers on crafts, art education and enhancing children's learning. She appears weekly as the crafts expert on *Noonday,* a featured television series on NBC-affiliate WXIA-TV in Atlanta, Georgia. Robyn holds a bachelor of visual arts in art education and has taught art and served as arts coordinator in a variety of settings from elementary school to adult education. She lectures extensively and conducts workshops on teaching parents how to creatively motivate their own children. She is a featured columnist for the *Atlanta Jewish Times* and is married, has two children and lives in Atlanta, Georgia.